1981

# Violence
# in the Family

*Under the Advisory Editorship of*
ROBERT BIERSTEDT
*Professor of Sociology*
*University of Virginia*

# Violence in the Family

EDITED BY

**Suzanne K. Steinmetz**
UNIVERSITY OF DELAWARE

**Murray A. Straus**
UNIVERSITY OF NEW HAMPSHIRE

HARPER & ROW
NEW YORK  HAGERSTOWN  SAN FRANCISCO  LONDON

# Preface

This book has its origins in the 1970 meeting of the National Council on Family Relations. The theme of that conference was "Violence and the Family." As chairman of the Research Section of the Council for 1970, one of us (Straus) had the responsibility for securing reports of research on this topic for presentation at the meeting. A number of the papers presented at that meeting were published in the November, 1971, issue of *Journal of Marriage and the Family* and some are reprinted in this book.

Despite the publication of papers such as these, the literature on violence and the family is nowhere well covered. We have therefore tried to help fill the gap by editing this book. Each of us has searched the literature intensively. The result of this search was a bibliography of over 400 items.[1] From this list we have selected what seems to us to be an impressive array of thoughtful theoretical articles, reports of original research, and summaries of research. Sometimes (as in the case of the child abuse literature) the choice was merely a question of picking an appropriate selection from a very large number of possibilities. Sometimes, even our 400-item bibliography did not contain suitable material and we had to undertake a renewed search. This was particularly the case with material on husband-wife violence. Even a simple example like a passage from a novel depicting a fight or other violence between husband and wife proved extremely difficult to locate. We found lots of violence in non-family contexts and also found novels depicting husband-wife murders, but—even after checking about twenty different novels—found no fights, slappings, or throwing things between husband and wife.

We think that says something about the extent to which husband-wife violence is unconsciously repressed by novelists. Even anthropologists seem to avoid material on husband-wife violence. As Paul Bohannan wrote to our colleague Amnon Orent: "There are two reasons for this, it seems to me. One is that the middle-class anthropologists . . . share the middle-class horror of violence. . . . A second point [is that] . . . the people in colonial situations . . . do not misbehave in the anthropologist's presence; they are even shy of telling about violent episodes for fear that they will be considered misbehaving."

There are other reasons why, even with the present national concern with violence, violence *within the family* has received relatively little attention from social scientists. Some of these reasons are discussed in the introduction to this book. Nevertheless, the contents of the book will show that more study has been done on the subject than either we or Bohannan thought. By bringing together these materials, we hope to help create a larger public

[1] To obtain a copy of this bibliography, see p. 22.

awareness and understanding of the violence which occurs within families. At the same time, we also hope that certain obvious gaps in knowledge will be revealed by our book, and that this will encourage social scientists to devote the effort to the study of intra-family violence which the importance of the issue merits.

SUZANNE K. STEINMETZ
MURRAY A. STRAUS

## ACKNOWLEDGMENTS

Large organizations tend to be depreciated these days. But this book is an illustration of the contribution an organization can make. The 1970 meeting of the National Council on Family Relations had as its theme "Violence and the Family." It was participation in that conference which stimulated our interest in intra-family violence and which led to this book. We are therefore indebted to Harold Feldman for suggesting violence as a theme for the conference and to Gerald Leslie who, as President-Elect of the Council, organized such an outstanding program.

We are also indebted to many colleagues with whom we have discussed the issues; to Stuart Palmer for alerting us to important work in the sociology of violence; to Peter Dodge and Richard J. Gelles of the University of New Hampshire and Charles H. Woodford of Dodd, Mead and Company for aid in revising the introductions; to Dudley Dudley for aid in the bibliographic searching; and to Serene Klumpar, Jean Wild, and Colette Skeehan for painstaking work in preparing the manuscript for the printer.

Suzanne Steinmetz especially wishes to thank Professor Wallace E. Maw of the University of Delaware and Robert A. Rodgers of the Vocational Rehabilitation of Delaware for their encouragement and support during her undergraduate years.

Finally, we are grateful for the financial support of the National Institute of Mental Health. Our work on violence in the family was carried out partly with the aid of grant number MH 15521.

# Contents

# PART THREE
# Violent Parents

# PART FOUR
# The Family as Training Ground for Societal Violence

# Violence
# in the Family

# PART ONE
# Overview

# CHAPTER ONE
# Intra-Family Violence

## 1. General Introduction: Social Myth and Social System in the Study of Intra-Family Violence

### SUZANNE K. STEINMETZ AND MURRAY A. STRAUS

At one time almost all the major institutions of our society had the right to use violence. Corporal punishment was the rule of the day in the courts and prisons; masters could use physical punishment on apprentices; the church turned heretics over to the civil authorities for burning at the stake. Today, only the police and parents have a clear legal mandate to use violence as a means of social control. In fact, it would be hard to find a group or institution in American society in which violence is more of an everyday occurrence than it is within the family.

To describe the family in this way is jarring for most of us, since our view and hopes for the family define it as an arena for love and gentleness rather than as a place for violence. As a result, it is extremely difficult to see what is actually going on in the family. We tend to overlook the violence which occurs there. Or, if it cannot be ignored, we tend to repress the memory of it. Yet the facts are clear. Studies of murderers and their victims, for example, show that the most frequent single category of murderer-victim relationship is that of family relationship. Another well-documented form of intra-family violence is the use of physical punishment by parents. In every state of the union, it is legal for parents to strike children—that is, to use physical punishment. Indeed, most Americans see a moral obligation for parents to use physical punishment as a means of controlling children if other means fail (Stark and McEvoy, 1970) and a goodly proportion see it as the most desirable means of controlling children. "Spare the rod and spoil the child" is not a dead way of life in contemporary America, even though it is no longer the dominant ideology.

It can be objected that physical punishment is not really the same as other violence. We agree that it is not the same. But it is violence none the less. In certain respects, it has the same consequences as other forms of violence, despite good intentions. For example, the research on parents' use of physical punishment (see Part Four, "The Family as Training Ground for Societal Violence") shows that parents who use physical punishment to control the aggressiveness of their children are probably *increasing* rather than decreasing the aggressive tendencies of their child. Violence begets violence, however peaceful and altruistic the motivation.

It is not altogether rare for violent tendencies thus built into the person-

3

ality of the child to be turned against the parents, as in the case of Lizzie Borden who, in 1892, as the famous rhyme goes:

> . . . took an ax
> And gave her father 40 whacks.
> When the job was neatly done
> She gave her mother 41.

Most of the violence we will be describing is less bloody than what is attributed to Lizzie Borden. For example, we already mentioned the most common of all forms of intra-family violence: the use of physical punishment by parents. But irrespective of how extreme the level, the central focus of this book is on *physical* violence between family members.

Our focus on interpersonal physical violence does not mean that other related behaviors are unimportant. Aggression, for example, is closely related to violence. There are many ways to be aggressive, that is, to do something which will injure another. The use of physical force is only one of them. One can be excruciatingly cruel without ever lifting a finger to strike another person. Therefore, we should stress that our focus is not just on cruelty or aggression, but on the expression of aggression and cruelty by physical means.

Similarly, as Etzioni (1971) notes, there is a difference between coercion and violence. One can coerce by many means: money, threats of loss of a job, or manipulating symbols, such as those involved in excommunication. But there is a large difference between *violent* coercion and coercion by other means. Coercion of any kind is generally undesirable. However, the use of physical force, or threats to use physical force, form a special class of coercion having a particular set of antecedents and consequences; and, again, it is on these that we have chosen to focus.[1]

Our choice of physical violence as the central focus does not mean that destructiveness, aggression, cruelty, and non-physical coercion are omitted from consideration altogether. Rather, it means that we will consider them only insofar as they are related to physical violence. We are concerned with the man who batters down a door, but only if it is related to his battering down a person. Since the two are likely to be related, in a certain sense this book *will* consider these related phenomena but, as we have said, they do not form the central focus.

Obviously, we see this book as contributing to an understanding of violence. At the same time, we also see it as advancing the understanding of

---

[1]To define "violence" precisely is extremely difficult. What violence is has been debated at length by philosophers (Schaeffer, 1971). For our purposes, we think of violence as the intentional use of physical force on another person. This physical force can be used for a variety of purposes, including: (1) to cause pain or injury as an end in itself (what might be called "expressive violence"); (2) the use of pain or injury or physical restraint as a punishment to induce the other person to carry out some act (what might be called "instrumental violence"). In addition to considering whether violence is either instrumental or expressive (or some combination of them), for some purposes it is also important to take into account whether or not the violence under consideration is "legitimate" according to the rules of the society in which it takes place (such as spanking a child in most societies, or shooting an enemy soldier in time of war) or "illegitimate" (such as spanking a disobedient wife in contemporary society, or shooting a soldier of one's own country).

the family. Violence, as will be indicated later, is a widespread and enduring feature of human societies. In principle, any such widespread and enduring aspect of society should be related to other widespread and enduring features of society, such as the family. Thus, to understand or explain the occurrence of violence in a society, we need consider the family as one of the factors influencing the level of violence. The argument also cuts the other way. To fully understand what goes on in the family, we need to consider the role which force and violence play in family life.

## SOCIETY AND CONFLICT

Conflict is a fundamental and often constructive part of social organization. It is a primary engine for social change and development, for the underdog —blacks, women, and children, for example—to gain greater rights. A "conflict theory" view of society is also extremely helpful in understanding intrafamily violence.

A conflict theory perspective on the family is both a radical view and an old view. It is radical in that it does not take the usual comfortable, more pleasant, conflict-free view of society. It is radical in that it challenges a viewpoint which labels violence, abrupt change, tension, and struggles between subordinate and superordinate individuals as deviant or abnormal situations. The conflict perspective is also radical because it views as normal the struggles between individuals and groups, and considers tension or violence between people (e.g., family members) as natural. It sees conflict and change as necessary parts of the individual growth and societal development process. Such a conflict approach to society is also an old tradition in sociology, going back at least to Ibn Khaldun, the great medieval social philosopher of the Islamic world, and held by many others such as Thomas Hobbes, Karl Marx, George Simmel, Robert Park, Rolf Dahrendorf, and Louis Coser.

The conflict theory view of society is not, however, the most popular or generally accepted one in Western or academic sociology. That the conflict-free, consensus view is generally preferred is understandable since it is more consistent with what most people assume to be the desirable state of society. We tend to view as normal in society only those aspects which are perceived to benefit the majority and to consider deviations from the traditionally accepted norms as temporary. Also, there exists a certain amount of security in the known and familiar, and accepting or even acknowledging a situational change can be perceived as threatening.

Conflict and tension are usually considered to be detrimental to group cohesiveness and as states to be avoided. The greater the importance attached to the maintenance of a particular group—the family being the foremost example of such a group—the more carefully its members protect its cohesiveness from conflict and tension. Frequently, however, the conflict and tension are not eliminated, but are merely covered up or ignored until they reach uncontrollable proportions.

As Coser (1963, 1966) points out, group members tend to regard conflict as so harmful that the emotions which result from it are stifled. Perceived wrongdoings are suffered in silence. When these "unpleasant" emotions finally surface, they may cause unrepairable damage since to show them is so against the Western middle class norm regarding marriage and family.

In view of the more generally accepted consensus view of society, it is understandable why many people are a little puzzled by the idea of a book on violence in the family. We tend to see the family, even more than the society as a whole, as a center of solidarity and love rather than of conflict and violence. Of course, everyone knows about the relatively few but horrible cases of child abuse and about the occasional sensational cases of wife or husband, child or parent murder. We also know about drunken brawls and occasional loss of control. But the tendency is to consider all of these cases as abnormalities—as exceptions to the usual state of affairs.

A more accurate view is that these sensational events are just the tip of the iceberg. Underneath the surface is a vast amount of conflict and violence —including bitter feelings, anger, hatred, much physical punishment of children, pokes and slaps of husbands and wives, and not altogether rare pitched battles between family members. A survey by the National Commission on the Causes and Prevention of Violence found that about a third of the population had been spanked frequently as children (and almost all at some time) and one out of five husbands "could approve of slapping a wife's face."

This and much other evidence make us believe that violence is a fundamental part of all family life. The articles by William J. Goode (p. 25), George R. Bach and Peter Wyden (p. 98), and Jetse Sprey (p. 110) suggest that a focus on conflict and violence may, in fact, be a more revealing approach to understanding the family than a focus on family consensus and solidarity. Yet, as we have just pointed out, this aspect of the family is typically ignored. If violence in the family is considered, it is usually considered in the context of abnormality—as something which involves the study of sick people or abnormal families. Contrary to this view, we see the potential for violence in the family as being as fundamental as the potential for love. This does not mean that we approve of violence. But because we do not approve of something does not mean it isn't there. It *is* there and it needs to be studied and understood. We hope that the material brought together in this book will contribute to such an understanding.

To see the family as a place in which conflict and even physical violence are a regular part of the pattern of family life takes some effort. It takes this effort because the attitudes, values, and rules of behavior about the family all point in the opposite direction. There is a discrepancy between the idealized picture of the family and what it actually is.

## SOME MYTHS ABOUT VIOLENCE IN THE FAMILY[2]

The idealized picture of family life is a useful and perhaps even a necessary social myth. The utility of the myth results from the fact that the family is a

[2]An earlier version of this section was presented at a round table discussion at the 1971 meeting of the American Sociological Association. Substantially the same material is presented in our article "Five Myths about Violence in the Family" (1973). We would like to thank Howard M. Shapiro for comments and criticisms which aided in revising the manuscript.

tremendously important social institution. Therefore, elaborate precautions are taken to strengthen and support the family. In Western countries one of these supportive devices is the myth or ideology of familial love and gentleness. This ideology helps encourage people to marry and to stay married. It tends to maintain satisfaction with the family system despite the stresses and strains of family life (Ferriera, 1963). Thus, from the viewpoint of preserving the integrity of a critical social institution, such a mythology is highly useful.

At the same time, the semi-sacred nature of the family has prevented an objective analysis of the exact nature of intra-familial violence. To begin with there is the tendency we discussed above to deny or avoid consideration of the widespread occurrence of violence between family members in what are generally considered to be "normal families." This is the myth of family consensus and harmony. Another myth which is critically discussed in several of the articles which follow might be called the "psychopathology myth." This is the idea that husbands who hit their wives and parents who abuse their children are mentally ill. No doubt some are. But the studies of child abuse by R. J. Gelles (p. 190) and Sidney Wasserman (p. 222) indicate that such actions more often reflect the carrying out of a role model which the abusing parent or the violent husband learned from his parents and which is brought into play when social stresses become intolerable.

Although there are probably many other myths about violence in the family, we have selected the following as particularly important:

(1) The class myth: intra-familial violence is primarily a lower or working class phenomena.
(2) The sex myth: sexual drives are violence-producing mechanisms.
(3) The catharsis myth: the expression of normal aggression between family members releases the tension and prevents severe violence.

Each of these is a myth because it oversimplifies the social context of the behavior. The conditions under which each myth and its opposite apply will be discussed.

THE CLASS MYTH

The evidence for concluding that working class and lower class families are more violent than middle class families is by no means clear. There are studies which show such differences. For example, George Levinger's study of divorce applicants (p. 85) found that 40 per cent of the working class wives indicated that "physical abuse" was a reason for seeking divorce, but only 23 per cent of the middle class wives reported this reason. Nevertheless, the almost one out of four middle class women reporting physical abuse hardly indicates a lack of violence in middle class families.[3] A national

[3]These statistics are subject to widely varying interpretations, depending on the reader's assumptions. For example, one could discount the differences reported between middle and working classes with respect to physical abuse as a reason for seeking divorce as being purely a reflection of the relatively greater cost of divorce to working class couples (i.e., the expense, time, and fear of the legal system may be greater deterrents to divorce).

sample survey conducted for the Violence Commission (Stark and McEvoy, 1970) found that over one-fifth of the respondents approved of slapping a spouse under certain conditions. More directly relevant is the fact that there were no social class differences in this approval of slapping, nor in reports of having ever spanked a child. At the same time, almost twice as many low education respondents reported spanking *frequently* (42 per cent) than did high education respondents (22 per cent).

Other research on physical punishment is also contradictory. Most studies report more use of physical punishment by working class parents (Bronfen-brenner, 1958; Kohn, 1969), but some find no difference. A recent study by Straus (see p. 159) found no social class differences in a sample of college students in which about half reported physical punishment or threats of physical punishment during their senior year in high school. These findings were replicated by Steinmetz for two other samples of college students (see p. 166).

A recent comprehensive review of studies of social class differences in the use of physical punishment concluded that although the weight of the evidence supports the view of less use of this technique among the middle class, the differences are small (Erlanger, 1972). Sizeable differences only occur when the analysis takes into account differences within classes of such related structural factors as race, the sex of the child and of the parent (Erlanger, 1972), parental ambition for the child (Pearlin, 1971), and the specific nature of the father's occupation (McKinley, 1964; Pearlin, 1971; Steinmetz, 1972). Thus, variation *within* social classes is at least as important as differences *between* classes.

Despite the mixed evidence, and despite the fact that there is a great deal of violence in middle class families, we believe that research will eventually show that in the recent past intra-family violence has been more common as one goes down the socioeconomic status continuum.[4] This is not because of the existence of a lower class "culture of violence" which encourages violent acts, and an opposite middle class culture which represses violence. Although such cultural elements are well documented (Wolfgang and Ferracuti, 1967), we see them as a response to more fundamental forces which affect

---

Thus, more middle class couples may part relatively amicably before the conflict escalates into a violent phase. On the other hand, one could interpret these data as underestimates if it is assumed that violence is more shocking to middle class persons. If this assumption is correct, then much of the working class violence would not be reported to interviewers because it is just part of life, whereas, the same "minor incident" occurring in a middle class family would be vividly remembered and reported. Finally, there may be a difference in reporting rather than in behavior. Middle class wives may believe physical abuse is contranormative more than working class wives do and therefore be less inclined to report it. Obviously more detailed research on representative samples is needed to settle this issue. See also n. 4.

[4]It is possible that what we sense as an underlying class difference in the actual frequency of intra-family violence may be only an artifact of such things as: (1) a lack of privacy in lower class families, making their fights more visible than fights which occur in more affluent sectors of the population; (2) a tendency to call in social *control* agencies, such as the police, to deal with extreme situations rather than social *support* agencies, such as marriage counselors or child psychologists. Both of these factors make violence in lower class families more likely to be noticed both by recorders of official statistics and by social observers making speculations such as those in this paper. See also n. 3.

families at all social levels. The class difference comes about because these structural factors impinge more frequently on the lower and working classes. In this introduction we will mention only two of these factors: the resources available to a family member, and the amount of frustration inherent in the familial and occupational roles.

*The Resource Factor.* We believe that the willingness and ability to use physical violence is a "resource," in the Blood and Wolfe sense (1960). A family member can use this resource to compensate for lack of such other resources as money, knowledge, and respect. Thus, when the social system does not provide a family member with sufficient resources to maintain his or her position in the family, violence will tend to be used by those who can do so. Some indication of this is given in a study by John E. O'Brien (p. 65), which concludes that ". . . there is considerable evidence that the husbands who . . . displayed violent behavior were severely inadequate in work, earner, or family support roles." Although such lack of resources appropriate to a position which must be maintained is more likely to characterize lower class families than other strata, it is by no means confined to that stratum. A recession such as occurred in 1970–71, with high rates of unemployment among middle class occupational groups (e.g., aerospace engineers), would provide an opportunity to test this theory. In such a case, the resource theory of violence would predict that intra-family violence on the part of the husband would be greater among the unemployed than among a comparable middle class group who have not lost their jobs.

Such research remains to be done. But some indication that the predicted results might be found is suggested by a report of a British study. Statistics for Birmingham, England, showed a sharp rise in wife-beating during a six-month period when unemployment also rose sharply: "Frustrated, bored, unable to find a satisfying outlet for their energy, Britishers who are reduced to life on the dole meet adversity like men: they blame it on their wives. Then, pow!!!" (*Parade*, 1971: 13).

*The Frustration Factor.* In a society such as ours, in which aggression is defined as a normal response to frustration, we can expect that the more frustrating the familial and occupational roles, the greater the amount of violence. Evidence for this is to be found in research by McKinley, which shows that the lower the degree of self-direction a man has in his work, the greater the degree of aggressiveness in his relationship with his son. McKinley also found that the lower the job satisfaction, the higher the percentage using harsh punishment of children. This relationship held even when social class was controlled (McKinley, 1964: 132–150).

Severe dissatisfaction with one's job and being an educational dropout at one level or another were also found to contribute to a husband's use of physical violence on his wife (see p. 65). The frustration theory of violence would predict that with middle class educational expectations of at least one college degree, college dropouts may experience more frustration and job dissatisfaction, and thus resort to physical violence as a problem-solving device more often than do individuals who have completed the amount of education they desire.

The husband is not the only family member whose position may expose him to much frustration. The same principle applies to wives. But since the main avenue of achievement for women has been in familial rather than in occupational roles, we must look within the family for likely frustrating circumstances for women. An obvious one is the presence of a large number of children in the home. Another is a high degree of residential crowding. Both these factors have been found to be related to the use of physical punishment (see p. 25). As in the case of lack of resources, frustrations of this type are more common among the lower class. Since lower class wives are less likely to be provided with material means of carrying out family functions—few home appliances, little money for food—this would make her family role frustrating. As a result, intra-family violence is likely to be more common among the lower class.

On the basis of both the theoretical considerations and the empirical findings just described, we conclude that although intra-family violence is probably more common among lower class families, it is erroneous to see it as primarily a lower class or working class phenomenon. What we have called the "class myth" overlooks the basic structural conditions (such as lack of adequate resources and frustrating life experiences) which give rise to intra-family violence and which are present at all social levels, though to varying degrees.[5] The class myth also overlooks the fact that differences *within* social classes are at least as important as sources of variation in violence, as are differences *between* classes. The class myth is an example of group stereotyping by social scientists. Granted that there is a theoretically important relationship between the use of violence and social classes, one cannot conclude from these relatively small differences (as many social scientists have done) that the use of violence in the family is characteristic or typical of the working or the lower class, but not of the middle class. Some kinds of intra-family violence are typical of *both* the middle and the working class (e.g., hitting children), even though the rate may be lower for middle class. Other kinds of intra-family violence are typical of *neither* class (e.g., physical fights between husband and wife), even though the rate is probably greater for the working class and especially the lower class.

THE SEX MYTH

Violence in sexual relations is directly related to violence in the family because the family is the main way in which sexual intercourse is made legitimate. That is not to say that sex is confined to the family—either in this age of supposed "sexual revolution," or probably in any other age or society. But

---

[5]Although our general stance is to regard violence as undesirable, we do not mean to imply that violence is entirely negative. See in this connection the essay by Coser on the social functions of violence (1966), and our discussion on pp. 16 and 322. Under certain circumstances, the ability to use violence may be necessary for survival, or at least adequate functioning, as in the case of a child growing up in an urban slum. Indeed, this fact is well recognized by slum parents, who take steps to "toughen" their children. Even among middle class parents, there are many who use physical punishment as a first rather than last resort. Such parents feel that it is better for the child to spank him and settle the matter there and then. On the basis of studies such as those of Sears, Maccoby, and Levin (1957), we think this is incorrect, but obviously, much additional research is needed to settle the question.

at the same time, satisfaction of sexual needs is one of the major things which people seek through marriage. If, then, sex is a fundamental aspect of the family, and if sex and violence are related, there is something to be learned about violence in the family by looking at the linkage between sex and violence. In a certain sense, when we look at the connections between sex and violence, we are looking at a biological basis for violence within the family.

There is abundant evidence that sex and violence go together—at least in our society and in a number of others. At the extreme, sex and warfare have been associated in many ways, ranging from non-literate societies which view sex before a battle as a source of strength (or in some tribes, as a weakness) to the almost universally high frequency of rape by soldiers, often accompanied by subsequent genital mutilation and murder. In the fighting following the independence of the Congo in the early 1960's, rape was so common that the Catholic church is said to have given a special dispensation so that nuns could take contraceptive pills (Rubin, 1969). Most recently, in the Pakistan civil war, rape and mutilation were an everyday occurrence (Singh, 1971). In Viet Nam, scattered reports suggest that rapes and sexual tortures have been widespread (Hersch, 1970). Closer to home, we have the romantic view of the aggressive he-man who "takes his woman" as portrayed in westerns and James Bond type novels. In both cases, sex and gunfights are liberally intertwined.

Then there are the sadists and masochists, individuals who can only obtain sexual pleasure by inflicting or receiving violent acts. We could dismiss such people as pathological exceptions. But it seems better to consider sadism and masochism as simply extreme forms of a behavior which is widespread. Moreover, the sex act itself typically is accompanied at least by mild violence and often by biting and scratching (Ford and Beach, 1951).

Nevertheless, despite all of this and much other evidence which could be cited, we feel that there is little biological linkage between sex and violence. It is true that *in our society* and in many other societies, sex and violence are linked. But there are enough instances of societies in which this is not the case to raise doubts about the biological linkage. Consequently an intriguing issue is to determine the *social* conditions which produce the association between violence and sex.[6]

*The Repression Theory.* The most commonly offered explanation attributes the linkage between sex and violence to repressive sexual norms. Empirical evidence supporting this theory is difficult to establish. Societies which are high in restriction of extramarital intercourse are also societies

---

[6]It is also important to differentiate between mutually enjoyable sexual violence (biting, pinching, etc.) and one-sided aggressive acts—rape followed by mutilation and murder being an extreme example of such an act. Ford and Beach (1951:73), in discussing painful stimulation and sexual activity, make three very relevant conclusions from their survey of the anthropological literature. The first is that ". . . only when the interaction is bilateral does it generally assume the proportions of a genuine sexual stimulus." Second, societies considering this type of stimulation normal are also societies which permit relatively free and unrestricted sexual expression by the young. Third, they are also societies in which women are seen as active, vigorous participants in all things sexual. Thus, the symbolic meaning of painful acts accompanying sexual intercourse tends to be reversed in sexually restrictive and sexually permissive societies.

which tend to be violent—particularly in emphasizing military glory, killing, torture, and mutilation of an enemy (Textor, 1967). But just how this carries over to violence in the sex act is not clear. Our interpretation hinges on the fact that sex is both restricted and defined as intrinsically evil. This combination sets in motion two powerful forces making sex violent in societies having such a sexual code. First, since sex is normally prohibited or restricted, engaging in sexual intercourse may imply license also to disregard other normally prohibited or restricted aspects of interpersonal relations. Consequently, aggressively inclined persons will tend to express their aggressiveness when they express their sexuality. Second, since sex is defined as evil and base, this cultural definition of sex may create a label or an expectancy which tends to be acted out.[7]

By contrast, in societies such as Mangaia (Marshall, 1971) which impose minimal sex restrictions and in which sex is defined as something to be enjoyed by all from the time they are first capable until death, sex is nonviolent. Exactly the opposite of the two violence-producing mechanisms just listed seem to operate. First, since sex is a normal everyday activity, the normal standards for control of aggression apply. Second, since sex is defined as an act expressing the best in man, it is an occasion for altruistic behavior. Thus, Marshall says of the Mangaia: "My several informants generally agreed that the really important thing in sexual intercourse—for the married man or for his unwed fellow—was to give pleasure to his partner; that her pleasure in orgasm was what gave the male partner a special thrill, separate from his own orgasm." (Marshall, 1971: 70.)

*The Sex Antagonism and Segregation Theory.* Socially patterned antagonism between men and women is at the heart of a related theory to account for the association of sex and violence. This line of reasoning suggests the hypothesis that the higher the level of antagonism between men and women, the greater the tendency to use violence in sexual acts. However, if it is not to be tautological, such a theory must also contain related propositions which account for the sex role antagonism.

In societies such as our own, part of the explanation for antagonism between the sexes is probably traceable to the sexual restrictions and sexual denigration which were just discussed. The curse placed by God on all women when Eve sinned (Gen. 3: 16) is only the earliest example in our culture of the sexually restrictive ethic, the placing of the "blame" for sex on women, and the resulting negative definition of women—all of which tend to make women culturally legitimate objects of antagonism and aggression. The New Testament reveals much more antipathy to sex than the Old and contains many derogatory (and implicitly hostile) statements about women (I Cor. 7: 8–9 and 14: 34).

The present level of antagonism between sexes is probably at least as great as that indicated in these earlier examples. One can find numerous instances in novels and biographies and in everyday speech. For example,

[7]This assertion is based on the "labeling" and "expectancy" theory perspectives. See Aronson and Carlsmith, 1962; Dinitz, Dynes, and Clark, 1969; DiVesta and Bossart, 1958; Schur, 1972.

words indicating femaleness, especially in its sexual aspect (such as "bitch"), are used by men as terms of disparagement for other men; and terms for sexual intercourse, such as "screw" and "fuck," are used to indicate an aggressive or harmful act. On the female side, women tend to see men as exploiters and to teach their daughters that men are out to take advantage of them.

It would be a colossal example of ethnocentrism, however, to attribute antagonism between the sexes to the Western Judeo-Christian tradition because cultural definitions of women as evil are found in many societies. Obviously, more fundamental processes are at work, of which the Christian tradition is only one manifestation.

A clue to a possibly universal process giving rise to antagonism between the sexes may be found in the cross-cultural studies which interrelate sex role segregation, socialization practices, and sexual identity (Barry, Bacon, and Child, 1963; B. Whiting, 1965). Whiting, for example, concludes: "It would seem as if there were a never-ending circle. The separation of the sexes leads to a conflict of identity in the boy children, to unconscious fear of being feminine, which leads to 'protest masculinity,' exaggeration of the differences between men and women, antagonism against and fear of women, male solidarity, and hence back to isolation of women and very young children" (Whiting, 1965: 137). This process can also be observed in the matri-focal family of the urban slum and the Caribbean (Rodman, 1968), where the relationships between the sexes have been labeled by Jackson Toby as "compulsive masculinity" (see p. 58) and vividly depicted in Eldridge Cleaver's "Allegory of the Black Eunuchs" (1968). Slightly more genteel forms of the same sexual antagonism are to be found among middle class men, as illustrated by the character of Jonathan in the movie *Carnal Knowledge* (1971).

Obviously the linkages between sex and violence are extremely complex and many other factors probably operate besides the degree of restrictiveness, the cultural definition of sexuality, and the antagonism between sexes.[8] But even these factors are sufficient to indicate that it is incorrect to assume a direct connection between sexual drives and violence because such an assumption disregards the socio-cultural framework within which sexual relations are carried out. It is these social and cultural factors rather than sex drives *per se* which may give rise to the violent aspects of sexuality in so many societies.

[8]Among these factors might be listed the general level of aggressiveness of the society and the opportunities and expectations for expressing aggression in other spheres of life. Analysts such as Bettelheim (1967) hold that our society so restricts the expression of aggression that it tends to spill over in unexpected ways. Thus, Bettelheim argues that uncontrolled and destructive violence can be minimized if the society affords culturally sanctioned modes of expressing aggression. Such a "catharsis" theory, however, is based on the questionable assumption of an innate level of human aggressiveness which seeks expression. By contrast, a "social learning" theory of aggression and violence concludes that societies in which aggression and violence are common will tend to be societies in which sexuality is also violent because interpersonal relations involving sexual acts will reflect the dominant behavior modalities of the society. See the discussion of the catharsis myth in the next section of this general introduction.

## THE CATHARSIS MYTH

The catharsis myth asserts that the expression of "normal" aggression between family members should not be bottled up. If normal aggression is allowed to be expressed, tension is released and the likelihood of severe violence is therefore thought to be reduced. This is a view with a long and distinguished intellectual history (see p. 303). The term "catharsis" was used by Aristotle to refer to the purging of the passions or sufferings of spectators through vicarious participation in the suffering of a tragic hero. Freud's idea of "the liberation of affect" to enable the reexperiencing of blocked or inhibited emotions and Dollard *et al.*'s view that "the occurrence of any act of aggression is assumed to reduce the instigation of aggression" (1939) are modern versions of this tradition.

Applying this approach to the family, Bettelheim urges that children should learn about violence in order to learn how to handle it. Under the present rules (at least for the middle class), we forbid them to hit, yell, or swear at us or their playmates. Children must also refrain from destroying property or even their own toys. In this learning of self-control, however, Bettelheim holds that we have denied the child outlets for the instinct of human violence and have failed to teach them how to deal with their violent feelings (see p. 299).

By contrast with assertions of this type, the empirical evidence bearing on the catharsis theory is almost overwhelmingly negative. Exposure to vicariously experienced violence has been shown to increase rather than decrease both aggressive fantasy (Berkowitz, 1964) and aggressive acts (Bandura, 1961; Walters, Thomas, and Acker, 1962). Similarly, experiments in which children are given the opportunity to express violence and aggression show that the experimental children express more aggression after the purported cathartic experience than do the controls (Kenny, 1952; Hicks, 1965).

The theoretical arguments against the catharsis view are equally cogent. The instinct theory assumptions which underlie the idea of catharsis have long been discarded in social science. Modern social psychological theories —including social learning theory, symbolic interaction theory, and labeling theory—would all predict the opposite of the catharsis theory. From any of these non-instinctual theories one would expect that the more frequently an act is performed, the greater the likelihood that it will become a standard part of the behavior repertory of the individual and of the expectations of others for that individual.

In the light of the largely negative evidence and cogent theoretical criticism, the persistence of the catharsis theory becomes itself an interesting phenomenon which may prove rewarding to consider. There seem to be at least five factors at work in accounting for the persistence of the catharsis myth:

*(1) The prestige and influence of psychoanalytic theory.* Albert Bandura and Richard H. Walters (p. 303) suggest that the persistence of the catharsis view is partly the result of the extent to which psychoanalytic ideas have become part of both social science and popular culture. Although we share this view, one must also ask why this particular part of Freud's vast writings?

After all, much of what Freud wrote has been ignored, and other parts have been dropped on the basis of contrary evidence.

A sociological perspective on the issue suggests that whenever an element of cultural belief (such as the catharsis theory) persists in spite of seemingly sound reasons for discarding it, one should be alerted to look for ways in which this belief is part of a system of social behavior for which the belief may have latent consequences (Merton, 1967). There is likely to be behavior which is at least partially congruent with the "false" belief, or social patterns which need to be justified by the holding of such a belief. The remaining four of the factors which we feel account for the persistence of the catharsis myth are all factors of this type:

*(2) The catharsis myth justifies patterns of violence which actually exist.* Intra-family violence is a recurring feature of the family system of our society despite the cultural commitment to *familial* non-violence (Goode, 1971). For example, 93 per cent of the national sample studied by the Violence Commission experienced physical punishment at some time, and a third were spanked frequently (Stark and McEvoy, 1970). There has been no comparable investigation of husband-wife violence in a cross section of the population, but certain data suggest that the frequency may also be high. Over one out of five of the respondents in the Violence Commission survey *approved* of slapping a spouse under appropriate conditions. Among the divorce applicants interviewed by Levinger, over one out of three reported physical abuse as a problem in their marriage leading to divorce. Undoubtedly others used violence even though they do not approve of it, and other divorced couples experienced violence but did not mention it as a factor leading to divorce.

The probable high frequency of actual intra-family violence is something which needs to be explained. It is not farfetched to assume that, in the circumstances, the catharsis theory which (in effect) justifies sporadic violence will be attractive to a population engaged in sporadic violence.

*(3) The catharsis theory is congruent with the positive value of violence in non-family spheres of life.* Although the *familial* norms depreciate or forbid intra-family violence, the larger value system of American society is hardly non-violent. In fact, the overwhelming proportion of American parents consider it part of their role to train sons to be tough. This is reflected in the Violence Commission survey finding that 70 per cent of the respondents believed it is good for boys to have a few fistfights (Stark and McEvoy, 1970). Thus, a social theory which justifies violence as also being psychologically beneficial to the aggressor is likely to be well received.

*(4) The catharsis theory is congruent with the way in which familial violence often occurs.* Given the anti-violence family norms, intra-family violence typically occurs as a climax to a repressed conflict. As Coser (1969) points out:

Closely knit groups in which there exists a high frequency of interaction and high personality involvement of the members have a tendency to suppress conflict. While they provide frequent occasions for hostility (since both sentiments of love and hatred are intensified through frequency of interaction), the acting out of such feelings is sensed as a danger to such intimate relationships, and hence there is a tendency to suppress rather than to allow expression of hostile feelings. In close-knit groups, feelings of hostility tend, therefore, to accumulate and hence to intensify (pp. 218–219).

At some point the repressed conflict has to be resolved. Frequently, the mechanism which forces the conflict into the open is a violent outburst. This is one of the social functions of violence listed by Coser. In this sense, intra-family violence does have a cathartic effect. But the catharsis which takes place comes from getting the conflict into the open and resolving it, rather than from releasing deeper intra-psychic tension, as posited by catharsis theorists. Thus, the crux of the "art of family fighting" (referred to by Bach and Wyden, p. 98) and the management of conflict (Sprey, p. 110) does not center on the tension-releasing effects of violent incidents *per se*, but on the ability to recognize these as warning signals and to deal with the underlying conflict honestly and with empathy.

*(5) Confusion of immediate with long-term effects.* There can be little doubt that a sequence of violent activity is often followed by a sharp reduction of tension, an emotional release, and even a feeling of quiescence. Thus there is often an *immediate* cathartic effect. But to the extent that tension release *is* produced by violence, this immediate effect is likely to powerfully *reinforce* the violence which preceded it. Having reduced tension in one instance, it becomes a mode of behavior likely to be repeated later in similar instances. An analogy with sexual orgasm seems plausible. Following orgasm, there is typically a sharp reduction in sexual drive, most obvious in the loss of erection on the part of the male. But at the same time, the experience of orgasm is powerfully reinforcing so that successful orgasm has the long-term effect of increasing the sex drive. We believe that violence and sex are similar in this respect. The short-term effect of violence is, in one sense, cathartic; but the long-term effect is a powerful force toward including violence as a standard mode of social interaction.

MYTHS AND STEREOTYPES

Like stereotypes, the myths we have just examined contain a kernel of truth but are oversimplifications. Thus, although there are probably differences between social classes in the frequency of intra-family violence, the class myth ignores the high level of intra-family violence present in other social strata. The sex myth, although based on historically accurate observation of the linkage between sex and violence, tends to assume that this linkage is biologically determined and fails to take into account the social and cultural factors which associate sex and violence in many societies. The catharsis myth seems to have the smallest kernel of truth at its core. An attempt to understand the reasons for the persistence of the latter myth in the face of devastating empirical and theoretical criticism suggested that its persistence may be due to factors such as the subtle justification it gives to the violent nature of American society and to the fact that violent episodes in a family can have the positive function of forcing a repressed conflict into the open for non-violent resolution.

Myths such as the ones we have just outlined, while they in some ways contribute to preserving the institution of family, also keep us from taking a hard and realistic look at the family and taking steps to change it in ways which might correct some of its problems. Clearly, the approach of this book is the opposite. We want to examine a tabooed aspect of the family—violence —in a realistic way.

## ORIGINS OF VIOLENCE

Any social pattern as widespread and enduring as violence must have fundamental and enduring causes. Ethologists and anthropologists such as Konrad Lorenz (1967) and Robert Audrey (1967) have studied the evolutionary and biological forces which presumably have shaped the human organism in a way which builds a predisposition to violence into the genes. Neurologists, physiologists, and endocrinologists are doing important work on the possible association of body chemistry and gene structure with violence. A great deal has been learned from these approaches and more is to come in the future. But there are limits to these approaches. Alexander Alland's recent book (1972) demonstrates that the work of the widely read ethologists contains many unwarranted extrapolations from animal to human behavior. Our point of view is that knowledge of genetic and other biological factors associated with violence is tremendously important. However, such knowledge must be combined with knowledge of social factors because most aspects of violence, like most aspects of other human behavior, are the product of social forces interacting with basic human potentialities.

We have tried to suggest some of the social forces which act as antecedents and consequences of familial violence in Figure 1. This figure is intended to show that we are dealing not with one-directional influences but with a whole *system* of mutually influencing and interacting forces, with each part of the system providing feedback to the others (Buckley, 1967; Hill, 1971). That is, societal violence is in a two-way interaction with familial variables. It influences the amount and type of violence in the family and, at the same time, the level and type of intra-family violence affects the pattern of violence in the society as a whole. Similarly, within the family, variables such as those we show in box A affect the level and type of familial violence and, at the same time, intra-family violence affects these variables.[9]

[9]To call this a "system" model in the sense used by Walter Buckley is something of an overstatement because Buckley's view of system requires that the feedback be more than just mutual or reciprocal causation. The feedback referred to in such a system model is part of a process whereby information from each part of the system goes through a control unit which monitors and directs the feedback in relation to the goals of the system. A working paper presenting a "general systems" or cybernetic model of the processes which maintain, diminish, or escalate violence in family interaction has recently been published (Straus, 1973). Complex as Figure 1 may seem, it omits a great many of the factors involved in family violence. Our aim in presenting it is to illustrate rather than to present an exhaustive accounting of the factors included. Finally, even though the flow chart specifies a feedback system, it has a directional emphasis going from familial variables to other variables. The directionality reflects the fact that the purpose of this book is to illuminate the familial aspects of violence. This expository emphasis is not meant to imply that the primary direction of flow is from familial to other variables.

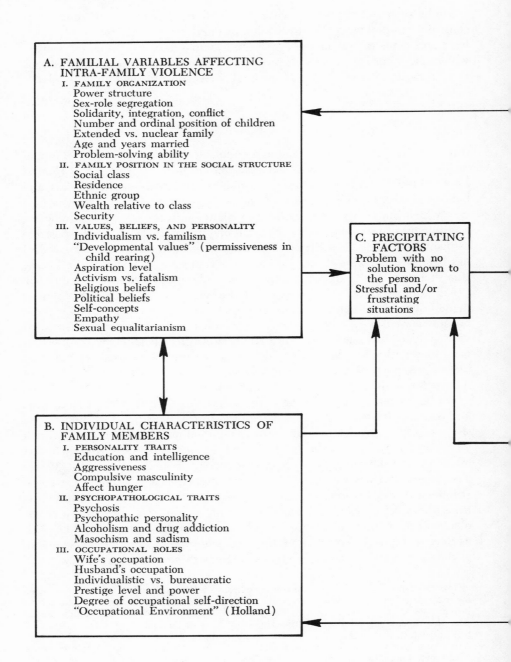

A. FAMILIAL VARIABLES AFFECTING
   INTRA-FAMILY VIOLENCE
   I. FAMILY ORGANIZATION
      Power structure
      Sex-role segregation
      Solidarity, integration, conflict
      Number and ordinal position of children
      Extended vs. nuclear family
      Age and years married
      Problem-solving ability
   II. FAMILY POSITION IN THE SOCIAL STRUCTURE
      Social class
      Residence
      Ethnic group
      Wealth relative to class
      Security
   III. VALUES, BELIEFS, AND PERSONALITY
      Individualism vs. familism
      "Developmental values" (permissiveness in
         child rearing)
      Aspiration level
      Activism vs. fatalism
      Religious beliefs
      Political beliefs
      Self-concepts
      Empathy
      Sexual equalitarianism

C. PRECIPITATING
   FACTORS
Problem with no
   solution known to
   the person
Stressful and/or
   frustrating
   situations

B. INDIVIDUAL CHARACTERISTICS OF
   FAMILY MEMBERS
   I. PERSONALITY TRAITS
      Education and intelligence
      Aggressiveness
      Compulsive masculinity
      Affect hunger
   II. PSYCHOPATHOLOGICAL TRAITS
      Psychosis
      Psychopathic personality
      Alcoholism and drug addiction
      Masochism and sadism
   III. OCCUPATIONAL ROLES
      Wife's occupation
      Husband's occupation
      Individualistic vs. bureaucratic
      Prestige level and power
      Degree of occupational self-direction
      "Occupational Environment" (Holland)

*FIGURE 1. System Model of Intra-Family Violence*

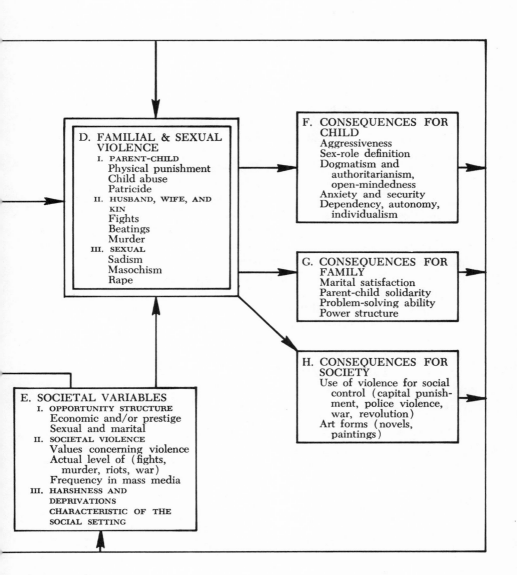

D. FAMILIAL & SEXUAL VIOLENCE
I. PARENT-CHILD
Physical punishment
Child abuse
Patricide
II. HUSBAND, WIFE, AND KIN
Fights
Beatings
Murder
III. SEXUAL
Sadism
Masochism
Rape

E. SOCIETAL VARIABLES
I. OPPORTUNITY STRUCTURE
Economic and/or prestige
Sexual and marital
II. SOCIETAL VIOLENCE
Values concerning violence
Actual level of (fights, murder, riots, war)
Frequency in mass media
III. HARSHNESS AND DEPRIVATIONS CHARACTERISTIC OF THE SOCIAL SETTING

F. CONSEQUENCES FOR CHILD
Aggressiveness
Sex-role definition
Dogmatism and authoritarianism, open-mindedness
Anxiety and security
Dependency, autonomy, individualism

G. CONSEQUENCES FOR FAMILY
Marital satisfaction
Parent-child solidarity
Problem-solving ability
Power structure

H. CONSEQUENCES FOR SOCIETY
Use of violence for social control (capital punishment, police violence, war, revolution)
Art forms (novels, paintings)

If we are to really understand or explain the occurrence of intra-family violence, the whole system must be considered. If one wants to change the occurrence of violence in the family, it is not sufficient to deal directly with such aspects of intra-familial violence as child abuse and fights between husband and wife. To confine attention to such events and their immediate antecedents is analogous to treating the symptoms of a disease. A much more fundamental approach is needed, one which recognizes that family behavior is embedded in the society and its workings. The poverty and frustration which the structure of society creates for millions of families must be reduced if there is to be any substantial reduction in the level of intra-family violence. The models of violent behavior presented on television and the models embodied in the actions of public figures who "retaliate" by saturation bombing of cities and towns cannot continue if we are to have less violence in family relationships.

To deal with the problem of violence within the family also requires recognizing that the family itself constitutes a system. Thus, as we suggested in discussing the class myth, an excessive number of children (in relation to desires and resources) tends to increase the level of intra-family violence. To the extent that this is true, providing all families with the contraceptive knowledge and skills which will enable them to control the size of their family will make a contribution to the reduction of violence. More direct aid is also obviously needed—particularly information on child rearing techniques and managing the normal phenomena of family conflict. Programs such as those described by Morton Bard (p. 127) have a dual function: they aim both to reeducate marital partners and also to deal with future violence by educating police officers, and professional and community aides, in family crisis intervention work. However, admirable as such programs are, our guess is that they are likely to have only limited success unless there are also changes at the societal level—for example, changes in norms and practices to replace the existing patterns in child rearing, mass media, criminal punishment, and international relations with patterns of non-violence.

Equally fundamental, and equally important for their potential in reducing familial violence, are changes in such basic aspects of the family as the power structure—especially the male dominance and *machismo* values and norms which form a subtle but powerful part of our sexual and family system. For example, the "status sex" norms described by Desmond Morris (1969) and the "compulsive masculinity" described by Jackson Toby (p. 58) are a powerful force toward violent sexuality. Aside from sex, the male-dominant ideology of our society also plays a part in producing violence. Take the norms which require male economic superiority in occupation and income, for instance. These serve as powerful sources of frustration for those men who, because of social restrictions or personal characteristics, cannot meet the cultural expectations. New, less frustrating, and therefore less violence-producing, norms would emphasize, instead, how well one did a job and how much enjoyment was received from an occupation—not the prestige of selected jobs or the amount of income received relative to the wife. These norms should be flexible enough to allow males to assume the homemaker role (while the wife was employed outside the home) if couples found this to be a better, more satisfying arrangement. The article by Robert N. Whitehurst on "Alternative Family Structures and Violence Reduction" (p. 315) deals directly and systematically with these issues. But even this brief sketch should indicate the major point: one must view intra-family violence as only one element of a complex system if we are to engage in meaningful attempts to reduce the level of violence in the family.

## PLAN OF THE BOOK

Although considerable work has been done on the relationship between family patterns and violence, the resulting articles and reports are scattered in books, magazines, and scientific journals of many fields. This material is largely inaccessible to all but the professionally trained, and even for them, it is accessible only with much digging. We hope that bringing a selection of articles together will not only be a convenience, but will also contribute to the advancement of our understanding of violence by suggesting relationships which might not otherwise be seen.

The organization of the book is simple and at the same time consistent with life as an ongoing developmental process. Part One contains an overview article by William J. Goode entitled "Force and Violence in the Family." The article was first delivered as a paper at the meeting of the National Council on Family Relations when Goode received the 1970 Ernest W. Burgess award for outstanding contributions to research on the family. The careful review of the literature and theoretical synthesis in this paper provides added proof of the appropriateness of that award.

Following Goode's overview, we turn in Part Two to a fundamental aspect of intra-family violence, "Violence Between Spouses and Kin." Aside from sexual drives, the social intimacy and involvement of family members with each other creates an intensity of involvement which is rarely found in other spheres of life and which, if things go wrong, can easily spill over into violence—including murder and sometimes the injury or death of those trying to help. Parnas' study of the "Police Response to Domestic Disturbance" (1967) cites FBI figures which show that in 1960–65 more police officers were killed responding to "disturbance" calls than in any other category of police action (21 per cent of the 278 policemen killed in this period).

Part Three, "Violent Parents," is devoted to another fundamental aspect of intra-family violence: the rearing of children. The kind of intense involvement which characterizes the husband-wife relationship may be even more characteristic of the relations between parents and their children. So when things go wrong, the potential for violence may also be greater. Furthermore, at least early in life, the power of the parents is almost absolute. Parental rights include the legal right to use limited violence: physical punishment. Parents differ in their use of physical punishment and in their ability to abandon it as the child grows older. What are the causes of these differences between parents and what are their consequences? These important questions, and also the question of parents who physically abuse their children, will be considered in Part Three.

The fourth and final part of the book, "The Family as Training Ground for Societal Violence," looks at the consequences of violence within the family—both for the individual and for society as a whole. Part Four considers such things as the effect of physical punishment on the child's personality and, especially, the child's aggressiveness; the relationship between violence in the family and violent crime; and the relationship between family violence, social policy, and social action such as revolution and war. In a final, all too brief section in this part, we deal with the possible consequences for interpersonal violence of certain widely heralded changes in the structure of the family. We do not know if such alternatives to the present form of the family will even become widespread. But if man is to take control of his own destiny, he should do so, at least in part, on the basis of the best information social science can provide concerning possible consequences of the alternatives. The discussion by Robert N. Whitehurst (p. 315) of what these alternative family structures might contribute to reducing the level of violence is an example of the kind of theoretical examination of the future of society which is much needed if social science is to be more than an elegant commentary on the status quo.

In each of the four parts, our first aim is to describe the facts: just how much violence is there in family life and what forms does it take? But description is not sufficient. What is most needed is understanding—of the factors which bring about violence between family members, of factors which inhibit or limit intra-family violence, and of the consequences for society and its members both of high and low levels of intra-family violence. Research on these critical issues of cause and effect is scarce. The need for further knowledge is tremendous.[10] Despite this, we have managed to find and bring together a substantial amount of information which gives a greater understanding of the causes and consequences of violence in the family than is now possessed by either the general public or most social scientists. Finally, each of the four parts provides material on steps which can be taken to reduce violence between family members. The scientific basis for some of these steps to reduce violence is minimal. But, as we point out in the editors' Postscript, most of these proposed means for reducing violence consist of social changes which are, themselves, desirable. Implementing such changes will move us closer to a just and good society even if we cannot be sure

---

[10]To aid others in research on violence, we have made available two bibliographies. The first consists of the over 400 references which we uncovered in the course of our search for materials to include in this book. The second consists of a computer-produced set of abstracts provided for us by the National Clearing House for Mental Health Information of NIMH. A copy of each of these bibliographies has been deposited with the National Auxiliary Publications Service (NAPS) of the American Society for Information Science. A copy may be obtained by ordering Document Number 02182 (374 pp.) and remitting $1.50 for a microfiche copy or $58.85 for a photocopy to ASIS National Auxiliary Publications Service, c/o Microfiche Publications, 305 East 46th Street, New York, N.Y. 10017. Make checks payable to Microfiche Publications.

that they will be effective in moving us toward the goal of a minimally violent society.

## REFERENCES

References to articles reprinted in this book are omitted.

Alland, Alexander Jr.
    1972    *The Human Imperative.* New York: Columbia University Press.
Ardrey, Robert
    1967    *The Territorial Imperative.* New York: Atheneum.
Aronson, Eliot and J. M. Carlsmith
    1962    "Performance Expectancy as a Determinant of Actual Performance." *Journal of Abnormal and Social Psychology* 65: 178–182.
Bacon, M. K., H. Barry, and I. L. Child
    1963    "A Cross-Cultural Study of Correlates of Crime." *Journal of Abnormal and Social Psychology* 66 (4): 291.
Bandura, Albert, Dorothea Ross, and Sheila A. Ross
    1961    "Transmission of Aggression Through Imitation of Aggressive Models." *Journal of Abnormal and Social Psychology* 63 (3): 575–582.
Berkowitz, Leonard
    1964    "Aggressive Cues in Aggressive Behavior and Hostility Catharsis." *Psychological Review* 71: 104–122.
Blood, Robert O. and Donald M. Wolfe
    1960    *Husbands and Wives: The Dynamics of Married Living.* Glencoe, Illinois: Free Press.
Bronfenbrenner, Urie
    1958    "Socialization and Social Class Through Time and Space." Pp. 400–425 in E. E. Maccoby, T. M. Newcomb, and E. L. Hartley (eds.), *Readings in Social Psychology*, third edition. New York: Holt, Rinehart, and Winston.
Buckley, Walter
    1967    *Sociology and Modern Systems Theory.* Englewood Cliffs, New Jersey: Prentice-Hall.
Cleaver, Eldridge
    1968    "White Woman, Black Man: The Allegory of the Black Eunuchs." Pp. 145–192 in Eldridge Cleaver, *Soul on Ice.* New York: Dell.
Coser, Lewis A.
    1956    *The Functions of Social Conflict.* Glencoe, Illinois: Free Press.
Coser, Lewis A.
    1963    "Violence and the Social Structure." *Science and Psychoanalysis* 6: 30–42. (Also reprinted on pp. 71–84 in Shalom Endleman (ed.), *Violence in the Streets.* Chicago: Quadrangle Paperbacks, 1970.)
Coser, Lewis A.
    1966    "Some Social Functions of Violence." Pp. 8–18 in Marvin E. Wolfgang (ed.), *Patterns of Violence: The Annals of the American Academy of Political and Social Science*, Vol. 364 (Philadelphia: American Academy of Political and Social Science, March, 1966).
Coser, Lewis A.
    1969    "The Functions of Social Conflict." Pp. 218–219 in Lewis A. Coser and Bernard Rosenberg (eds.), *Sociological Theory: A Book of Readings.* New York: Macmillan.
Dinitz, Simon, Russell R. Dynes, and Alfred C. Clarke
    1969    *Deviance: Studies in the Process of Stigmatization and Societal Reaction.* New York: Oxford University Press.
Dollard, John, Leonard W. Doob, Neil E. Miller, O. Hubert Mowrer, and Robert R. Sears
    1939    *Frustration and Aggression.* New Haven: Yale University Press.
DiVesta, Francis J. and Phillip Bossart
    1958    "The Effect of Sets Induced by Labelling on the Modification of Attitude." *Journal of Personality* 26: 379–387.

Etzioni, Amitai
1971    "Violence." Chapter 14 in Robert K. Merton and Robert A. Nisbet (eds.), *Contemporary Social Problems*, third edition. New York: Harcourt Brace Jovanovich.

Ferreira, Antonio
1963    "Family Myth and Homeostatis." *Archives of General Psychiatry* 9: 457–463. (As reprinted in Normal W. Bell and Ezra F. Vogel [eds.], *The Family*. New York: Free Press, 1968.)

Ford, Clellan S. and Frank A. Beach
1951    *Patterns of Sexual Behavior*. New York: Harper.

Hersch, Seymour M.
1970    *My Lai 4*. New York: Random House.

Hicks, David J.
1965    "Imitation and Retention of Film-Mediated Aggressive Peer and Adult Models." *Journal of Personality and Social Psychology* 2: 97–100.

Hill, Reuben
1970    "Modern Systems Theory and the Family: A Confrontation." *Social Science Information* 10 (October): 7–26.

Kenney, D. T.
1952    "An Experimental Test of the Catharsis Theory of Aggression." University of Washington, unpublished Ph.D. dissertation.

Kohn, Melvin L.
1969    *Class and Conformity: A Study in Values*. Homewood, Illinois: Dorsey Press.

Lorenz, K.
1966    *On Aggression*. New York: Harcourt Brace.

Marshall, Donald S.
1971    "Too Much in Mangaia." *Psychology Today* 4 (February): 43–44+.

McKinley, Donald Gilbert
1964    "Work and the Family." Pp. 118–151 in *Social Class and Family Life*. New York: Free Press.

Merton, Robert K.
1967    "Manifest and Latent Functions." Chapter 3 in Robert K. Merton, *On Theoretical Sociology*. New York: Free Press—Macmillan.

Morris, Desmond
1969    "Status Sex." Pp. 100–123 in Desmond Morris, *The Human Zoo*. New York: McGraw-Hill.

Parnas, Raymond I.
1967    "The Police Response to the Domestic Disturbance." *Wisconsin Law Review* 914 (Fall): 914–960.

Pearlin, Leonard I.
1970    "Parental Discipline." Pp. 99–122 in *Class Context and Family Relations: A Cross-National Study*. Boston: Little, Brown.

Rodman, Hyman
1968    "Family and Social Pathology in the Ghetto." *Science* 161 (August 3): 756–762.

Rubin, David
1969    *Everything You Always Wanted to Know About Sex—But Were Afraid to Ask*. New York: David McKay. (Also New York: Bantam Books, 1971).

Schur, Edwin M.
1972    *Labeling Deviant Behavior: Its Sociological Implications*. New York: Harper and Row.

Shaffer, Jerome A. (ed.)
1971    *Violence: Award-Winning Essays in the Council for Philosophical Studies Competition*. New York: David McKay.

Singh, Khushwant
1971    "Why They Fled Pakistan—And Won't Go Back." *New York Times Magazine* (August 1): 12–15.

Steinmetz, Suzanne K. and Murray A. Straus
1973    "The Family as Cradle of Violence." *Society* (formerly *Transaction*) 10 (Sept.-Oct.): 50–58.

Stark, Rodney and James McEvoy III
1970    "Middle Class Violence." *Psychology Today* 4 (November): 52–65.

Straus, Murray A.
1973    "A General Systems Theory Approach to a Theory of Violence Between Family Members." *Social Science Information* 12.

Textor, R. B.
   1967   *A Cross-Cultural Summary.* New Haven: Human Resources Area Files Press.
Walters, Richard H., E. Llewellyn Thomas, and Charles W. Acker
   1962   "Enhancement of Punitive Behavior by Audiovisual Displays." *Science,* 136: 872–873.
Whiting, Beatrice B.
   1965   "Sex Identity Conflict and Physical Violence: A Comparative Study." *American Anthropologist* 67 (December): 123–140.
Wolfgang, Marvin E. and F. Ferracuti
   1967   *The Subculture of Violence: Toward an Integrated Theory of Criminology.* London: Tavistock.

# 2. *Force and Violence in the Family*
## WILLIAM J. GOODE

At several points in our general introduction we made reference to the near universality of violence in the family. Goode goes even further and asserts that the family, like all social units, rests ". . . to some degree on force or its threat. . . ." The focus of his analysis is in showing why this is so. The theory he puts forth in this article can be called a *social control* or a *resource theory* of family violence. This theory argues that violence is a resource which can be used to achieve desired ends. It tends to be used when other resources (such as money, respect, love, shared goals) are lacking or found to be insufficient.

There are, of course, other theories or explanations for the near universality of violence in the family, some of which have already been mentioned. These include *conflict theory,* which emphasizes violence as a means of bringing about social change and thus maintaining the viability of a social unit or institution; *cultural theory,* which emphasizes the approval of violence in the value system of the society and the social norms which indicate when and under what circumstances violence is to be used; and *general systems theory,* which emphasizes the cybernetic or control mechanisms which regulate the level of violence in the family system and the goal-seeking properties of the family. In addition, the articles on child abuse in Chapter VI will focus on *psychopathology theory,* which argues that violence between family members occurs because of abnormal psychological characteristics of a family member.

Goode's article does not deny the importance for producing violence of the processes highlighted by these other theories. In fact, some are subsidiary parts of his analysis. Rather, his purpose is to show that whatever else may be operating to bring about violence, human society requires a minimum degree of social order and control if it is to survive. Among the resources which are used to maintain the social order are force and violence or the implicit threat of their use.

SOURCE: Reprinted with permission from *Journal of Marriage and the Family* 33 (November, 1971): 624–636. Presented as the Fifth Annual Ernest W. Burgess Award Lecture of the National Council on Family Relations, Chicago, October 9, 1970. The author wishes to acknowledge the help of Joel L. Telles and Mary E. Curran in preparing this paper. The work was facilitated by a grant from the National Science Foundation and a Senior Science Award from NIMH.

Like all other social units or systems, the family is a power system. All rest to some degree on force or its threat, whatever else may be their foundations. Perhaps many rulers have believed that their regimes did not, and that they used physical force only on those who were evil, but those at the bottom of the power and class system, the disadvantaged, the deprived, women, and children have always known better.

Our aim of applying this bit of folk wisdom to the family is handicapped because in no field of social science have systematic observations been made about how force or its threat affects day-to-day interaction among human beings. Sociologists have not filled this gap, since they have been mainly exploiting the fact that much of social behavior is determined by norms, attitudes, and values, by the evaluations people make, by what people want or dislike, approve or deprecate. However, observation of the phenomenon is difficult, and I cannot fill that gap here. At this stage, I shall rather examine the problem theoretically, and analyze the empirical data on only one sub-segment, which is expressed in overt force or violence. On the other hand, a theoretical statement will at least point to the sets of forces that I believe can be observed and that if understood properly would interpret social behavior more adequately.

I should prefer to use the term "power" here but unfortunately that has come to mean a ragbag of phenomena and forces, usually the ability to impose one's will upon another in spite of his resistance. Since one can impose one's will with a variety of resources, from love to murder, the term is too broad.[1] Since all of us have *some* power, even when someone has imposed his will upon us, the term is also too narrow. The term is tempting, since it carries a penumbra of references to strength, force, and domination, and indeed is often used to suggest force. However, I shall forego the use of the term because of these objections, and shall use the phrase, "force and its threat." For the sake of simplicity I shall use the term "force" as my substitute, and "overt force" when I want to refer specifically to the actual exercise of physical force.

Force or its threat is used in all social systems because it is one of four major sets of resources by which people can move others to serve their ends. Three of these have played a large role in grand social science theory because they are also the major bases of all stratification systems: i.e., economic variables, prestige or respect, and force and its threat, sometimes called power. A fourth can be called likability, attractiveness, friendship, or love.[2] All of these are major elements in all family systems, or any other social system. All are necessary social means for the ends of both individuals and groups. All can be acquired and expended; all can be exchanged to some degree for each other. Some people and groups possess more of these social resources than others do, and are thereby better able to achieve their goals.

Of these, force and its threat have been in poor repute among social phi-

---

[1]See, for example, the conceptual analysis in Cartwright (1959).

[2]All of these can be found, under one label or another, in most of the classical theorists. For a more recent use of them, see Etzioni (1961).

losophers, social analysts, and especially family counselors. However my aim is not to praise or condemn, but to explore their impact on human action. Napoleon is given credit for wisdom because he is supposed to have commented that one can do anything with a bayonet except sit upon it. However thoughtful, the remark must at least be qualified by the obvious historical fact that his regime was nevertheless founded on force and fell apart when he could no longer muster enough.

Rulers officially deplore force because they are convinced that their domination is based on justice, but they use force just the same. Philosophers deplore force because they see people are most tempted to apply it when they wish to gain more than others believe they ought to have, i.e., when they wish to impose injustice on others.

Social analysts often try to prove that force is simply an ineffective way of controlling others. This is partly incorrect, as thousands of years of conquest, imperialism, exploitation, and injustice prove amply. They also miss the main point, since no society is ever based on force *alone*. We pose the question falsely if we ask whether the family or any other system will survive if its sole foundation is force, since no such system is likely to occur or to last long if it does. Alone, it *is* ineffective.

But this is very different from asking how useful force is in getting things done, or where it is to be observed in the family system. This is the focus of my inquiry here.

In the analysis that follows, we wish to examine both the legitimate and the illegitimate applications of force in the family, i.e., both force and violence, and also the more subtle elements of family structure where force plays a role, though no overt use of force is actually visible. I believe these latter cases are much more important, but I want to explain all these patterns, both illegitimate and legitimate, violent and peaceable, by the same set of variables, within a framework of exchange theory.

Force is primarily thought of as a deterrent, i.e., it stops others from doing something we disapprove, either at the time they do it, or in the future because of a punishment in the past or a threatened punishment in the future. It is equally obvious, however, that force or its threat can persuade others to *do* something, not merely to avoid doing something. It is evident that we can at a minimum stop a weaker person from a disapproved act by holding him, or any one at all by killing him. Even if we never go so far, we can by the threat of force at least alter the other person's calculation of the anticipated gain from a specific action. In our effort to gain compliance we may offer both a reward—love, respect, or money—and a threat of force, and we know that the latter will be one of the variables influencing the decision. The threat may be unwise or ineffective at times, but it does alter the person's view of his possible cost/reward ratio. As an element in social exchange, it alters the perceived payoffs.

But this way of expressing the general relationship between force and compliance in the family still suggests, because its language is imprecise, that both parties in the social interaction are conscious of force, and that we presume the actual use of overt force will be visible. It also suggests that force only occurs when someone wants to prevent another from carrying out some deviant, improper, or wrong act, as when a child must be forced to obey. In fact, force may be used in favor of an act, and even one disapproved by the society.[3] And most force is not visible; we observe few acts of violence in any given day.

Because people have been socialized to accept the family structure in which they live, and because they take that social structure for granted, they do not test whether force would be applied if they challenged it. They know in advance they would fail. In most families, the structure is not overthrown, because it is viewed as inalterable or at best the only real alternative. Thus, force plays a role even when no deviant act is actually committed. The rebellious child or wife knows that the father or husband is stronger, and can call upon outsiders who will support that force with more force. Knowing the costs and the certainty of failure, the individual sees no likelihood of altering the terms of exchange.

Let us consider a few of such family patterns where we are unlikely to observe the application of force, but where its threat creates a relatively stable, unchallenged set of understandings, behaviors, and imbalances of influence or dominance. For example, if in a patrilineal polygamous society an older woman were to announce that she is henceforth to be treated as the leader of her patriline, tried to sell its cattle, started to give orders, set dates for rituals, or choose a chief, very likely she would be beaten or treated as insane. Similarly, if a child in our own society were to claim the headship of his family, give orders to his parents or siblings, try to write checks on his father's account, to trade in the automobile for a new one, the same result would occur.[4] That is, not only can his parents overpower him physically as a rule, but even if he is physically stronger they can call on superior force from other members of the family, as well as from outsiders such as policemen and juvenile authorities. The force or threat they command is not only their own strength but that of the community, which will back up the traditional family patterns.

Similarly, the mother who abandons her children, the father who runs off with the children, the wife or husband who takes a second spouse, the child who beats up his mother, the adolescent girl who wishes to spend a weekend with her boy friend against the will of her parents, the wife who wishes to change the family domicile without the consent of her husband, all can be and sometimes are restrained by either force or its threat, if not from fam-

---

[3]E.g., parents may use the threat of force to persuade a child to finish his homework; a parent may whip a child to force him to lie to outside authorities.

[4]Note that in some cases of this type, the son's physical possession of his father's credit cards or other documents does not give him the power to engage in such transactions: specifically, he would have no recourse if a clerk or salesman refused. On the other hand, ultimately the real owner of such documents can call upon the courts and other agencies (e.g., corporations which would not wish to lose his business) and thus obtain recognition of his rights. Since everyone knows all this, clerks and salesmen behave as they do, i.e., they will not ordinarily treat the son as a surrogate for the parent without parental authorization.

ily members then at their request by the community through its command over force.[5]

Such a list is not meant to be exhaustive. Rather it alerts us to the many and diverse mandates and restrictions on all of us in our family roles, which are ultimately backed by force. They include parental rights and obligations, laws of custody, property rights, traditions and laws about the freedom of children, the mutual rights and obligations of husbands and wives, and testamentary laws and traditions, among others, and they define to a considerable extent the institution of the family in our society. They do so in other societies as well.[6]

They function to shore up those family patterns by imposing strong sanctions when an individual tries to reject them. They are often expressed in laws, and thus are ultimately backed by the courts and the police system. They are similar to the force that maintains the economic system: the individual cannot invade the monopoly of a public utility, import forbidden goods, take over another person's property, sell drugs without quality controls, and so on. We do not ordinarily *see* force applied in these situations, because most people take this structure for granted, as part of the cosmos; they know they are likely to lose if they challenge it.

But such family patterns are backed not only by the state, just as laws generally are not supported only by policemen. Friends, neighbors, members of the community, in-laws and relatives, and other members of the conjugal family are also likely to intervene.[7] They are most likely to intervene with their resources of friendship, prestige, or even economic services and goods, either as promises or threats. Nevertheless, they can and do intervene with force and its threat as well.[8]

We should also see a further distinction here, between the weakness of a family member because he cannot command as *much* force as another—the adolescent boy commands *some* because of his own strength and can also defend himself from brutality by calling on outsiders—and the weakness because of an inability to command others to move in the desired direction. Thus, a husband can no longer sell his wife's property, as he once could,

[5]An interesting illustration of this occurred when the Soviets tried to change the family structure of Soviet Central Asia through immediate liberation of the Moslem women. Husbands' control over wives, which had been absolute, was declared officially ended by a series of emancipation laws. Control by force remained the crucial variable, however, since husbands were able to prevent their wives physically from going to the civil authorities. See Massell (1968).

[6]A recent summary of laws of this type may be found in Clark (1968); the European case is stated in Boschan (1963).

[7]Where outside community controls are not effective, force is much more visible. Oscar Lewis' (1965) study of Puerto Rican slum dwellers provides an example: "In the Rios family, uncontrolled rage, aggression, violence and even bloodshed are not uncommon." Numerous specific instances of this are related throughout the long record of participant observation of this extended family.

[8]Note the control implicit in the common pattern of pounding on a common apartment wall, when a family (usually husband and wife) is having a violent argument. It is a threat to call in outside authorities such as the police; it is also a reprimand, since "nice people" do not engage in such arguments. When individuals are persuaded to lower the noise level of their quarrel, violence is less likely to occur.

because her signature is required. He cannot successfully command her to vote as he wishes, or even to stop having movie dates with a friend whether male or female. This distinction is not, of course, an analytic one, since ultimately they both center on relative amounts of force, but pragmatically they differ, since the person who is commanded does not ordinarily have to act, to fight back actively; he or she need only fail to comply, and outsiders will not act in support of the command.

I do not think it is necessary but I shall repeat, that individual families and family systems are not maintained by force alone, any more than other social systems are. Daily role interaction also rests upon the constant flow of respect, affection, and services or gifts each family member makes to the others. We can nevertheless carry out the mental experiment of imagining away *all* the supports of force I have mentioned, or imagining entirely different ones.

If, for example, no husband were able to use his own force or that of family members, relatives, neighbors, or the community to press his children toward obedience at any age, to eject from his house a man who is courting his wife, to threaten his wife for welcoming flirtations or going on dates with another, to press her to stay in the domicile he has chosen, to persuade her not to abandon the children when she would like to go off alone, to take care of the home and children, to avoid running up bankrupting bills with their creditors, it is easy to see that substantial part of the structural strength of the family would be undermined. This is comparable to the place of deterrence in criminal actions: we know not everyone would suddenly begin robbing and stealing, if no force were usable—but many *would*, and many others would soon follow, upon seeing that those who took this greater freedom were not punished or deterred.

## SOCIALIZATION

Of course, most people have not only been trained to know that these structures are real and strong, and must therefore be accepted, but they have also been socialized to believe they are both right and desirable. In addition, the day-to-day social exchanges, shaped as they are by the existing force-based structures, offer better payoffs to those who do comply. On the other hand, it is equally important to emphasize that force and its threat have perhaps even more impact on the process of socialization than in normal adult interaction within the family. In this process by which we transform infants into people, inculcating in them the values, norms, and role habits of the family and society, or more specifically by which children come to accept as right and desirable the family patterns we approve, not only do we use force and threat in order to socialize our children, we also teach them thereby that force is useful, and we do in fact train them in the use of force and violence.[9]

---

[9] "It is in daily life, and especially in the life of children that the human propensity for violence is founded; we now suspect that much of that excess of violence which distinguishes man from animals is created in him by those child-training methods which set one part of him against another" (Erickson, 1969).

Observational studies of childrearing are understandably rare, but no very sharp eye is needed to know that American parents typically use force on their children from the earliest ages on. As against the widespread denunciations of permissiveness and love in childbearing over the past generation—Agnew is only the most recent, loud-mouthed, and ill-formed—and in spite of a probable slow decline in violent beatings over the past half-century or more, in fact love and permissiveness have not displaced force as a prime basis for molding U.S. children. Indeed, since parents themselves were trained to use and especially to threaten force, they cannot easily cast off that lesson when they confront an unwilling child.

Like other animals, man learns quickly from punishment. Doubtless this is a genetic inheritance of great survival value in the evolution of the species. An animal that did not learn almost instantaneously that fire burns, falls kill or maim, or a powerful male will slash if opposed, would stand little chance of living long. Punishment also constricts, since the fear it generates inhibits exploration: as Twain remarked, the cat that sits on a hot stove won't sit on a hot stove again, but may never sit on a cold one, either. In any event, the learning is quick and powerful.

The learning is also not merely cognitive, not simply a prediction. It is also emotional. The child learns that punishment will follow, but he also acquires a revulsion against a wide range of forbidden acts, an anxiety when he thinks of doing them, a feeling that they are undesirable and not pleasant. This effect is most striking, perhaps, in the area of sex, where early punishments color and distort later expressions of love, sexuality, and trust throughout the adult's life. However, the effect is general, and accounts for the depth of our commitment to the norms by which we live and by which we judge others morally and ethically.

I want to emphasize, however, that I am not speaking only of beatings, spankings, or blows, but any form of force or its threat. To underscore this, childrearing among the Japanese may be noted in passing. By contrast with the United States, one almost never sees a youngster being hit, but many Americans have marveled at what they see as the docility and "good behavior" of Japanese children. On the other hand, the child is not left alone, is not typically commanded from several rooms away, is guided through ritual bowing and other movements, is severely restricted in his explorations —in short, he learns early that the social space in which he will not be deterred, confined, or moved is very small indeed. He will rarely be left alone.[10]

The Japanese case is especially instructive, since it points up the great difficulties in measuring force when it so rarely expresses itself in overt physical shoving, hitting, or hurting. In every social system, the same measurement

---

[10]A brief sketch of "Japanese Family Structure and System of Obligations" can be found in Caudill (1952). "The main teaching and disciplinary techniques are teasing and ridicule—physical punishment is seldom used" (p. 30). A field study of "Taira: An Okinawan Village" by Thomas and Hatsumi Maretzki (1963) corroborates this, adding that threats are much more common than the actual occurrence of spanking or other physical punishment. See also the studies reported in *Families East and West* (Hill and Konig, 1970).

problem faces us. For example, the captain of a modern ship has a great deal of power (e.g., he can order the confinement of a crewman or passenger), but only rarely does he feel called upon to express it by the actual use of physical force. In socialization, parents may only rarely spank a child, but the child at least knows that he can be overwhelmed. As the columnist Jimmy Breslin remarked, in a discussion of the modern student revolt, "Why shouldn't I have been afraid of my parents? They were bigger and stronger than I, and I didn't have a nickel in my pocket." The problem is intensified, as noted earlier, by the fact that compliance is elicited from others not only because of force or the threat of force, but also through the daily exchanges of services, gifts and money, deference and respect, and love or affection. Consequently, we cannot measure the amount of force by simply noting the amount of compliance or conformity.

On the other hand, we can at least note in passing two sets of relationships: (1) between the command of power or force and other social resources; and (2) between physical punishment in childrearing and various other family variables. These do not solve our problem, but at least give us some information with which to think more productively about the place of force in the family as it shapes the terms of exchanges there.

Within the family itself, the harsh fact must be faced that the member with the greater strength and willingness to use it commands more force than others do. This is usually the father,[11] and in most cases it will also be the parents as compared with the children.[12] Since more husbands and parents are willing to use overt force in the lower class, they possess thereby an advantage as compared to their counterparts in other classes.[13]

On the other hand, they may be impelled to use overt force because they lack other resources that yield power or force to middle or upper class parents and husbands. Most people do not willingly choose overt force when they command other means because the costs of using force are high in any social system, but especially in the family, where it may destroy the possibility of achieving other goals than mere conformity, e.g., spontaneous affection and respect. Consequently, it is a general rule that the greater the other resources an individual can command, the more force he *can* muster, but the less he will actually deploy or use force in an *overt* manner. The husband in the middle or upper class family commands more force, in spite

[11]Lewis (1965) reports in the lower class Puerto Rican case that "The women show more aggressiveness and a greater violence of language and behavior than men." The women are also more likely to have greater resources in jobs and control of their families' loyalty.

[12]A summary of studies of the relation of class differences in socialization to differences in childrearing practices can be found in Bronfenbrenner (1958). He concludes that middleclass parents tend to use less punishment and rely more on appeals to guilt and the threat of the withdrawal of love.

A more recent study of 709 mothers in the city of Nottingham, England, showed that 56 percent of the mothers of one-year-olds in the highest class studied claimed they never hit their children as opposed to 35 percent in the lowest class (Newson, 1963).

[13]Note however that this relationship may change in late adolescence; when the boy may become bigger and stronger than either parent. In most nonindustrial societies, the boy was given some adult responsibilities then or earlier. In industrial societies, they are sent away to schools and colleges, or allowed to take jobs independently. This is also a period when severe challenges to parental authority occur, if youngsters stay at home.

of his lesser willingness to use his own physical strength, because he possesses far more other social resources. His greater social prestige in the larger society and the family, his larger economic possessions, and his stronger emphasis on the human relations techniques of counter-deference, affection and communication give him greater influence generally, so that he does not have to call upon the force or its threat that he can in fact muster if he chooses, through kin, neighbors, or the police and courts.

However, we can at least assert that the same variables generate a greater command of force in family relations as create more of what is usually called "influence" in the larger society: success, prestige, and position outside the family; age; being male; control over property, money, gifts, jobs and services; living up to the ideals of the family and thereby engendering trust and loyalty; skills in understanding and communicating with others; political authority; intelligence and relevant information; friendship, love and attractiveness; and so on. Such resources command force within the family and also yield more outside support (both force and other kinds) when a direct family confrontation takes place. Of course the family member who possesses more of them can also have greater impact on the socialization process when he chooses.

Because family analysts deplore the use of physical force on children, they have carried out many studies designed to ascertain its effects. Few studies have obtained data from children, and I know of none that have reported the opinions of children about its consequences. In any event, since measures of the amount and frequency of force used are lacking, the results could not be expected to be very consistent from one study to another. I shall at this time merely list in passing a number of the hypotheses that have described the relationship between physical, punitive, or harsh socialization practices and other family variables, including of course the effectiveness of socialization. Without discussing their meaning in great detail, I shall simply present them as correlations.

Firm discipline and harsh punishment by the father is associated with his lower I.Q., occupational level, and class.

Restrictiveness and firm discipline by the father are associated with higher scores on ethnocentrism, conservative political attitudes, and authoritarianism in the child.

Harsher discipline is used on the first-born child than on later-born children.

Boys are subjected to more physical punishment than are girls, who are more often disciplined by love-oriented techniques.

The use of physical punishment is associated with the development in the child of a moral orientation based on fear of authority.

The Oedipus complex is more likely to occur in a severe form in societies where physical punishment is used more often.

Aggressive boys are more likely than others to have been encouraged by their parents in their aggression.

Younger mothers are more likely than older mothers to urge their children to fight back when attacked by others.

Although I have abstracted many propositions on the relationship between aggression outside the home and aggression directed toward parents, the findings are highly contradictory. In general, however, high permissiveness for aggression toward parents is associated with aggression; lower-class children are given less punishment for outside aggression and more for aggression against parents; mothers who accept the child's dependency are less likely to punish their children for aggression toward parents than other mothers are; mothers who permit their children to direct aggression against parents are more permissive; middle-class boys are punished more by their mothers but not by their fathers for peer-directed aggression, than are lower and upper-class boys. On the other hand, some authors have suggested that there is no relation between social class and the severity of parental punishment for parent-directed aggression.

Middle-class parents are more likely to use psychological punishments than physical punishments, as compared with lower-class parents.

When the social and economic bonds among members of community are strong, children are more likely to be punished for peer-directed aggression. Catholic parents are more likely to use physical punishment than are Protestant parents; and Italians are less permissive of aggression toward parents than are Jews; in general, mothers are more permissive of aggression toward themselves than are fathers.

The ability of the child to resist temptation is not correlated with severity of punishment for the child's aggression. The use of physical punishment is correlated with authoritarian control by the father, the boy's identification with the father, and stricter sexual control.

When parents spend more time in explaining the family rules, the child is less aggressive.

When parents disagree on discipline, one being lax and the other punitive, the child is more likely to be aggressive.

The more controlling and punitive the discipline of the father over the son, the more likely the son is to become alcoholic; this type of discipline is also associated with other anti-social behavior such as stealing, lying, or truancy from school.

Fathers are more likely to use physical punishment on boys if all their siblings are brothers than if their son has only sisters and no brothers.

Large families are more likely to use physical punishment in socialization.

Adolescents whose parents use less authoritarian or punitive childrearing patterns are more likely to be satisfied with those parental policies.

Parents who use explanation more often as a childrearing technique are more likely to carry out their threat of physical punishment if such a threat is actually made. The use of praise is negatively associated with use of physical punishment.

Parents of repeater criminals (recidivists) are more likely than those of ordinary criminals, to have used physical methods of punishment. Mothers who use physical punishment are likely to have less warmth for and more hostility toward their husbands than mothers who do not.

Mothers of homosexuals are likely to have been harder on their sons in matters of discipline, and to have given more physical punishment.

The severity of parental punishment for disobedience is paralleled by a belief in supernatural punishment for disobedience to the gods.

When parents of aggressive boys stress masculine behavior, they are less likely to be warm and acceptant of their spouses than those who do not stress such behavior.

Husbands are, in general, inclined to believe that their wives are not strict enough with the children, and the wives tend to believe that their husbands are too strict.

The father's approval of physical punishment correlates with marital conflict.[14]

Most of these are well-known. In spite of their inadequacy they suggest several general conclusions (apart from specific findings) about the use of force in socialization. (1) Although there are many restrictions on it, it is widely used, and it does *seem* to "work." At the worst, most children who have been subjected to physical punishment will in fact grow up to become adequately functioning adults in this society. (2) It is more likely than some alternative techniques to create some effects that are judged by our contemporary values to be less desirable as outcomes of childrearing: e.g., a lesser amount of emotional spontaneity and freedom, of creativity, of communication and even a lesser willingness to give love. (3) However, it will continue to be used, because those who have been so reared are likely to rear their own children similarly, and because in any family confrontation between parents and children, some parents will at times resort to what is after all one effective way of eliciting obedience.

My first emphasis in this paper was on force embodied in continuing family roles and structures, the traditions and laws, that are accepted because people come to understand (whether or not they believe in their rightness) that others will defend them successfully with force if they are challenged. Most family members rarely reject these elements of the family structure.

My second emphasis was not only on that type of force which does not often become immediately visible, but also overt force, physical force actually applied, in the molding of children during the socialization process.

## VIOLENCE

In the final section I wish to explore a third aspect of force which emerges into violence within the family, appearing as assault, murder, or child abuse. Here, too, I wish to utilize the same framework of exchange variables so as to illuminate further the pervasive effect of force in the family, without at all denying the impact of other causes.[15] I shall first comment on assault and homicide, although certainly the dynamics there also apply to child abuse.

As we know, man is not a killer by instinct, because in the technical sense he has no instincts. But equally he is not restrained at all, as other great predators are, by automatic, nearly reflex mechanisms that prevent him from killing when his opponent quits. He is socialized not to kill, but that very socialization makes him care deeply about principles and honor, fairness and possessions, fidelity and self-respect; indeed, these emotional commitments are so great that he will risk or even give his life for them. It cannot be so surprising that he will also murder for them.

As I have already emphasized, parents and other moral authorities constantly exhort young children against violence, but their own behavior

[14]All of these were abstracted from William J. Goode, Elizabeth Hopkins, and Helen M. McClure (1971).

[15]In this section I shall draw upon my paper, "Violence Between Intimates" (1969).

belies that advice. We are all trained for violence. The child does learn that force is very effective at stopping others, and that force or its threat can change other people's calculations of profit and loss. They can be persuaded to obey when faced with such consequences. The child experiences this directly, and watches it in others—the fright of his mother when his father is furious, arguments and threats among neighbors, the battles with his own siblings, and so on.

The child also learns to make differentiated responses, depending upon the number of variables: he learns to gauge, however incorrectly, which people seem more willing and able to fight. He learns which kinds of situations call forth a greater amount of violence, within the family or outside it. For example, to challenge his father by aggressing against him is almost certain to elicit violence, but perhaps not a challenge against a playmate. A boy should not punch a girl, or a younger or weaker boy, but he may punch a bigger boy, and especially if the other started the battle. He learns that some acts so dishonor a person that violence is the only appropriate answer. In former days, of course, some kinds of acts justified duels.

He also learns, as part of this training for violence, that others are more or less likely to justify his violence; that is, others may support his own evaluations. In a slum area, to back down in a violent argument is to lose more face than is tolerable. Violence to protect one's sister's honor is praised by family members. He also learns *when* force (as distinct from other controls that might be available) will be more or less effective. He learns in addition how to call on the help of outsiders, whether kin, friends, or policemen, which laws might support or punish his use of force, and so on.

Little of this training justifies homicide, but much does justify the kinds of feelings, responses, traditions, evaluations, and actions that lead to violent assault and even homicide. Thus it is that family processes set in motion many patterns that ultimately generate violence: they inculcate the evaluations that make people want to force others to act in certain ways even at the risk of danger; they present models of the use of force and violence; they teach the various gradations of violence for different occasions; and they teach a set of rationalizations and justifications for violence.

Implicit in these comments is also a notion which is only now beginning to receive systematic attention: the contribution of the *victim* to the dynamics of violence. Typically, neither the victim nor the attacker *wills* the total outcome, whether it is a murder or a simple beating, but both contribute to it through the ongoing actions and counteractions of their daily lives. This is obviously so within the family, where from 40 to 50 per cent of all homicides are carried out, but it is not only the victim that contributes to his own demise. Other members of the family and the neighborhood contribute as well, since they create the field of forces that play upon the main participants in the drama.

These social linkages between evaluations, social pressures and propensity to assault also generate some of the major differences in assault and homicide rates that have been widely reported in the research on violence: rates are higher in the South than the North, younger adults are more prone to violence than older adults; men kill more than women: blacks than whites, the poor more than the middle class; and so on. However, we believe that the same variables operate in much of family violence, whether the rates are high or low.

Some part of that variance we have just discussed, by noting the extent to which training for violence occurs, how strong a field of violence exists within the family and neighborhood, how effective the family may be in training its members to solve problems through nonviolent techniques, or how deeply they are taught to care about certain ends, so that they might risk violence to achieve them.

Most of those variables are essentially socialization processes, i.e., the extent to which family members are taught as children to avoid or use force and violence, and which costs justify it in a set of social exchanges. Since the repression of violence in middle class families is much stronger, more consistent, and backed by more resources, middle class people *are* less likely to resort to homicide or assault. However, we also suppose that almost everyone is capable of violence. Almost every family member is from time to time enraged to murderous impulses by other family members. If so, we should look at the dynamics that generate such responses, whether or not they issue in murder or assault. For it is likely that these underlying processes operate in creating such lethal feelings at all class levels.

In any continuing family structure, people are bound to one another through an ongoing flow of transactions which may in part be viewed as exchanges. When family members fight about what one has done to the other, they are likely to refer to these actions as exchanges, and comment on what each owes the other. In the enraged family, very likely most members feel the others owe a great deal, and pay out little, whether it is love and deference, personal services, or gifts.

Even in the more harmonious family, of course, the objective observer might not always see that each person's contribution is equal. The wife works hard, but in economic terms contributes less than the husband; the children do not pay in as much love as the parents do; or the husband demands and gets much personal service, but gives none. On the other hand, if what each gives is valued by the others, and they agree roughly on these evaluations, over a period of time they may feel no necessity to count in close terms what each owes to the other. A husband knows he works hard, but enjoys the respect, loyalty, and love that others express; a child feels constricted, but enjoys the protection and affection he gets; and so on.

Over time, however, many family relations turn sour, what each values more or less will alter, and what each is willing to do for the other may diminish, so that one or more members feel a growing sense of anger and frustration, of being in fact cheated by the exchanges in which they engage. A wife's ability or willingness to give love may decline, and a child's willingness to obey or pay respect may lessen. A brother-in-law's success may lead him to demand respect that a man cannot easily give. Family members come to feel diminished, put upon, punished unjustly, or short-changed by others.

We are all exhorted to talk out such problems, to be wise in presenting our grievances and listening to those of others. Most of us are not wise, however, and in any event the underlying problem is that both sides may honestly feel that they are being cheated in the flow of family transactions. If both believe they are already paying out more than they should be, it is difficult to alter the terms without perpetrating more injustice.

At the same time, since both are already emotionally close, they know the other's weaknesses, and have acquired great skill at neatly hurting the other, or bludgeoning the other with a flood of counter-attacks. Moreover, they cannot easily retreat to the masks and formulas that mere acquaintances or business friends can use to pass over the conflict. As I have commented elsewhere,

Locked in but suffering from it couples may engage in fighting that is savage and even lethal. Many men and women have finally come to the conclusion that homicide is a cleaner, neater solution than the dragged out acerbic destruction of ego and dignity that is inherent in breaking off. (Goode, 1969: 958)

These dynamics also create two additional traits of man that increase the risk of violence among family members: the unwillingness of human beings either to submit or to escape. In this, man is like some of his domestic creations, such as gamecocks, pit bulldogs, and fighting bulls. He does not willingly escape or submit, as does the wild animal when another wins a battle. Man does not submit because thereby all that gives meaning to his existence is lost, i.e., values, norms, traditions, and moral or ethical beliefs. It is especially in the family that he cannot or will not escape easily, because his emotional investment in these relations is great, the costs of leaving are high, and the social pressures to maintain his kin ties are strong.

Thus it is that many family members continue to take part in an ongoing set of social transactions in which they feel they are paying more than they get in return, but self-respect and commitment to what they believe is fair keeps them from submitting, while no satisfying alternatives emerge elsewhere.

Shrugging one's shoulders and accepting the loss is also a difficult action to take. Even if a family member sees that he is constantly losing, the odds are poor, and change is unlikely, from time to time pleasurable exchanges do happen, and once more the hope is kindled that the other person will see the light and alter his behavior. Meanwhile, as against the situation of some payoff, there may be a few alternatives that look better. In addition, the peculiarity of family relations, like that between lovers and close friends is that they are *unique*. No other person can exactly substitute.

In the immediate situation of conflict, the emotions aroused are often high enough, even among those who are pacifically inclined, to call for a strong resolution. The conflict as it finally appears in the war of words is so sharp, the feeling of betrayal and loss so great, that redress must be physical and destructive. This impulse is the stronger because the person who wins the war of words—often the woman since she is perhaps ordinarily more facile verbally—is not necessarily the person with the greatest sense of outrage or even with the better case to present. The person who is least fair may be most competent in verbal attack.

A further general peculiarity of all conversations, emphasized by ethnomethodologists, exacerbates the conflict. Social customs dictate, often without explicit rules, how to end conversations of different kinds,[16] but perhaps none exists for ending conflict interaction. Among intimate friends, the formula may call for specifying when and where the next meeting will occur. At a cocktail party, a gesture or stating the need for another drink may be sufficient.

Unfortunately, conflict calls for peaceful resolution as an ending, and often that is not possible. Fighting conversation, being so unsatisfactory because it exposes still more disagreements and hostility as it progresses, does not easily lend itself to a safe completion. As already noted, two possible resolutions for the entire relationship, running or submission, seem difficult, and this holds for the conflict conversation as well. Escalation to the point of attack *is* one kind of end to the conversation, and often seems easier than tediously working through to some new harmony. Crushing the other can become a more tempting resolution to the interaction than any alternative. And, as a consequence, as the family member reviews in his mind all his injuries in the past, hurting the other can be a life-affirming act.

These dynamics also explain in part why so much assault is never reported to the police, and why the outsider finds it difficult to reconstruct just what took place. Both parties have contributed to the violence, not only over the long run but also within the ultimate conflict situation.

The process analyzed here also suggests a basis for Wolfgang's finding that women commit homicide more often in the kitchen and secondly the bedroom in order of frequency, and one-third of female victims were killed in the bedroom. It is in the bedroom where unresolved conflicts can burst out because both husband and wife finally go there for the evening and cannot easily leave as a way of ending the conversation. To some degree this is also true for the kitchen where in lower-class homes many family members are likely to spend much of their time (Goode, 1969: 126). The high emotion generated may also be seen in the finding that husband-wife slayings are more common than any other category if we consider only murders that were accompanied by a great deal of violence such as repeated shootings or beatings.

Although to discuss the general field of social forces that create different homicide and assault rates in different classes or ethnic groups takes us too far afield into the general problem of violence we should at least note that people who grow up in such social settings acquire a higher predisposition to violence because the norms against it are less stringent, punishment for resorting to it is milder, and training for it is stronger. Males are reared to believe that backing down is to deny one's masculinity, and bystanders are more likely to egg the conflicting parties on to a higher level of conflict.

Perhaps of more importance in this analysis is the fact that family members in such settings typically have fewer alternative resources of any kind that will help them to redress the balance of exchanges with their relatives or family members, and fewer alternative sources of pleasure and contentment, as compared with say, middle-class family members. Lower-class

---

[16]See Emmanuel A. Schegloff and Harvey Sacks, "Opening Up Closings," paper delivered at the annual meetings of the American Sociological Association, San Francisco, September, 1969.

people have less prestige, money, and power, and consequently they suffer greater frustration and bitterness. They can make fewer decisions that do not depend upon their friends or spouses. They generally command fewer resources with which to achieve their aims, with outsiders or intimates. Receiving less respect during the day from their experiences outside the home, they have less ability to withstand hurt and frustration in the home. They have less ability in talking out difficulties or mediation, whether the problem is one of sexual adjustment or family budgets.

A major consequence of these class and ethnic differences is the greater resort to violence among the disadvantaged members of the lower social strata in this and other societies. However, it is clear that these broader differences express themselves in the imbalances of transactions within the family, and the greater difficulty of improving the flow of services or gifts, loyalty and deference, or love and affection. They are more likely to feel that no other alternative to the satisfying use of force exists, and thus to be more easily tempted by it as a resolution if not a solution.

## CHILD ABUSE

It is not possible here to review the growing literature on child abuse,[17] but it is evident that the foregoing analysis also applies to this type of fanatical violence, as well. Although most people view child abusers as little short of psychotic fiends or mad killers, such parents do not hurt casually, and are typically not sadists. Their behavior is not explained, of course, so much by social pressures of their daily lives, as by their prior socialization, in which they were deprived of motherliness or tenderness, from mothers or fathers.

Abusing parents demand far higher performances from their children than ordinary parents. What they demand is beyond the capacity of their children even to understand, much less perform. Typically they become angry because the child will not stop crying, eats poorly, urinates after being told not to do so, and so on. In fact, they feel righteous about the punishments they have inflicted on their children.[18] They avoid facing the degree of injury they have caused, but they justify their behavior because they feel their children have been "bad."

Essentially, they approach the task of child care with the wish to do something for the child, a deep need for the child to fill their own lacks, to salve their own hurt self-esteem, to give them love, and a harsh demand that the child behave in a certain way. Failing that, the child demonstrates thereby his lack of respect, love, affection, goodness, and so on. The parents' high standards—e.g., that a six months' child must stop crying if the parent commands him—create an inevitable failure on the part of the child to show his virtue, and thus his concern for the parent himself. The parent is thus, at a deeper level, asking that the child not merely learn to eat, drink, control his crying and urination, etc. as an older child would, but that the child satisfy the parents need for counterpayments of devotion and concern.

---

[17]See David G. Gil, *Violence Against Children: Physical Child Abuse in the United States,* Harvard University Press, 1970.

[18]In this section, I have drawn especially upon Brandt F. Steele and Carl B. Pollock (1968). See also David G. Gillan and John H. Noble (1969).

Typically, such parents were themselves given little love or tenderness as children, so that their underlying hunger is for a response that will redress the imbalances of their past lives. They therefore force the child to engage in a set of transactions or exchanges in which they set a high price on what they do, and the child cannot pay back adequately. For this failure, the child is punished. Of course, violence of this kind is not effective in eliciting either the warmth the parents need, or the performance they require—though eventually, if the child lives, he may indeed try to meet at least the behavioral standards out of fear.

I am not suggesting here that such parents are healthy, happy people who feel they have received a poor bargain. They do suffer from emotional problems. However, what is striking is that those problems have usually been generated by precisely the experience of an unsatisfying imbalance in their own childhood transactions with their parents. In turn, their daily experience with the children they abuse takes that form once again, a form that parallels the dynamics of assault and murder among family members described in the previous section: nothing less than severe punishment will right the injustice they have experienced.

### FINAL COMMENTS

To analyze force or its threat in several of its guises is to emphasize those aspects of family life that violate not only our personal ideals but also, at times, the goals of family members themselves. Typically, family members want spontaneous affection from each other, not calculated obedience or compliance. If a family member conforms to rules because of the force they embody while resenting it, others are both hurt and angry. Each wants the others to *want* to offer services, pay respect, cooperate and help, give loyalty or obedience. If members discharge their role obligations because that is the best bargain they can get in the face of superior force, the foundations of the family are fragile and labile indeed.

But though I have reiterated the fact that family systems rest on customs and tradition, deeply held beliefs and values, and the constant exchange of *other* resources than force or its threat, we cannot on that account ignore this pervasive set of processes in family life and social actions generally. I have focused on three main faces of this power: (1) the family structures that are ultimately backed by force though few challenge them and instead accept them as given, not to be questioned. Ordinarily, force is not visible here unless some family member rejects part of the structure, whereupon one or more family members, kinsmen, neighbors, or the community in the form of court and police will intervene to reassert the rules. Most people have been socialized to believe the rightness and reality of these patterns, but it would fly in the face of fact to suppose, as we cannot for any other social patterns, that the removal of these supports would not reduce compliance, first among the antagonistic or less committed and eventually among others.

With references to that socialization itself, as a second theme, we have pointed out that from the start it is based on overt physical force or threat, since the child begins his life with no commitment at all to family values. He does not know them or believe in them. Here again, almost all parents use love and its withdrawal, the pleasure of food and other comforts, and gifts or money to inculcate those values in the child. But in no societies do parents find these to be enough. They use physical punishment or its threat, restrain the child by force from hurting himself, bring him back home if he runs away, and so on. As one result, he learns that violation of a wide range of rules will be met with force. The lesson is not lost on him and is rather extended to other social rules as well.

Finally, we have probed the dynamics of violence in the family, which here has referred to overt but illegitimate force. This we have placed in the same framework of exchanges within the family, specifically those which yield a continuing residue of resentment because of felt injustice.

These exchanges are made between family members on the basis of the evaluation each brings to or accepts within the family, so that in a harmonious domestic unit each feels the exchanges are more or less equal in value. The child brings in no income, but does pay loyalty, obedience, and respect to his parents. The mother gives affection, salves hurt egos and supervises or carries out household tasks, and so on. As long as each values what he gets as roughly equal to what he gives, all are fairly content, and their feelings are reinforced by outsiders, who share the same values. Most do not calculate the pay-offs and investments. When, however, one or more family members begins to feel a continuing imbalance, they start to engage in conflict about them, and for various reasons noted in the paper they may also feel they cannot submit, escape, or right the balance. Such conflicts can escalate to the point of violence because no simpler or easier resolution emerges. The dynamics outlined earlier go some distance toward explaining the variations of assault and homicide rate among different classes, ethnic groups, the two sexes, age groups, or neighborhoods.

With reference to child abuse, which has only recently begun to be studied carefully, because it was to some extent hidden from view, it seems likely that the processes sketched here also apply, though to an extreme degree.

Finally, although we do not believe it is possible to take seriously an imaginary utopia in which force would not play a role, we do not at all suppose the amount of force now applied in these various areas of family life or social life in general is either necessary or desirable. It is not only possible but we think likely, that some part of every social system is pervaded by force if only because some or many of its participants believe the system is unjust: therefore, those who dominate must use force to maintain it. Women, children, slaves, Colonials, lower castes, and other disadvantaged segments of any society are constrained more than others by force—although all are to some extent—or they are enjoined to refrain from its use, simply because the existing structures would change without these buttresses.

However, as the worldwide revolutionary temper of our era amply shows, when the disadvantaged learn how much of the social structure is not embedded unchangeably in the cosmos but is held in place by force wielded by human beings, they become less willing to comply with its traditional rules. Perhaps one could even say, as a challenge to superordinates everywhere, that we could test whether and where justice is to be found, by removing more and more physical force as a support. The system which needs least support of this kind would, I think, be a closer approximation of justice than any we know.

## REFERENCES

Boschan, Siegfried
    1965    *Europaisches Familienrecht Handbuch.* Berlin: P. Vahlen.
Broffenbrenner, Urie
    1958    "Socialization and Social Class Through Time and Space." Pp. 400–424 in
        E. E. Maccoby, T. M. Newsomb, and E. L. Hartley (eds.), *Readings in
        Social Psychology.* New York: Henry Holt.
Cartwright, D.
    1959    "Power: A Neglected Variable in Social Psychology." Pp. 1–15 in Dorwin
        Cartwright (ed.), *Studies in Social Power.* Ann Arbor: Research Center for
        Group Dynamics.
Caudill, W.
    1952    "Japanese Structure and System of Obligations." In *Japanese-American Per-
        sonality and Acculturation.* Genetic Psychology Monographs 45 (February):
        29–33.
Clark, H. H.
    1963    *The Law of Domestic Relations in the United States.* St. Paul: The West
        Publishing Co.
Erikson, E.
    1969    *Gandhi's Truth.* New York: W. W. Norton and Company, Inc. Pp. 234.
Etzioni, A.
    1961    *A Comparative Analysis of Complex Organizations.* New York: The Free
        Press.
Gil, David G. and John H. Noble
    1969    "Public Knowledge, Attitudes and Opinions about Physical Child Abuse in
        the United States." Child Welfare 48 (No. 7): 395–401, 426.
Goode, William J.
    1969    "Violence Between Intimates." Pp. 126, 941–979 in D. J. Mulvihill, Melvin
        M. Tumin, and Lynn A. Curtis, *Crimes in Violence.* Washington: United
        States Government Printing Office.
Goode, W. J., Elizabeth Hopkins and Helen M. McClure
    1971    *A Propositional Inventory in the Field of the Family.* Indianapolis: Bobbs-
        Merrill.
Hill, Reuben and Rene Konig (eds.)
    1970    *Families East and West.* Paris: Mouton.
Lewis, Oscar
    1965    *La Vida.* New York: Vintage Books.
Maretzki, Thomas and Hatsumi
    1963    "Taira: An Okinawan Village." Pp. 363–540 in Beatrice Whiting (ed.), *Six
        Cultures: Studies of Child Rearing.* New York: John Wiley and Sons, Inc.
Massell, G. J.
    1968    "Law as an Instrument of Revolutionary Change in a Traditional Milieu: The
        Case of Soviet Central Asia." *Law and Society Review* 2 (October): 179–
        228.
Newson, John and Elizabeth
    1963    *Infant Care in an Urban Community.* New York: International Universities
        Press, Inc., pp. 194–201.
Steele, Brandt F. and Carl B. Pollock
    1968    "A Psychiatric Study of Parents Who Abuse Infants and Small Children."
        Pp. 103–147 in Ray E. Helfer and C. Henry Kempe (eds.), *The Battered
        Child.* Chicago: University of Chicago.
Whiting, Beatrice (ed.)
    1963    *Six Cultures: Studies of Child Rearing.* New York: John Wiley and Sons,
        Inc., pp. 363–540.

# PART TWO
# Violence Between Spouses and Kin

At an 1886 meeting of the Philadelphia Social Science Association, an address was presented which helps us to see things about violence between family members which might be more difficult to perceive with more familiar and contemporary materials. We gain a certain detachment because of the historical nature of the address and its quaint language. But the issues are very contemporary. It is a prime illustration of society's uses of violence to control violence:

## WIFE BEATING AS A CRIME, AND ITS RELATION TO TAXATION.

During the session of the legislature of Pennsylvania, for 1885, a constituent put in my hands the following bill to be placed on the statute book:—

LEGISLATURE OF PENNSYLVANIA,

### FILE OF THE SENATE,

No. 26, SESSION OF 1885.

Mr. Adams in place, January 16th, 1885.

Mr. Lee, judiciary, special, January 29th, 1885.

NEGATIVE RECOMMENDATION.

### AN ACT

To provide for the infliction of corporal punishment upon all male persons convicted of wilfully beating their wives, and the manner and place of inflicting the said punishment, and the officers by whom the same is to be inflicted.

SECTION I. Be it enacted by the Senate and House of Representatives of the Commonwealth of Pennsylvania in General Assembly met, and it is hereby enacted by the authority of the same, that whenever hereafter any male person shall wilfully beat, bruise or mutilate his wife, the court before whom such offender shall be tried and convicted, shall direct the infliction of corporal punishment upon such offender, to be laid upon his bare back to the number of lashes not exceeding thirty, by means of a whip or lash of suitable proportions and strength for the purpose of this act.

✿　　✿　　✿

In 1883 the Legislature of Maryland passed a bill to punish wife beaters by whipping them, and the District Attorney of Baltimore informed the writer that after the first conviction the crime ceased as if by magic, in that state. With this last unanswerable testimony, the writer closed his argument in favor of the establishment of the whipping post for the offence of wife beating, feeling fully persuaded that the sentiment which undoubtedly exists to a certain extent against whipping as a punishment, will, as did his own individual feeling, change when the facts are known, and when it is well understood that corporal punishment is to be inflicted solely in cases of wife beating.

(Adams, 1886)

The author of this address was confident that twenty or thirty lashes on the bare back would deter husbands from beating their wives.[1] He was apparently unaware that such a procedure carries a dual message. The direct message is that the society disapproves of violence against wives. The indirect message is that when dealing with a crucial matter, violence is the most effective tool. It is a question of "do as I say versus do as I do," and we believe that the latter message carries the day. Thus, despite Adams' confident assertion that similar legislation in Maryland completely eliminated wife-beating, wife-beating has remained a part of the social scene in Maryland, as elsewhere.

Just how much wife-beating there is now, almost a century after Adams' proposed law (which was not passed), is unknown but it is probably considerable. Some hint of just how common physical violence is between husband and wife can be gleaned from the data reported by Parnas (1967: 914) for Chicago. Parnas estimates that more police calls involve family conflict than do calls for all criminal incidents, including murders, rapes, non-family assaults, robberies, and muggings. It seems as though we should be at least as concerned with "violence in the home" as we are with "crime in the streets."

Since it takes an unusual combination of events to have the police called in, one cannot tell from these data on police calls just what proportion of husbands and wives have had physical fights. The closest we can come to such an estimate is to be found in the studies by John E. O'Brien (p. 65) and George Levinger (p. 85). Both these researchers studied applicants for divorce. O'Brien found that 17 per cent of his cases spontaneously mentioned overt violent behavior; Levinger found that 23 per cent of the middle class couples and 40 per cent of the working class couples he studied gave "physical abuse" as a major complaint.

Our guess is that both these figures are underestimates of the amount of physical violence between husbands and wives because there were probably violent incidents which were not mentioned or which were not listed as a main cause of the divorce. Perhaps these figures should be at least doubled. Even then we are far from knowing the extent of husband-wife violence among all couples. It should be noted that there is a considerable discrepancy between the O'Brien and the Levinger figures. Moreover, these figures apply to couples who have applied for divorce. It may be that physical violence is less common in a cross section of couples or it may be, as we suspect, that the difference between divorcing couples and other couples with respect to amount of physical violence employed is not very great.

In a study restricted to working class families, Komarovsky found that 17 per cent of the husbands with a high school education and 27 per cent of

---

[1]Adams had other reasons for advocating corporal punishment. He considered this method of reprimanding an offender as more humane than existing prison conditions. Adams and his supporters also felt that it was more humane to keep families intact, which could be accomplished if corporal punishment were adopted. Finally, there would be a monetary saving to the individual taxpayer as compared with support of the offender while imprisoned, and his family, hence the title of the address.

those with less education mentioned a physically violent quarrel in the course of the interview. Of the wives, only four per cent of the high school graduates reported such fighting, but the figure reached 33 per cent for wives with less than a high school diploma (Komarovsky, 1964: 363).

The closest thing to data on a cross section of the population is to be found in a survey conducted for the National Commission on the Causes and Prevention of Violence which deals with what violence people would approve (Stark and McEvoy, 1970). These data show that 25 per cent of the men in this survey and 16 per cent of the women would approve of slapping a wife under certain conditions. As for a wife slapping a husband, 26 per cent of the men and 19 per cent of the women would approve. Of course, some people who approve of slapping will never do it and some who disapprove *will* slap, or worse. Probably the latter group is larger. If so, we know that husband-wife violence at this minimal level occurs in at least one quarter of American families. When we do not have even simple descriptive information about how much violence of this type occurs, the need for research is obviously very great.[2]

## SELECTIVE INATTENTION

The aspect of intra-family violence for which the most extensive and accurate data is available is not slaps and fights, but murder and child abuse. The selectivity shown in the available data is, in itself, instructive. It reflects the myths about the family presented in the general introduction. Since the family is seen by the society as the focus of love and gentleness, there is a tendency not to perceive or attend to the actual level of conflict and violence which occurs within the family. It is only when violence reaches the extremes of murder and severe injury to a child that society is willing to acknowledge the existence of violence in the family. This selectivity in perception of the family seems to be as true for social scientists and novelists as it is for the man in the street. It is an example of what Dexter (1958) calls "selective inattention" arising out of the value commitments of social scientists.

We had originally hoped to open Part Two with a brief passage from a

[2]As a result of the huge gap in knowledge concerning husband-wife violence, we decided to make this area the first priority in our own empirical research on intra-family violence. Four studies are in progress. The first is a reanalysis of the Violence Commission data which, with appropriate subcategorizing, we think can be made to yield information on intra-family violence. Unfortunately, because of the way the Violence Commission data was gathered, it is not possible to separate husband-wife violence from violence between other adult members of a family. The second study is therefore a questionnaire survey designed to obtain such information. A pilot run of this survey reveals that about one out of six couples used physical force on each other during a single year. The third study is being conducted by Richard Gelles using informal interview techniques. Eighty couples have been interviewed. Of these, 56 per cent mentioned at least one incidence of husband-wife physical violence (Gelles, 1973). It is obvious that there is a large discrepancy between the preliminary results of these two studies. We suspect that the 56 per cent figure from the informal interview study may be closer to the correct figure than is the 16 per cent figure of the questionnaire survey. The fourth study, by Suzanne Steinmetz, compares husband-wife, parent-child, and sibling violence within each family to give a total family configuration of violence.

novel depicting a fight between husband and wife. This proved impossible. We did find fight scenes in some plays, notably in *Who's Afraid of Virginia Woolf*. But the bare script, we felt, did not produce the dramatic effect of the famous fight scene from this play. In the twenty novels or so recommended to us by others as containing such a scene, the only suitable passages dealt with situations in which the wife was murdered; or they depicted foreigners, blacks, slum residents, alcoholics, or drug addicts or others on the fringes of American society.

There has been a similar absence in the social science literature. As O'Brien notes in "Violence in Divorce Prone Families" (p. 65): "in the index for all editions of *The Journal of Marriage and the Family*, from its inception in 1939 through 1969, not a single article can be found which contains the word 'violence' in the title. During that same period, discussions and studies of 'conflict' in the family were quite common. But apparently violence, as such, was either assumed to be too touchy an issue for research or else thought to be so idiosyncratic as to be unimportant as a feature in 'normal' families."

Why then is there a fairly extensive literature—both in fiction and in social science—concerning husband-wife murder and child abuse? At least in part, it is because the society *cannot* ignore these acts. In the case of husband-wife murder, there is unavoidable legal or physical evidence. A body is there and the coroner must be called. So such acts get entered into the official statistics and legal processes. In the same way, child abuse is the aspect of parental violence which cannot be ignored because the battered child is in the doctor's office or the hospital. Similarly, the reason why the only good data on non-lethal husband-wife violence describes divorced couples is probably their vulnerability to study as a result of the legal action.

As a result of the unignorable physical evidence produced by murder and child abuse, researchers such as Stuart Palmer have been able to analyze husband-wife murder (see his article on "Family Members as Murder Victims," p. 91); and historians such as Richard Hofstadter and Michael Wallace (1970) have been able to analyze violent feuds between kinsmen. Probably, even the official statistics on murder are a considerable underestimate of the extent of husband-wife murder. For example, there is evidence suggesting that car accidents are a frequent means of murder and suicide, and that husbands and wives are probably more vulnerable to this mode of being murdered than non-related persons (Mulvihill, Tumin and Curtis, 1969).

CAUSAL FACTORS

The state of knowledge about factors which produce high levels of intrafamily violence is no better than our knowledge of the frequency with which it occurs. In addition, most of what has been written is based on events which could not be hidden, or on persons who were not in a position to conceal. The article by Israel W. Charny on "Marital Love and Hate" (p. 52) is based on his work as a psychotherapist and marriage counselor and appeared in a journal devoted to such issues. The article by Jackson Toby on "Violence and the Masculine Ideal" (p. 58) is based on interviews with prisoners, and the article by Mabel Sewell on "Some Causes of Jealousy in Young Children" (p. 82) is largely based on cases brought to a social welfare agency. Even the article by Robert N. Whitehurst on "Violence in Husband-Wife Interaction" (p. 75), although it uses some survey data, is primarily based on cases from Whitehurst's practice as a marriage counselor and from police and court records. Despite the limitations imposed by data based on such special populations, we think that the general principles uncovered in these special circumstances apply to the rest of us. However, only future studies of "normal" situations can tell if this is so. Even more important is the need to go beyond descriptive studies to get a more complete picture of the social and psychological origins of violence between kin and between husband and wife.

Given both the limited data on the occurrence of such intra-family violence and the unrepresentative samples on which they are based, plus the scarcity of social science research on the causes of such violence, it is obvious that the material included in the section on "Approaches to Controlling Violence" must be regarded with considerable caution. The article by George R. Bach and Peter Wyden on "Why Intimates Must Fight" (p. 98) is based on their clinical experience. The principles they advocate are plausible and in accord with our values. But they have never been subjected to even the minimal standards of proof customary in contemporary sociology and psychology. Similarly, the article by Jetse Sprey on "Management of Marital Conflict" (p. 110) is an incisive *theoretical* analysis based in part on the work of ethologists such as Konrad Lorenz (1969) and Niko Tinbergen (1968).

Although the principles set forth in Sprey's article also have not been tested by research, our confidence in both his conclusions and those of Bach and Wyden is strengthened by the convergence of the two articles. Bach and Wyden base their work on clinical experience and theory. Sprey bases his on ethology and sociology. Thus, they draw on very different scientific traditions. Yet they come to some quite similar conclusions, notably an emphasis on learning to fight constructively (which these authors all feel can strengthen a marital relationship) rather than fighting violently and destructively.

A different sort of caution applies to the article by Melvin Cohen *et al.* on "Family Interaction Patterns, Drug Treatment, and Change in Aggression" (p. 120). The caution here does not concern the absence of evidence or the research procedures used to get the evidence. The research by Cohen *et al.*, in fact, represents a degree of experimental control and simultaneous consideration of social factors which is exceedingly rare. Rather, our concern is with the general issue of reliance on drugs to control anti-social behavior. In fact, the very effectiveness of chemical agents in manipulating behavior, although a short-run boon to mankind in such things as enabling a dramatic reduction in the mental hospital population between 1960 and 1970, is a potential long-term threat. First, to the extent that violence is social in its origin, the use of drugs enables us to avoid dealing with the underlying social realities which produce violence. Thus, the fundamental problems of society can be ignored in favor of a symptom-focused mode of dealing with their manifestations.

A second danger is that as chemical agents become more sophisticated, a society committed to drugs for therapy will be tempted to use drugs for social and political control. Even without drugs, there is a tendency to use psychotherapy and mental hospital commitment to deal with social and political deviants (Szasz, 1963; Scarf, 1971). It is much easier to control deviants with drugs than with therapists and hospitals as the agents of social control. We can already see this starting to take place in the recent trend toward almost indiscriminate use of tranquilizing drugs on troublesome children in slum schools (Witter, 1971). Most recently, Kenneth B. Clark, in a presidential address to the American Psychological Association, urged that we consider giving drugs to political leaders to prevent them from committing a society to war (Rensberg, 1971). If this were ever done to the heads of states, the likelihood of using drugs to control the ordinary citizen would be extremely great. In addition, such use of chemical agents implicitly assumes that the present structure of international relations is sound; only the heads of state need to be treated. Here, as in the case of personal violence, our conviction is that the more fundamental problem is with the social structures which produce violence and war, rather than with supposedly abnormal individuals who are violent or hawks. Clearly, there is an enormous task facing social scientists if we are to uncover these fundamental causes of violence and, on the basis of that knowledge, alter the features of society which lie at the roots of violence.

REFERENCES

Adams, C.
1886    *Wife Beating as a Crime and Its Relation to Taxation.* Philadelphia: Philadelphia Social Science Association, pp. 3 and 17.
Dexter, Louis A.
1958    "A Note on Selective Inattention in Social Science." *Social Problems* 6 (Fall): 176–182.
Gelles, Richard J.
1973    An Exploratory Study of Intra-Family Violence. Durham, New Hampshire: Unpublished Ph.D. Dissertation.
Hofstadter, Richard and Michael Wallace
1970    "The Hatfields and the McCoys." Pp. 397–400 in Richard Hofstadter and Michael Wallace, *American Violence: A Documentary History.* New York: Knopf.
Komarovsky, Mirra
1964    *Blue-Collar Marriage.* New York: Random House.
Lorenz, Konrad
1969    *On Aggression.* New York: Bantam Books.
Mulvihill, Donald J., Melvin M. Tumin, and Lynn A. Curtis
1969    *Crimes of Violence.* Staff Report to the National Commission on the Causes and Prevention of Violence. Washington, D.C.: U.S. Government Printing Office, Appendix 10, "Suicide and Violent Auto Fatality Data and Computational Method."
Parnas, Raymond I.
1967    "The Police Response to the Domestic Disturbance." *Wisconsin Law Review* 914 (Fall): 914–960.

Rensbergh, Boyce
 1971     *New York Times* (September 5): Section 1, p. 1, column 4.
Scarf, Maggie
 1971     "Normality is a Square Circle or a Four Sided Triangle." *New York Times Magazine* (October 3): 16ff.
Szasz, Thomas
 1963     *Law, Liberty and Psychiatry.* New York: Macmillan.
Tinbergen, Niko
 1968     "On War and Peace in Animals and Man." *Science* 160 (June): 1411–1418.
Witter, Charles
 1971     "Drugging and Schooling." *Transaction* 8 (July, August): 30–34.

# CHAPTER TWO
# The Origins of Violence
# Between Spouses and Siblings

## 3. Marital Love and Hate
### ISRAEL W. CHARNY

Charny is one of a growing number of marriage counselors who feel that aggressiveness and conflict in marriage is a necessary life force, a challenge to be met rather than avoided. The goal of marriage counseling, therefore, should be to teach couples to experience the *positive* effects of fighting rather than to try to eliminate fighting. The alternative of suppressing conflict and aggression can lead to a marriage which is increasingly demoralizing, destructive, and violent.

Although Charny's view is based on many years of experience as a marriage counselor, some cautions against accepting it without qualification are in order. First, the kind of fighting Charny advocates excludes physical fighting; in fact, a main point made in the article is that by fighting things out fairly, violence can be avoided. Second, we need scientifically valid evidence to know if families who suppress conflict really have worse marriages than those who seek to experience the positive effects of fighting. On purely theoretical grounds, a good case can be made for either approach. Clinical evidence (i.e., case histories of couples who have been under treatment) is notoriously undependable. For example, there were a huge number of case histories showing the efficacy of blood-letting, a standard treatment for many ailments until the nineteenth century. "Fighting fairly" may be only a modern psychological version of blood-letting—harmless, but useless in some instances and injurious in others. Only a controlled experimental study can provide the needed factual evidence. But even if such a study were to come out against the practical recommendations which seem to follow from Charny's approach, his presentation of the combination of love and hate which characterizes the family would still be a valuable description of the human condition.

For all practical purposes, the working theory of desirable marriage in our contemporary mental health literature speaks of marital communication, cooperation, and relatively little fighting; and if fighting, certainly not too intense or regressive.

In marriage counseling or various individual or family psychotherapies, troubled couples in effect are invited to consider just what are the personal sources of immaturity that lead them to be too angry, or how they are failing

SOURCE: Reprinted with permission from *Family Process* 8 (March, 1969): 1–3 and 17–24. Edited and slightly revised. This article was expanded by Dr. Charny into a book for the general public, *Marital Love and Hate* (1972), which was adopted both by general book clubs and by book clubs in the social sciences.

to communicate their feelings in more respectful and mature ways; most treatment aims at eliminating fighting rather than helping and teaching people to experience the possible positive effects of fighting.

Many other "patients" of the mental health professions who present themselves for help for any of a variety of other kinds of symptoms of emotional problem are also led to discover and acknowledge the destructive consequences of the marital fighting and/or dissension that are all-too-soon discovered in their lives.

While all of these notions have *some* validity, in the long run these orthodoxies of our contemporary mental health world miss and obscure these essential truths:

1. "Nearly all" marriages are "disturbed," including those that *are* arriving at a reasonably mature state of development, because the business of marriage is inherently a disturbing one—no less than the state of being a human being is inherently troubling and difficult.

2. For a marriage to be reasonably productive a couple needs to arrive at a balance of "love *and* hate, honor *and* dishonor, obedience *and* disobedience."

3. The goal of marriage counseling should be to teach people how to be strong enough to be honestly loving *and* hating, how to extend themselves enough to support *and* confront each other, not to be volatile and violent but *how* to fight, with much of that fighting very much in front of the children.

In discussion with colleagues we find that none of these principles is entirely new to many psychotherapists and marriage counselors. However, in most cases these ideas must grow for each therapist out of his own maturing ability to give up the make believe of his training days that so-happy, stable marriages await the mentally healthy and well analyzed. (So often the therapist's learning follows on cynical but also frightening observations of the despairs and divorces of his own senior teachers, let alone wise observations of his own patients and counselees and of course himself in his always-demanding marriage.)

The therapist who is open to learning will also find some support in here-and-there fragments in the psychological literature, especially in connection with writings that speak to the inherent *challenge* of all life and the inevitability of *anxiety, conflict,* and yes, *despair* too through the entire spectrum of man's journey from the miracle of his beginning to his inevitable death. There are also some statements in the clinical literature of marriage difficulties that speak to the inevitability of conflict, and even to the constructive role of aggression in marriage; and recently too some recommendations as to *how* couples might fight with each other productively; but as we shall see, there is rarely a frank, decisive statement of a theory of marriage as an inherently tense, conflict-ridden interpersonal system whose successful fulfillment demands not resolution of conflict so much as it requires a constructive living out or tapping of conflict for generating energy for creative living in both partners—and their children.

In developing a theory of marriage as a wise balancing of love and hate, we will tap evidences from several sources or levels of human experience.

. . . The literature of the traditional mental health concept of marital adjustment . . . has been evolving an increasingly sophisticated concept of the reciprocity and complementarity of marital partners' problems, but . . . there still persists the myth that marital difficulties are largely the lot of "sick" people or those who are not really "mature." [By contrast,] . . . we will conclude that empirically it cannot be denied (as our culture overall and even our mental health world vainly attempt) that the largest majority of marriages are riddled with profound destructive tensions, overtly or covertly.

We shall then argue from the logic of pragmatism that even if one believes that there are a few mature people for whom marriage *might* become a more enduringly cooperative, loving relationship, or even if one dreams that man may someday evolve to a state of potential for such interpersonal peacefulness and respect for one another, at the moment it is folly to shoot for anything other than effective fighting marriages—or how to be a "happy, unhappy husband or wife" (with appreciation to one of my patients who phrased this goal so simply).

Finally, we cite naturalistic evidence for the inevitability of aggressive tension in all human affairs, indeed in the life process itself; that aggression is not only inevitable but desirable for stimulating pleasure, productivity, and creativity. On this basis, we argue that the institution of marriage (and its derivative role of child rearing too) in no ways is exempt from this truth of life: that all living inherently draws from and creates anew profound tension and problems. . . .

## AGGRESSIVENESS AS A CONSTRUCTIVE FORCE IN MARRIAGE

So far, we have been reluctantly yielding to the fact of aggressiveness as a sadly inescapable quality of existence. However, the fact is that there are some aspects of aggressiveness that are really quite positive. We tend to forget these because so often aggressiveness ends up in destructive expressions that are so devastating that we naturally fear the very sources of such power without realizing that much aggressiveness can be constructive in its nature.

Thus, Coser (1) a sociologist, has pointed out how from a larger point of view of social organization aggression plays at least three positive functions: as a form of achievement as in the violence of revolutions against oppression; as a danger signal—a good example in our own time would be the demonstrations of American Negroes; and as a catalyst.

In biological life, we have learned that aggression plays key *life-serving* roles in survival of the fittest (the basic Darwinian concept, of course); also for spacing out or apportioning territory to the species (1, 5); also as a tonic for the stimulation and effecting of the whole symphony of drives (5); and even as a basis for the evolution of a bond of affiliativeness—and love (5).

This last function of aggression is especially remarkable for our purposes. It is fantastic to see that only among those animals who show significant aggression within their species does there also evolve a love bonding; that without hating-killing there is no emerging counterpoint of loving. Shades of human lovers!

In psychological affairs, too, we have increasing evidence of the significance of aggressiveness as a life force; its absence marks weakness, lack of energy for projecting oneself, lack of stamina for creativity, lack of zest for recovery from emotional problems.

Aggressiveness is the hum of life, the spirit of being.

This has long been understood in popular, instinctive psychology: We are forever curiously gauging another man's real strength by the vitality of his bearing and manner. In projective test studies of people, we look for indications of drive and affect strength.

In treatment of various serious emotional disorders and mental illness, we find so often not only an excess of anger that is burning up the person himself, but an excess that in many ways is built on a basis of improper release or utilization of the natural aggression one needs for successful living. Much of the treatment process is intended to teach people how to feel anger, and share their anger with their family and associates without fearing that their anger will in fact destroy another.

In treatment of various sexual disorders, we frequently find fears of one's aggression inhibiting the flow of sexual vigor; in treatment an effort is made to help people be angry at the very person they love and desire; also, on another level, to be physically penetrating and vigorous towards their sexual partner.

This last point is particularly significant for our consideration of the marital relationship. For it reminds us that in the cornerstone area of the basic sexual contract of marriage there is to be a never-ending aggressiveness—a never-ending fusion of anger with loving feeling. It is surprising that we have been so long in coming to an extrapolation of this principle to the broader range of the marital relationship; that the couple who can hate each other *and* love each other may stay together, with some real satisfaction no less, for all that they too must indeed endure many painful low points and troubling unsure experiences of bitterness with each other.

Let us consider specifically some of the positive values of aggressiveness in the marital union:

1. Our spouse is a colleague, critic, teacher, and supervisor.

2. Our spouse is a reacting, stimulating, catalyzing force, often irritating and provocative perhaps, but challenging us to be more wise and creative.

3. From what we know of the structure of marriages, given the particular characteristic of most marital unions as involving people who differ quite dramatically on certain key psychological characteristics, there is the possibility of each partner teaching the other those qualities in which the one partner is quite strong and in which the second partner is particularly weak.

A simple example is that the fair young maid who is socially more comfortable and winning may be able to bolster the shakier, more socially withdrawing man to dare experiment with becoming more winning socially. Since the oppositeness of people often also implies a degree of extremeness even on the part of the mate who seems blessed with the more positive side of a trait, conflict between spouses may also help reduce the too-good extreme. Thus, the sociable lady may also be a person who is too driven to socialize; and in conflict with a mate who tends to be more withdrawn but also possibly more given to inner depth, she may learn to quiet down, and search for more inner value in her interpersonal relationships.

4. An even more subtle but we believe important point about the opposite-ness of marriage partners is that by and large we know that underneath whatever extreme is represented in the overt stance of a human being, there is so often an unconscious oppositeness in that person himself. In the con-flicting interchange between mates, there is also a struggle around these unconscious opposites, and hopefully, if the marriage struggle moves along constructively, there is also change developing on this level of the secret emotional understructure of each spouse.

For example, take the generally fair mate and the characteristically unfair mate in fights. The one generally seeks to pacify and to be reasonable. The other generally attacks and carries on as an unrelenting "hawk." Yet, often we find deep in the hawk considerable fairness and sensitivity; and in the fairer, more righteous fate, so often underneath there is a heck of a lot of unreasonable anger.

5. There is often value in a clash of forces insofar as it creates energy.

We now take for granted the miraculous physics of electrical potential as it involves plus and minus elements. So too may it be that the interplay of complementary qualities within us as individuals produces the energy of a search for a balanced expression of ourselves. And so too does the clash of various levels of difference and oppositeness between peoples such as a couple in marriage produce energy, vitality, zest, and power for life, for them and for their children stimulated by this environment.

Needless to say, if the wires are uninsulated, or if the amount of electricity transmitted is excessive for the wiring, or if you're standing in a puddle when you touch the hot wire, or if you do any of the other kinds of things that are wrong when you're dealing with electricity, you can burn yourself up! But if you learn to tap the energy, wire it, channel it appropriately to its goal points for activating other machinery, create on and off switches, circuit breakers, dimmers and whatnot, then there is the possibility of getting to a more creative state precisely because you do have power machinery work-ing for you, and not just your own old hand tools!

## THE "HOW" OF MARITAL FIGHTING AND LOVING

This is not the place for an extensive discussion of how couples might love and hate well. Interested readers are referred to a more popular presentation of this paper in which there is a fuller discussion of working "Principles for Survival in the Inferno" (3).

Some techniques and attitudes for marital fighting are these:

1. It is natural and right to feel anger.

2. There is much to be gained from learning how to fight with one's spouse openly, saying what we feel but not promiscuously, sharing our angers, but not overwhelming one another.

3. It is very much wrong to hurt another person, overtly, in *acts* against the other's person, but to *feel* like hurting another is a natural expression of anger.

4. Feelings are not the same as actions; our feelings of anger in no way really punish or hurt the other party in a literal sense.

5. Husbands and wives are far better off when they learn that in the course of marital fighting a good deal of unfairness, exaggeration, and extremes is natural.

6. Our minds operate much like computers searching through all the accumulated data for just what we want to say; in a good, heated marital fight the machinery tries out many bits, including such part-truths or truths-of-the-moment as "I wish I had never married you." We should not believe that anything our rival spouse says is *fully* intended or the *whole* truth of his feelings, nor should we believe anything we think of is the full measure of what we feel and believe.

7. For one's own sake, above all, and then too for the sake of one's children and for one's spouse, it is all to one's good to be committed increasingly to stay with one's marriage if at all possible—to work hard at reducing undue pain and at gaining the best this union can grow to create. Such commitment offers a sense of security and meaning to oneself and to one's family, especially when the going gets rough, as it always does.

8. Even when we hate, we love. Even the moments filled with our bitterest hate contain our love at one and the same time. How good to know this before one acts too strongly and realizes too late the damage done a person and a relationship one loves very much. An excellent emotional exercise in the heat of marital battle is to conjure up (silently! for Macys doesn't really tell Gimbels!) just how much one cares for one's now quite-hated-spouse; so as to experience one's hate and love as coexisting streams of feeling.

9. We would be wise to feel grateful for the stimulation of confrontations and challenges by our spouse.

10. Never fight in front of the children? On the contrary, fight fairly often in front of the children!, but fight wisely and well. The trick is not to put anger away so much as to show the children that when anger is experienced, it does not destroy either party, it is not acted out in overt violence, and that even certain regressive fighting behaviors that the parents allow themselves in the somewhat greater privacy of their away-from-the-children fighting are put aside out of respect for the child to whom they both are loyal.

There is much more to be said and much to be learned about effective marital fighting. As noted previously, at this writing we have been promised a major work is forthcoming from Bach (2), who has previously reported on his teaching couples how to fight as the key focus of his group therapy approach to marital disorders. In general, we would suggest that the *how* of marital fighting and loving will yet be worked out through the efforts of many family researchers. The critical point of the hour, we have felt, is the need for a theory of marriage that acknowledges once and for all that marital fighting is inevitable, necessary, and desirable—not simply an unhappy byproduct of emotional immaturity or disturbance. The latter make for ineffective and immature fighting, or for a suppression of fighting with all their marriage-shattering consequences, but not for the fighting *per se* that is the legacy of all of us Adams and Eves.

A FINAL PERSPECTIVE: MARRIAGE AS A SMALL SCALE
BATTLEGROUND OF MAN'S CHOICES OF WAR OR PEACE

A final thought for twentieth century couples: In our marriages each of us is
given a chance to participate in a worldwide and mankind-wide panorama
of choices as to whether or not each man will allow his aggressiveness to
mount into destructive, warring forms, or whether each of us will learn to
feel angry and aggressive in *feelings* but not in violent destructive *action*.

In each marriage the choice is not between happiness and unhappiness,
but between a respectful, cooperative state of nonviolent tension, where
quite often we must experience anger though often we may also enjoy a more
positive, empathising love; or a state of increasingly violent, demoralizing,
depersonalizing destruction of one or another. And so it is in all of our
universe that we must face as collective groups of people learning how to
live with our differences, expecting there will be disagreements all the time
and much anger, but learning how to create a lawful machinery for the expression and resolution of these differences, rather than succumbing to the
age-old impulses to destroy and be destroyed.

REFERENCES

1. Ardrey, R., *The Territorial Imperative.* New York, Atheneum, 1966.
2. Bach, G., Symposium, "Hate and Aggression." *Voices: The Art & Science of Psychotherapy,* 1 (1965).
3. Charny, I. W., "Love and Hate, Honor and Dishonor, Obey and Disobey." In cooperative, nonviolent tension: the need for a revised marriage contract and a revised
   offer of help by the marriage counselor. Presented to the Family Workshop, Family
   Service of Chester County, Pennsylvania, September 27, 1967.
4. Coser, L. A., "Some Social Functions of Violence." Pp. 8–18 in Marvin E. Wolfgang
   (ed.), *Patterns of Violence: The Annals of the American Academy of Political and
   Social Science,* Vol. 364 (Philadelphia: American Academy of Political and Social
   Science, March, 1966).
5. Lorenz, K., *On Aggression.* New York, Harcourt, Brace & World, 1966.

# 4. Violence and the Masculine Ideal: Some Qualitative Data

## JACKSON TOBY

In the discussion of the sex myth in the general introduction, it was suggested that one of the social conditions which tends to make sex and violence
occur together can be traced to a need on the part of boys to overcome their
unconscious fear of being feminine by means of "compulsive masculinity."

The compulsive-masculinity theory suggests that anxiety over demon-
strating one's masculinity is likely to be greatest in female-headed house-

SOURCE: Reprinted with permission from Marvin E. Wolfgang (ed.), *Patterns of Violence: The Annals of the American Academy of Political and Social Science,* Vol. 364
(Philadelphia: American Academy of Political and Social Science, March, 1966), pp.
20–27.

holds. In these families, the entire care of the child is the responsibility of the mother and there is no adequate male role model available. Since there are more female-headed households in the lowest strata of society than in other strata, one would also expect to find more compulsive masculinity and hence more husband-wife violence in lower class families. The following article provides a case example of a lower class young man who typifies the resulting compulsive masculinity and husband-wife violence.

What inference should be made from the observation that males are more likely than females to behave violently in Western societies? That biology predisposes males to violence? Or that something in the organization of Western society encourages masculine violence more frequently than feminine violence? Evidence from cultural anthropology seems to rule out the biological inference; primitive peoples exist where violence is very rare on the part of both sexes, and in some cultures females are more prone to violence than males.[1] In contemporary societies, regional, urban-rural, and other social variations in the incidence of violence also suggest the fruitfulness of a sociocultural explanation. In the United States, for example, the South has more violent crimes per capita than the North and West; Negroes have a higher arrest rate for violent crimes than whites; middle-class persons are less violent, on the average, than working-class persons; and rural areas —with some regional exceptions—produce less violence than urban areas.[2] Such variations can be explained better by social organization than biology, thus reinforcing the inclination to look for sociocultural factors underlying the sex difference in the incidence of violence.

## COMPULSIVE MASCULINITY AS A CAUSE OF VIOLENCE

Professor Talcott Parsons has developed an analysis of the family structure of urban industrial societies capable of explaining (1) why violence is more likely to be a masculine ideal in *modern* societies than in *preliterate* societies and (2) why violence is more likely to be regarded as a *masculine* rather than a *feminine* characteristic in modern societies.[3] He calls attention to the tendency in such countries as the United States, Canada, West Europe, the Soviet Union, and Japan for extended kinship relations to diminish in importance. That is to say, family life is almost synonymous with the nuclear or conjugal family in these societies, partly because the small family system is more compatible with an urban society characterized by rapid population mobility. Children are brought up in households where there are usually no more than two adults —and, in cases of divorce, separation, or widowhood, only one. Furthermore, the father typically works at some distance from the place of residence of his

---

[1]Margaret Mead, *Male and Female: A Study of the Sexes in a Changing World* (New York: William Morrow, 1949).

[2]See United States Department of Justice, *Uniform Crime Reports—1964* (Washington, D.C.: U.S. Government Printing Office, 1965) for data on the incidence of criminal homicide, aggravated assault, forcible rape, and robbery.

[3]Talcott Parsons, "Certain Primary Sources and Patterns of Aggression in the Social Structure of the Western World," *Psychiatry*, Vol. 10 (May, 1947), pp. 167–181.

family; hence the major responsibility for socializing both male and female children falls on the mother. Parsons hypothesizes that these structural features of contemporary societies create a problem of masculine identification. Boys initially identify with and depend on their mothers, but they realize that they must, when they grow up, become men and not women. Much of the exaggerated roughness and toughness of preadolescent and adolescent boys should be understood, according to this hypothesis, as the result of unconscious needs to repudiate a natural identification with their mothers. Parsons labels this effort on the part of boys to clear up possible misunderstandings of their sexual identification "compulsive masculinity."

The compulsive masculinity hypothesis goes far to explain a variety of observations: (1) Large numbers of adolescent boys are fascinated by weightlifting and body-building—as evidenced by the various magazines devoted to these activities; (2) males make extensive use of profanity, symbolically associated with masculinity, in fear-provoking situations—such as combat—where there is danger that they may respond in ways appropriate to women;[4] (3) some males require endless heterosexual conquests to reassure themselves of their own virility; and (4) seemingly senseless violence is perpetrated by delinquent gangs in response to implicit or explicit charges of cowardice.[5] These observations can each be explained in other ways than by invoking compulsive masculinity, but the compulsive masculinity hypothesis is provocatively parsimonious. We need not believe that the majority of males in urban industrial societies have serious problems of masculine identification—only that there are sufficient numbers of males with this problem to influence the cultural ideal of masculinity.

## PREDICTIONS DERIVED FROM THE COMPULSIVE MASCULINITY HYPOTHESIS

If the compulsive masculinity hypothesis has merit, it ought to generate testable predictions about the occurrence of violence that prove correct. Here are a few such testable predictions.

(1) Boys who grow up in households headed by a woman are more likely to behave violently than boys who grow up in households headed by a man. Some students of delinquency have noted (a) that matriarchal families (and broken families) are more characteristic of Negroes than whites and (b) that violent crimes are more frequent among Negroes—and have hypothesized that female-based households tend to produce such delinquency.[6] This hypothesis would be strengthened if it could be shown that Negoes committing *violent* crimes (forcible rape, murder, aggravated assault) come more

[4]Henry Elkin, "Aggressive and Erotic Tendencies in Army Life," *American Journal of Sociology*, Vol. 51 (March, 1946), pp. 408–413. See also an argument for one alternative to profanity in Ashley Montagu, "Should Strong Men Cry?", *New York Times Magazine*, May 26, 1957, pp. 17–18.

[5]Lewis Yablonsky, *The Violent Gang* (New York: Free Press of Glencoe, 1962) and David Matza, *Delinquency and Drift* (New York: John Wiley & Sons, 1964), pp. 53–59, 156–157; for a fictional account, see Warren Miller, *The Cool World* (Boston: Little, Brown, 1959).

[6]Walter B. Miller, "Lower Class Culture as a Generating Milieu of Gang Delinquency," *Journal of Social Issues*, Vol. 14, No. 3 (1958), p. 9.

frequently from matriarchal families than Negroes committing nonviolent crimes (pilfering or burglary)—or even that the higher rate of Negro criminality as compared with white criminality is directly attributable to Negro family situations. These demonstrations have not yet been made, to my knowledge.

(2) Boys who grow up in households where it is relatively easy to identify with a father figure are less likely to behave violently than in households where identification with a father figure is difficult. Thus, other things being equal, the younger the father at the birth of the boy and the more time he spends with his son, the less likely it is that the boy will behave violently. The greater availability of farmer fathers as role models as contrasted with urban fathers, who usually work at considerable distance from the family residence, should make for less compulsive masculinity among sons of farmers. We do not have systematic studies bearing on this problem.

(3) Boys whose development toward adult masculinity is slower than their peers are more likely to behave violently than boys who find it easy to think of themselves as "men." Thus, boys in whom secondary sex characteristics appear early ought to be less violent than boys in whom secondary sex characteristics appear late. Similarly, adolescent boys compelled to wear juvenile clothing, or assigned household responsibilities usually considered "girls' work," or denied adult privileges such as staying out late at night and possessing a key to the house ought to be more prone to violence. Again, data are lacking.

(4) Masculine ideals emphasize physical roughness and toughness in those populations where *symbolic* masculine power is difficult to understand. Thus, middle-class boys ought to be less likely than working-class youngsters to idealize strength and its expression in action and to be more likely to appreciate the authority over other people exercised by a physician or a business executive. We do not know whether weightlifting has a greater appeal to working-class or middle-class boys, but there is little doubt that what Professor Wolfgang calls the "subculture of violence" is concentrated in segments of the American population having little opportunity to wield symbolic power—among adolescents rather than adults, in the working class rather than the middle class, among deprived minority groups rather than white Protestant Anglo-Saxons.[7]

At the present time the evidence is so fragmentary that these predictions cannot be rigorously evaluated. The scanty data that exist, however, are compatible with the predictions. Furthermore, case studies abound which suggest that violence is not merely a response to frustration but is felt by the perpetrator to be required by the demands of the male role. As an illustration of such case studies, I am including excerpts from a tape-recorded interview with a 25-year-old reformatory inmate. His attitudes are obviously not typical of American males or even necessarily of American offenders. Nonetheless, I suggest (1) that Jimmy's willingness to resort to violence reflects his

[7]See Marvin E. Wolfgang, *Patterns in Criminal Homicide* (Philadelphia: University of Pennsylvania Press, 1958) and Menachem Amir, "Patterns in Forcible Rape," unpublished Ph.D. dissertation, University of Pennsylvania, 1965.

participation in the subculture of violence and (2) that this subculture teaches a masculine ideal in terms of which violence may be the most appropriate way to protect one's honor, to show courage, or to conceal fear, especially fear of revealing weakness. In the excerpts from our conversation reproduced below, Jimmy was responding on two levels: the personal one, in terms of which he depended on and cared for his wife and the subcultural level, in terms of which tough and perhaps violent behavior was expected.

## THE SUBCULTURE OF VIOLENCE FROM THE VIEWPOINT OF A PARTICIPANT

JAMES: *(Long pause)* Let's put it this way. I know that I took my wife for granted, like she was there all the time.

DR. TOBY: Yes.

JAMES: She'll stick to me through anything. This I know. Now, if you take nine guys out of ten here that are married, their wives—as soon as they get busted—boom, they scrammed or they shacked up with somebody else. Nobody can tell me nothin' about this. And I know that some of them went out on the streets, too. By takin' somebody for granted, you know they're always there, but, now, because I'm in here, taken away from her, I never realized how much I needed her. I'm not the type of guy to tell her this, but I'll show her in my own way. . . .

JAMES: I know all kinds of guys here, a few guys from the street, and a few guys that I didn't know. Like one of the guys in particular that I know from my tier, he got a letter from his wife. She told him that she don't want to be bothered with him. And another guy got a letter from his wife practically telling him that she is shacking up with somebody else and that she doesn't care what he thinks. But my wife—my wife writes me every day, and she comes up here every visiting day, and she is always down at my mother's house. Now you gotta appreciate this or you're a crumb. So, like I said, you don't realize what you've got until it's taken away. See, I was never taken away from her before. I've been in jail before, but this was before I met her. So maybe she's got more influence on me than we both know.

DR. TOBY: She doesn't attempt to put real pressure on you though, apparently. And you say it wouldn't work if she did.

JAMES: Well, she did say to me in jail that, "Jim, if you come out and get in trouble any more, you can forget about me."

DR. TOBY: Did she say that?

JAMES: I felt like slapping her in the mouth right then and there. Like I said, I know that she's a good kid, but being married to a guy of my type makes a good kid a bad kid.

DR. TOBY: What does that mean—"your type"?

JAMES: Just that I'm in jail. If you keep coming back to jail, she gets the impression, "The son of a bitch don't give a shit about me." Then the first guy that'll come along and say a kind word to her, she'll go for him. You know that.

DR. TOBY: Let me tell you a story about a guy I met, not at this jail, but in the Middlesex County Workhouse. . . . While he was gone, his wife shacked up with another guy. When he learned about this he was furious. He wanted to kill this other guy.

JAMES: Why the other guy?

DR. TOBY: What would *you* have done?

JAMES: Cut her face, cut her all open. Slashed her face.

DR. TOBY: That's interesting that you say that. Do you think she did something so bad?

JAMES: In my opinion?

DR. TOBY: Yes.

JAMES: Because. Because if she's a good girl, she stays with you no matter what. I don't say she should wait if you get locked up for fifteen years or twenty years. But if you're only doing a year bit or a two-year bit, it's like going in the service. . . .

DR. TOBY: It's two years now since he went back, and things are working out very well with them.

JAMES: I don't see how.

DR. TOBY: No?

JAMES: Nah, I couldn't do it. After your wife did that, I don't believe in that shit.

DR. TOBY: You'd expect more from your wife than you think she should expect from you.

JAMES: Right. I guess so. I guess I'm selfish.

DR. TOBY: Much more.

JAMES: That's right, much more. This is my *wife*. You know, this is not one of the bitches; this is my wife. This is the mother of my kids. I don't want her walking down the street, and every guy she says hello to, I wonder if this is a guy that went to bed with her. I'd wind up killing her eventually.

DR. TOBY: He was terribly upset. As a matter of fact, the way I learned of it was that he didn't have anybody to talk to about this, and he wrote to me about it. I suppose that you would say that I gave him very bad advice. Not that I thought that he would take it.

JAMES: You know you could cause that girl to get killed by makin' him make up with her.

DR. TOBY: I didn't make him make up with her. He asked me for an opinion, and I told him that I thought that he had it coming to him.

JAMES: Why? Listen, maybe he did have it coming to him, but the best thing for him to do is just get away from her, as far away as possible. Because me, myself, they might bullshit me around, "Jimmy it's your own fault. She's a young girl." But this stays on my mind. Sooner or later I know what's gonna happen. So it would be better for me to stay away from her.

DR. TOBY: Jimmy, let me see what this means. This means that you are expecting your wife to be on a different level from you. You're a human being, but she's got to be an angel. . . .

JAMES: What did this guy do? Did he give her anything?

DR. TOBY: I don't know.

JAMES: Just a fly by night.

DR. TOBY: Probably so. She was pretty bored and tired; and she needed a kick, I guess. You talk about needing a kick; she needed a kick. She didn't have any babysitters——

*(Jimmy had previously recounted his own extensive infidelities.)*

JAMES: She should have stayed home with her kid.

DR. TOBY: She couldn't stand it.

JAMES: When a girl starts fooling around like that, somebody is going to get hurt. If she wants to go out to movies with her girlfriends, that's all right, but not with another guy. Like my wife, she's a bug for bingo. She conned me into going to bingo with her one night, and I went. I didn't like it but the other shit, it just ain't her. They got faults, everybody has faults—that's only human. My wife's a little heavy. So what about me? I'm a little skinny—what are you gonna do? You take it as it comes. She probably has a lot of faults that I just overlook because they're not important. Sure, I can see that. I don't say it's right what I want—that it's all right for me to do it and not her. I don't say it's right, you understand? That's the way it's gotta be with me.

DR. TOBY: Yes.

JAMES: That isn't saying that after I get out of here—I haven't got that much time to do—I know what to do now; I could probably tell you. You might have heard all this shit before. That don't mean that I expect her to be just right. She might be doing a lot of things wrong, but that doesn't mean that you break her head for it. You got to live with her, and besides I probably do a lot of things wrong, little things. No one's going to stop her from goin' out with a girlfriend one night and comin' home late. I'd probably break her head if she came home drunk. But this is life and you gotta live it. *(Long pause)* But I ain't gonna do what I've been doin'. As far as her going out with another guy, I'll tell you one thing and you can believe this or not. If she shacked up with some guy, she'll be dead—even if they give me the chair—that you can believe. When I'm mad I don't think. That would really hurt me. You can't hurt me no worse than that. That's the way I am, that's the way I'll always be as far as she is concerned. . . .

DR. TOBY: You're putting an awful lot of importance on sex. Isn't it sex?

JAMES: Listen, all right, it's sex. I don't know how to put it: this is the worst thing that a woman could do. As far as your wife is concerned, going to sleep with another guy. I imagine that it really isn't that bad—like you said, it takes only five minutes but, shit, you've got to live with it.

DR. TOBY: *You* could go to these bags, and yet——

JAMES: Yeah, that's right. *(Laughs)*

DR. TOBY: You expect things from her that you don't expect from yourself. It's quite different, isn't it?

JAMES: Yeah, but so is the man from the woman. Let me tell you something. Me or you can go out with, say, fifteen different bitches, fuck every one of them. You can come down the street naked, cockeyed drunk, and fall flat on the ground. You get up. And let a woman do it, and she's finished.

DR. TOBY: I'm not sure that I get your point.

JAMES: If a man fools around, some people will admire him. They'll say he knows how to bullshit a broad. Let a woman do it? What is she? She's a fuckin' whore. . . .

CONCLUSION

Given the family structure common in urban industrial societies, it is less easy for boys to grow up confident of their fundamental masculinity than for boys in the extended families of preliterate societies. One response to doubts about masculinity is *compulsive* masculinity: an exaggerated insistence on characteristics differentiating males from females. Superior strength and a readiness to exhibit it obviously fills the specifications. This analysis explains why violence, though punishable by law and condemned by custom, nevertheless remains a clandestine masculine ideal in Western culture. The assumptions of this ideal are most explicitly formulated in certain subcultures within the larger culture—and especially among these segments of the population unable to wield symbolic power. Excerpts from a tape-recorded interview with an imprisoned armed robber illustrate these assumptions.

# 5. Violence in Divorce-Prone Families
**JOHN E. O'BRIEN**

In the general introduction, we take the position that the greater amount of violence between family members found in the lower class is fundamentally traceable to the social conditions faced by lower class families rather than to cultural norms approving of violence. To the extent that such norms exist and are maintained, they occur because they reflect common life experience of the lower class—experiences such as excessive numbers of children, inadequate income, unemployment, lack of respect by the rest of society, etc. If our theory is correct, then whenever these conditions are found, irrespective of social class, violence should also be found. Thus, the article which follows is important because it is a study of a population "devoid of any sizeable number of poor families and of black families." Within this population O'Brien finds that the families reporting husband-wife violence tend to be families which have experienced precisely the kinds of goal blockages and inability to fulfill culturally prescribed roles that are so often experienced by the poor. O'Brien concludes that, for the husbands in the families he studied, violent behavior represents the use of physical force to maintain the social position of superiority expected by the society, when the husband lacks other resources to maintain this position.

Although concern over the occurrence of violence in the family may not be new, the study of it appears to be a relatively recent issue for scholarly endeavor. For instance, in the *Index* for all editions of the *Journal of Marriage and the Family*, from its inception in 1939 through 1969, not a single

SOURCE: Reprinted with permission from *Journal of Marriage and the Family* 33 (November, 1971): 692–698. This is a considerably revised version of a paper presented at the annual meeting of the National Council on Family Relations, Chicago, Illinois, October, 1970. The research was supported in part by Midwest Council for Social Research in Aging, Institute for Community Studies, Kansas City, Missouri, and by the Institute for Research on Poverty, the University of Wisconsin, Madison, Wisconsin.

article can be found which contains the word "violence" in the title. During that same period, discussions and studies of "conflict" in the family were quite common. But apparently violence, as such, was either assumed to be too touchy an issue for research or else thought to be so idiosyncratic as to be unimportant as a feature in "normal" families.

There is no logically implicit relationship between conflict and violence. As used here, violence is defined as any behavior which threatens or causes physical damage to an object or person. It may be the product of some idiosyncratic individual characteristic or it may be the product of social interaction.

Conflict, on the other hand, is more generally a product of social interaction and typically is a special form of effort directed at the resolution of a decision making impasse. Violent behavior may or may not emerge from conflict and may or may not be characteristic of individuals who are otherwise involved in extensive conflict ridden interaction.

As has been pointed out before, the concern for conflict in the family has frequently been premised on the assumption that it represents a deviation from family "harmony" or "equilibrium." This position, by no means shared by the present writer, is probably invalid (Sprey, 1969).

But whether conflict in the family is inherently undesirable because it shatters a needed state of "harmony," or whether the family is inherently a "conflict managing" system is not of issue here. Rather, taking violence in the family as a researchable phenomenon, the analytic problem was to attempt to ascertain those kinds of family structural characteristics which were associated with the occurrence of violent behavior between family members. No data was gathered which might be used to determine the social-interactional dynamics which may have also been characteristically associated with the violent behavior.

## THEORETICAL BASIS FOR THE STUDY OF VIOLENCE

Outside the family, violent behavior has become an ever present aspect of the contemporary scene. Because of that presence, a great deal of consideration is currently being given to the phenomenon of collective violence as a major dynamic in our social and political institutions. (See, for instance, Volume 391, the *Annals*, 1970, entire issue.) Certain of the generalizations arising from the study of violence in the larger society are clearly applicable to a discussion of violence in the family.

In the opinion of most analysts, conflict ridden, violent acts are generally thought to be goal directed and problem solving in design. At least in the mind of the actor or actors, violence is typically intended either to bring about some needed change in the social order (Marx, 1970) or else to reaffirm in a ritualistic sense, the existing structurally differentiated status quo (Neiburg, 1970).

Conflict in a social group is thought to be most likely to occur during the decision making process. Such a process is conducted according to some established authority pattern that is vested in a status hierarchy. Assignment of individuals to the status hierarchy is based on their classification according to one or another social category. Hence, from an external perspective, violence is most often seen to be constituted of actions through which the incumbents of different status positions are maneuvering for control of some decision outcome. In the process of that struggle, if the members of the subordinate status position fail to concede the decision, then the superior group will typically exert coercive power in order to influence the outcome of the decision.

In short, violence in the larger society most frequently occurs between persons who are differentiated as superior-subordinate based on their respective positions in some social category and tends to erupt in times when less extreme forms of conflict resolution are found to be unworkable (Grimshaw, 1970).

It should be further noted that, at least according to Georg Simmel, whose work lies at the apex of most sociological discussions of conflict, the stability of any social system is at best tenuous. As he described it, either the incumbents of the different status categories which compose the structure of the system are in open conflict or else are in some more or less temporary state of accommodative interaction. In general, however, Simmel asserted that since all social systems are structurally based on hierarchies, then all social systems are inherently prone to conflict (Simmel, 1955).

If Simmel was correct in his thinking, that conflict and violence are endemic in the structure of any social system, the question to be answered is not: "Why do conflict and violence periodically shatter the complacent status quo?" Rather, the question of greater concern ought to be: "How does peace and tranquility ever prevail in any social system?"

The answer appears to lie in the dynamics of the process by which legitimacy and value consensus are learned in early socialization and thereby transmitted via the culture base of each particular social system as part of its value system.

Although this is not the place to detail the process of socialization (for such a review see Chapter V in Defleur *et al.*, 1970), a brief comment on one of its effects is central to this discussion.

In any social system, the members of the superordinate status categories are (or at least in terms of the history of any particular culture group, *were*) the holders of superior skills, talents or resources. The distribution of freedom of access to the goods and services possessed or controlled by the dominant status group to those in subordinate positions does (or *did*) result in the return of support and a sense of perceived legitimacy for the status structure (Dahrendorf, 1959). The process of learning to accept the legitimacy of the structure is central to the socialization process.

As has been noted elsewhere, if for any reason, the members of the superordinate status lose their advantaged skills, talents or resources, or if those at the top of the structure cannot or will not distribute access to the goods and services which they control to those in the subordinate positions, then conflict and, in extreme cases, violence are likely to ensue (Grimshaw, 1970: 19 ff.).

This form of analysis has been advanced as helpful in explaining the violence associated with such phenomena as the student and black "revolutions" which have been so much a part of recent events in the United States (Short and Wolfgang, 1970).

## FAMILY PROCESSES AND VIOLENCE

The family is a social system in which dominance patterns are based upon the social categories of age and sex. At least according to the culture shared by most persons in the United States, the adult (parent) group is *ipso facto* superior to the young (children) group and the male (husband) is superior to the female (wife).

The basis for the age graded pattern of dominance by the adults over the young in the family is reasonably obvious. Further, the large collection of research which repeatedly demonstrates the operation of a "mating gradient" among couples who marry in the United States is quite conclusive (Leslie, 1967: 433 ff.). According to this "mating gradient," men tend to marry women who are younger, less intelligent and of lower social status.

Applying the ideas from the earlier discussion of conflict in the larger society to the family, one should find that violence is most common in those families where the classically "dominant" member (male-adult-husband) fails to possess the superior skills, talents or resources on which his preferred superior status is supposed to be legitimately based. Hence it was expected that violent behavior would be disproportionately prevalent in families where the husband-father was deficient relative to the wife-mother in achieved status characteristics.

## RESEARCH METHOD

The data for this report come from that gathered for a larger project on the problems and processes of pre-divorce family life. The major purpose of the study was to determine the nature of the phenomenon of family instability in the early versus the later stages of the life cycle.

A sample of families was selected from the population of those in which one of the spouses had initiated a divorce action during the first nine months of 1969. The study was conducted in a midwestern standard metropolitan area which is dominated by a state government-state university complex. The area is devoid of any sizeable number of poor families and of black families.

Only one spouse was interviewed in each family; 48 per cent were men and 52 per cent, women. Stratified by a three factor index of social status (McGuire and White, 1955), the families studied were 24 per cent upper-middle class, 29 per cent lower-middle class and 47 per cent working class. This particular status index is a modified Werner measure which takes into account the husband's job, source of income and education. The "working class" consists, most typically, of regularly employed blue collar workers, who are paid on an hourly rate and who hold a high school diploma or its equivalent. On this scale, the critical difference between the "working class" and the "lower class" is whether or not the head of household is regularly employed. Since chronic unemployment was not prevalent in the area of the study, the "lower class" was not represented in sample as drawn.

In order to maximize the long versus short durational differences, families formed by marriage between 1957 and 1963 were excluded from the study. A total of 150 interviews were conducted with 79 spouses in the short-marriage group (range: 0 to 5 years; mean = 2.7 years) and 71 spouses in the long marriage group (range: 13 to 37 years; mean = 20.6 years).

There was no direct inquiry about the occurrence of overt violence among the family members. There seemed to be little wisdom in asking a man whether or not he ever beat his wife or children. Nonetheless there were two particular points in the detailed, semi-structured interview when reports about violent behavior were noted. One series of questions concerned the events by which the actual initiation of the divorce action was precipitated. The other place was at the end of the interview when the respondent was asked to globally describe what it was, in his or her opinion, which accounted for the deterioration in the marriage and the subsequent divorce action. For purposes of this analysis, violence was defined as the occurrence of behavior which openly threatened the physical wellbeing of some member of the family. Those interviews in which overt violence was mentioned were isolated and analyzed for this paper. Hence what is being discussed here is violent behavior of an intensity sufficient in impact to prompt the person who reported it to claim that it was central to the initiation of a divorce action.

The problem, of course, is that there is no basis for the claim that violent behavior, as we identified it, did not occur in those families in which relatively spontaneous reports about it were not made. For that reason, based on these data, one would not be justified in attempting to estimate the incidence of violent behavior in divorce prone families in the general population.

Spontaneous mentions of overt violence were recorded in 25 of the 150 interviews. It was more often mentioned by respondents from the long (64 per cent) than the short (36 per cent) marriage group of respondents. Most of the reports of violence (84 per cent) came from women.

By way of summary, the most commonly reported form of violence was that the husband was physically abusive to his wife. There were twelve such cases, of which two-thirds were voiced by women from the long marriage group of respondents. In addition there were three cases of asserted suicide attempts, two cases of infant child beating, two cases of father-teen age child problems (one was a physical battle between a man and his teen age son, the other involved a father who, having caught his teen aged step-daughter in bed with her boy friend, physically evicted the young man from his home), and two cases where the husband purportedly threatened his wife and family, at gun point, with annihilation. Finally, there was a single case where a rather classically described sado-masochistic sex relationship became more extreme than the wife found tolerable and one instance where a husband displaced his aggressive behavior from his wife, and starved her pet cats to death.

The precise etiology of the violent behavior was difficult to infer. But based on the assertions of the respondents, 48 per cent of the behaviors were later classified as indicative of a "life style." That is, the behavior had occurred, chronically, from time to time throughout the marriage. The remaining 52 per cent of the violent behaviors reported had been acute, one time events and hence were classified as behaviorally extreme, social "exclamation points."

Only three of the acute events were reported to have followed the decision to initiate the divorce action. As an interesting note, both of the "gun point –showdown" events followed this pattern.

Because all the respondents in this study were involved in a divorce action, it is obvious that there was some kind of severely faulty functioning in their families. But certainly there are many non-violent ways by which family harmony could deteriorate. Yet the fact was that in one out of six cases, overt violent behavior was reported. Hence we were interested in what might be inferred to account for the violence which was reported. An answer was sought by comparing the subgroup of families in which violence was reported to the total sample of divorce prone families which were studied.


## POSSIBLE EXPLANATIONS FOR FAMILY-CENTERED VIOLENCE

Since this process of explanation was conducted on a post hoc basis, the inferences to be drawn must be viewed as hypotheses for further research.

According to our earlier model, violent interaction is generally seen to involve the direction of coercive force by the superior status group in a social system toward those in lower status categories. That coercive force is expected to be most often applied in times when there is a threat to the innate legitimacy accorded those in the superordinate positions by those in the subordinate positions.

The relative placement of individuals into those different positions is typically based upon gross membership in social categories and is referred to as ascribed status. One of the most common situations leading to a rejection of the legitimacy of those in high status is when their achieved status fails to measure up to their ascribed status. This condition is a special form of the phenomenon called "status inconsistency" (Lebowitz, 1969).

As mentioned earlier, in the family, the husband-father role has a higher ascribed status than do the wife-mother or child roles. That higher ascribed status of the husband was traditionally supported by his superior competence (relative to his wife and children) in handling the world at large, and specifically in the work or earner role. In our analogy, comparing the processes within the family to those in the larger social system, one should expect family violence to most commonly involve the use of physical force on the part of a husband-father who is either underachieving in the work/earner role or otherwise identifiable as a real or potential underachiever relative to other members of his family and particularly relative to his wife. The data available support this hypothesis.

As can be seen in Table 1, the husbands in the "violence" sub-group of families showed evidence of underachievement in their work roles as well as achievement potential which is deficient to that which their wives might expect. That is, compared to those from the non-violence segment of families in the study, the men who reportedly exhibited violent behavior were more often seriously dissatisfied with their job, more often educational drop-outs at one level or another (from either high school or college) and more often brought home earnings which were the source of serious or constant conflict. In addition, in comparison to the background of their wives, the men in the violence group were more often less educated than their wives and more often the holders of jobs with an occupational status classification lower than that of their wife's father.

*Table 1. A Comparison of the Achievement Status of the Husbands in the Violence and Non-Violence Subgroups of Unstable Families*

|  | *Prevalence in:* | |
|---|---|---|
|  | *Violence* | *Non-Violence* |
|  | *Subgroup (N = 25)* | *Subgroup (N = 125)* |
|  | % | % |
| 1. Husband was seriously dissatisfied with his job | 44 | 27 |
| 2. Husband started but failed to complete either high school or college | 44 | 18 |
| 3. Husband's income was the source of serious and constant conflict | 84 | 24 |
| 4. Husband's educational achievement was less than his wife | 56 | 14 |
| 5. Husband's occupational status was lower than that of his father-in-law (Wife's marital mobility downward) | 37 | 28 |

This data clearly support the hypothesis that family centered violence is associated with the occurrence of a condition in a family where the achievement ability of the husband is less than or inconsistent with his proscribed, superior status. Hence, at least from these findings about violent behavior, one might conclude that the family, as a social system, functions in close dynamic analog to that of the society at large.

An alternative position suggests that the family, as a system, responds or depends upon the conditions and dynamics in the larger society in which it is located. The same data presented above could be used to support this alternative position. That is, the men in the violence subgroup of families apparently were not fulfilling the obligations connected with the work/earner role. One could expect that this inability to gain adequate economic rewards from the larger world would have been a source of frustration. At this point, the Miller and Dollard thesis seems relevant concerning the like-lihood that aggressive behavior will ensue if individuals are constantly frus-trated in their efforts to be socially effective (Dollard *et al.*, 1939); that is, the violent behavior which was reported may have represented the family centered venting of the aggressiveness on the part of the husband which had its antecedence in frustrations encountered in the larger structures of the social and economic world.

There is no way to test between those positions. Either explanation is con-sistent with the widely held proposition that adequate job-earner achieve-ment is essential in order for men to have a meaningful involvement in the family (Aldous, 1969). But these data clearly do not support any notion that underachieving men are necessarily disposed to passively withdraw from the family and let their wives take over.

In either case, the association stands between underachievement on the part of the husband and his use of violent, harmful behavior in his family life.

As pointed out at the onset, this report is not directly concerned with con-flict or with the interactional dynamics of conflict management or resolution. But by way of collateral information, brief mention will be made of the rel-ative coincidence of conflict and violence in the families which were studied.

At different points in the interview, each respondent used separate Likert-scale devices to report the relative levels of "pleasure and satisfaction" and of "conflict" across an 18 item list of carefully selected behaviors (O'Brien, 1970).

Because the study did not employ any specific methodology for assessing the occurrence of violent behavior, it is not judged as appropriate to employ sophisticated analytic techniques by which to assess the inter-relationship between violence and marital conflict or marital satisfaction. But, as shown in Table 2 and Table 3, the individuals who reported violent behavior were

*Table 2. Mean Item Score on Marital Satisfaction Over Five Selected Behaviors*[a]

|  | Mean Marital Satisfaction Score For: | |
|  | Violence | Non-Violence |
|  | Subgroup (N = 25) | Subgroup (N = 125) |
| --- | --- | --- |
| Marital Behavior: | | |
| 1. Spending an evening together at home | 2.00 | 2.87 |
| 2. Going out together and doing things for recre-ation | 2.25 | 3.01 |
| 3. Children | 3.33 | 4.04 |
| 4. Having sexual relations with the spouse | 1.95 | 3.32 |
| 5. Planning together for the future of the family | 1.96 | 2.96 |

[a]The study employed five point Likert scales. On any item, a score of one (1) was the lowest level of satisfaction, and a score of five (5) was the highest level of satisfaction.

*Table 3. Mean Item Score on Marital Conflict Over Five Selected Behaviors*[a]

| Marital Behavior: | Mean Marital Conflict Score For: | |
| --- | --- | --- |
| | Violence Subgroup (N = 25) | Non-Violence Subgroup (N = 125) |
| 1. Spending an evening together at home | 2.66 | 2.23 |
| 2. Going out together and doing things for recreation | 3.15 | 2.54 |
| 3. Children | 3.34 | 2.38 |
| 4. Having sexual relations with the spouse | 3.42 | 3.32 |
| 5. Planning together for the future of the family | 2.76 | 2.27 |

[a]The study employed five point Likert scales. On any item, a score of one (1) was the lowest lever of conflict, and a score of five (5) was the highest level of conflict.

also consistently lower in marital pleasure and satisfaction and consistently higher in marital conflict across the set of marital behaviors which are listed.

Implicit in the study of violent behavior is the desire to curtail it. Based on the association discussed above, one could make a case for social intervention of a type intended to strengthen the earning and achievement potential of husbands. Inferentially, at least, were that to be done, the occurrence of status inconsistency of the type we defined would be less prevalent and then the incidence of family centered violence would decrease.

Kate Millett and other proponents of the "Women's Liberation" movement would certainly object to such a strategy. Why, they might ask, should the superior, ascribed status in the family of men over women be programatically supported? Rather, why not reestablish the basis of power and status distributions in the society in general and the family in particular, such that achievement and ability rather than membership in one or other social category (in this case, one's sex) would determine the ordering of the members in the structure (Millett, 1969).

A second important ramification of this study concerns the popular notion that there is a strain toward violence unique to the ethos of the poor (Black) ghetto. This belief is often supported by the use of statistics showing a high incidence of homicides and assaults in ghetto areas (Gibbons, 1969) and by ethnographic studies of the characteristics and effects of the "subculture" of poverty (Green, 1946; Freedman, 1964; Moynihan, 1965; Valentine, 1968; Schultz, 1969).

Interestingly enough, however, in the present study, not a single family could be classified as belonging to the "lower-lower" class and none were located in a neighborhood in any way similar to the typical urban ghetto. Yet there was a high incidence of violent family centered behavior. Hence it appears possible that the greater incidence of violence which occurs in ghetto areas reflects, not a subcultural disposition toward violence, but rather a greater incidence of men in the father/husband role who fail to have the achievement capacities normally associated with this role.

CONCLUSION

In conclusion, a study of spouses who were involved in a divorce action revealed a significant incidence of violent family behavior. Under analysis, the violent behavior was found to be most common in families where the husband was not achieving well in the work/earner role and where the husband demonstrated certain status characteristics lower than those of his wife. This was viewed as a special form of status inconsistency. One interpretation for that violent behavior was that it represented the use of coercive, physical force by the husband in an effort to reaffirm his superior ascribed sex-role status vis-à-vis the other family members.

Enactment of public policy designed to support the status of husbands by increasing their achievement ability was suggested as likely to promote a reduction in family violence. Such a plan was also suggested as likely to be viewed by those in support of the "Women's Liberation" movement as a blatant reinforcement of male supremacy.

The fact of the high prevalence of violence in this study of non-poor, non-ghetto families was further presented in support of the premise that the popular notion of an ethos of violence associated with the "subculture" of poverty may be unfounded. Rather, it appeared likely that violence in the family, as with violence in the larger society, most often represents a response to certain status imbalances in the social structure.

REFERENCES

Aldous, Joan
    1969    "Occupational Characteristics and Males' Role Performance in the Family." *The Journal of Marriage and the Family* 31 (November): 707–712.
The Annals
    1970    "Collective Violence." 391 (September).
Dahrendorf, Ralf
    1959    *Class and Class Conflict in Industrial Society.* Stanford, California: Stanford Press.
DeFleur, M. L., W. V. D'Antonio and L. B. DeFleur
    1970    *Sociology: Man in Society.* Glenview, Illinois: Scott, Foresman and Company.
Dollard, J., N. E. Miller, L. W. Doob, O. H. Mower and R. S. Sears
    1939    *Frustration and Aggression.* New Haven, Connecticut: Yale University Press.
Freedman, Lawrence Z.
    1964    "Psychopathology and Poverty." Pp. 363–371 in A. B. Shostak and W. Gomberg (eds.), *Blue-Collar World.* Englewood Cliffs, New Jersey: Prentice-Hall, Incorporated.
Gibbons, Donald C.
    1969    "Violence in American Society: The Challenge of Corrections." *American Journal of Correction* 31 (March-April): 6–11.
Green, Arnold W.
    1946    "The Middle Class Male Child and Neurosis." *American Sociological Review* 11 (February): 31–41.
Grimshaw, Allen D.
    1970    "Interpreting Collective Violence: An Argument for the Importance of Social Structure." *Annals* 391 (September): 9–20.

Lebowitz, Barry D.
1970    "Research in Status Inconsistency: A Synthesis and Appraisal." Department
        of Sociology, Portland State University, Mimeo.
Leslie, Gerald R.
1967    *The Family In Social Context.* New York: Oxford Press.
Marx, Gary T.
1970    "Issueless Riots." *Annals* 391 (September): 21–33.
McGuire and G. D. White
1955    "The Measurement of Social Status." Research Paper in Human Development,
        No. 3, Department of Educational Psychology, University of Texas.
Millett, Kate
1970    *Sexual Politics.* Garden City, New York: Doubleday and Company.
Moynihan, Daniel P.
1970    *The Negro Family: The Case for National Action.* Office of Policy Planning
        and Research, U. S. Department of Labor.
Neiburg, H. L.
1970    "Agonistics–Rituals in Conflict." *Annals* 391 (September): 56–73.
O'Brien, John E.
1970    "The Decision to Divorce: A Comparative Study of Family Instability in the
        Early Versus the Later Years of Marriage." The Library of the University of
        Wisconsin, Madison, Wisconsin.
Schultz, David A.
1969    *Coming Up Black.* Englewood Cliffs, New Jersey: Prentice-Hall, Incorporated.
Short, J. F. and M. E. Wolfgang
1970    "On Collective Violence." *Annals* 391 (September): 1–8.
Simmel, Georg
1955    *Conflict and the Web of Group Affiliations.* Translated by K. H. Wolff and
        R. Bendix. Glencoe: The Free Press.
Sprey, Jetse
1969    "The Family as a System in Conflict." *Journal of Marriage and the Family* 31
        (November): 699–706.
Valentine, Charles A.
1968    *Culture and Poverty.* Chicago, Illinois: University of Chicago Press.

# 6. *Violence in Husband-Wife Interaction*
## ROBERT N. WHITEHURST

On the basis of the previous two articles, one might conclude that as a society becomes more equalitarian, there will be less violence between husbands and wives. That may be the long-run sequence of events. But in the
following article, Whitehurst suggests that the *short run* is likely to be very
different—even opposite. This is because the idea of male superiority is still
the dominant ideology in our society. Consequently, changes which bring
about greater equality between the sexes (such as changes in legal rights,
increases in female employment, and economic and technological changes
such as the second car and the "pill") will result in strain and frustration for
males attempting to retain their superior position. If this analysis is correct,
it will not be until a generation of men and women reared under equalitarian
conditions and subscribing to equalitarian rather than male-superiority norms

SOURCE: This is a revised version of a paper originally presented at a roundtable discussion at the National Council on Family Relations, Chicago, Illinois, October, 1970.
Reproduced by permission of the author.

takes over that we can expect to see a reduction in violent encounters between spouses. In the meantime, Whitehurst suggests that the conflict between the emerging equalitarian social structure and the continuing male-superiority norms will tend to increase rather than decrease conflict and violence between husbands and wives.

In the last decade, a series of events, violent in extreme, have caused us to look closer at the general problem of man's inhuman and violent treatment of his fellow man. Since the early part of the century when Freud, through observation, case study, and speculation came to ascribe sexuality and aggressiveness as basic characteristics of man's nature, interest in the problem has increased.

Although the recent work of anthropologist Lionel Tiger has been concerned with male-female differences rather than with violence of males *per se*, his effort to show differences has been instructive in its implications for male aggressiveness (Tiger, 1970). He cites evidence that at the onset of puberty, males produce 20 to 30 times more of the male hormone, testosterone, than do females. Although the total amounts produced in the body are minute, Tiger claims that the effects on differentially aggressive male behavior cannot be forgotten nor written off as simply culturally induced differences. To understand male violence, then, we must begin with the presumptions that there is some kind of biological difference and that this difference does matter for our comprehension of male behavior, whether it comes from body build, hereditary predispositions, hormones, or endocrinology.

It must also be recognized that a consideration of the violence involving husbands and wives must take account of the heavy interactional investments both have made in building and sustaining a relationship, most of which has not been (presumably) characterized by violent responses to each other.

Husbands who turn to violence in dealing with wives in general experience a serious inability to control a specific situation to their satisfaction and perceive the situation as polarizing even further, thus precluding a self-concept of "being in control." In fact, this felt inability to control and to feel any realistic possibility of instituting an accommodative possibility in the relationship is a *sine qua non* of marital violence. How these situations arise in such a large number of marriages, their implications for both the society and individuals will make up the major portion of our discussion.

As we have said, the general problem of violent responses of husbands *vis-à-vis* wives involves failure on the part of the husband to perceive himself as in control. Several factors add to the problem—some general, some specific —but in general we cite the following. We are entering an age of equality; and equality for females is so new and so threatening for so many males that we have inadequately understood the magnitude of change for either males or females. Most of the literature points out that males of the lower socioeconomic classes are most fearful of meaningful interaction and equality in wives (Rainwater, 1959). The impact of the media, especially television, cannot be underestimated in terms of its impact on freedom-seeking females.

This datum, if we interpret it correctly, should cause us to predict an increase in male to female violence in the future; for there appears to be no way to move in terms of Women's Liberation except forward to increased equality between sexes. Whether or not this equality revolution in fact has already caused much of an increase in male violence is poorly understood. As husbands retreat from relationships with wives who are seeking more freedom, increasing polarization and loss of control (by husbands) is compounded. Increased female labor participation in the market as well as more vocal demands for equal pay are additional factors tending to weaken the control of husbands at home. Add to these the factor of certain structural changes in society which give women increased freedom and infinitely greater mobility to roam freely, and we further complicate some husbands' problems with wives. The confluence of the second auto, television, the pill, and free time granted by the addition of gadgetry in the household have all created wives of a different order than previously. If wives are not now substantially different, their husbands' potential fear of loss of power due to the new structures seems real. This potential equality, ever demanding and showing itself in new ways, has had no counterpart in the history of man. Men simply have no culturally approved ways of coping with "uppity" women who want to be really free.

A further culturally derived problem manifests itself in male-female relationships that bode ill for the wife who violates (or whose husband defines her as violating) the sexual norms of a double-standard society. Whereas wives have some normative protections built into wifely roles when husbands deviate sexually, no such comparable set of norms exist to protect the male. A wife can understand, if she cannot forgive, a husband's sexual indiscretions; for men are often felt to be "that way." Perhaps when we learn from such studies as Masters and Johnson that women are as sexy as men, alteration of the norm that "men are like that" will provide for lessening the violence-potential within marriage by husbands who are affronted.[1] As of now, husbands have little choice but to become irate when wives are unfaithful since we have no real emergent set of norms defining women as the same as men in terms of sexual prowess. It is no doubt a function of male insecurity that this double-standard tradition persists—just one more bit of irrational behavior holding society together in a tenuous and unhealthy way. Throughout most of mankind's history on earth, man has had the force of law on his side if he killed either his wife, her lover, or both if he caught them in an act of adultery; the present sense of rage as men which is a vestigial remain of this

[1]We should be cautious about interpreting such findings about human sexuality in terms of their actual impact, however. Robert Merton has noted that sociological insights and data do not make men instantly free (or rational in their responses to life). The point is that however much we may "find" some things to be true (e.g., that women are at least as sexy as men), making these new findings fit into an ideological framework of a society is quite another problem; one of the major functions of society is to provide us with ready-made sets of symbolic categories which give us *answers*—not necessarily truth. The answers we are given may or may not have anything to do with the kinds of truth sociologists claim to seek, but the answers do have much to do with the maintenance and control of society and its members. In this case the more obvious function of the myth of female sexuality (or at least lesser-intense sexuality) has much to do with control and perhaps societal maintenance, almost nothing to do with truth.

double standard is not only dysfunctional but is destructive to any human-izing possibility.

Not only have men had the force of tradition and law influencing them in regard to violence potential but current socialization practices feed into this as well. When all other sources of masculine identity fail, men can always rely on being "tough" as a sign of manhood. Handling wives in aggressive ways is in some respects an extension of the normal ways men learn to handle a variety of problems in the subcultural setting.

Most interpersonal violence of a marital variety carries heavily learned components coupled with felt inadequacy of the male to cope with a wife in less drastic terms. Although the normative view of wives as sometimes "deserving" of physical abuse is essentially lower class, elements of this belief seem to be diffused into all males of all social classes. Most males seem to believe at some level that a woman will behave better and may even enjoy in some sense being put in her "rightful" (subservient) place by physical punishment. Part of the male folklore has it that women really enjoy a male domination-female submissive relationship. Like so many other things in life, this belief is sometimes true; and the selective perceptions of males coupled with their need to control makes the violent outcome more likely when they meet with selective reinforcements to their belief that women enjoy a little violence.

Although violence in males has been characterized as essentially a lower class male phenomenon, it is the contention here that this is a vastly over-simplified view of the problem of domestic violence (Toch, 1969). In re-viewing all of the evidence available at this time, our conclusion is tentatively that violence in families is ubiquitous but highly variable in its patterning and outcomes. The discussion to follow points out the logic and the ratio-nales for broadening the view of violence to include middle class husbands and wives.

Little evidence other than cases of counselors and non-legal agencies can be adduced to show the relationship of middle class families to violence re-actions. Skimpy evidence leads us to the tentative conclusion that nearly *all* families at some time or another deal with violence-reactions of some sort or other, basically making middle class families different only in matter of degree of violence, frequency, and reactions to the outcome. Middle class wives are probably more prone to feed into the violence-production in a less passive manner than lower class wives; in part this is due to their enhanced verbal capabilities and their unwillingness to play the subservient role as often as the lower class wife.

In terms of violent reactions, middle class husbands are more prone to hit or strike out at a wife only once and then immediately to regain control—perhaps because of inadequate socialization in calculating responses to vi-olence and long training in non-violence as a physical release. Once he strikes, the middle class male is likely to fairly immediately reassess the situa-tion in terms of the total consequences to himself. The involvement of the law is a much more real threat to his occupational identification—and the intrusion of other relatives, neighbors, and friends is more of a real source of social control over his devious actions—than is the case for the lower class male. Once the middle class male becomes violent, his well-trained sense of guilt and shame for his actions are more likely to cause the violent incident to be redefined, accommodated, and assimilated within the family context, rather than externalized and brought to the attention of the community, the law, and the courts. For these reasons, no one has a very real idea as to the actual amount or frequency of middle class family violence. Lower class families, having fewer resources of a social-psychological nature within the family structure to assimilate such experiences, more often turn to outside agencies for help. The controls over violence-limitation are thus different for middle class and lower class families. Violence-responses are much more built into the lower class subculture as a means to achieve some goals, to assert independence and masculinity; and in general they carry positive sanctions in ways not at all acceptable in the middle classes. Another factor described by Dietz (1969) has to do with the "sure winner" syndrome. Some men low in the status hierarchy seem to only exercise violence when they are assured of a victory. Whether sure winners are both lower and middle class is problematical, but the pattern is one that cannot be ignored.

Sex and jealousy get mixed into relationships often with highly complex outcomes. Trainer (1968) describes many cases in which violence is associated with jealousy of the husband; in many of the cases, husbands reached a false conclusion about their wives, assuming unfaithfulness on the basis of little or no evidence that they had been having affairs.

Although it is usually assumed in the literature that it is mostly lower class males who accuse their wives on the basis of little evidence of having affairs, we actually know little about these ratios or frequencies. The dynamics of the mild forms of paranoia that husbands and wives generate within their relationships—each suspecting the other of having affairs—is almost certainly one of the highly destructive aspects of modern marriage that will only increase with time. Given the freedom to range far from home that both spouses now enjoy, if we do not begin to develop some new norms of openness and non-jealousy, we might expect more potential violence within marriage in the future.

Another emergent pattern that appears to cut across social class lines involves the pattern of swinging relationships. Bell (1970) has described mates who attend weekend parties for purposes of trading sexual partners. Often, it is the husband who suggests that the pair enter into swinging activities. When it is the husband who wants to discontinue the swinging relations and the wife who does not—it is a new ball game. The stage is set for hostile interaction.

It is relatively easy for males—especially young ones who consider themselves "with it," modern, and non-traditionalist—to fail to recognize their problem. It is easy to commit oneself to a single-standard relationship with a female in a marriage when no other males are around to seek sexual favors of the spouse. This intellectual commitment to the idea often flies out the window when it is necessary to follow through with a real emotional commitment to the situation when it occurs. Working through this kind of problem is a usual part of life for many young marrieds and is likely to become more prevalent; it is a problem in part because the culture provides no ready-made set of norms by which people can assimilate a sharing experience with others outside marriage. Perhaps new life styles emerging will inform and educate the new generation. In the meantime, there is more violence-potential in the response of husbands struggling with an idea they can often accommodate themselves to intellectually, but not actually, when it comes to the crunch.

Survey information from a study by the author has shown that threats of violence are frequent among husbands as a means to controlling wives. When asked to respond to a question (by agreeing or disagreeing) involving their own level of jealousy if a spouse were to admit an extramarital situation, over half of the sample of husbands claimed that they could not help being jealous and would probably respond with some form of violence. Just over one-third of the sample also claimed (in another question) that no kind of extramarital situation is worthy of creating serious jealousy or violence. Again, it seems that the intellectual commitment to non-jealous reactions is fairly easy to make—so long as it is someone else's spouse involved. It is easier to claim people should not get jealous than it is to look at one's own real or even projected self-situation. Survey data shows that about 20 per cent of all respondents claimed that violence is a part of life and cannot be eliminated. In a Canadian survey by Goldfarb (Macleans, 1970), some subjects saw positive effects of family fights and felt that conflict could be a sign of love as well as hostility. Possibly one of the underlying indicators of the cultural naturalness of conflict can be gleaned in the response to a question about the basic nature of men. Over 61 per cent felt men should be tough and not back away from a fight (these were mostly middle class people who are presumably trained to think and to reason). If the potential violence indicated in these middle class responses is not atypical, perhaps we can understand how very real and culturally normative is the pattern of violence socialized into males at all stages of their life cycle.

Wives seem to have some knack for expressing their violence: potential in passively hostile ways which comes out fairly clearly in court cases. Gestures of defiance, remarks made during the heat of argument, and subtly hostile-appearing techniques are frequently observed. We must simply note as a social fact that husbands are often complemented in the creation of hostile and aggressive responses to wives by a great number of subtle interactions, signs, cues, and passively hostile acts that build the violence-possibility in a marriage.

It has been noted by Watzlawick, *et al.* (1967, 103), that in the case of lovers, men can become violent in response to felt rejection of their affectionate intentions by women. An attempt to give love which is thwarted by the female can create immediate frustration in the male aggressor, who has few ways to internalize his rejection; again, this is part of a situation in which the male is unable to retain a self-concept of being in control and often leads to violent reactions.

Sometimes, being in control for the male involves his sense of masculinity as perceived in relation to his wife's overall satisfaction level. One husband, a medical doctor in his thirties, had always defined his sexual prowess as superior and felt that his wife should be more than satisfied with sex from him and never be attracted to other men on this count. On learning that another man had been in the apartment with his wife one day, the doctor struck her in a rage, promptly felt badly, made love to her, and then developed a definition of the situation as one that could not possibly occur again. A few weeks later, he happened home at an odd time in the afternoon and found his wife in bed with another man—a friend of his, also a doctor. He set upon the two of them in a jealous rage—the other man first, then the wife. In this case, the husband's own need to control his wife and feel superior, because of his wife's unfaithfulness, was simply too much of an emotional burden for him to handle without recourse to violence.

It is a virtual unknown how much husbands and wives develop a mutually hostile relationship that may have sexual overtones for their own relationship, apart from the overt causes of the problem. Toch (1969) notes that for some men violence can become a substitute orgasm. It is also common among marrieds to note that sex after battle implies an increased intensity, for making up can be great fun according to folklore and admission of most marrieds themselves. How much wives and husbands may subtly encourage each other in violence for sexual purposes is not known; but hypothetically, some cases might get carried away by their own game, overreact, and lose control of the intended lesser reaction.

*Conclusion.* Noting that there are certain concomitant biological problems in understanding male aggressiveness, we have attempted to show that there are a number of social and social-psychological factors involved in the violence reactions of husbands to wives. Berkowitz (1962, 319) claims that males who had a long history of both physical and psychological frustrations as a child, many illnesses, and much harsh treatment—when coupled with poor learning of social restraints—feed into the male system of violence. The "learning" of the pattern of violence thus seen tends to spring from several sources.

The general condition presumed to underlie husbands' violent reaction to wives involves the notion of control of the wife in terms of self-concept of husband. Husbands who neither project sexual fantasies, affairs, nor other situations onto wives in a threatening manner will probably have less need to control wives in most situations. The smaller the need of the husband to control his wife and the fewer his projections, the less likely is a violent encounter. Since an increasing number of wives are seeking and finding some freedom, this situation is seen as likely to create tensions—and possibly more liberalizing forces to act on husbands—but as the double standard remains in effect, this latter possibility is rather uncertain.

REFERENCES

Bell, Robert R. "Sexual Exchange of Marriage Partners." Paper presented with Lillian Silvan at the Society for the Scientific Study of Social Problems meeting, Washington, D.C., September 1, 1970. Also, see the *Philadelphia Magazine*, September, 1969, pp. 76–160.
Berkowitz, Leonard. *Aggression: A Social Psychological Analysis.* New York: McGraw-Hill, 1962.

*MacLean's* magazine (Toronto). "We're More Violent than We Think," August, 1970, pp. 25–28.

Rainwater, Lee, Richard P. Coleman, and Gerald Handel. *Workingman's Wife.* New York: Oceana Publications, 1959.

Tiger, Lionel. "Male Dominance? Yes, Alas. A Sexist Plot? No." *New York Times Magazine,* October 25, 1970, pp. 35–36.

Toch, Hans. *Violent Men.* Chicago: Aldine and Co., 1969.

Trainer, Russell *Sex and Love Among the Poor.* New York: Ballantine Books, 1968.

Watzlawick, Paul, Beavin, Janet, and Jackson, Don D. *Pragmatics of Human Behavior.* New York: Norton, 1967.

# 7. *Some Causes of Jealousy in Young Children*
MABEL SEWELL

The relationship of a brother and sister, like other family relationships, carries with it a high potential for violence. This is not only because of the closeness and intimacy of the relationship, but also because each sibling is a real or potential rival for the care and affection of the parents. Sibling rivalry is therefore a widely acknowledged aspect of family violence. But like many other aspects, it has rarely been studied systematically. One of the few such researches is reprinted below. In this research, Sewell studied 70 children in nursery schools and preschool clinics. She used both case records and visits to the homes to obtain her information. In the report of her findings, she distinguishes between overt and more subtle forms of jealousy and tries to pinpoint some of the factors which lead to overt jealousy. It is important to keep in mind that this study is limited to a specific type of sibling rivalry: that between a young child and his newborn brother or sister. As a result, we only see the aggressiveness and violence which preschoolers direct toward an "intruder" and can only hypothesize the interaction between two or more older sibs. For children of elementary school age the figure may even approach 100 per cent. We make this guess because preliminary data from a study by Straus reveals that during the senior year in high school 62 per cent of the over 500 students in that study had used physical force on a sibling in the course of a conflict.

There was, first, a large group of children who exhibited what was considered jealousy by bodily attacks on the younger sibling. For example, the following case:

When Myron Conway was five years old his baby sister was born. At this time, Myron had whooping cough and was told by the doctor not to cough near the baby "or else she will get sick and then you won't have a baby sister any more." Several times after this, the mother found Myron coughing into the baby's face.

At another time, he poured salt into the young child's eyes and on another occasion pushed the bassinet over.

SOURCE: Reprinted with permission from *Smith College Studies in Social Work* (1930): 6–22.

One day his mother taught him to pat the baby's face. He did this, and when his mother's back was turned he slapped the baby hard and bit her finger.

In contrast to this case in which jealousy was so apparent, the following shows how subtly jealousy may manifest itself:

Rachel Levine had been the only child for two and a half years when Harry was born. Her behavior following the birth of her brother was of such a nature as to cause her parents and other people to suspect mental retardation.

Her mother, a rather intelligent Jewish woman of thirty, brought Rachel to the clinic for advice on handling her. She said that previous to the birth of Harry, Rachel had been a very "good girl," easy to manage. Her eating and sleeping habits had been well established, and she had already partially learned how to dress herself. Her mother told of Rachel's present behavior in a tone of mingled censure, apprehension, and discouragement.

She said Rachel refuses to feed herself. She insists on being fed. It takes the combined efforts of father and mother to get her to eat, and then they must feed her.

She likewise refuses to try to dress or undress herself. In the morning when she is called to get up she starts screaming.

She is very restless at night, occasionally has night terrors and talks much in her sleep.

She breaks all her toys into bits. She jumps around on the furniture and beds and seems delighted when she has succeeded in breaking something.

She picks her nose or bites her nails constantly all day long. She runs in and out of the apartment, and if she finds the door locked she kicks it violently instead of ringing the bell or knocking.

Her spells of temper are becoming more frequent and more severe. She is very negativistic and impudent toward her parents.

She hits her playmates so that she has become very unpopular in the neighborhood.

She has a very lively imagination and tells stories of bears, lions, and other animals chasing her, of riding in an aeroplane and large pieces of the sky falling out and killing people, about punching people in the nose "till the blood squirts," about scaring people by looking like an old man, etc. These stories the mother interprets as meaning the "child is crazy."

At no time has she expressed her jealousy of her brother by attacking him. She goes rather to the other extreme—whenever anyone asks her about her brother she denies having one.

As soon as the problem of jealousy was recognized and dealt with, the behavior difficulties began to grow less and finally disappeared. From the fact of their disappearance following such treatment it may perhaps be inferred that they were chiefly symptoms of the conflict that had arisen over her jealousy of the younger child. . . .

The results of this study showed that jealousy seemed to be associated with certain age differences between the child and the sibling. These age differences of 18–24 months for girls and 30–36 months for boys were the ages found to have the greatest amount of resistance and negativistic behavior. The one factor, however, which accounted for the greatest differences in jealousy was inconsistency in discipline or parental control of the child. . . .

Closely connected with the question of the attitude of the mother toward her child is that of the type of discipline which she uses with him. To gain obedience some mothers use fear, some corporal punishment, some unfavorable comparisons; others nag, bribe, threaten, or use still other methods. But whatever the method used the primary distinction, so far as the effect on the child is concerned, is whether the discipline is consistent or inconsistent.

*Table 13. Consistency of Discipline as Related to Presence or Absence of Jealousy*

| Children's Attitudes | Type of Discipline | | | | | |
|---|---|---|---|---|---|---|
| | Consistent | | Inconsistent | | Total | |
| | No. | Per cent | No. | Per cent | No. | Per cent |
| Jealous | 5 | 18 | 34 | 80 | 39 | 56 |
| Not Jealous | 22 | 82 | 9 | 20 | 31 | 44 |
| Total | 27 | 100 | 43 | 100 | 70 | 100 |

Disregarding the methods of discipline entirely, the seventy homes were studied to see into which of these categories the discipline would fall. In twenty-seven the discipline was found to be consistent; in forty-three it was found inconsistent—that is, the parents at one time disregarded or smiled upon, and at another severely punished certain types of behavior. Table 13 shows to what extent these differences in discipline were related to the presence of jealousy.

Inconsistency of discipline seems to be a factor closely associated with jealousy. Just about a fifth of the homes characterized by consistent discipline and four-fifths of those characterized by inconsistent discipline contained jealous children.

The factors making for jealousy seem thus to lie largely in the home situation. Whether the child is or is not told that a baby is expected seems to be immaterial—at least, the mere fact of telling is not sufficient to prevent jealousy. As has been suggested above, it may be that his attitude is conditioned by the way in which he is told this fact.

Neither sex nor intelligence is a factor of importance in the production of jealousy. The child's age at the birth of the younger sibling makes some difference in his attitude, the points of danger being eighteen months to 24 months for girls, 30 to 36 months for boys. The number of other children in the family is also of some importance. Poverty and its associates produce more than the average number of jealous children. But the overwhelming cause of jealousy seems to be the lack of consistency in discipline, and this is closely linked to other factors that point to familial maladjustment.

# CHAPTER THREE
# Patterns of Violence
# Between Spouses and Kin

## 8. *Physical Abuse Among Applicants for Divorce*
**GEORGE LEVINGER**

It is often true that the most simple and "obvious" things are the hardest to pin down. This appears to be the case with physical fights between husbands and wives. Amazing as it may seem, we could not locate even one research giving figures for a representative sample of the percentage of couples who get into such fights—to say nothing of studies of how often this occurs or how intense such fights are. Since just about every other aspect of family life has been the object of many studies by social scientists, this glaring omission is probably not an accident. We have already commented on some of the possible reasons for this omission (see p. 3). Whatever the reason for the lack of data on husband-wife fights, it leaves a big gap in what we know about violence in the family. The available research that comes closest to filling this gap is the study which follows of applicants for divorce. It shows that 37 per cent of wives who applied for divorce in one metropolitan area gave "physical abuse" as one of their complaints. This data provides a clue to what might be true for other families. Perhaps the figure for a cross section of all families would be lower, but we suspect that it is not lower. Clearly, how much physical fighting occurs between husband and wife is one of the elementary problems concerning violence in the family which urgently awaits the attention of social scientists.

. . . The most extreme case of marital complaint occurs when partners are seeking dissolution—when a husband and wife are applying for divorce.

The present paper will deal with two general questions. First, to what extent do such husbands and wives differ in the bases of their marital dissatisfaction? Second, what differences can be noted across socioeconomic lines?

### METHOD

The findings are based on a sample of 600 couples who were divorce applicants, representing marriages at the brink of dissolution. All these people

SOURCE: Reprinted from George Levinger, "Source of Marital Satisfaction Among Applicants for Divorce," *American Journal of Orthopsychiatry* 36 (October, 1966): 804–806. Copyright 1966, The American Orthopsychiatric Association, Inc. Reproduced by permission.

This work was supported in part by grants from the Cleveland Foundation and the National Institute of Mental Health (MH–04653).

Appreciation is owed to officials of the Court of Common Pleas, Cuyahoga County, Ohio; particularly to Dr. Mandel Rubin, director, and others of the staff of the Department of Marriage Conciliation. Strict anonymity of applicants' names was ensured.

were residents of Cuyahoga County, Ohio (i.e., greater Cleveland). All had one or more children under 14 and had been seen jointly by an experienced marriage counselor at the Conciliation Department of the Domestic Relations Court of Cuyahoga County. The interviews were of a mandatory nature, required by rule of Court for all divorce applicants with children under 14. The interview records of the marriage counselors were kept according to a standardized printed schedule.

The counselors' records were made available to us for analysis and a large number of characteristics were coded. Among the codable data, there was considerable information about each spouse's complaints about his partner.

Spouses' complaints were coded in one of the following 12 categories, with an intercoder reliability of 88 per cent:

1. *Neglect of home or children:* frequent absence, irregular hours, emotional distance.
2. *Financial problems:* either inadequate support (by husband) or poor handling of family's money.
3. *Physical abuse:* committing overt physical hurt or injury to other partner.
4. *Verbal abuse:* profanity, name-calling, shouting.
5. *Infidelity:* attachment to an alternate partner, frequently sexual in nature, which excludes spouse; adultery.
6. *Sexual incompatibility:* reluctance or refusal of coitus, inconsiderateness and other sources of dissatisfaction.
7. *Drinking:* drunkenness or excessive drinking.
8. *In-law trouble:* interference or pressure by in-laws, spouse's excessive loyalty to parental kin.
9. *Mental cruelty:* suspicion, jealousy, untruthfulness, and vague subjective complaints.
10. *Lack of love:* insufficient affection, communication, companionship.
11. *Excessive demands:* impatience, intolerance, strictness, possessiveness.
12. *Other:* miscellaneous category.

RESULTS

Let us examine the findings of the study. First, did husbands and wives differ in the number and nature of their complaints?

Concerning the number of complaints, wives' reports exceeded husbands' by a ratio of almost 2:1. The 600 wives averaged 3.05 separate complaints; the husbands expressed a mean of 1.64 complaints.

As to the nature of complaints, Table 1 shows that wives complained 11 times more frequently than husbands about physical abuse. That is, 36.8 per cent of the wives and only 3.3 per cent of the husbands said that their partner hurt them physically. Wives complained four times as often about financial problems and about drinking; three times as much about their spouse's verbal abuse. Wives' complaints significantly exceeded husbands' on three other categories, neglect of home and children, lack of love, and mental cruelty, but these ratios were less one-sided.

Husbands' complaints exceeded those of their mates on two counts. They were more apt to mention in-law trouble, by a ratio of 5 to 2; and they more often brought up sexual incompatibility in a ratio of 3 to 2.

Let us now look at some social-class comparisons. Did complaint patterns differ across socioeconomic lines? The answer is a clear "yes."

*Table 1. Marital Complaints among 600 Couples Applying for Divorce, Classified by Sex and by Social Position of Respondents*

| | Proportion of Complaints by Respondent Groups | | | | | |
| | | Hus- | Social Position of | | | |
| | *Wives* | *bands* | *Wives* | | *Husbands* | |
| *Complaint* | *Total[a]* | *Total[a]* | *Middle[b]* | *Lower[c]* | *Middle[b]* | *Lower[c]* |
|---|---|---|---|---|---|---|
| Physical abuse | .368[d] | .033 | .228 | .401[e] | .029 | .035 |
| Verbal abuse | .238[d] | .075 | .200 | .245 | .048 | .082 |
| Financial problems | .368[d] | .087 | .219 | .402[e] | .124 | .079 |
| Drinking | .265[d] | .050 | .143 | .294[e] | .048 | .051 |
| Neglect of home or children | .390[e] | .262 | .457 | .374 | .200 | .276 |
| Mental cruelty | .403[e] | .297 | .372 | .408 | .267 | .306 |
| In-law trouble | .067 | .162[e] | .038 | .074 | .200 | .153 |
| Excessive demands | .025 | .040 | .057[f] | .018 | .057 | .035 |
| Infidelity | .240 | .200 | .324[f] | .223 | .114 | .198[f] |
| Sexual incompatibility | .138 | .200[e] | .124 | .141 | .267 | .120 |
| Lack of love | .228[e] | .135 | .324[e] | .206 | .200[f] | .188 |

[a] N = 600; all husbands or wives.
[b] N = 105; "Middle" refers to Class I–III on Hollingshead's Index of Social Position.[1]
[c] N = 490; "Lower" refers to Class IV–V on the Hollingshead Index. Note that 5 cases could not be categorized for position, by dint of insufficient information.
[d] p < .001, indicating a significant difference in favor of the lettered number in the pair, by t test (two-tailed).
[e] p < .01.
[f] p < .05.

To examine the matter, frequencies of complaints from 490 lower-class pairs—Class IV and V, according to Hollingshead's Two-Factor Index—were compared with adjusted frequencies for 105 middle-class pairs (Class I-III).

In mean number of *total* expressed complaints, there was no difference between spouses from lower and those from middle socioeconomic position. However, Table 1 indicates that lower-status wives were considerably more likely than middle-status wives to complain about financial problems, physical abuse and drinking. Middle-class wives were significantly more prone to complain about lack of love, infidelity and excessive demands. Middle-class husbands paralleled the wives in their significantly greater concern with lack

[1]Hollingshead, A. B. 1957. Two Factor Index of Social Position. New Haven, Conn., multilithed.

of love; on the other hand, they were significantly *less* likely than lower-class husbands to complain of the wife's infidelity.

Considering the sexual relationship, one may note that "sexual incompatibility" was a more frequently voiced complaint by middle-class than by lower-class husbands, while the reverse was true for wives. The opposite was found for "infidelity."

In general, the evidence indicates that spouses in the middle-class marriages were more concerned with psychological and emotional interaction, while the lower-class partners saw as most salient in their lives financial problems and the unsubtle physical actions of their partner. . . .

# 9. *Criminal and Civil Liability in Husband-Wife Assaults*
## ROBERT CALVERT

Americans are particularly prone to viewing the law as a means of bringing about desirable social change. Most of us have some inkling of the fact that, in previous times, husbands had the right to use physical punishment on their wives, just as parents now have this right in respect to children. There is also a tendency to assume that the long series of laws which have gradually given more and more equal rights to women were the means by which the rights of husbands to use physical force on their wives was called to a halt. But this article makes clear that the change did not occur in this way. If there has been a reduction in wife-beating (and we are inclined to think there has been), it has come about through gradual increases in the socio-economic level and education of the population rather than by legislation. The decisions reached by judges and juries have tended to reflect these changes in social practice. Thus, although neither the rights of husbands to use physical force, nor the parallel rights of parents to use force have ever been repealed by statute, the courts no longer tolerate "chastisement" of erring wives. At the same time, it is also important to remember that even though the courts no longer tolerate a husband using physical punishment on a wife, just as they will not tolerate theft, in neither case does the illegality of the act mean its absence.

References may be found in ancient law to the right of the husband to "chastise" his wife with a "whip or rattan no bigger than my thumb, in order to enforce the salutory restraints of domestic discipline" (Bradley v. State, Walker, 156, Miss. 1824). However, such authority was doubted in Blackstone's time and the holding in a Mississippi case stated:

Perhaps the husband should still be permitted to exercise the right to moderate chastisement, in cases of great emergency and to use salutary restraints in every case of misbehavior, without subjecting himself to vexatious prosecutions, resulting in the discredit and shame of all parties. (Bradley v. State, Walker, 158)

source: Edited for this volume by Murray A. Straus from draft papers prepared by Robert Calvert. We are grateful to Professor Lenore J. Weitzman for help in securing Mr. Calvert's contribution to the book.

This holding of the Mississippi court that some "moderate chastisement" should still be the "right" of the husband was overruled in Harris v. State (14 S 266, 1894).

There is no specific time which one can point to as the year or decade when the husband lost his authority to beat his wife. The courts are reluctant to get into every family squabble, but they do recognize that the inhumane treatment of the wife will not be allowed. The North Carolina court stated:

We may assume that the old doctrine that a husband had a right to whip his wife, provided he used a switch no bigger than his thumb, is not the law in North Carolina. Indeed, the courts have advanced from that barbarism until they have reached the position that the husband has no right to chastise his wife under any circumstances. (State v. Oliver, 70 N.C. 60, 1874)

Even this enlightened court qualified its holding by stating that in order to preserve the sanctity of the domestic circle, the Courts will not listen to trivial complaints (State v. Oliver, 70 N.C. 61, 1874). The court did go on to define in a negative manner what a trivial complaint consisted of:

If no permanent injury has been inflicted, nor malice, cruelty nor dangerous violence shown by the husband, it is better to draw the curtain, shut out the public gaze, and leave the parties to forget and forgive. (State v. Oliver, 70 N.C. 60, 61.)

In general today, the states will allow the wife to bring criminal action against the husband who inflicts injury on her, but not to the same extent that the state criminal laws protect a third party from unwanted injury. For a husband to be guilty of the battery of his wife something more than unpermitted touch or even minor injury is required("Rape and Battery Between Husband and Wife," 6 *Stanford Law Review* 719). Some states have enacted specific husband-wife assault statutes and these laws denote that the injury to the wife must be *more* than what is required for battery (Cal. Penal Code S 273d).

Among the cases reviewed, some dealing with divorce suits, all speak to the right of the wife to bring criminal action for battery against her husband. There is no enlightened period in history that can be designated as the time the woman's right was elevated. One can only speculate as to whether the husband ever had an unrestricted right to beat his wife or whether certain activities of the husband were sanctioned by the courts and the general public. Also, there was never a time when the wife would not dare speak up to her husband, let alone bring a criminal action against him in a court of law.

In the case of torts (civil actions to recover damages or injury), the situation is in some ways more clear and in others less so. The state laws are divided into two basic viewpoints: (1) the majority view which upholds the common-law immunity of the husband from law suits by his wife; and (2) the minority view which treats the rights of the married woman as if she were single (Hinkel, 1970). Like any general rules, there are many exceptions.

To understand the difference between the majority and minority views, one must examine the common-law rule and the rationale behind inter-spousal immunity. The leading commentary on the common law, *Blackstone Commentaries* 442 (1768), states:

By marriage the husband and wife are one person in law, that is, the very being or legal existence of the woman is suspended during marriage or at least is incorporated and consolidated into that of the husband.

The reasoning followed that since the husband and wife were legally one, the law would not allow one person to sue himself. This view of the merging of the spouses was primarily a political move to settle property claims and the subsequent right of the husband to handle the family fortune regardless of whose fortune it was prior to marriage.

The Married Woman's Acts began to be passed by the individual state legislatures after the Civil War, and today such acts have been enacted in every state. Initially introduced to protect and maintain equitable separate estates, most statutes deal with a wide variety of matters concerning the legal rights of the wife. However, even the passage of these acts did not immediately render the husband liable to suit for striking his wife. Kanowitz (1969) notes that a response in some states was to change the basis for the immunity of spouses from torts. He notes that ". . . the new reason for denying them the right to sue one another for personal injuries was allegedly to prevent damage to domestic tranquility. . . . A husband could beat his wife mercilessly, . . . but the law in its rectitude denied her the right to sue her husband because such a suit, it claimed, could destroy the peace of the home" (Kanowitz, 1969: 77–78). Thus, even today the only recourse for a wife is the criminal law or divorce. The former is difficult to invoke and the latter is an extreme step. Nevertheless, despite the ambiguity of the law on this matter, it seems as though the right of husbands to use physical punishment is no longer present. But husbands have lost this right by change in customary usage more than by legal change.

REFERENCES

Blackstone, Sir William
    1768    *Commentaries on the Laws of England.* London: Houghton Mifflin.
Hinkel, David B.
    1970    "Intrafamily Litigation—Husband and Wife." *Insurance Law Journal.*
Kanowitz, Leo
    1969    *Women and the Law: The Unfinished Revolution.* Albuquerque, New Mexico: University of New Mexico Press.
Cases on criminal liability:
    State v. Oliver, 70 N.C. 60, 1874.
    State v. Mabrey, 64 N.C. 592, 1870.
    Goodrich v. Goodrich, 44 Ala. 670, 1868.
    Moyler v. Moyler, 11 Ala. 620, 1846.
    Commonwealth v. McAfee, 108 Mass. 458, 1871.
    Bradley v. State, Walker 156, 1824.
    Harris v. State, 14 S 266, 1894.
    Cal. Penal Code 273d.
Cases on tort:
    Thompson v. Thompson, 218 US 611.

Shiver v. Sessions, 80 S 2d. 905, Florida, 1955.
Corren v. Corren, 47 S 2d. 774, Florida, 1950.
Bencomo v. Bencomo, 200 S 2d. 171, Florida, 1967.
Brown v. Brown, Conn., 1914.
Peters v. Peters, 103 P 219, Ca., 1909.
Self v. Self, 376 P 2d. 65, Ca., 1962.
Klien v. Klien, 376 P 2d. 70, Ca., 1962.
Brandt v. Keller, 109 N.E. 2d. 729, Ill., 1952.
Apitz v. Dames, 287 P 2d. 585, Oregon, 1955.
Mosier v. Carney, 138 N.W. 2d. 343, Mich., 1965.

## 10. *Family Members as Murder Victims*
### STUART PALMER

In this article Palmer summarizes the data on the amazing extent to which murder victims are family members. He also makes clear some of the dynamics underlying these statistics. In the section on "victim-precipitation" he shows the frequency with which murder victims help to precipitate their own demise by the nature of their interaction with the murderer. The cumulative spiral of antagonism, ultimately ending when ". . . one participant breaks that process by bringing about the death of the other," is especially likely to occur in families because it is so difficult to end the spiral by other means. It is hard to ignore relatives, and even harder to ignore a husband, wife, or child. Finally, Palmer provides a graphic case example of the gradual escalation of husband-wife violence and antagonism to the point of murder.

The nature of the immediate situations and circumstances surrounding homicidal violence is of much importance in any rounded understanding of the phenomenon. Regarding the victim-offender relationship: As a rule the two individuals are friends or acquaintances and often they are biologically related or are marital partners.[1]

A cross-cultural study indicates that in the vast majority of non-literate societies analyzed, 41 out of 44, homicidal victims and offenders are rarely if ever strangers.[2] Among 550 Philadelphia homicide cases, Wolfgang found that victim and offender were close friends in 28.2 per cent of the killings; in 24.7 per cent they were relatives; in 13.5 per cent they were acquaintances; in another 9.8 per cent they were paramours; and in but 12.2 were they strangers. (The remaining percentages included homosexual partners,

SOURCE: Reprinted with permission from Stuart Palmer, *The Violent Society* (New Haven, Conn.: College & University Press, 1972), pp. 40–49.
[1]Marvin E. Wolfgang and Franco Ferracuti, *The Subculture of Violence* (New York: Barnes and Noble, 1967).
[2]Stuart Palmer, "Murder and Suicide in Forty Non-Literate Societies," *Journal of Criminal Law, Criminology, and Police Science* (Sept., 1965), pp. 320–324. In some instances, societies are so small and isolated that victims and offenders are bound to know each other. Generally, however, strangers within or without the given society are abundant.

police officer-felon relationship, and so on.[3] For the United States as a whole, 29 per cent of all murders in 1966 occurred between offender and victim who were members of the same family.[4] Slightly over half of those cases involved one spouse killing the other; in about one seventh of the cases, parents killed their children.

When victims and offenders have never met, the offender is nonetheless likely to be familiar with the victim's characteristics or with the characteristics of individuals like the victim. For example, two young men despise middle-class values. They choose a family well known in the locality for its personification of those values. The men are not personally acquainted with the family but they know much about them. They go to the family's home and kill all members.[5] Again a college student who feels out of place and snubbed by his peers climbs to the top of a campus tower. He shoots to death a number of students crossing the yard below. While they have been individually unknown to him, the victims represent, personify, those whom he sees as his frustrators. . . .

VICTIM-PRECIPITATION

In the United States and elsewhere as well, homicide tends to occur in the context of a quarrel or where insult or jealousy is clearly present.[6] Two major patterns emerge here. First there is a sudden argument between two persons who, while they know each other, do not interact daily. One resorts to extreme violence. For example two men run across each other in a bar. One accuses the other of having molested his wife some time ago. They fight; one pulls a knife and kills the other. This is less usual than the second form where there is a daily mounting buildup of argument and insult over weeks, months, or years.[7] Finally, one participant breaks that process by bringing about the death of the other.

Often it is difficult to determine to what extent the victim "conspires" with the offender, helping to bring about his own demise.[8] Tarde wrote at some length of the phenomenon of victim-precipitation.[9] More recently von Hentig,[10] Wolfgang,[11] and Schafer[12] among others have given the matter sustained attention. Wolfgang has made the most extensive empirical investigation.[13] Of 588 homicidal cases in his analysis, 150 or 26 per cent were

---

[3]Wolfgang, *op. cit.*, p. 207.

[4]Federal Bureau of Investigation, *Uniform Crime Reports, 1966* (Washington, D.C.: U.S. Government Printing Office, 1967), p. 6.

[5]Truman Capote, *In Cold Blood* (New York: Random House, 1965).

[6]Palmer, *A Study of Murder*; Wolfgang, *op. cit.*; Wolfgang and Ferracuti, *op. cit.*

[7]Palmer, *op. cit.*

[8]This may apply also to assault, rape and robbery victims, among others.

[9]Gabriel Tarde, *Penal Philosophy* (Boston: Little, Brown, 1912).

[10]Hans von Hentig, *The Criminal and His Victim* (New Haven, Conn.: Yale University Press, 1948).

[11]*Op. cit.*, Ch. 14.

[12]Stephen Schafer, *The Victim and His Criminal* (New York: Random House, 1968).

[13]*Op. cit.*

victim-precipitated. Wolfgang confined his definition of victim-precipitation to those interchanges resulting in death where the victim was the first to use physical force. If he had been able to include serious psychological provocation, the percentage of victim-precipitated cases would undoubtedly have been considerably higher.

In any event, Wolfgang found offenders tended to be female and victims to be male. Both victims and offenders were more likely to be black than white. Offenders and victims were often related. Moreover, Wolfgang found that in a disproportionately large number of victim-precipitated slayings, offenders were wives and victims were their husbands. Typically the male lashed out assaultively at the female and she retaliated in the extreme.[14] The spiral of conflict was broken by a final clash, physically initiated by the victim, that had within it elements of an inverted reciprocity: victim and offender were cooperating in the former's death.

## WEAPONS, PLACES, AND TIMES

Apart from whether victim-precipitation is involved, especially lethal weapons such as firearms, knives, and clubs are typically used to carry out the homicidal act.[15] Generally these weapons are employed in a frenzied attack upon the victim. And not infrequently the attack is more than sufficient to kill.[16] However, less physically aggressive means, poisoning for example, are not uncommon.[17] Whatever the weapon, the carefully planned, highly rational killing is a rarity in the United States and in most other societies.[18]

To what extent the unavailability of firearms and other weapons might decrease homicide rates is largely unknown.[19] Ready access to lethal weapons may in some instances serve to convert what would have been assaults into criminal homicides.[20] However, many potential weapons are likely to be near at hand unless precautions are taken that unduly restrict ordinary activities of everyday life. For example, female offenders frequently make violent use of carving and other knives from the kitchen. To place bans on the possession of those would hardly be practicable.

Homicide seldom occurs in highly public places. The usual site is a home or other non-public place.[21] The bedroom and the kitchen are common scenes of attacks.[22] Apart from dwelling places, the car is a fairly frequent setting.[23] . . .

14*Ibid.*
15Palmer, *op. cit.*; Wolfgang, *op. cit.*; Wolfgang and Ferracuti, *op. cit.*
16Wolfgang, *op. cit.*
17Wolfgang and Ferracuti, *op. cit.*
18Palmer, *op. cit.*
19Wolfgang and Ferracuti, *op. cit.*
20*Ibid.*
21Alex D. Pokorney, "Human Violence: A Comparison of Homicide, Aggravated Assault, Suicide, and Attempted Suicide," *Journal of Criminal Law, Criminology, and Police Science*, 56 (Dec., 1965), pp. 488–97; Wolfgang, *op. cit.*
22Wolfgang, *op. cit.*
23Pokorney, *op. cit.*

THE CASE OF LOUELLA FEARY

There follows the case of an aging woman, Louella Feary. The killing of her husband is an apt example of victim-precipitated homicide. Interviewed by the author in prison, she tells her story:

"What kind of a man was Feary? He was a son-of-a-bitch, that's what he was. A regular son-of-a-bitch. I don't usually use such words but with him I can't help myself. Oh, he was so nice on the outside, you know. He was one of those people, butter wouldn't melt in his mouth, and underneath he was as dirty and rotten as they come. He owned a farm up there, two hundred and forty acres, and you'd have thought he was something the way he put on. He was going to take me away from all of the trouble I'd seen. He took me in, I will say that for him. He took me in. Anyway we were married in the summer of 1940 and I moved up to the farm to live with him. Well, it was a mess, I tell you. Nice house on the outside but nothing inside. Furniture all broken down. I moved in my furniture, some of it pretty good. Feary had been short of money all along, and he told me one night soon after I'd moved in that he was planning on burning the barn.

"See, he was one of these people that would work pretty hard for a week or so and then he'd go off on a drunk for a couple of weeks. That's the way he did all the time. Work hard when he worked, drunk as a pig when he drank.

"The first while, him and me got along pretty good even with his drinking. But then pretty soon he got to cussing me out. No matter what I did he'd cuss me out. Why he's called me a whore more times than there's whores in the whole state. And that's plenty, believe me. Called me stupid, called me a liar, a cheat, thief, anything you can think of and a lot more. He called me them things time after time till I got sick and sick of hearing it. And like I told you, I'm sensitive and it made me feel awful.

"Feary and one friend or another was always taking off in the truck, the farm truck. Going somewhere or another to have a good time, get liquored up. I lived with that man for eight years and I tell you, life was nothing but one hell all of the time. He'd come home drunk and he'd cuss me out, and he'd hit me. One time he almost choked me to death. He was six foot-two, weighed a hundred and ninety pounds and there wasn't a thing I could do.

"Then as the time went on he got so he was mean even when he wasn't drinking. He'd sit there in the kitchen and cuss me up one side and down the other. Tell me what a whore I was, what a thief I was, a liar and all the rest of it. Many's the time I thought to myself, I could kill him. And most all this time I kept on working for one family or another. Doing housework and getting good money for it, too. Most of what we lived on came from what I made.

"Then in 1948 it was, I'd had enough. I couldn't take it from him any more and I left. Went to live in Toland. I was there five months when Feary came around just as sweet as you please. Oh, he was going to be so different. Butter wouldn't melt in his mouth. He wasn't going to touch a drop of liquor. Ever. He was going to treat me nice. Never call me names. Never cuss me out, swear at me again. Well, like a fool I believed it. I went back to live with him.

"Wasn't ten days after I'd been back he was cussing me out just like he had before. Calling me every filthy name in the book. Drinking again, threatening to beat me. I remember one time we got in an argument about something and Feary came up to me and stood there in front of me and he just kept taking his right fist and smashing it into his left fist and saying, 'I ought to kill you.'

"Then, a couple of months later my son came to live with us. His wife had died and he didn't want to be alone. A week after that Feary decided he was going to take the cows down and sell them at this auction. So he got my son to help him get the cows loaded in the truck. Feary's way of getting cows in a truck was to drive the truck up to a stone-wall, back it up to the stone-wall, drop the tail-gate and let the cows climb in as best they could. Well this time he backed it up to a manure pile and he tried to get the cows in. There was three of them. They wouldn't go. They weren't having any part of it. But finally he got two of them in. The third one—the black one— wouldn't go and Feary was getting madder and madder. He was cussing me out to beat the band, cussing my son out and screaming at the cow.

"Finally Feary got a rope and he put it around the cow's mouth so the cow could hardly breathe. He told my son to take one end of the rope and get up in the truck and my son got up there. Then Feary, he got the pitchfork, and he got behind the cow and he started jabbing at her with the pitchfork. That cow could hardly breathe. You could hear it wheezing. But the cow wasn't having any part of going up in that truck. Well, Feary kept at it with the pitchfork but that cow wouldn't move up in the truck. Jabbing, jabbing, jabbing. Harder and harder. And Feary bellowing all the time. After five or ten minutes of that the cow fell down. You could hear it still wheezing. Then all of a sudden it shuddered and it lay still.

"My son called out, 'You killed her!'

" 'Serves the goddamned thing right,' says Feary.

"And he had killed it too. He killed it with that pitchfork. When he'd seen that he killed it he raised the pitchfork up over his head with both hands and brought it down on the head of that cow. He brought it down so hard he broke the handle of the pitchfork. The police chief, he got that broken pitchfork later, but he wouldn't bring it into court because he was one of Feary's boozing friends.

"Well, Feary got in the truck and he was bound and determined to take the other two cows down to the auction. 'Lou, get in the truck,' he yelled at me, not calling me Louella like he should.

"I just stood there. 'Lou, get in the goddamned truck,' he yelled again. I still didn't move and he jumped out of the truck. He came up to me, grabbed me by the shoulders and said, 'Now get in the goddamned truck or you'll be laying there just like that cow.'

"I got in, feeling numb all over from what he'd done to that cow. We went down the road, a dirt road it was, sixty miles an hour. Those two cows were laying down in the back but they were bouncing off the floor of the truck by as much as a foot. That's how fast he went down that dirt road. Wild man, that's what he was.

"When we got home I was sick, sick from seeing that cow killed like it was. I had to go to bed. I was shaking all over. Well, Feary went out drinking that night. And when he got home he came in the room and said, 'You're getting out. I'm having no more to do with you. I've got other women I can get to live here. I don't need you.'

"I told him I'd had the doctor earlier that evening, which I had. And he says, 'That don't make no difference. You're getting out.'

"For the next couple of days I couldn't eat a thing. I was so nervous I couldn't touch food. Then on the third day after that my son had to go to Toland and I got up and made breakfast for him. He could hardly eat himself from the thought of that cow and I couldn't eat anything. Feary was out drinking somewhere. He'd been out all night. I got my son off to Toland. That afternoon Feary came in, drunk as a skunk. He started cussing me out again. Knocking me around. I'd had just about enough. So later that afternoon I drove into town and on the way back I stopped and got me a nice little pistol in the gun store. I brought it home and put it in the dresser in my room.

"I wasn't planning on killing him, you see. I got it just to defend myself against him.

"Well, the next evening Feary came in to his dinner and I didn't have dinner ready. I didn't know he was coming in at that time. He yelled, 'Where the hell is dinner?' And so I told him how I'd been sick and he said, 'I told you to get out.' Well, he started abusing me once again. He started calling me every name in the book. Oh, what a whore I was and all of that stuff.

"I just slipped into my room and I took that pistol out of the dresser drawer and I loaded it. I slipped it into the pocket of my skirt underneath my apron. So he couldn't see it. I went back out into the kitchen. He was sitting in that big chair where he always sat and he started to cuss me out again.

"I went over to him, trying to put my arm around him, trying to make up. I was giving it one more try. Well, as I tried to put my arm around him he raised up and swung at me and hit me along side the head with his fist.

"I reeled back and then I pulled the gun. I hadn't had the safety catch on and I fired at him point blank. He was standing up as the bullet hit him and he staggered and went around the room in a big circle, tottering, and came right back to where he'd been before. 'You've done it now, Lou,' he said. 'You've really done it.' And with that he fell down straight out on the floor. Flat on his face. I took the gun and fired at him once more. Don't know what made me do it the second time. I guess I was just so mad at him for all the trouble he'd caused me.

"Then after I'd shot him for the second time I sat down in kind of a daze. I sat there not knowing what was going on. The fire went out and it grew awful cold. It must have been four or five hours later I came to, and almost freezing to death. The dog was there in the kitchen whimpering and whining away. I opened the door and he went out and we never saw him again. He wouldn't go back to the kitchen.

"I went into my room and laid down. And I was thinking to myself: Well, Feary, you got yours and got it good and you deserved it for all you've done to me. The next morning my son came home and he saw what I'd done.

"How do I feel about it, now? Killing him? He deserved it. Can you say different? That man was the meanest man on this earth. He made my life one hell from the day I met him."

# CHAPTER FOUR
# Approaches to Controlling Violence

## 11. Why Intimates Must Fight
### GEORGE R. BACH AND PETER WYDEN

Although the concluding section of Israel W. Charny's article on "Marital Love and Hate" (p. 56) contains a list of ten techniques for "marital fighting and loving," his article is basically oriented to *explaining why* conflict is a normal state in marriage. By contrast, Bach and Wyden's *The Intimate Enemy,* from which the following article was taken, is primarily oriented to providing *advice and guidance* to couples. To do this they skillfully interweave a series of case examples and illustrations into their general discussion so that the reader can visualize himself in the situations portrayed. They present examples of how *not* to fight as well as suggestions for fighting constructively.

An important aspect of this approach is that it is directed to all families, not just those who are 'fighters" or who seek aid from a marriage counselor. Bach and Wyden are skeptical of the middle class ideal of a family exercising a high degree of self-control and avoiding display of emotions. They feel that this tends to produce outwardly harmonious marriages ("they never exchange a harsh word") which suddenly disintegrate. There are undoubtedly many such cases, but as we noted on p. 52, there is no scientifically valid evidence which demonstrates that couples who follow their suggestions disintegrate any less frequently than those who follow the traditional middle class prescriptions. Still another possibility is that the styles of family interaction depicted in this article will, as they claim, open new vistas for individual and family development for *some* families. For others they could prove traumatic and destructive. A skilled marriage counselor can presumably sense which type he is dealing with and adapt his treatment accordingly.

Verbal conflict between intimates is not only acceptable, especially between husbands and wives; it is constructive and highly desirable. Many people, including quite a few psychologists and psychiatrists, believe that this new scientific concept is an outrageous and even dangerous idea. We know otherwise, and we can prove it. At our Institute of Group Psychotherapy in Beverly Hills, California, we have discovered that couples who fight together are couples who stay together—provided they know how to fight properly.

SOURCE: Reprinted by permission of William Morrow and Company, Inc., from *The Intimate Enemy* (New York: Morrow, 1968), pp. 17–33. Copyright 1968, 1969 by George R. Bach and Peter Wyden.

The art of fighting right is exactly what we teach couples who come to us for marriage counseling. Our training methods are not simple and cannot be successfully applied by everyone. They require patience, good will, and the flexibility to adopt some challenging and unconventional ways for dealing with humanity's most personal drives. Most of all, they demand hearts and minds that are open—open to reason and to change. The great majority of our clients master the art of marital combat quickly. For them, the payoffs are warmly rewarding, and we believe that any couple with honest and deep motivation can achieve the same results.

When our trainees fight according to our flexible system of rules, they find that the natural tensions and frustrations of two people living together can be greatly reduced. Since they live with fewer lies and inhibitions and have discarded outmoded notions of etiquette, these couples are free to grow emotionally, to become more productive and more creative, as individuals in their own right and also as pairs. Their sex lives tend to improve. They are likely to do a better job raising their children. They feel less guilty about hostile emotions that they harbor against each other. Their communications improve and, as a result, they face fewer unpleasant surprises from their partners. Our graduates know how to make the here-and-now more livable for themselves, and so they worry much less about the past that cannot be changed. They are less likely to become victims of boredom or divorce. They feel less vulnerable and more loving toward each other because they are protected by an umbrella of reasonable standards for what is fair and foul in their relationship. Perhaps best of all, they are liberated to be themselves.

Some aspects of our fight training shock trainees when they first begin to work with us. We advocate that they fight in front of their friends and children. For many couples we recommend fighting before, during, or after sexual intercourse. Some people who learn about our work by way of hearsay get the impression that we encourage trainees to become expert at the sort of sick and chronic insult exchanges that proved so readily recognizable to audiences of Edward Albee's play and movie, *Who's Afraid of Virginia Woolf?*. But this we never, never do. People fight in the *Virginia Woolf* style before we train them, not afterward.

The wild, low-blow flailing of *Virginia Woolf* is not an extreme example of fighting between intimate enemies; in fact, it is rather common in ordinary life. Let's listen in on a fight that we have heard, with variations, literally hundreds of times during nearly 25 years of practicing psychotherapy. We call this a "kitchen sink fight" because the kitchen plumbing is about all that isn't thrown as a weapon in such a battle.

Mr. and Mrs. Bill Miller have a dinner date with one of Bill's out-of-town business associates and the associate's wife. Mrs. Miller is coming in from the suburbs and has agreed to meet Bill in front of his office building. The Millers have been married for 12 years and have three children. They are somewhat bored with each other by now, but they rarely fight. Tonight happens to be different. Bill Miller is anxious to make a good impression on the visiting firemen from out of town. His wife arrives 20 minutes late. Bill is furious. He hails a taxi and the fun begins:

HE: Why were you late?

SHE: I tried my best.

HE: Yeah? You and who else? Your mother is never on time either.

SHE: That's got nothing to do with it.

HE: The hell it doesn't. You're just as sloppy as she is.

SHE *(getting louder)*: You don't say! Who's picking whose dirty underwear off the floor every morning?

HE *(sarcastic but controlled)*: I happen to go to work. What have *you* got to do all day?

SHE *(shouting)*: I'm trying to get along on the money you don't make, that's what.

HE *(turning away from her)*: Why should I knock myself out for an ungrateful bitch like you?

The Millers got very little out of this encounter except a thoroughly spoiled evening. Trained marital fighters, on the other hand, would be able to extract from this brief volley a great deal of useful information. They would note that while the trigger for this fight was legitimate (the lady *was* very late), it was also trivial and not indicative of what was really troubling this couple. The aggression reservoir of the hapless Millers was simply so full that even a slight jar caused it to spill over. Both partners had been keeping their grievances bottled up, and this is invariably a poor idea. We call this "gunnysacking" because when marital complaints are toted along quietly in a gunny sack for any length of time they make a dreadful mess when the sack finally bursts.

Our graduates would also be able to point out that Bill Miller quite unfairly reached into the couple's "psychiatric museum" by dragging the totally irrelevant past (his mother-in-law's tardiness and sloppiness) into the argument; and Mrs. Miller added to the destruction when she escalated the conflict by going out of her way to attack Bill's masculinity. She did this when she castigated him as a poor provider (we call this "shaking the money tree").

Obviously, both of these fighters would benefit from the principal recommendation we make to our trainees: to do their best to keep all arguments not only fair but up-to-date so that the books on a marriage can be balanced daily, much as banks keep their debits and credits current by clearing all checks with other banks before closing down for business every evening. Couples who fight regularly and constructively need not carry gunny sacks full of grievances, and their psychiatric museums can be closed down.

By studying tens of thousands of intimate encounters like this one between the Millers, we designed a system for programming individual aggression through what we call constructive fighting. Our system is not a sport like boxing. It is more like a cooperative skill such as dancing. It is a tool, a way of life that, paradoxically, leads to greater harmony between intimates. It is a somewhat revolutionary notion, but we believe that it can serve not only to enrich the lives of husbands, wives, and lovers; it could become the first step toward controlling the violent feelings that lead to assassinations and to aggressions between entire peoples. A Utopian dream? Perhaps. But we submit that humanity cannot cope with hostilities between nations until it learns to hammer out livable settlements for hostilities between loved ones.

About eight years ago our Institute pioneered in the management of intimate aggression. We have worked successfully with more than 250 couples, and many therapists throughout the United States and abroad now use our system. But, since our methods are still widely misunderstood, we would like to emphasize that our kind of "programming" is neither as precise nor as rigid as the type achieved by computers. Anyone who tries to "program" people in a machinelike way is either kidding himself or trying to play God.

Our system amounts to a set of experimental exercises. We suggest format, but not content; the frame, but not the picture. The picture is filled in by each couple as they fight. This is known as the heuristic approach to education, a system that trains students to find out things for themselves. We train attitudes and suggest directions for further inquiry through trial and error. We formalize and civilize impulsive or repressed anger; but we preserve the spontaneity of aggressive encounters. This is vital because no fight is predictable and no two are alike.

We will describe the at-home fight exercises that we offer our clients; when, where, and how to start a fight; when and how to finish it when it has gone far enough; how couples can regulate their "closeness" to each other while they are between fights; how to score 21 kinds of results of an intimate battle. Our program does not, however, offer hard-and-fast recipes in cookbook style. It can be tried, always with due consideration for the vulnerability of the partner, by anyone without a therapist. But when a therapist is present, as is always the case at our Institute, he is no distant father figure. He participates as trainer, coach, referee, cheerleader, model, and friend.

Some readers may wonder whether all this adds up to complicated machinery constructed by psychologists who cannot bear to keep things simple. Our clinical experience suggests otherwise. Many intelligent, well-to-do trainees tell us of fights that are so abysmally crude and hurtful that it is impossible to doubt the need for fight training. But these kitchen-sink fighters are not the ones who are worst off. We have far more clients who live in a style that can be infinitely more threatening to intimate relationships. Again paradoxically, these unfortunates are the partners who fight rarely or not at all.

Although the Bill Millers, for example, sustained painful emotional injuries in their taxicab fight, they became aggressors ("hawks") under pressure. This is a point in their favor, not against them, for even this destructive encounter produced one positive result. In its way, the taxicab fight gave the Millers a rough—very rough—idea of where they stood with each other, which is the essential first step toward the improvement of any relationship. This knowledge placed them way ahead of many couples. Approximately 80 per cent of our trainees start out as natural nonfighters or active fight-evaders ("doves"), and these people usually know much less about each other than the Millers did. After their fight the Millers knew at least how far apart they were and how far each would go to hurt the other.

In intimate relationships ignorance is rarely bliss. At best it leads to the monumental boredom of couples who are living out parallel lives in a state of loneliness *à deux*. The quiet that prevails in their homes isn't really peace. Actually, these people are full of anger much of the time, like everyone else on earth. After all, what is anger? It's the basic emotional and physiological reaction against interference with the pursuit of a desired goal; and an expression of strong concern when things go wrong. When partners don't fight, therefore, they are not involved in an intimate relationship; honest intimates can't ignore their hostile feelings because such feelings are inevitable.

One typical evening in the home of nonfighting pseudo-intimates began like this:

HE *(yawning)*: How was your day, dear?

SHE *(pleasantly)*: OK, how was yours?

HE: Oh, you know, the usual.

SHE: Want your martini on the rocks?

HE: Whatever you want to fix, dear.

SHE: Anything special you want to do later?

HE: Oh, I don't know . . .

In this fight-phobic home nothing more meaningful may be exchanged for the rest of the evening. Or practically any evening. For reasons to be discussed shortly, these partners won't level with each other. Their penalty is emotional divorce.

There is another group of fight-evaders who do exchange some important signals with their mates, but usually with unfortunate results. We call them the pseudo-accommodators. Here is one such husband who is about to dive into appalling hot water:

WIFE *(settling down comfortably for a sensible discussion)*: Mother wants to come visit from New York.

HUSBAND *(shrinking away and accommodating)*: Why not?

The dove-husband in this case was saying to himself, "Oh, my God!" He did not say it out loud because he "can't stand hassling." So his mother-in-law arrives and the fights triggered by her presence are far more terrible than the original fight with his wife which the husband managed to avoid. This husband was also practicing another technique that is popular among intimates. He expected his wife to *divine* how he really felt about the mother-in-law's visit. He was saying to himself. "If Emmy loves me she will know that I don't want her mother to come until later in the year when I'll have less pressure on my job." Too bad that most people are not talented in the extrasensory art of divining. But they're not, and many intimates therefore never really know "where they're at."

Throughout this book we will demonstrate how they can find out. Here we would only like to demonstrate the dangers of not trying.

Surprisingly few couples seem to realize how their failure to level with each other can lead to a totally unexpected, dramatic marriage crisis and perhaps even to divorce. This is what happened to another pair of doves, Mr. and Mrs. Kermit James. While making love, many husbands and wives pretend more passion than they really feel. In some marriages, both partners engage in this charade. In the case of the James family, the wife was the one who did the pretending. True intimates would confess their sex problems to each other. Pseudo-intimates, on the other hand, just go on pretending. The trouble is that unless two partners are really beyond the point of caring what happens to their union, the pretending eventually wears dangerously thin.

The Jameses had been married for eight years. One night after they had sexual intercourse Mr. James patted himself innocently on the back for his skill at love-making. Mrs. James happened to be furious at him because at dinnertime he had refused to discuss an urgent financial problem and later he had left his clothes strewn messily all over the floor. Normally she ignored such provocations just to keep things peaceful. This time, her anger at her husband got out of control. She was ready to "let him have it." She had been gunny-sacking so many additional grievances for such a very long time, however, that she reached unthinkingly for the trigger of an atomic bomb. The danger of a nuclear explosion hovers over every nonfighting marriage. Mrs. James unleashed the lethal mushroom cloud when she casually said: "You know, I never come. I fake it."

Marriages have split up with less provocation. The Jameses gradually repaired their relationship by entering fight training at our Institute. One of the first bits of advice we gave them, incidentally, is that wise marital combatants always try to measure their weapons against the seriousness of a particular fight issue. Nuclear bombs shouldn't be triggered against pea-shooter causes; or, as we sometimes warn trainees: "Don't drop the bomb on Luxembourg!"

Fight-evading can also lead to disaster without any blowup whatever. A somewhat extreme example are Mr. and Mrs. Harold Jacobson, a prosperous suburban couple who had been married for more than 20 years. They had raised two children and were socially popular. Everybody thought they had a fine marriage. Mr. Jacobson was a sales manager with an income of well over $20,000. His wife dressed well, played excellent bridge, and did more than her share for local causes. Both were considered well-informed conversationalists in their set, but at home Mr. Jacobson rarely said much. Peacefully, he went along with whatever his wife wanted to do.

Shortly after their younger child went off to college, Mr. Jacobson packed his clothes while his wife was out shopping and left home without leaving a note. It took Mrs. Jacobson some time to discover through her husband's lawyer that he meant to leave for good. As usual, he just hadn't felt like arguing about it. His wife was incredulous and then horrified. Their many friends were flabbergasted. None would have believed that this marriage could break up. Over a period of weeks, several of them brought sufficient pressure to bear on the Jacobsons to enter our fight-training program.

Mr. Jacobson was persuaded to start first. He joined one of our self-development groups, along with eight other individuals who were involved in marital crises but were not yet ready to work on their problems in the presence of their mates. The senior author of this book was the therapist. Together the group convinced Mr. Jacobson that the "silent treatment" which he had given his wife was not cooperation or strength but noncooperation or something worse: hostility camouflaged by phony and misleading compliance. He admitted that he had never leveled with his wife, and never clearly communicated his feelings about the way she dominated most of the family decisions; it riled him no end when she decided what they should do to "have fun," to "be creative," and all the rest. Almost invariably he went along, even though he resented it terribly in what we call the "inner dialogue" (conversations and fights which all of us keep going within ourselves). On the few occasions when Mr. Jacobson did protest mildly—always without making the true depth of his feelings clear—he found that his wife became even more assertive when she was resisted. So he became even more quiet.

At first Mr. Jacobson resisted fight training. He said that it would be "undignified" to let himself go and engage his wife in "useless" arguments. It was against his "values." It turned out that his German-born mother had taught him the virtue of the old adage, *"Reden ist Silber, aber Schweigen ist Gold"* (Talk is silver, but silence is golden). Mr. Jacobson still lived by this peasant saying, which was useful in feudal times when speaking up was indeed dangerous for serfs. He therefore believed that self-control was more virtuous than his wife's "noisy dominance."

In the course of six weekly sessions, the group thawed out this typical case of "etiquette-upmanship." We were able to convince Mr. Jacobson that speaking up in a good cause is more effective and valuable than "golden silence" that leads only to hopelessness. In his therapy group he then practiced "speaking up" and "fighting back" on a particularly domineering lady who became, in effect, a substitute for his wife. He reasoned with her. He argued. He refused to be squelched. He was elated when finally he succeeded in getting through to her, and boasted that she was "much worse than my wife."

Then Mr. Jacobson entered a second type of group. Here, four to six married and unmarried intimates work at their problems not as individuals but as couples. Having learned the value of asserting himself aggressively in the self-development group, Mr. Jacobson found that he could now face Mrs. Jacobson on a new basis. During the group sessions he noticed that the wife whom he had always considered overwhelmingly argumentative and domineering could be managed, even tamed. To his surprise, he discovered that she actually *preferred* him to speak up assertively and to share the responsibility for family decision-making. It also made him generally more attractive and stimulating to her, with pleasing sexual fringe benefits for both.

Eventually, Mr. Jacobson, like most intelligent people, came to enjoy the give-and-take of true intimacy. He dismissed his divorce lawyer and, most likely, will carry on his marriage for another 20 years, but on a fresh, realistic basis. We felt that the Jacobsons had gained a brand-new marriage without a divorce.

Like most people today, Mr. Jacobson considered "aggression" a dirty word, just as "sex" used to be. Most people feel secretive about their anger and their fights. When we first initiated fight training, we asked couples to put some of their fights on tape at home and bring us the tapes for interpretation and discussion. This system did not work too well. Some partners were too clever; they turned on the tape recorder only when it was to their supposed "advantage" and turned it off when they felt like acting as censors. Other couples resisted the tape-making at home simply because they were too embarrassed to put their anger on record and then listen to it.

The fact is that anger is considered taboo in modern society. It isn't "gentlemanly." It isn't "feminine." It isn't "nice." It isn't "mature." This is supposed to be the age of sweet reason and "togetherness." The very word "fighting" makes most people uncomfortable. They prefer to talk about "differences" or "silly arguments." And they will go to considerable lengths to maintain the quiet that isn't peace.

Partners say, "Darling, I love you too much to fight with you; you're not my enemy!" But they usually say this in their inner dialogue, not out loud to their partner. Then, when they get angrier, their next step may be a demand, also directed toward the partner but still usually unspoken: "Act nice, no matter how angry you feel!" When an intimate feels even more threatened, he may finally speak up with a plea: "Don't get angry with me!" Or he may demand to turn the partner off: "I can't take you seriously when you're angry!" In an extremity, he may link his demand to a threat: "Don't raise your voice—or else!" All this is part of the strategy of "peace at any price."

The wish to be above personal animosity is fed by many mistaken beliefs. Control of anger, rather than its expression, is considered "mature." Hostility feelings toward an intimate are not only considered the antithesis of love ("If you really love me you should tolerate me as I am"); often such "hate" emotions are considered "sick," requiring psychiatric care. If an angry partner is not seriously enough afflicted to be led away to the head doctor, he is considered at least temporarily irrational. After all, everybody "knows" that what is said in anger cannot be taken seriously; a "mature" partner discounts it as the gibberish of an emotionally upset person, much like the ranting of a drunk.

Nonfighting marital stalemates are rooted in the romantic belief that intimates should take one another as they are. Folklore and etiquette insist that one should not try to change the beloved but accept him or her, warts and all, and "live happily ever after." Once one somehow acquires the magic ability to accept the other's frailties, automatic bliss is supposed to ensue. This charming idyll is promoted not only in fiction and on the screen but even by some marriage counselors and other professionals.

The dream of romantic bliss is an anachronistic hangover from the Victorian etiquette that tried to create gentlemen and gentleladies by social pressure. But the notion that a stress- and quarrel-free emotional climate in the home will bring about authentic harmony is a preposterous myth, born in ignorance of the psychological realities of human relationships. Fighting is inevitable between mature intimates. Quarreling and making up are hallmarks of true intimacy. However earnestly a mature person tries to live in harmony with a partner, he will have to fight for his very notions of harmony itself and come to terms with competing notions—and there are always competing interests.

Everybody has his own ideas about what makes for harmonious living. Being human, one likes one's own ideas to prevail except perhaps in cases of aggression-phobic fight-evaders or excessively submissive partners who act like doormats. The mature partner may yield some of his notions, but usually not without a fight. The classic battle about where to take the family on vacation is a perfect example of such an authentic encounter.

"The mountains are most relaxing," shouts the husband.

"The beach is more fun," shouts the wife.

Such conflicting notions make it perfectly natural for everybody to be angry at his mate some of the time.

Yet many couples still consider intimate conflict revolting. "We never fight," they tell us indignantly. They are, in truth, afraid of fighting. Sometimes they fear just the stress of "hassling"; few couples know about the modern research that shows stress is valuable for keeping the nervous system toned up in the psychological sense. More likely, intimates fear that anger is a Pandora's box. They fear they "can't afford to fight" because they have so many years invested in each other. They worry that if one partner raises his voice, the other must raise his. There might be tears. The fight might escalate out of control. It could lead to rejection, even separation!

As a matter of fact, our trainees find that they tend to feel closest after a properly fought fight. Only our newest recruits wonder whether we're being facetious when we tell them, "A fight a day keeps the doctor away."

Fascinating new experiments document this paradoxical-sounding thesis. In one famous series, Dr. Harry Harlow of the University of Wisconsin reared several generations of monkeys and showed that an exchange of hostilities is *necessary* between mates before there can be an exchange of love. Harlow's calm, mechanical, totally accepting and nonfighting monkey mothers raised off-spring who grew up "normal" except that they couldn't and wouldn't make love.

Another distinguished researcher, Konrad Lorenz, made similar observations about "bonding" (loving) behavior: "Among birds, the most aggressive representatives of any group are also the staunchest friends, and the same applies to mammals. To the best of our knowledge, bond behavior does not exist except in aggressive organisms. This certainly will not be news to the students of human nature. . . . The wisdom of old proverbs as well as that of Sigmund Freud has known for a very long time how closely human aggression and human love are bound together." Indeed, one of the leading theorists on emotional maturity, Erik Erikson of Harvard University, blames the failure to achieve human intimacy on "the inability to engage in controversy and useful combat."

Oddly enough, anger can be useful just *because* it pours out with a minimum of forethought. Unless a partner hides it behind a falsely neutral or false-friendly (and ulcer-producing) façade, his anger—like spontaneous laughter or spontaneous sexual arousal—cannot be dishonest. Making a person angry is the surest way to find out what he cares about and how deeply he cares. Since intimates keep measuring and remeasuring how much they care for one another ("Are you getting bored with me?"), they can make each other angry in normal but usually unconscious tests of the depth of their involvement.

The process starts right in the early phase of courtship when one partner tries to get the other "sore," not necessarily to "pick a fight," but just to "tease," to test the other out. How far can he go? What does she care enough about to get her "good and angry"? These fight games can be informative if they are played fairly and in a spirit that seeks not to inflict hurt but to resolve realistic conflicts. Lovers also find out by this process that affection grows deeper when it is mixed with aggression. Both feelings then become part of a natural, genuine relationship that allows for expression of the bitter as well as the sweet side of emotional involvement.

We believe, then, that there can be no mature intimate relationship without aggressive leveling; that is, "having it out," speaking up, asking the partner "what's eating" him and negotiating for realistic settlements of differences. This does cause stress, but our successful trainees learn to accept one of the realities of the human condition: the pain of conflict is the price of true and enduring love. People simply cannot release all their love feelings unless they have learned to manage their hate.

"Hate" sounds like too strong a word, but it isn't. When a partner performs according to one's expectations, one is "turned on" and feels love. When these expectations are frustrated, one is "turned off" and feels hate. This is what people recognize as the ups and downs of marriage. We call it "the state of marital swing." Unfortunately, it is usually a state viewed with vast resignation; hence the saying. "You can't live with 'em and you can't live without 'em." This hopelessness is unwarranted. At our Institute we discovered: (1) It is not a partner's sweet and loving side that shapes his bond with an intimate; it is the talent for airing aggression that counts most. And (2) aggression management not only can be learned; it can be used to *change* a partnership constructively.

Contrary to folklore, the existence of hostility and conflict is not necessarily a sign that love is waning. As often as not, an upsurge of hate may signal a deepening of true intimacy; it is when neither love nor hate can move a partner that a relationship is deteriorating. Typically, one partner then gives up the other as a "lost cause" or shrugs him off ("I couldn't care less"). Indifference to a partner's anger and hate is a surer sign of a deteriorating relationship than is indifference to love.

The problem of regulating personal aggression is rarely discussed. It hovers too uncomfortably close to home for most people. Almost everybody has a greater or lesser "hang-up" about admitting hostile feelings, even to himself. It is part of humanity's embarrassment about its inborn aggressive side. Frequently, therefore, people displace their hostilities onto others. We call this "blamesmanship " or "scapegoating," and intimates usually find the process baffling and infuriating.

Suppose it's Wednesday night. Mrs. Jones has had a trying day. She doesn't feel like making love and has decided to withhold sex from her husband. Instead of negotiating with him, she contaminates the situation with an extraneous issue and engages in blamesmanship between the sheets.

SHE: Not tonight, dear. Besides, I can't ever feel anything anyway. Your stomach is in the way.

HE: That's just your excuse. It all depends on the position.

SHE *(heatedly)*: You know perfectly well that I can't make it with those acrobatics. Everything would be very simple if you'd just stop stuffing yourself.

HE *(furious)*: I'm comfortable the way I am and you're not going to take my gourmet tastes away from me.

SHE *(icily)*: Well, something's got to give.

HE *(angry but resigned)*: Oh hell, there we go again. . . .

Children are a favorite target when intimates displace their own fights onto other people. Most parental fights about children, for example, are not about children at all. The disagreement is between the parents; the child is only the battleground. Tom and Myra Robinson learned this when they conducted the following fight before one of our training groups:

SHE: You simply must start to enforce discipline around here and make the kids toe the line.

HE: Why me?

SHE: Because I want you to be the power in this house!

HE: I like to be and I am.

SHE: No, you're not—I am! I have to be!

HE: No, you don't have to be, and you're not!

SHE *(getting angrier)*: Don't be stupid! Who disciplines the kids? Me! Who takes all the responsibility for discipline—me!

HE *(pacing and pulling hard on cigarette)*: I am glad you do, but that just makes a cop out of you . . . it doesn't really impress the kids at all.

SHE *(very red in the face)*: You're driving me out of my mind! That's my point! You let me do all the dirty work. That makes me a "mean mother" in the eyes of the kids. You get all the goodies: you're their loving "super daddy." I don't like it!

HE *(flopping resignedly into an armchair)*: Why shouldn't you like it when the kids and I have a terrific relationship? I don't understand you. That's one of the main attractions for coming home. I love those kids and you'll never make a "heavy" out of me!

SHE: OK! But I can't do it all! You have to back me up and you never do! Listen to what they just did today. . . .

HE *(disgusted with her but not with his children)*: Cut it out!

SHE *(totally exasperated)*: Why? Don't you want to hear? Don't you want to be part of this family? Don't you want to take any responsibility?

HE *(getting up again to counterattack)*: I take enough responsibility earning our living. And I don't like you when you tattle on the kids! In fact, I can't stand it. . . .

The Robinsons thought they were battling about their ideas of "parental authority," "doing a good job of raising the kids," and the role of the "man of the house." But these are only superficial cultural stereotypes. Once the therapy group began to probe what was really bothering Tom and Myra, we discovered some much deeper intimate issues which the couple did not dare confront.

It developed that Myra was jealous of Tom's love for the kids because he was not making enough passionate love to her. Tom, in turn, was not making love to Myra because since the kids came she had been a disappointment to him. She did not conform to his definition of a "good mother." What turned him off completely was her tattling because this aroused a strong memory of ugly, angry emotions from his past. His mother used to tattle to his father about his own misdeeds, and his father used to beat discipline into him every Saturday morning after his mother, behind the boy's back, had presented the father with a list of misdeeds!

Myra is also bitter because, since the kids came, the husband turned off loving her. She thinks that he thinks that she thinks: "I love my kids more than him. I only used the man to have a father for my kids, who are my joy and pride and who fulfill me." She therefore thinks: "He is jealous of my love for the kids and punishes me by withholding his love from me. He does not want to share me with anybody."

In our training group this spiral of misconceptions collapsed as the facts were exposed. By using techniques to be discussed in the next chapter, the Robinsons learned to level about their real feelings, wants, and expectations. The issue of disciplining the children never came up again. It was spontaneously handled by one partner or the other, as the situation demanded. . . .

We believe that the inability to manage personal conflicts is at the root of the crisis that threatens the structure of the American family. Communications between children and parents are breaking down. More and more young people are "turning out" by escaping into the world of drugs and other short-lived emotional kicks. One out of every three marriages ends in divorce. In our largest and most "advanced" state, California, the figure is approaching an almost incredible one out of every two.

Millions of other couples continue to live together physically and legally, yet emotionally apart. Atrophy, boredom, casual infidelities, and false-front façades "for the children's sake" are no longer exceptional. No one knows how many couples are emotionally divorced. We do know that millions of husbands and wives live in card houses held together by fantasy; by social, religious, economic, or legal pressures—or by the fear of change. . . .

When Dr. Eric Berne's book, *Games People Play*, became a runaway best-seller, publishing experts were surprised. They shouldn't have been. America's living rooms and bedrooms are full of partners who are too weak or frightened or not sufficiently knowledgeable to tolerate authentic encounters with their supposed intimates. They recognized their own camouflaging rituals in Dr. Berne's somewhat cynical and overly flip but essentially accurate descriptions. Remember "Uproar," the pointless fight that is provoked by a husband or wife early in the evening merely to avoid sex later? It is all but a national pastime. So are such marital games as "If it weren't for you" and "Look how hard I've tried." . . .

Constructive fighting makes for game-free living. It is a liberating, creative alternative that works. Since we introduced fight training, the rate of reconciliation among our Institutes problem couples has increased sharply. Follow-up studies indicate that most of our graduates are living much more satisfying (if perhaps noisier) lives than before. And for the most tragic victims of our psychological ice age, the children, the benefits are incalculable. For them, a sense of genuine family closeness is as important as food and drink. When a "nest" cools or disintegrates, children can grow only amid enormous handicaps. Young children especially thrive on intimacy and starve emotionally when they cannot share and learn it. We regard the neglect of intimacy and the absence of intimate models within many families as principally responsible for the current "generation gap." Those who are deprived of an intimate nest may never care to build or to protect one for themselves.

For intimate partners, perhaps the richest payoff of well-managed conflict comes with yielding after a fight. Any intimate relationship implies some readiness to yield one's own self-interest when it clashes with that of the partner. Everybody knows that the give-and-take of trying to get along with someone often means bending one's own will to the wishes of the other. This is never easy because the psychological price of yielding to another is a loss (however temporary and partial) of one's own identity. Realistic intimates find that this is a small price as long as it is part of an equitable, mutual process and leads to an improved relationship.

The final benefit of yielding is the tremendous feeling of well-being that comes from making a beloved person happy. This is why it feels so delicious to make one's wife or husband laugh. It also explains why "It is better to give than to receive." In true intimacy, it really is. Which is one more reason why intimacy is worth fighting for.

## 12. On the Management of Conflict in Families
### JETSE SPREY

The work of ethologists on "pair bonding," avoidance-attack mechanisms, and threat rituals has captured the imagination of both social scientists and laymen. This is not to say that their work has been universally accepted (see, for example, Alexander Alland's criticisms in *The Human Imperative*, 1972), but the basic assumption that by studying the behavior of animals many insights can be gained into human behavior seems valid. In the following paper, Sprey applies a number of the findings of ethologists to the analysis of conflict in the human family. Certain instinctive violence-limiting mechanisms such as the avoidance-attack mechanism and the use of "threat ritual" are absent in humans. Hence the potential for conflict and violence in long-

SOURCE: Reprinted and abridged with permission from *Journal of Marriage and the Family* 33 (November, 1971): 722–732.

term intimate groups like the family is very high. Sprey therefore suggests that family relationships might be aided by non-competitive supportive, extra-marital relationships. A similar point is made in Robert N. Whitehurst's article "Alternative Family Structures and Violence-Reduction" (see p. 315), in which the presence of other "family" members may reduce the violence potential found in the intimate, other-excluding, nuclear family.

. . . The conflict approach followed here has been introduced in an earlier paper (Sprey, 1969). Within its analytical context familial and marital harmony are seen as problematical rather than normal states of affairs. The family process *per se* is conceived of as a continuous confrontation between participants with conflicting—though not necessarily opposing—interests in their shared fate. The theoretical focus thus centers around the ways in which members of families, and marital dyads, negotiate the issues that arise from their joint participation in the institutions of marriage and the family. . . .

In his treatment of the stranger Simmel gets at the most crucial questions which can be raised about reciprocity between individuals: what exactly *is* a human relationship? How deep can it penetrate? What happens when two people become close?

. . . the unity of nearness and remoteness involved in every human relation is organized, in the phenomenon of the stranger, in a way which may be briefly formulated by saying that in the relationship to him, distance means that he, who also is far, is actually near (1950: 402). . . .

A human bond, as is implied in the above quote, and as conceptualized in this paper, is a paradox. Moving closer to another person also, by necessity, means moving apart. That is, increasing intimacy brings with it an increasing awareness of, and confrontation with, the uniqueness of the other. The more special two people become to each other the greater may be the pressure, from both sides, to possess the other totally, or in popular phraseology, to "become one." And that indeed, would mean the end of reciprocity. Intimacy, to be viable, thus requires the awareness, and acceptance, of the stranger in the other.

It is this paradox, this synthesis between nearness and remoteness in every relationship that provides the clue to our analysis of the management of conflict in bonds. The closer the bond, the more exclusive of strangers it becomes, the greater is also its vulnerability and its strength. Its strength is a consequence of its vulnerability, that is, the strain resulting from the inability of its members to be indifferent to one another. "The more we have in common with another as whole persons . . . the more easily will our totality be involved in every single relation to him. Hence the wholly disproportionate violence to which . . . people can be moved within their relations to those closest to them" (Simmel, 1955: 44).

Lorenz sees personal bonds as belonging to the "aggression-inhibiting, appeasing behavior mechanisms." Aggression within bonds is, in his opinion, redirected toward strangers (1969: 132). In Turner's view "the most important effect of intense bonds is not to heighten conflict but to provide incentives to avoid and conciliate it" (1970: 136). He considers Simmel's premise that the closer the relationship the more intense the conflict as "transparently ridiculous," however. But it is only through the intensity of the strain towards conflict in intimate bonds that the "incentives to avoid and conciliate," Turner speaks of, are created. He seems to have missed Simmel's point.

The relevance of the foregoing to the analysis of marital and family relationships seems obvious. Conjugal love, the bond of marriage, is the most exclusive of all in our society, and presumably should last a lifetime. Parent-child relations involve, as a rule, many years of cohabitation, and also provide a life-long bond. In contrast, there are few such lasting bonds among animals. Most familial arrangements do not continue beyond the reproductive season —if they exist at all—and, often in a one-parent form, for a relatively short time afterwards. This leaves us with two questions: why do we still find life-long bonds in human society? And, how are such relationships possible?

## AGGRESSION AND APPEASEMENT

One of the more relevant aspects of animal aggression is the dearth of it. Fighting, and aggressive behavior rarely occur without provocation, and only as a last resort. Tinbergen observes that man is, among the thousands of species that fight their own kind, the only one in which fighting is frequently disruptive and destructive (1968: 1412).

This raises the question: destructive to what? And, why would human conflict be more destructive than its animal counterpart? Is it because human bonds, such as love, friendship, and companionship, have less tolerance for conflict? Is it the extended duration of some of these bonds that becomes self-defeating over time? Or is it because humans do not know how to regulate their conflicts properly?

To answer such questions for situations of marital and familial conflict we need to differentiate between disruptive and constructive acts of overt conflict. There is some clinical evidence in support of the assertion that fighting, and other forms of aggressive conduct, can be a constructive, stabilizing, factor in marriages (Bach and Wyden, 1968). Most family sociologists, however, see such behavior as destructive by definition. It is considered to indicate a breakdown of the marital process, rather than as a potentially constructive part of it.

The fact that many families do continue in the face of a good deal of overt, recurring, strife is generally accounted for by the premise that in such cases "positive behaviors" (Bernard, 1964: 675), the right kind of love (Ryder, 1971) or the proper "identity orientation" (Turner, 1970: 135) will overcome the disruptive consequences of conflict. Family continuity, in this view, becomes a matter of the plusses outweighing the minusses. The family process is seen as one of exchange, that is, one in which the inputs of all members should, over time, balance each other, so that the kind of interpersonal harmony deemed necessary to family stability is maintained.

The exchange idea itself is not challenged here, on the contrary, it is basic to the conflict approach. What *is* questioned are the definitions of the plusses and the minusses. To postulate two analytical entities within the family process, the forces of good and evil, so to speak, seems unwarranted. The conceptualization of the family process as one of recurring interpersonal negotiation does not allow for an analytical distinction between subprocesses that lead, respectively, to order and disorder. Instead, our analysis must focus on what it is within the balance of the familial process that may, or may not, lead to a successfully negotiated order of affairs.

As such, the distinction between what should be considered plusses or minusses can not be made—analytically or empirically—through the designation of certain types of behavior, such as aggression, hostility, conciliation or love, as either constructive or destructive. Whether or not a given interchange between family members is to be seen as positive or negative should depend on its strategic appropriateness.[1]

In order to better understand the requirements of our conceptual framework, another brief look at some ethological findings in the realm of animal aggression will be fruitful. To explain the regulation of animal conflict ethologists view acts of aggression and appeasement as possible occurrences within an adaptive system. When placed in a conflict situation *two* drives are aroused in animals, namely the need to attack and the need to retreat. Animals are instinctively conditioned to attack when this is, under the circumstances, appropriate, and therefore constructive. The ethologist Tinbergen (1968: 1413) sees the regulation of conflict among animals, especially the control of intra-species fighting, as being guided by an "attack-avoidance" system. This explains why so little actual damage is done in animal conflicts, since the attack of the one is normally balanced by the retreat of the other. Even in those situations where both animals have a "legitimate" reason to attack, the ensuing battle is rarely settled by the destruction of the losing party. Other inhibitions operate to prevent the fight from continuing after the issue is settled. Mechanisms of this nature cause the loser to concede, while inhibiting further unnecessary aggression by the winner (Eibl-Eibesfeldt, 1961). Fights like this are, therefore, not decided on the basis of strength alone, but also on the merits of the situation. A large male Cichlid, for example, that strays into the territory of a much smaller specimen will retreat quickly when challenged.

In a situation like the above, however, two "mistakes" are possible, each one destructive in its own way. The intruder may refuse to retreat, or the rightful owner may refuse to challenge. Both of these possibilities are a great deal more characteristic of human than of animal conflict. Tinbergen points out that the "ruthless fighter who knows no fear" has no place in the animal scheme of events, since his actions interfere with the reproductive potential of the species. A male Cichlid who fails to defend his territory, on the other hand, eliminates himself, and his potential offspring, from the reproductive process. The regulation of animal conflict cannot be understood to serve the interests of either one participant, but rather as the most effective way of

---

[1]The term strategic appropriateness is not to be equated with the concept of function, since it has no teleological implications. A fruitful analogy would be that of "preferred strategy," as that term is used in the analysis of games.

handling a given conflict situation, and others like it in the future. Animals are, of course, not aware of this, but seem conditioned to select the most appropriate course of action when in conflict with members of its own kind. During the phylogenetic history of each species destructive behavioral strategies have been selectively eliminated. If this had not happened the species itself would, in all likelihood, no longer exist. It would be instructive to raise the question: what happened to the species Homo Sapiens? One thing seems certain, the guidance that was provided once by instinct is no longer present. It is, therefore, imperative to find out what, if anything, has been developed to take its place.

## THE CONCEPT OF THREAT

A threat is a message—verbal or non-verbal—which indicates unfavorable consequences, for all concerned, resulting from failure to comply with its demand. It may be implicit or explicit. To be effective, however, it needs to be understood by both its sender and receiver. It is argued here that threats, in the above sense, are a necessary part of the successful management of familial and marital conflict, and that a meaningful conceptualization of it is essential to the understanding of the negotiating process.

In our attempt to arrive at such a conception animal conflict behavior again may serve as a source of insight. When two aggressive, territorial animals—two male Cichlid fish, for example—meet at the border of their respective domains attack and retreat drives will be aroused equally in both. Consequently, each will be in a state of considerable "emotional" turmoil and excitement. Under these circumstances inappropriate behavior, such as fighting, or bullying, might occur. Instead, we see that species-specific, mutually understood, threat rituals have evolved. These routines provide an emotional outlet, and take the place of unnecessary fighting.[2] Such a threat ritual functions as a conflict regulatory mechanism, and affects both parties. For if the threat, for some reason, goes unheeded, *both* animals must face the consequences and fight.

The parallel between the foregoing and a range of marital and familial conflict situations is apparent. A threat to sue for divorce may mean different things to each spouse, but affects both. The same holds for many other ones, such as the limitation of sexual access by one spouse, separation, non-support, and the like. It is clear that for each of these the possible deprivation for one spouse may be greater than for the other, but it is also evident that, depending on the quality of the relationship, both parties may either win or lose depending on whether or not the threat is heeded.

In view of this, it is noteworthy that in the growing social science literature on the use of threats in conflict situations this aspect of mutuality has been ignored. Instead, threat is defined unilaterally: as a force exerted upon a person to coerce him to act as the source wishes (Tedeschi, 1970: 101).

---

[2]If, in one way or other, this threat ritual is interferred with, or prevented, fights till death are likely to result.

Threat thus is seen as a clear "if-then" signal which promises some form of punishment in case of non-compliance. Consequently the research on the phenomenon of threatening—most of it conducted by means of quasi-experimental designs—omits two aspects of the situation that are crucial to the family sociologist. The implications to its sender are ignored, but also the fact that the receiver may be aware of its consequences to *both* parties is not taken into account. As a result of this the stabilizing potential of threatening within an interpersonal negotiating process remains unexplored.

This may be further illustrated by a brief discussion of a well-known research experiment by Deutsch and Krauss (1960).[3] In a two-person nonzero sum game both parties were given the potential to threaten the other unilaterally. Three separate experiments were conducted: (1) both participants were given the option to threaten, (2) one was given the option to threaten unilaterally, (3) neither was given the option. The results proved interesting in that only under the no-threat condition both parties gained. In *both* other instances, both participants lost. The worst losses, to both, occurred when *each* was given the option to threaten the other unilaterally. These findings lead at least one author to conclude that:

. . . the less opportunity for threat any two parties have in negotiating a settlement, the more likely they are to share a profit in their negotiations. International settlements would be more profitable if neither party were able to threaten the other with war. Under certain conditions unions might even fare better without strikes . . . (Gergen, 1969–70).

Following this line of reasoning one would have to conclude that marriages would be better off if neither spouse could threaten with divorce. In contrast, the position taken here is the reverse: married couples presumably are better off if they have access to a variety of threats, assuming however, that they know how to threaten properly.

The differences between Gergen's stance and ours is a result of the different ways in which the concept of threat has been defined, and is illuminating in that respect. If a threat has no direct repercussions for its sender it may indeed become no more than a means of unilateral coercion, and as such, in all likelihood, do no more than inhibit the desire to compromise and negotiate. This is the way in which Deutsch's findings must be interpreted. Threats of this nature seem associated with zero sum type conflict situations, rather than with nonzero sum ones. Most human conflict situations resemble the latter type, however. It is hard to conceive of the kind of war in which one party has nothing to lose, or the kind of labor issue in which a strike would not affect *both* labor and management. While in the study of conflict management in small, intimate, permanent bonds such as those found in marital dyads and families, a unilateral conception of threat seems analytically useless.

It is interesting and indicative of the manner in which family sociologists approach the study of family interaction that in a recent, quite thorough review paper on the study of family power structure the concept of threat

---

[3]This particular piece of work received an American Association for the Advancement of Science Award for outstanding research in the behavioral sciences.

did not feature at all (Safilios-Rothschild, 1970). As a matter of fact, the question *why* one would wish to study family power structure, or what a theory of family power structure would contribute to our understanding of the family process, was not raised. Instead, a perusal of the sixty-seven sources cited leads one to conclude that family power, and decision-making in families is studied in a static, structural, frame of reference. The focus is on the *outcomes* of power relations in families, in quasi-experimental and natural situations. Even studies aimed to get at familial bargaining *behavior*, end up attempting to fit their findings into a structural type of formulation. Olson (1969), for example after observing the decision making processes of 35 couples, limits his discussion to questions about what spousal *role* contains most authority, appears dominant, and the like. To know this and understand it in a given social setting is of course, important. On the other hand, the presumed association between a dominant role, or even a dominant personality, and "winning" in the family negotiation process, becomes irrelevant, or at best tangential to the understanding of this process if we assume that the dominance of a given role is not to be equated with a dominant *strategy*. In other words, the question becomes: what can we learn about the way a game is played by limiting our attention to its outcome? Especially if this game, as in the case of marriage resembles a nonzero sum game, that is, a game in which both parties can either win or lose?

It should be understood that the above question in no way negates the structural importance of the familial power structure. It merely accentuates its theoretical limitations. Another brief illustration may clarify this further. In the above cited paper, Olson documents the existing discrepancy between what spouses *say* they will do in conflict situations and the actual outcomes of such decision making processes. Within the framework of this paper such a discrepancy is hardly surprising. After all, given two equally matched chess players, who is to predict the outcome of their game? The outcome does become predictable *only* if one player, for some reason, feels obligated to *let the other win*.

This obligation "to let the other win" is, of course what Olson and many others have been getting at in their role analysis of family power. Position or role, seems a good predictor of conflict outcomes as long as spouses accept and refer to its prescriptive norms. In view of this one of the conclusions of a recently published, nation-wide survey of marital satisfaction seems worthy of mention:

. . . despite the companionate activity prescribed in the egalitarian marriages of college-educated groups, the affiliation motive is irrelevant to marital role reactions . . . The prescription for mutuality and sharing called for in marriages of the college-educated seems to lead to the arousal of power goals for the more educated women. Perhaps what is being shared is influence and authority rather than companionship (Veroff and Feld, 1970: 334).

In other words, the "prescription for mutuality" that is becoming increasingly associated with middle class family role behavior can be expected to undermine the predictive worth of our traditional role prescriptions. It will thus provide an increasing challenge to the ability, and motivation, of contemporary spouses and parents to negotiate and re-negotiate their mutually shared arrangements.

## THE EXTRAMARITAL ASPECTS OF CONFLICT MANAGEMENT

Some species of fish are so intolerant toward their own kind that pair-bonding is virtually impossible. Even in a large tank a pair will fight till one is eliminated. To allow for courtship and reproduction the presence of other fish, of the same or closely related species, is necessary. If that condition is filled even quite aggressive specimens can be kept and raised without too much trouble. Territories are established, bonds formed, and on neutral ground threat ritual replaces most actual fighting. The strain associated with pair-bonding is, apparently managed through the presence of others. A question inspired by this brief illustration is: are the differences that exist between animal and human bonds sufficient to warrant the assumption that conflict management in close human relationships can, even under the best of circumstances, be handled from within?

The answer to this query is, to my knowledge, not yet known. Many professionals in the fields of marriage and the family seem to answer it similarly, however. When a given marriage is suffering from a "lack of love," their prescription is: more love. This leads us to more questions: how much love, affection, or friendship, can a given bond withstand? What happens to a relationship if one, or both, of its participants infuse more love, affection, or friendship, into it? These are theoretical questions, and, therefore, ultimately require empirical answers. To get at the proper facts, however, the questions must make more sense. To that the rest of this section is devoted.

Husbands and wives, parents and children, are, in our society, considered to be, by others and themselves, quite special to each other. This quality of "specialness" is dependent on the existence of others who can be excluded. A close, permanent, bond, like marriage, requires a continuous re-affirmation. This process—which may be experienced by the spouses as one of continuous mutual rediscovery—in its turn depends on the ongoing extramarital involvements of both spouses. Or, to put it differently, the continued presence of the "extra" in the marital—be it in reality or fantasy—is seen as crucial to the harmony and stability of the marital bond.

This viewpoint is opposed to that which holds that outside involvements compete, categorically, with the marital relationship. Levinger, a spokesman for this widely shared stance, defines marital cohesiveness as the total field of forces acting on the spouses to remain in it (1965: 19). Marital stability then is the outcome of an interplay of three sets of forces: internal cohesive factors, barrier strength, and sources of outside attraction. Consequently, marital strength becomes a "direct function of the attractions within and barriers around the marriage, and an inverse function of such attractions and barriers from other relationships."

It is clear that in the above framework the logical possibility that an outside relationship could be a source of strength is excluded by definition.

Levinger does recognize the existence of non-competing, and perhaps supportive, alternative involvements, but only to the extent that such bonds do not become too strong:

... an extreme commitment to such a relationship would interfere with the marriage; as would also, of course, a commitment to a third party that fully excludes the spouse (1965: 20).

Empirical support of the above contention seems lacking, however. Moreover, its question-begging potential also is apparent. Should, for example, a given outside involvement be found to interfere with a marriage, it can simply be *defined* as "too strong," or too exclusive of the spouse, depending on what the investigator wishes to prove. As long as outside relationships are found not to interfere, however, they can be categorized as compatible, or weak.

Does the companionship, friendship, or perhaps love, that a person may share with colleagues, or other outsiders, somehow deplete a limited supply, so that the marital or family bonds will be shortchanged? The answer to this depends on whether or not we view the human capacity to love, like, or hate, as limited. This seems unlikely. Still, there is the belief—reflecting a great deal of accumulated human experience—that true love can exist only between two individuals at the time, that real friendship can be shared only by a few, and that one cannot love other's children as one loves one's own. Implicit in all this is, again, the view that conjugal love should be protected from outside competition. Married individuals, for example, are expected to withdraw from outside, heterosexual, involvements as soon as such bonds become "too personal." Again, a paradox, and once more the clue towards its understanding can be found in the nature of the process of bonding.

Given the premise that the human potential to love, to like, and to hate, seems virtually unlimited, a social mechanism to *prevent* everyone from loving, or hating, everyone else is highly desirable. Bonding, it has been repeatedly stated, is such a mechanism, since it depends on the exclusion of others, and thus rations our social uses of love, friendliness, animosity, and hatred. Rather than to claim that conjugal love needs protection from the competitive potential coming from outside, one might reverse the issue and suggest that the outside world benefits, and perhaps depends on, the containment of love, and hate, within the confines of marriages and families. To use an analogy, a secret would be meaningless, and really not worth guarding, if no one was interested in its content. It is the fact that people wish to *know* the contents of a given secret that provides both its vulnerability and its strength. The same holds true for the sanctity of conjugal love, its continued strength must be derived from the challenge of competition. . . .

IN CONCLUSION

What does the foregoing have to do with the management of conflict in families? The answer is twofold. There is, firstly, the fact that the successful management of conflict requires the ability to negotiate, bargain, and cooperate: a range of behavioral skills. To study, and ultimately explain such phenomena, the concepts of aggression, appeasement, and threat were proposed as essential analytical tools.

In the second part of this paper, a very tentative attempt was made to come to grips with the question: what exactly enters into a marital and familial relationship, what remains outside, and what is the interdependence between these two categories? The answer to this question is crucial to the understanding of how people manage to exist peacefully with specific others within the bonds of marriage and the family. In this context it was suggested that it is the vulnerability to unresolved, that is, unmanaged, conflict which provides the major source of "motivation" towards negotiation and compromise in families, while the openness and inherent weakness of the marital bond is seen to furnish its major strength as a voluntary, reciprocal interpersonal commitment.

## REFERENCES

Aldous, Joan
    1969    "Occupational Characteristics and Male's Role Performance in the Family." *Journal of Marriage and the Family* 31 (November): 707–713.
Bach, George R. and Peter Wyden
    1969    *The Intimate Enemy.* New York: William Morrow.
Deutsch, M. and R. M. Krauss
    1960    "The Effect of Threat Upon Interpersonal Bargaining." *Journal of Abnormal and Social Psychology* 61, 181–189.
Eibl-Eibesfeldt, Irenaus
    1961    "The Fighting Behavior of Animals." *Scientific American* (December).
Gergen, Kenneth J.
    1969    *The Psychology of Behavior Exchange.* Reading, Mass.: Addison-Wesley.
Levinger, George
    1965    "Marital Cohesiveness and Dissolution: An Integrative Review." *Journal of Marriage and the Family* 27 (February): 19–28.
Lorenz, Konrad
    1969    *On Aggression.* New York: Bantam Books.
Olson, David H.
    1969    "The Measurement of Family Power by Self-report and Behavioral Methods." *Journal of Marriage and the Family* 31 (August): 545–550.
Ryder, Robert G.
    1971    "Communal Life Styles." Paper presented at the 1971 Annual Meeting of the Groves Conference, in San Juan, Puerto Rico (May).
Safilios-Rothschild, Constantina
    1970    "The Study of Family Power Structure: A Review 1960–1969." *Journal of Marriage and the Family* 32 (November): 539–552.
Simmel, Georg
    1955    *Conflict and the Web of Group-Affiliations.* New York: The Free Press.
    1959    "How Is Society Possible?" Pp. 337–356 in Kurt H. Wolff (ed.), *Essay on Sociology, Philosophy and Aesthetics.* New York: Harper Torchbooks.
Sprey, Jetse
    1969    "The Family as a System in Conflict." *Journal of Marriage and the Family* 31 (November): 699–706.
Tedeschi, James T.
    1970    "Threats and Promises." Pp. 155–187 in Swingle (ed.), *The Structure of Conflict.* New York: Academic Press.
Tinbergen, Niko
    1968    "On War and Peace in Animals and Man." *Science* 160 (June): 1411–1418.
Turner, Ralph H.
    1970    *Family Interaction.* New York: John Wiley and Sons, Inc.
Veroff, Joseph and Sheila Feld
    1970    *Marriage and Work in America.* New York: Van Nostrand.
Wolff, Kurt H. (ed.)
    1950    *The Sociology of Georg Simmel.* Glencoe, Ill.: Free Press.

# 13. Family Interaction Patterns, Drug Treatment, and Change in Social Aggression

## MELVIN COHEN, NORBERT FREEDMAN, DAVID M. ENGLEHARDT, AND REUBEN A. MARGOLIS

Family therapy, as opposed to individual treatment, is rapidly becoming the dominant mode of dealing with many psychological and marital problems. This approach views the family as a social system in which the behavior of each member is contingent on the behavior of the other members in a cyclical fashion. Clinical studies indicate that the problem is frequently not with the individual member, but with the network of relationships between family members. For example, studies of child abuse suggest that if an abused child is removed from the home, another child may become the target of parental abuse, or husband-wife violence may increase. Other studies illustrate how family members may actually reward and reinforce aggressive behavior (see p. 308). The study reprinted below is an example of such a social system approach. The authors found that merely treating the aggressive family member with a tranquilizing drug had little effect *if* non-aggressive behavior was inconsistent with the family interaction patterns; that is, when the patient's home was characterized by conflict and tension, non-aggressive behavior on the part of the patient was inconsistent with the family interaction patterns. This resulted in family members provoking further aggressive behavior from the patient in order to restore the family "system," counteracting the effect of the drug. On the other hand, the tranquilizer was effective if the family pattern was consistent with the effect of the drug—i.e., one of low conflict and tension.

Psychiatric literature is abundant with studies reporting the effectiveness of phenothiazine treatment in altering the behavior of mentally ill patients. When such studies are conducted within hospital or laboratory settings they are performed under relatively controlled environmental conditions which are usually conducive to behavioral change among patients. However, when studying the effects of treatment among a population of clinic patients, those who are living at home while receiving medication, the environment in which the anticipated behavioral change is expected to occur may differ according to variability in family culture. The basic assumption underlying this paper is that the . . . patterns of social interaction between family members . . . will modify the effects of phenothiazine treatment. The specific behavior studied was the alteration of social aggression among a sample of chronic schizophrenic outpatients receiving either chlorpromazine, promazine, or placebo treatment. . . .

The relationship between the family unit as a closed social system and drug effectiveness has been discussed by Lennard.[1] Basically, a social system

SOURCE: Reprinted with permission from *Archives of General Psychiatry* 19 (July, 1958): 50–56. This study was supported by grants from the National Institute of Mental Health, Public Health Service (MH 01983 and MH 05090). Copyright 1958, American Medical Association.

[1]Lennard, H. L. A Proposed Program of Research in Sociopharmacology. Symposium presentation on "Psychological Approaches to Social Behavior" at the Harvard Medical School, April, 1963.

may be defined as one in which members show some responsiveness towards each other, some awareness of each other's actions and reactions, and maintain some level of affective input. Systems make different demands upon their members according to both the *degree* (greater or lesser), and *type* (positive or negative) of intrasystem inputs required. Therefore, according to Lennard the differential demand for affective input in diverse family systems should be reflected in the effects of drug treatment on affective behavior.

The variable which we have chosen as a measure of the level of negative affective input required in a family system is the degree of conflict and tension which is characteristic of the interrelationships between the patient and other family members. The measure of conflict and tension in the home is not viewed as indicating a temporary crisis situation, but rather as a reflection of a predominant mode of interaction among the family members.

A family unit characterized by a high degree of conflict and tension requires a greater amount of aggressively oriented behavior from its members than one which is low in conflict and tension. In a high conflict and tension family, not only is there a higher tolerance of aggressive behavior, but such behavior is the expected mode of social interaction. Thus, the effects of a purportedly aggression-reducing drug, such as chlorpromazine, should be minimized when administered within the context of an aggression-demanding environment (high conflict and tension). The same drug administered within a family system which required less aggressively oriented behavior from its members (low conflict and tension) should prove more effective in the reduction of such behavior.

## METHOD

*Subjects.* The subjects were 54 male and 72 female psychiatric patients selected from a population of over 500 patients attending a community outpatient clinic utilizing psychotropic agents. The sample of 126 patients consisted of those patients who had obtained high intake scores on a measure of social aggression at home, and who had remained in treatment for at least three months. All patients had received a primary diagnosis of schizophrenic reaction with evidence of schizophrenic symptoms of at least one year's duration. The age range was 18 to 42 years.

## TREATMENT PROCEDURE

Using a double-blind procedure, patients were randomly assigned to one of three drug treatments; chlorpromazine, promazine, or placebo. The patient also received supportive therapy from the psychiatrist. The double-blind drug administration was maintained with provisions for flexible dosage administration. Mean daily dosage level for patients on active drug was approximately 180 mg with a range from 100 to 400 mg. Several checks were employed to ascertain that patients were in fact taking their medication as prescribed (reports by the patient and family members, periodic urine examinations, etc). Patients were seen weekly for the first month of treatment and biweekly thereafter.

SOCIAL BEHAVIOR INTERVIEW

A close relative of the patient was interviewed at intake and at the end of three months. The interviewer, using an open-ended questionnaire, attempted to ascertain from the relative the patient's behavior at home and in the community as perceived by that relative. We specifically used open-ended questions so that the relative could give us any information which he felt was relevant, without being restricted as to specific behaviors on the part of the patient. The interviews were coded independently of the interviewer, and the patient was given scores on the various items. The measures of conflict, tension, and social aggression were derived from the information given by the relative.


MEASURE OF CONFLICT AND TENSION IN THE HOME

The measure of conflict and tension in the home was derived from the intake interview with the relative. The items comprising this measure are concerned with the amount and locus of stress in the relationship between the patient and significant others (e.g., parent, sibling, or spouse), and therefore, refer to relatively stable and habitual modes of behavior within the family unit. They measure the need within the family system for negative affective input. One end of the scale represents a low need for stressful input, as reflected in ratings indicating either complete absence of tension or tension not attributed to significant others; the other end of the scale indicates the presence of a high degree of tension within the family unit.

The four items derived from the relative's response which comprise the conflict and tension scale are:

1. *The person whom the patient likes the most.* A low score represents that the patient likes everyone and gets along well with everyone at home; a high score indicates that the patient does not get along with anyone or the liked person is out of the home.

2. *What characteristic of the patient does the relative most like.* A low score represents the frequent occurrence of some liked behavior; a high score indicates that the liked behavior occurs rarely or never.

3. *The person whom the patient dislikes the most.* A low score indicates that the patient gets along with everyone or the person the patient dislikes does not live with the patient; a high score means that the disliked person is someone who lives with the patient.

4. *What the patient does to give the relative a "hard time" (something which the relative perceives as negative).* A low score represents a minor complaint involving, in the relative's estimate, trivial "misbehavior"; a high score represents a strong complaint about what the relative perceives as highly negative behavior.

The scores for each item were equally weighted and summed to give one score as a measure of conflict and tension in the home. The range of scores was from 0 to 8. The correlation between baseline and three month scores for the clinic population was 0.65 ($r_{tet}$, $P < 0.001$), indicating that this is a reliable measure of the degree of conflict and tension in the home.

## MEASURE OF SOCIAL AGGRESSION

A series of social traits was derived from the information given by the relative in the interview. . . .

Explicit opposition (EO) is used as a measure of the patient's social aggressiveness at home. The trait is operationally defined as any report by the relative that the patient has been speaking or acting abusively or violently in the home. Examples of such socially aggressive behavior would be: "She screamed at me all morning"; "He woke up angry—everything made him jump at you"; "He hits the children for no reason at all." The patient population chosen for this study were those exhibiting high social aggression, i.e., those whose intake score on EO was 20.0 or above (somewhat above the median 18.4 for the entire clinic population). Change in social aggression was measured after three months of treatment.

## RESULTS

We have predicted that the characteristic patterns of interpersonal behavior between the patient and other family members will determine the effectiveness of specific drugs on modifying the patient's aggressive behavior after three months of treatment. The measure of conflict and tension in the home was chosen as a reflection of the patterns of family interaction. The results of the analysis of variance of change in social aggression by drug treatment and level of conflict and tension are presented in Table 2. There is a significant interaction between these two independent variables ($F = 5.08$, df $= 2/120$, $P < 0.01$), indicating that the patient's response to drug was different within the two contrasting social situations. For the high conflict and tension sample, mean change in social aggression after three months of treatment is the same whether the patient received active drug (chlorpromazine, $-5.67$; promazine, $-7.48$, or placebo, $-6.50$). For the low conflict and tension sample, however, there is a significantly greater reduction in social aggression among those patients who had received chlorpromazine treatment ($-15.13$) than among those who had received either promazine ($-4.24$) or placebo ($-5.36$) treatment. In fact, a series of $t$-test analysis show that the reduction in social aggression of the chlorpromazine treated patients in the low conflict and tension conditions is not only significantly greater ($P < 0.01$) than the decrease observed in the comparable promazine and placebo treated patients, but is also significantly greater than the reduction in social aggression observed in the chlorpromazine treated high conflict and tension group. Though there is a general decrease in socially aggressive behavior after three months of clinic attendance, a significantly larger decrease occurs among those patients who were being treated with chlorpromazine and living in a home characterized as low in conflict and tension.

Daily modal dosage of chlorpromazine prescribed for each patient was examined to exclude the possibility that differences in reduction of aggression were merely reflections of differences in drug dosage between the low and high conflict and tension samples. It was found that the average daily dosage was 185 mg for the low conflict and tension sample and 213 mg for the high

*Table 2. Mean Change in Social Aggression after Three Months of Treatment: Conflict and Tension by Drug*

| Conflict and Tension | N | Chlorpromazine | N | Drug Promazine | N | Placebo |
|---|---|---|---|---|---|---|
| High | 20 | − 5.67° | 21 | − 7.48 | 21 | − 6.50 |
| Low | 22 | − 15.13° | 21 | − 4.24 | 21 | − 5.36 |

| *Analysis of Variance†* | | | |
|---|---|---|---|
| Source | df | MS | F |
| Drug | 2 | 13.54 | 2.97‡ |
| Conflict and tension | 1 | 4.31 | — |
| Drug × conflict and tension | 2 | 23.17 | 5.08§ |
| Within | 120 | 4.56 | — |

°Baseline scores in Social Aggression were not significantly different between these two groups (high, M = 26.4; low, M = 27.3).
†Unequal in design.[4]
‡$P < 0.10$.
§$P < 0.01$.

conflict and tension sample. This difference (which was in the opposite direction) was *not* statistically significant ($t < 1.00$).

## COMMENT

In this paper we have attempted to demonstrate that the social milieu in which a psychotropic agent is administered must be taken into account in studying the effectiveness of the agent in modifying behavior. Our particular emphasis has been on the reduction of aggressive behavior with chlorpromazine treatment among a population of chronic schizophrenic outpatients. We found that in homes characterized as high in conflict and tension, in which aggressively oriented behavior is a predominant and apparently a necessary mode of adaptation, the aggressive patient who receives chlorpromazine does *not* show a significant reduction in aggressive behavior; whereas in a home characterized as low in conflict and tension, in which aggressively oriented behavior is *not* the predominant and apparently necessary mode of social adaptation, aggressive patients who are treated with chlorpromazine *do* show a significant reduction in aggressive behavior.

In the low conflict and tension home the patient's aggressiveness is dissonant with the general pattern of interaction among the family members. The home may be characterized as comparatively harmonious and tranquil. The relative perceives everyone as "getting along" with each other. There is a minimum amount of overt friction in the every-day interactional behaviors. It is possible, of course, that there is much denial and inhibition of aggressively oriented behavior—but the overt patterns of behavior are suggestive of a relatively tranquil and placid home environment. In this type of home environment, chlorpromazine, by reducing the patient's aggressiveness, reduces the dissonance between the patient's behavior and the predominant mode of social adaptation of the family unit.

The high conflict and tension home, on the other hand, is characterized by a great amount of aggressively-oriented behavior such as continual and persistent shouting and yelling in which the family members are constantly provoking each other. Each person's behavior is a stimulus for aggression in the others. In this type of social situation a reduction in social aggression by chlorpromazine would increase the dissonance between the patient's behavior and the predominant mode of social adaptation and the family would become more provocative of aggressive behavior in the patient in order to reduce the dissonance within the social unit.

The family mode of social adaptation may be seen in terms of a homeostatic balance which is upset by the reduction in the patient's aggression. Jackson[2] discusses the concept of "family homeostatis" in terms of communication theory; family interaction is depicted as a closed information system in which variation in output or behavior are fed back in order to correct the system's response. Therefore, in order to restore the balance, the patient's relatives should increase their role as aggression-inducing stimuli until the balance is restored and the patient's level of aggressiveness again fits into the family pattern.

A similar model of family behavior is proposed by Haley in terms of a self-corrective governed system.

If a family confines itself to repetitive patterns within a certain range of possible behavior, then they are confined to that range by some sort of governing process. No outside governor requires the family members to behave in their habitual patterns, so this governing process must exist within the family. . . . To describe families, the most appropriate analogy would seem to be the self-corrective system governed by family members influencing each other's behavior and thereby establishing rules and prohibitions for that particular family system. Such a system tends to be error-activated. Should other family members break a family rule, the others become activated until he either conforms to the rule again or successfully establishes a new one (p. 373).[3]

The model of a homeostatic balance as explaining the findings of the present study requires further support. We have not directly observed the patient's behavior in the family unit but have had to rely on an analysis of a report of it from a family member. Secondly, in this discussion we have employed the simplifying assumption that the measured mode of family adaptation characterizes all members of the family. It may well be that the predominant mode of family adaptation may vary as a function of the particular subunits of a family that is studied.[4]

The foregoing discussion is of special relevance when we consider the problem of therapeutic intervention in the situation where the patient lives in a family characterized by a high demand for aggressive behavior. Ideally, one may attempt to separate the patient from the family unit or help him to

[2]Jackson, D. D. The Question of Family Homeostatis. *Psychiat. Quart. Suppl.*, *31*, 79–90, 1957.

[3]Haley, J. The Family of the Schizophrenic: A Model System. *J. Nerv. Ment. Dis.*, *129*, 357–374, October, 1959.

[4]Walker, H. M., and J. Lev. *Statistical Inference*. New York: Holt, Rinehart and Winston, Inc., 1953, pp. 381–382.

participate in the family pattern at minimal personal cost. Such solutions are difficult to achieve in chronic schizophrenic outpatients under a regimen of psychotropic agents and brief supportive psychotherapy.

A more feasible strategy may be family therapy. If all the family members can be involved in the problem of modifying interactional patterns they may draw support from each other in this difficult task. Alteration of the family pattern to some degree may well alter the effectiveness of psychotropic agents on patients residing in such units. The degree of change necessary remains to be determined. One must also consider the possibility that this kind of social aggression which is generally viewed as symptomatic behavior may not at all be what brought this type of patient into treatment. Although the behavior is obvious and generally socially disapproved, the patient and his family may want help with other problems.


CONCLUSION

Chronic schizoprenic patients attending a community clinic were randomly assigned to one of three treatment conditions; chlorpromazine, promazine, or placebo and studied for change in aggressive behavior after three months of treatment. It was predicted that the degree of conflict and tension characterizing the patient's home milieu would be a factor in modifying the potential effectiveness of drug treatment on aggressive behavior. The results show that the most significant decrease in aggression occurred among the chlorpromazine treated patients from low conflict and tension homes. The decrease for chlorpromazine treated patients from high conflict and tension homes was the same as that for promazine and placebo treated patients, regardless of degree of conflict and tension. The results were interpreted as indicating that chlorpromazine will significantly reduce a patient's aggressive behavior if that behavior is dissonant with family interactional patterns (low conflict and tension) and will be less effective in those situations in which aggressive behavior is consistent with family interactional patterns (high conflict and tension).

# 14. The Study and Modification of Intra-Familial Violence
## MORTON BARD

Many factors which contribute to violence between spouses—such as poverty, low prestige, status inconsistency, insecurity, and the compulsive masculinity syndrome—are more prevalent in the inner-city ghetto and lower class families. Yet these families rarely seek out violence-preventive family counseling. To seek out such services requires money, sophistication, and an active rather than a fatalistic world view—all of which are likely to be scarce in the slums. An alternative is to bring the needed services to the family rather than expect the family to seek them out. A program which does this is described in the following article. This program makes use of the fact that policemen are called into a large number of family fights. Typically, policemen are not equipped to do more than separate the warring partners in such fights. The methods by which policemen in one New York City area were trained to provide more effective aid in family conflicts and the premilinary results of this program suggest that this may be an effective approach to helping the segment of the population most likely to engage in violent domestic encounters.

In the year 1965, seven brothers were slain by their brothers in New York City. But, also, two sisters were killed by their sisters, while eleven sons and thirteen daughters were murdered by their mothers; and five sons and one daughter, by their fathers. Forty wives were dispatched by their husbands and seventeen husbands by their wives. In all, close family relationships accounted for 35 per cent of all homicides in that year. Indeed, in fewer than 20 per cent of all homicides were the victim and perpetrator complete strangers (N.Y.C. Police Dept., 1966). About 40 per cent of aggravated assaults and rapes (constituting most of the serious crimes against the person) take place within the victim's home (Ennis, 1967). These statistics are close to the national average in both urban and rural areas. Cross-national studies yield similar findings throughout western society.

To put it succinctly, as Malinowski (1948) did, "aggression like charity begins at home (p. 286)." As our society debates the specter of mass violence, how surprisingly little more than the scriptural account of Cain and Abel have we to draw upon in understanding the origins of human aggression?

Down through the years aggression has occupied the attention of countless psychologists, sociologists, and anthropologists, and, more recently, the biologically oriented ethologists. The aggression debate has grown more heated . . . always seeming to rest in the same polarized position where: (1) aggres-

SOURCE: Reprinted with permission from Jerome L. Singer (ed.), *The Control of Aggression and Violence* (New York: Academic Press, 1971), pp. 149–164. The project described herein is supported in part by the Office of Law Enforcement Assistance, United States Department of Justice, Training Grant No. 157, with the co-operation and support of the New York City Police Department and The City College of The City University of New York.

sion is seen as the directly instinctual residue of evolutionary development and (2) aggression is regarded as being a directly learned or culturally conditioned response. The simple fact is that neither extreme position appears to apply to *human* aggression. In each case, the extremists choose to ignore multi-disciplinary evidence that human aggression is a highly complex phenomenon, involving *at least* elements of both positions.

Perhaps it would be useful to summarize briefly a selected number of the approaches among the different disciplines. The ethologists have assumed the most unambiguous and self-confident position. Both Lorenz (1966) and Ardrey (1966), reasoning from observations of animal behavior, have attempted to establish that aggression is an invariable, genetically determined, and highly specific response pattern. If learning is involved at all, they maintain, it is in the development of socially adaptive outlets for the discharge of instinctually-rooted aggressive impulses. While simplistically appealing, their position suffers from the failure to account for the enormous range of stimuli which can evoke aggressive responses in man or to account for, as Mead (1967) has suggested, the symbolic capacity of man to discriminate among a range of aggressive responses. Nevertheless, the position of the ethologists is clear—man is innately aggressive and his responses are purely and simply evolutionary extensions of his biological past.

Most prominent among the psychological theories are those of Freud and the schools of psychoanalysis, as well as those of a reawakened and popular behaviorist approach. The advocates of modern behaviorism generally emphasize the more specific aspects of aggression—they concern themselves entirely with determining aggressive habit strength as a highly specific learned response.

The psychoanalytic schools, on the other hand, have experienced some of their greatest disharmonies on the theoretical issue of aggression. Freud's ideas on the subject underwent constant change (Freud, 1948). At first, when totally absorbed with libido theory, he relegated aggression to a minor role as a largely instinctual consequence of the stages of psycho-sexual development. However, later, when he became concerned with the question of the "ego instincts," particularly with that of self-preservation, aggression was his major emphasis. He then theorized that aggressive urges were reactive rather than biologically instinctive. It was this position that was to become central in the frustration-aggression hypothesis of Dollard and his associates (Dollard *et al.*, 1939). Freud's final theory, however, was that of the "death-instinct" and was both a pessimistic and more inevitable view of the instinctive roots of aggression, and he remained in the end much more faithful to his essentially biological approach to behavior.

However, psychologists, in addition to theorizing about aggression, have devoted themselves to the scientific study of the phenomenon: most typically in the laboratory. Through ingenious experimental methods, a considerable literature has emerged; much of it, while rooted in scientific method, suffers the constraints of "control" and hence of "artificiality." As Megargee has noted, "generally the psychological experiments on aggression are disappointing . . . laboratory studies on aggression have largely been confined to unruly student behavior, hostile reactions to frustrating psychologists, and the willingness of students to give each other electric shocks (Megargee, 1966, pp. 29–30)."

The sociologists and anthropologists, on the other hand, have somehow managed to avoid the nature-nurture controversy in theory construction and in study. Not confined to rigorous and often artificial laboratory conditions in order to test their theories, sociologists and anthropologists have achieved a much greater consensus through intensive study of social process and cross-cultural observation: to them, the origins of aggression are more convincingly social and cultural. Of all disciplines, it is the field of social conflict which may have most significantly contributed to our understanding of aggression. In fact, the turn-of-the-century social theorist Georg Simmel (1955) showed himself to be remarkably congruent with the "reactive" period of Freud's speculations on the issue of human aggression.

Indeed, the theories of psychologist Freud and sociologist Simmel were in agreement with those of anthropologist Malinowski (1948, p. 286) and finally, surprisingly, with ethologist Lorenz (1966). For the purposes of this discussion, most relevant is Simmel's proposition that antagonism is a central feature of intimate social relations; that the closer and more intimate an association, the greater likelihood of aggression and violence. It should be noted that, while Simmel and Freud referred to aggressive *feelings* in the social context, it was the anthropologist Malinowski (1948, p. 286) who pointed out that aggressive *behavior* also occurs more readily in close social relations. Even Lorenz's observations of animal interaction led him to say that "intraspecific aggression can certainly exist without its counterpart, love, but conversely there is no love without aggression (Lorenz, 1966, p. 217)." The theories of all four, then, can be said to coalesce in the proposition: *the intensity of aggressive interaction is related to the closeness of relationships.*

Unfortunately, it is probable that no single theory will ever explain the wide variety of human aggressive behaviors. However, as social scientists we are obliged to continue our explorations and to extend our understanding of human behavior within its social and psychological matrix. Most academicians and most professionals are isolated from the fields of social action and, when they do venture into the community, they study safe and well-established social systems. There is a real reluctance to become involved in new sub-systems . . . usually rationalized by the deification of "pure" rather than "applied" research. Fairweather (1967) recently indicted academic psychologists as being particularly devoted to "pure" research in the mistaken belief that emulation of the methods of the physical sciences will make for greater respectability. But as Sanford (1965) has pointed out, "the psychologists' naive conception of science has led them to adopt the more superficial characteristics of the physical sciences." "This," he maintains, "has made it difficult for them to study genuine human problems. . . ."

The greatest impetus for the study of "genuine human problems" undoubtedly occurred with the report by the Joint Commission on Mental Health and Illness (1961). The Commission brought into focus the nation's overwhelming mental health problem, the manpower shortages in the field, the appalling disregard of preventive approaches, and the inadequacy of services available to the large "silent" segments of our society. The report and subsequent legislated financial support stimulated critical self-appraisal among social scientists in general and among mental health professionals in particular. "Community mental health" and "community psychology" were to become bywords largely related to the Community Mental Health Act of 1963. Early efforts to meet the intent of the Act saw traditional approaches cloaked in the vestments of novelty; the uncomfortable realization grew that the mental health professions were imprisoned by their traditional pasts in attempting to satisfy the terms of the Act. If anything, frustrating attempts at innovation revealed that perhaps other disciplines such as sociology and anthropology were more suited by tradition and training to respond to the need for imaginative community programs than were psychologists and psychiatrists.

The approach to be described here should be viewed in this evolutionary context. It rests on the conviction that preventive intervention as a service strategy enhances the community's availability as a research laboratory in ways which cannot be realized by hospital or clinic-based service programs; that existing community institutions which characteristically deal with "genuine human problems" can be effectively utilized to modify behavior while at the same time affording unprecedented study opportunities (Bard, 1969a).

In large urban centers, rapid social change, alienation, increasing population density, and ever more complex economic competition conspire to subject the family and the individual to exacting pressures. For the disadvantaged in urban society, the personal effects may be extreme. Frustration, despair, and hopelessness can make for a volatile aggressive mixture largely kept inert by a system of social regulation which is the very embodiment of control. The police may be regarded simply as a domestic army which keeps civilian order, or they may be regarded as individuals involved in highly complex functions that extend far beyond mere repression. Cummings (1968) recently pointed out that, "although the policeman stood for control, much of his role inevitably involved support (p. 175)" and that more than one-half of the appeals to the police involve requests for assistance with personal and interpersonal problems. On the other hand, the police are also the only social institution specifically charged with managing real or threatened violence. Their intimate knowledge of violence and aggression is unparalleled by any others concerned with human behavior. Indeed, a policeman's ability to understand and deal with aggressive potentials often has critical survival value for him . . . a factor certainly absent in the pure setting of the experimental laboratory. That policemen often fail in their efforts to judge aggressive potentials is attested to by the fact that 22 per cent of the policemen killed in the line of duty are slain while intervening in "disturbances" among people, most frequently in families (FBI Law Enforcement Bulletin, 1963).

The opportunity to develop a service program utilizing general police officers as psychological intervention agents offered the prospect of achieving the goals of both crime prevention and preventive mental health. In addition, such an approach held promise of revealing insights into aspects of human aggression and violence as it occurs in naturalistic settings. Also inherent in such an approach was the possibility of providing doctoral students in clinical psychology with an unusual consultative training experience; to have students exposed to atypical human problem situations, the kind precluded by traditional training in clinics and hospitals (Singer & Bard, 1969).

In recent years, there has been a growing recognition of the extent to which the family shapes the personalities of children and of the complexity by which that shaping occurs. The importance of the family environment in the genesis of behavior pathology is well documented. The results of these investigations suggest that early identification of an intervention in families where parents live in a perpetual state of hateful and sadistic involvement may have significant preventive mental health implications for their children. Most disordered families are diagnosed and treated only after breakdown has occurred and only after seeking help. Families who seek help are generally well educated and sophisticated in mental health matters; they come from the middle and upper classes and usually have the resources and awareness requisite to seeking help. Undoubtedly there are large numbers of families in difficulty whose class and educational limitations prevent their identification by usual mental health case-finding methods. The families who lack knowledge and sophistication in matters pertaining to mental health resources may be those most likely to involve the police when family crisis approaches breakdown (Bard, 1969b).

Consistent with the foregoing, a program in police family crisis intervention was designed to provide a unique service to a West Harlem community of about 85,000 bordering on The City College campus (Bard & Berkowitz, 1967). The residents are mostly working class and black, with a sprinkling of Latin Americans (8 per cent) and whites (2 per cent); a socially stabile, residential community.

The project consisted of three stages: Preparatory Phase, for selection of police personnel and their training; an Operational Phase, in which the Family Crisis Unit functioned with regular consultative support by the staff of The Psychological Center of The City College; and an Evaluative Phase for analysis of data.

PREPARATORY PHASE

During the first month of the project, 18 patrolmen were selected from among 45 volunteers. No effort was made to induce participation except by the offer of three college credits to be granted by the John Jay College of Criminal Justice of The City University. Selection was based on brief interviews to determine motivation, sensitivity, and stability. Applicants were required to have a minimum of three years' service and a maximum of ten. Nine white and nine black officers were selected for eventual bi-racial pairing.

For an entire month following selection, the men were released from all duties to engage in an intensive training program which included lectures, "self-understanding" workshops, field trips, discussion groups, and a unique opportunity to "learn by doing." Three brief plays depicting family crisis situations were specially written and performed by professional actors. Each play was performed three consecutive times with interventions by a pair of policemen in each instance. Each pair of policemen was unaware of the events which preceded their entrance. The plays had no scripted conclusions, the actors having been instructed to improvise to the behavior of the officers when they entered the scene. The value of the experience was to enable the members of the unit to see how the same set of circumstances could have entirely different outcomes, dependent upon the nature of their intervention. The technique proved particularly meaningful to the officers. The practice interventions were subjected to extensive critique and review by all members of the unit. Particular emphasis in training was placed upon sensitizing the men to their own values and attitudes about human behavior in general and about disrupted families in particular.

OPERATIONAL PHASE

At the conclusion of training, the Family Crisis Unit began its operations. For a 22-month period one precinct radio car was designated as the family car, to be dispatched on all family disturbance complaints regardless of the sector of their occurrence in the precinct. In other words, departing from usual practice, the family car could leave its own patrol sector even if the disturbance was within the jurisdiction of another sector car. A special duty chart permitted 24-hour-a-day coverage by members of the unit. A file of family disturbance reports was kept in the car for ready reference on the way to a dispute. This practice enabled the officers to know of previous interventions, if any, and their outcomes. During the 22-month study period, the policemen of a neighboring precinct have been completing family disturbance reports in all instances of domestic disturbance. We are hopeful that these data will be useful in evaluating the project.

An added feature of operations was the regularly scheduled consultation for each member of the unit. Once each week the eighteen men appeared on campus in groups of six for individual consultation and debriefing with advanced graduate students in clinical psychology. In addition, each six-man group met with a professional group leader for the purpose of on-going discussion of a broad range of issues relevant to family crisis intervention. Naturally, both experiences enhanced data collection, making possible additional, more in-depth information than could be provided by family disturbance reports alone.

EVALUATIVE PHASE

The project has just entered its evaluative phase, after two years. The unit continues to function as a regular feature of the 30th Precinct's service to the community. However, while the men no longer have regularly scheduled consultations, The Psychological Center staff maintains "on call" availability for any member of the Family Crisis Unit.

The project is over and the task of data analysis is in its earliest stages (Bard, 1970a). It is expected that the data will be subjected to multi-correlation analysis, providing us with deeper insights into intra-familial violence. In addition, data analysis will provide the basis for methodologic refinements of the relatively crude methods employed in this project. Perhaps it is wise to regard the present effort as a reconnaissance, "where the most we can expect is to isolate useful questions and promising avenues of exploration rather than to aim for definitive answers (Parad & Caplan, 1963, p. 316)."

During the course of the project's 22-month operational phase, the members of the Family Crisis Intervention Unit serviced 962 families on 1375 separate occasions. At the moment, this largely unanalyzed mass of data only suggests the wisdom of Tolstoy's observation in *Anna Karenina* that "happy families resemble one another; each unhappy family is unhappy in its own way." Eventually, however, we should be able to define the nature of at least the kind of unhappiness that requires police intervention.

In the 22 months of operation by the Family Unit, we have been impressed by the fact that there has not been a homicide in any family previously known to the unit. While family homicides in the precinct increased overall, in each case there had been no prior police intervention. Further analysis will be necessary to understand the significance of this finding, but at least one possibility suggests itself. Gilula and Daniels' (1969) recent distinction between aggression and violence may suggest an explanation. They define aggression as an entire spectrum of assertive, intrusive and attacking behaviors, including a range of overt and covert attacks. They regard violence, on the other hand, as the distinct intent to do physical damage . . . intense, uncontrolled, excessive, sudden, and seemingly purposeless. It may be that calls to the police occur in the context of a range of aggressive acts; the violence occurs with such sudden and unpredictable fury that it occurs before police intervention can be sought.

It may be also that "class-linked" aggressive patterns need to be more clearly understood. There may well be a distinction, for example, between the aggression of lower class life, which is regarded as "normal," and violence, which is regarded as "abnormal." [1] It is well known that child-rearing practices of the middle and upper classes proscribe overt aggression as unacceptable behavior. Unlike the lower class, "don't hit" is a primary parental prohibition. Class differences of this order would lead to the hypothesis that,

[1]There is a suggestion of this in Davis' classic paper on child rearing within class and ethnic structures in American society: "The lower classes not uncommonly teach their children and adolescents to strike out with fist or knife and to be certain to hit first. Both girls and boys at adolescence may curse their father to his face or even attack him with fists, sticks, or axes in free-for-all family encounters. Husbands and wives sometimes stage pitched battles in the home; wives have their husbands arrested; and husbands when locked out try to break in or burn down their own houses. Such fights with fists or weapons and the whipping of wives occur sooner or later in most lower-class families. . . . physical aggression is as much a normal, socially approved, and socially inculcated type of behavior as it is in frontier communities." (Davis, W. A., Child rearing in the class structure of American society. In M. B. Sussman (ed.), *Sourcebook of Marriage and the Family*. Boston: Houghton, Mifflin, 1963, pp. 225–231.)

while police may be called less frequently for domestic disputes in middle and upper class communities, when they are, the behaviors are likely to be more violently serious. That is, since even minimal aggressive expression is denied to the middle and upper classes, when aggression is expressed, it is likely to be "excessive, uncontrolled, and sudden." We hope in the future to test this hypothesis through the operation of police family intervention units in middle and upper class areas.

We have been particularly impressed by the remarkable absence of injury to the 18 men engaged in this highest hazard program. It is estimated that 40 per cent of injuries sustained by police occur while they are intervening in family disputes. In fact, most policemen regard a family dispute as among the most noxious and dangerous of all assignments. The 18-man unit, exposed for more than would ordinarily be the case to this dangerous event, sustained only one minor injury to one man during the course of the project. This re-markable absence of injury to a group of officers exposed to highly volatile aggressive situations strongly suggests the importance of the role played by the victim in the exacerbation of violence. Only recently, a new field of "victimology" has emerged in which the focus has begun to shift so that it is placed at least equally on the victim as well as perpetrator. Sarbin (1967) recently pointed out that danger connotes a relationship and that assaultive or violent behavior described as dangerous "can be understood as the pre-dictable outcome of certain antecedent and concurrent conditions (p. 286)." Sarbin believes that degradation procedures within role-relationships which transform an individual's social identity to the status of a "non-person" is evocative of dangerous behavior. Since a policeman's work is such that he is always ready to classify the conduct of others as potentially dangerous, he may engage in degrading kinds of power displays which provoke the ex-pected "wild beast" response. The officers in our project, through their sen-sitivity training, awareness of the language of behavior, and security in their mediation skills, may have learned to avoid fear-inspired premature power displays, thus avoided depriving their potentially violent clients of their social identity and hence avoided potentiating violence directed at *them-selves*.

Another possible explanation may be based on the medical concept of iatrogenesis: physicians have long recognized that an authority with the power of life and death has the capacity to induce profound and unexpected changes in the course of diagnosis or treatment. The term refers simply to a disorder resulting from the actions of the physician during his ministrations. In other words, the very actions undertaken to relieve a disorder may in themselves create still further disorder.

While the physician is an authority with the power of life and death in dealing with *physical* disorder, the policeman is a life and death authority in instances of *social* disorder. The implications in this analogy, if valid, suggest the necessity for a re-examination of some of the basic assumptions of law enforcement.

The experiment in family crisis intervention shows promise of demon-strating that policemen provided with skills appropriate to the complexities of today's social existence succeed in minimizing violence which might otherwise be exacerbated by their well-meant but inept performance. Consider for a moment the bizarre paradox in our urban ghettos that, while the police are hated, feared and envied, they are the ghetto resident's primary resource in times of sickness, injury or trouble. For the economically disenfranchised, long disillusioned by unfulfilled promises of help and service, the police officer represents the ordinarily unattainable: a reliable source of help, instantly available *for any human problem*. If, however, the helpseeker's expectations are met by simplistic behaviors of repression consistent with a bygone era of law enforcement, resultant frustration, bitterness, and resentment may easily escalate to a violent outcome.

It is increasingly clear that most of a policeman's daily activity in today's society centers upon interpersonal service; indeed, it has been estimated that as much as 90 per cent of his working time may entail such functions. Yet, little of the police officer's training prepares him to render these services with skill and compassion. In general, police training programs and police organizational structures are based upon questionable assumptions in the world of today. The notion that a policeman is simply a watchman over property or the strong repressor of the law breaker is just no longer realistic. Indeed, such ideas are just as outmoded as is the cherished fantasy of the legendary sheriff of frontier days, whose most valued posture was tough imperviousness to feelings and tight-lipped readiness to neutralize conflict by a quick draw in the middle of Main Street.

One can only speculate on the effects that such highly valued aspects of folk culture have had in shaping present-day police behavior. After all, films and television have furnished countless youngsters with simple formula solutions to the struggle between good and evil; outcomes which rest ultimately upon the triumph of good through the power of the six-shooter. Even casual observation of most American peace officers will testify to the modeling effectiveness of this steady diet of Hollywood "folk art." Just as young baseball players emulate the expressive movements of admired senior ballplayers, so do young policemen engage in a language of behavior which communicates the self-image of the determined, pistol-ready suppressor of evil.

If correct, such a limited law enforcement perspective, when supported by outmoded police organizational structures, has volatile potentials. It seriously limits the police officer's repertoire of response patterns and increases the likelihood of iatrogenic violence. Fantasy-based power displays, inappropriately applied in situations which call for a different kind of police response, are in themselves evocative of violence. Social conditions such as an exploding population, increased social mobility, and changes in family patterns have given the police responsibilities which require sensitive, reality-based skills unforeseen as recently as twenty years ago. To persist in training police for roles that are no longer viable is to contribute still further to social unrest and to encourage iatrogenic violence (Bard, 1970b).

Very recently, we completed a partial analysis of 300 interventions (i.e., 21 per cent of the total). It is interesting to note that of this preliminary sample, 32 per cent of the complainants reported physical violence, while 16 per cent reported the threat of violence. It is of further interest to note, however, that although violence is a factor in almost one-half of the complaints, on arrival at the scene, the police are most frequently (30 per cent) requested to arbitrate, mediate, or advise the disputants. In this connection, the specially trained officers have acquitted themselves well. In the comparison precinct, when police make referrals in family disputes, it is to the Family Court 95 per cent of the time. No referrals are made to social and mental health agencies. In the experimental precinct, 45 per cent of the referrals are made to Family Court and 55 per cent to twenty different social and mental health agencies. In addition, there were about 22 per cent fewer arrests in the experimental precinct than in the comparison precinct in relation to the number of family interventions. The lower rate of arrests in the experimental precinct is suggestive of the greater use of referral resources and of mediation. One can only speculate on the financial saving in reducing the burden on the courts by reducing the referral of inappropriate cases and by reducing the number of arrests. It is well known that upon reaching the courts, and long after the heated dispute has cooled, most complaints of this type are dropped anyway. Sophisticated police intervention can provide immediate mediation service but can also serve as a preliminary screening mechanism for final resolution of family disharmony.

The following case will illustrate the approach of two family unit patrolmen in one case involving threatened violence:

On arrival at a small apartment, the officers were informed by an older woman that her married daughter had become enraged, had begun throwing di⁻hes, threatened suicide by jumping out a window, and threatened the complainant and her own 12-year-old child with violence. The officers quickly calmed the agitated woman and learned that she had been depressed since her divorce six months earlier and on that particular day had returned from a frustrating visit to the bank, where she was unable to get her alimony check processed in less than 2 weeks. After decompressing the situation and eliciting the information, the officers took Mrs. C. to the bank, where they were able to arrange to have her checks processed in three days from then on.

Suspecting that Mrs. C.'s emotional difficulties extended beyond her financial difficulties, they suggested a psychiatric consultation and they then escorted her to the Medical Center. A psychiatrist found her to be profoundly depressed, suicidal, and homicidal and recommended immediate hospitalization. The patient readily accepted the suggestion and was accompanied to Bellevue by the officers.

In their report, the officers stated that it was their impression that Mrs. C. was profoundly depressed and that it had been precipitated by the divorce. They felt the incident at the bank reflected her inability to accept the reality of the divorce.

As in this case, many of the reports of violence are accompanied by the expectation that the police will remedy the grievance in the role of dispassionate third party. In fewer than 8 per cent of the preliminary sample was an initial request made to have the other person arrested. Clearly, then, appeals to the police are in the nature of requests for authority and objectivity in the resolution of conflict—not for enforcement of law. It would appear that, while aggression may be socially and culturally sanctioned, there may be self-regulated limitations to the permissibility of violence.

Our preliminary analysis of 300 cases indicates that the family dispute is largely a matter of marital dispute. In 80 per cent of the cases, the disputants were married (48 per cent legally, 24 per cent common law) or were separated (8 per cent). Violent confrontations between adolescents and a parent accounted for 15 per cent of the cases. In a surprising number of these cases it is our impression that parents appeal to the police to act as a more effective authority in disciplining or controlling an adolescent. A case in point:

Mr. S. called the police with the following complaint: "My daughter stayed out late and was drinking. I want you to talk to her—I can't do anything with her." The responding officers determined the following: the 17-year-old daughter went out, drank, and did not return until 11:30. The father struck her and then called the police. Father stated that this eldest of his 10 children is rebellious, will not help in the house, and generally is the most difficult of all the children. The daughter appeared to the officers to be intoxicated. The other daughters in the family described their father as overly strict and unwilling to let any of them leave the house in the evening.

The officers devoted considerable time to counseling the family. In the end, agreement was achieved by all concerned, including the daughter in question, to visit a local social agency for further counseling.

By the way, children were present in 41 per cent of the interventions. If this is typical, one can only speculate on the modeling effects of parental aggression on such children—not to speak of the effects of a variety of police behaviors on the perceptions of children in such situations. One of our students has become interested in learning about the effects of observing parental violence upon perceptual processes and fantasy in these children.

It is difficult to know the kind of impact the program has had on the community as a whole. There are indirect signs that its presence has been felt. For one thing, the number of calls for family disturbance intervention has steadily declined over the two-year period, while the number of calls in the comparison precinct has remained constant. One possible explanation is that successful resolution or referral of initial cases has cut down the chronic or repeat cases. Yet, at the same time, there have been referrals made to the police unit by families who have been served and, hence, some increase might have been expected. The neighborhood grapevine has it that there are some "special family cops" who are OK. In fact, the men have noted that, when their car rolls into a street (its number is apparently known), people fail to "freeze" as they would when just any police car appears. Also, after initial skepticism, other policemen in the area have grown to respect the work of the unit and to be grateful for its existence.

In no small measure, whatever the success the program has had is traceable to the fact that the professional identity of the officers has been preserved. They are not specialists in that they perform family crisis intervention to the exclusion of all other police functions. On the contrary, they are continuously engaged in regular police patrol but are available to provide family intervention when needed. In this instance, we have avoided role identity confusion—an often vexing problem when individuals are expected to provide services congenial with mental health goals. The policemen in the family unit have little doubt that they are policemen—they do not regard themselves as psychologists or social workers, nor do they perform as such. They restore the peace and maintain order, but it is "how" they do it that is the measure of their success.

We expect to learn a great deal about an aspect of social conflict resolution about which little is known. The nine teams of patrolmen in the unit have, in almost two years of operation, developed team styles of intervention. While we do not have detailed insight as yet, we do have certain impressions. There are some approaches which appear to be universal—for example, to separate the disputants, neutralize the potential violence, and then for each officer to engage in a dialogue with one of the disputants with as much privacy as possible. It is at this point that stylistic differences begin to show themselves. For instance, in one team of officers each characteristically then switches to the other disputant for a private chat and finally all four engage in a group discussion. Each takes a disputant as a client and then, with the two disputants watching, often in amazement, the two officers heatedly argue the case. This technique appears to sufficiently objectify the situation for disputants to permit meaningful discussion to follow.

One of the more satisfying dimensions of the project has been the opportunity to constructively utilize the unique qualities of policemen. The collaboration of police officers and social scientists to gain greater understanding of human behavior has proven itself to be quite tenable. Policemen have sharply-honed powers of observation; a skill with adaptive survival value for them. The successful employment of this skill in the service of the community and in the service of science has been only one of the exciting facets of this action research program.

We believe that this pioneering experimental social innovation involving a sub-system usually avoided by psychologists will encourage further research within existing community institutions. Even the present effort, which was more concerned with content than with elegance of form, will prove to be a forerunner of more sophisticated community psychology action research.

Our approach can be described as a relevant method for the study of human aggression and violence in its social and psychological matrix. It is action research—concerned with the world of real people, living as real people live. Clearly, if we are to understand the origins of violence and aggression, we must study the basic family unit, for there is undeniable evidence that violence is a family affair. Our method provided a novel research framework while at the same time it brought together the unlikeliest of bedfellows—law enforcement and mental health. But in both, the emphasis was on the prevention of crime and upon early and effective intervention and hence prevention of emotional disorder. But, above all, effective community psychology action research should be designed to effect change and innovation in existing social institutions while at the same time offering otherwise unavailable opportunities for research leading to the increase in our knowledge of man's behavior.

## REFERENCES

Ardrey, R. *The Territorial Imperative.* New York: Atheneum, 1966.

Bard, M. "Extending Psychology's Impact Through Existing Community Institutions." *American Psychologist,* 24 (1969a): 610–612.

Bard, M. "Family Intervention Police Teams as a Community Mental Health Resource." *Journal of Criminal Law, Criminology and Police Science,* 60 (1969b): 247–250.

Bard, M. *Training Police as Specialists in Family Crisis Intervention: Final Report.* Washington, D.C.: U.S. Government Printing Office, 1970a.

Bard, M. "Alternatives to Traditional Law Enforcement." In F. F. Karten, S. W. Cook, and J. S. Lacey (eds.), *Psychology and the Problems of Society,* Washington, D.C.: American Psychological Association, 1970b, 128–132.

Bard, M. and Berkowitz, B. "Training Police as Specialists in Family Crisis Intervention: A Community Psychology Action Program." *Community Mental Health Journal,* 3 (1967): 315–317.

Cummings, E. *Systems of Social Regulation.* New York: Atherton Press, 1968.

Davis, W. A. "Child Rearing in the Class Structure of American Society." In M. B. Sussman (ed.), *Sourcebook of Marriage and the Family* (2nd ed.). Boston: Houghton, Mifflin, 1963.

Dollard, J. *et al. Frustration and Aggression.* New Haven: Yale Univer. Press, 1939.

Ennis, P. H. "Crime, Victims and the Police." *Transaction* (June, 1967): 36–44.

Fairweather, G. W. *Methods for Experimental Social Innovation.* New York: John Wiley & Sons, 1967.

*FBI Law Enforcement Bulletin* (January, 1963): 27.

Freud, S. *Group Psychology and the Analysis of the Ego.* London: The Hogarth Press, 1948.

Gilula, M. F. and Daniels, G. "Violence and Man's Struggle to Adapt." *Science* 164 (1969): 396–405.

Joint Commission on Mental Health and Illness. *Final Report: Action for Mental Health.* New York: Basic Books, 1961.

Lorenz, K. *On Aggression.* New York: Harcourt, Brace & World, 1966.

Malinowski, B. "An Anthropological Analysis of War." *Magic, Science and Religion.* Glencoe, Ill.: Free Press, 1948.

Mead, M. "Alternatives to War." (In "The Anthropology of Armed Conflict and Aggression.") *Natural History* (Dec., 1967): 65–69.

Megargee, E. I. "Assault with Intent to Kill." *Transaction* (Sept./Oct. 1966): 28–31.

New York City Police Department. Press Release No. 30, March 31, 1966.

Parad, H. J. and Caplan, G. "A Framework for Studying Families in Crisis." In M. B. Sussman (ed.), *Source Book in Marriage and the Family* (2nd ed.). Boston: Houghton Mifflin Co., 1963.

Sanford, N. "Will Psychologists Study Human Problems." *American Psychologist* 20 (1965): 192–202.

Sarbin, T. "The Dangerous Individual an Outcome of Social Identity Transformation." *British Journal of Criminology* (July, 1967): 285–295.

Simmel, Georg. *Conflict and the Web of Group Affiliations.* Glencoe, Ill.: Free Press, 1955.

Singer, J. L. and Bard, M. "Community Consultation in the Doctoral Education of Clinical Psychologists." *The Clinical Psychologist* (Winter, 1969): 79–83.

# PART THREE
# Violent
# Parents

Tragic as was the death of four Kent State students who were killed in the spring of 1970 by National Guardsmen trying to control anti-war demonstrations, the fuller measure of the tragedy lies in the hundreds of thousands killed in Viet Nam and the mood of national violence created by that war. The national conflict over Viet Nam, however, has only intensified and brought to the surface tendencies which have characterized American society from the beginning. Americans have always had a propensity to use violence to achieve national and personal goals, ranging from the extermination of Indians who would not yield their land to the treatment of children (Graham and Gurr, 1969). A 1646 law declares:

If any child[ren] above sixteen years old and of sufficient understanding shall curse or smite their natural father or mother, they shall be put to death, unless it can be sufficiently testified that the parents have been very unchristianly negligent in the education of such children, or so provoked them by extreme and cruel correction that they have been forced thereunto to preserve themselves from death or maiming. . . .

If a man have a stubborn or rebellious son of sufficient years of understanding, viz. sixteen, which will not obey the voice of his father or the voice of his mother, and that when they have chastened him will not harken unto them, then shall his father and mother, being his natural parents, lay hold on him and bring him to the magistrates assembled in Court, and testify to them by sufficient evidence that this their son is stubborn and rebellious, and will not obey their voice and chastisement, but lives in sundry notorious crimes. Such a son shall be put to death. (Bremner, 1970:37)

There is no recorded case of a child ever having been executed under this statute. Nevertheless, the sentiment expressed is clear and remarkably similar to the sentiments which emerge from James A. Michener's account of the reactions to Kent State (p. 180)—as expressed by the citizens and the parents whose moral outrage over the war protests and the life styles of students at Kent State was so great that they felt it would have been better if a few more had been killed.

The parallel between the colonial period and modern America goes even further. In that distant period, as in our own time, children were the object of moral concern and outrage. Citizens then as now were concerned not just with destructive acts, but with the deviation of the younger generation from their own moral standards. It is not long hair, but the rejection and disobedience symbolized by long hair which outraged the citizenry in the 1660's (and in the 1960's) as the law just quoted and also the following section of a 1675 Massachusetts law makes clear:

Whereas there is manifest pride openly appearing amongst us in that long hair, like women's hair, is worn by some men, either their own or others hair made into periwigs, and by some women wearing borders of hair, and their cutting, curling, and immodest laying out their hair, which practise doth prevail and increase, especially among the younger sort:

This Court doth declare against this ill custom as offensive to them, and divers sober Christians among us, and therefore do hereby exhort and advise all persons to use moderation in this respect; and further, do empower all grand juries to present to the County Court such persons, whether male or female, whom they shall judge to exceed in the premises; and the County Courts are hereby authorized to proceed against such delinquents either by admonition, fine, or correction, according to their good discretion. (Bremner, 1970:38)

The fact that we do not know if any child was ever executed under the Massachusetts statute of 1646, or to what extent children then were punished for long hair and other such moral outrages against their parents, is representative of the limited knowledge most aspects of intra-family violence. Not only are specific figures scarce, even when they are available, but the data are typically difficult to interpret. This is because of such things as differences in the way events are defined or because the populations studied to get the figures are unrepresentative groups.

Take, for example, David G. Gil's estimate that there are about three million cases of child abuse of varying degrees of severity each year (Gil, 1971). The problem with such an estimate is that it depends on contemporary definitions of "abuse." An ordinary spanking or slap by a parent would not be counted as abuse. But if the parties involved were husband and wife, then a spanking or slapping would be considered abuse by most Americans. That has not always been the public attitude. Earlier in American history, it was considered quite appropriate for a husband to physically punish an erring wife. At some future time, we may also come to see what is now regarded as ordinary and permissible spanking of children as abuse. But whether we regard such acts as abuse or not, there is no question that they are violent acts.

## PHYSICAL PUNISHMENT

If we are content with determining the extent of the minimal level of parental violence, there is little difficulty because spanking of children is done by at least 93 per cent of all parents (Stark and McEvoy, 1970). Of course, many of these parents use physical punishment only rarely and only on young children. Even allowing for this, the frequency of physical punishment is far greater than most Americans would like to admit.

Information on the use of physical punishment is greatest for young children and suggests that spanking is almost universal for young children. There is little information on the middle years of childhood. However, studies by Murray A. Straus and Suzanne K. Steinmetz (p. 159, p. 166) show that as late as the last year in high school, about half of the students in their samples experienced physical punishment or threats of physical punishment. So we have information only for the beginning and the end of the period of childhood, and even the latter is based on samples of families who send their child to a major university—hardly a representative sample.

Despite these limitations, certain aspects of parental violence emerge clearly from the material in this part of the book. First, although physical punishment is still almost universal at some point in the child-rearing process, it has undoubtedly diminished since colonial times. At the very least, Samuel X. Radbill's "A History of Child Abuse and Infanticide" (p. 173) shows that, relative to certain other historical periods, ours is minimally violent to children. Since the focus of public and social concern is with the abuse of children, Radbill's article concentrates on situations of high rather than low violence toward children. On the other hand, if we knew which periods in history treated children relatively non-violently, it might be possible to uncover some of the social factors associated with such periods. These in turn could provide clues to steps which might be taken to further reduce the level of parental violence in our own time.

One could speculate that periods in history where there was great concern with intellectual and artistic development were relatively non-violent in their child rearing as compared with periods where heavy emphasis was placed on technological and material achievement. Following such a line of speculation, one might ask, was there more emphasis during the Greek classical period and the enlightenment on "humane" treatment of children than during periods of colonization and the industrial revolution? Supporting this speculation are analyses which suggest that while harsh, rigid punishment might be conducive to preparing individuals for battle, exploration, or the assembly line, it is not the type of socialization most likely to result in independent thinking, artistic and creative skills, and intellectual pursuits (Baumrind, 1967; Getzels and Jackson, 1962; Kohn, 1969; Miller and Swanson, 1958).

Returning to the colonial period and the "stubborn child law" which went so far as to prescribe the death penalty for a truly recalcitrant child, although it is doubtful if such a penalty was ever imposed, it is almost certain that extremely harsh punishments did prevail. Not only was life on the colonial frontier harsh and often violent, but the pressures toward harsh treatment of children were augmented by the equally harsh religious beliefs of the time. Susannah Wesley, mother of John Wesley, the founder of Methodism, wrote about her methods of child rearing as follows:

When turned a year old (and some before), they were taught to fear the rod, and to cry softly; by which means they escaped abundance of correction they might otherwise have had; and that most odious noise of the crying of children was rarely heard in the house; but the family usually lived in as much quietness as if there had not been a child among them. . . . As self-will is the root of all sin and misery, so whatever cherishes this in children insures their after-wretchedness and irreligion; whatever checks and mortifies it promotes their future happiness and piety. This is still more evident, if we further consider, that religion is nothing else than doing the will of God, and not our own: that the one grand impediment to our temporal and eternal happiness being this self-will, no indulgences of it can be trivial, no denial unprofitable. Heaven or hell depends on this alone. . . . (Gesell, 1930: 20–33)

The interrelation between religious beliefs and child-rearing practices suggested in the above passage is an example of the family as a system which exists in mutually influencing interaction with other subsystems of society (see Figure 1 on p. 18 and the accompanying discussion). Evidence supporting this interrelation is given in a study of 62 different societies by Lambert and Triandis and Wolf (1959). These researchers found a tendency in societies whose supernatural beings were punishing rather than benevolent, to be societies in which infants and children are treated punitively. Thus, the linkage between the religious system of society and violence in child rearing appears to apply to a great many societies, not just to eighteenth-century England and its colonies.

In neither case do we know which causes which. Do religious beliefs provide the model for parents to use in their god-like relations with their children? Or do people tend to model their conceptions of God on their early experiences with their parents? If we look at this issue in evolutionary perspective, we are inclined to see the sequence begin with some environmental adaptation problem which tended to produce relatively harsh patterns of child rearing. Adults brought up under such punitive conditions would tend to evolve a conception of God which is like the treatment they experienced as a child. But once the religious system is developed, it has an independent existence of its own, with feedback which influences each of the other parts of the social system, including, of course, the family.

## SOCIAL CAUSES OF CHILD ABUSE

Undoubtedly, some readers will not accept the idea that physical punishment is violence between family members. For such persons, the type of acts to be considered as violence are those committed by what have come to be called "child-abusing" parents, or parents of a "battered child." These are the parents described and analyzed in Chapter VII, "Helping Parents and Protecting Children."

We are somewhat uncomfortable with the term "abusive parents" because this term tends to focus on what is wrong with the parents as individuals, and to focus attention on treatment oriented to correcting the personal or familial defects of these particular parents. Nevertheless, this is the customary way of regarding extremely violent parents and is the perspective implicit in Leontine Young's description of the Nolan family (p. 187) and in Serapio R. Zalba's article on "Treatment of Child Abuse" (p. 212).

We do not doubt that parents such as the Nolans need the help of professionals to aid them in ending their mistreatment of a child. But, we feel that the roots of their behavior are to be found in the "normal" social patterns of the society. The Nolans represent an impermissible *extension* of these basic violent tendencies in American society. From this perspective, "abusive parents" are merely a special category because they are the ones who come to public attention as a result of medical care needed by their children.

"Ordinary" physical punishment is abusive, too, as David G. Gil argues in his article on the implications for social policy of extreme parental violence (p. 205). Gil holds that the present cultural approval of physical punishment is one of the factors which lays the groundwork for some parents to carry violence to the point where it causes severe injury to the child. For this and other reasons, he urges that an effort be made to gradually change social expectations. We should develop both informal and legal prohibitions of physical punishment and replace the use of physical force in child rearing with non-violent, constructive modes of parental influence.

## CHILD REARING WITHOUT VIOLENCE

Such a change will not come about easily. If, as William J. Goode concludes (p. 25), the use of force and violence is a fundamental part of the family system, it will be difficult for most of us to envision just how physical punishment can be eliminated without abrogating parental responsibility for producing a child who will be a constructive member of society.

Some observers feel that American parents do seem to be abrogating this responsibility. The evidence summarized by Urie Bronfenbrenner in his *Two Worlds of Childhood* (1970) does not portend well for either the welfare of our society or the personal happiness of its members. In a chapter on "The Unmaking of the American Child," Bronfenbrenner concludes that: "We leave our children to be brought up by their peers, in an atmosphere pervaded by subtle opposition to the standards of adult society, and by the television set, which significantly contributes to the likelihood of anti-social behavior. In truth, the freedom we claim to give our children is largely 'affluent neglect.' In short, the process of 'making human beings human' is largely breaking down in American society."

Assuming the accuracy of this description, and assuming the accuracy of Goode's (also Gil's) analysis of the fundamental role of force and violence in our family system, it is likely that a great many, if not most, Americans will respond to the "breakdown in the process of making human beings human" by calling for a return to the harsh patterns of parental discipline which characterized earlier historical periods. Indeed, we see such a trend in the harsh treatment not only of explicitly deviant "hippie" youth, but also in the events at Kent State, and in the growing call for "law and order" and less "permissiveness." The latter calls are unobjectionable if taken literally at their face value, but their real meaning is most often repressive and punitive.

Fortunately, as Bronfenbrenner shows, the alternatives are not limited to "affluent neglect" or a return to authoritarian parents and increased use of physical punishment—even assuming that the latter were possible. Bronfenbrenner offers a number of specific steps which can be taken to make the groups who deal with children, including the family *and* the peer group, effective in creating a responsible and non-violent citizenry. No part of Bronfenbrenner's carefully thought-through program involves physical punishment. Indeed, punishment of any type occupies only a minor place. Rather, the emphasis is on such things as providing children with a meaningful involvement in the real business of society, providing appropriate role models, and making children's peer groups a positive force in human development.

In giving emphasis to the larger social conditions from which physical punishment and child abuse arise, and the social conditions which determine the degree to which a child grows up to be an adequately functioning member of society, we do not mean to slight the importance of individual personality and individual family factors. Such factors are of tremendous importance. But they have so dominated discussions of child rearing and child abuse that we feel it is important to emphasize the social factors.

## INDIVIDUAL AND LEGAL APPROACHES

Despite the emphasis that should be placed on social conditions, it is clear that part of the approach to understanding and dealing with violence between parent and child must be based on an understanding of the individual child, his parents, and their interaction. Thus, a number of social scientists approach the problem at the family level rather than at the society level. The aim of these scientists is to understand what individual and family characteristics result in violence and to provide parents with aid and information on how to control their own and their children's violence.

The three articles in Chapter VII, "Helping Parents and Protecting Children," all deal with what can be done to help *parents* who are child abusers. As we have already emphasized, however, we feel that the societal-change perspective is a more fundamental one. This is because individual education, counseling, and treatment—although desirable in their own right—are not likely to have major effects unless they are part of fundamental social changes. Examples of the type of major changes needed include such things as a reduction in the frustrating life circumstances faced by millions of parents (especially the poor and those subject to racial discrimination) and in the cultural approval of the use of force and violence in the treatment of criminals and in international relations.[1] One can get some inkling of the social forces involved and the social changes necessary by considering how close in spirit is the medieval nursery rhyme:

> There was an old woman who lived in a shoe,
> She had so many children she didn't know what to do.
> She gave them some broth without any bread,
> And whipped them all soundly, and sent them to bed.

to the migrant worker father interviewed by Robert Coles (1970: 30):

"Now, they'll come back at me, oh, do they, with first one question and then another, until I don't know what to say, and I tell them to stop. Sometimes I have to hit them, yes sir, I'll admit it. They'll be asking about why, why, why, and I don't have the answers and I'm tired out, and I figure sooner or later they'll have to stop asking and just be glad they're alive.

Part of the overall social change necessary has already begun in the anti-poverty and child-protection legislation enacted in the last decade (Paulson, 1968). However, the fundamental problem of the legality of physical punishment is untouched by these laws. Indeed, it might be argued that we will not have progressed very far until all physical punishment is illegal. But too much cannot be expected from legal changes alone. The law *can* exert important influences on social patterns. But it cannot be too far ahead of the

---

[1]See in this connection, Brim (1959). This comprehensive review of a large number of parent-education programs failed to find any convincing evidence of their effectiveness.

population or it will be evaded or ignored. Prohibition is the most widely recognized example of this. Other examples abound. In Connecticut, the statewide police enforcement of the speeding laws was soon accompanied by a sharp increase in cases dismissed and sentences suspended because neither the courts nor the public were ready for this step (Campbell and Ross, 1968). Most recently, the court-ordered busing to achieve integration has met with massive movements out of the cities to avoid busing, thus aggravating the problem of racial segregation. In Norfolk, Virginia, for example, the white population of the schools dropped 21 per cent in the two years following the beginning of busing (Stevens, 1971). So we are back again to the basic social conditions which make us violent.

We will return to this theme, but look at it from a somewhat different perspective, in Part Four, "The Family as Training Ground for Societal Violence." Just as Part Three follows a social system perspective in emphasizing the relation of societal violence to intra-family violence, the same system perspective directs us, in Part Four, to consider the ways in which what goes on within the family influences the level of violence in the society as a whole.

## REFERENCES

Baumrind, Diana
    1967    "Child Care Practices Anteceding Three Patterns of Preschool Behavior." *Genetic Psychological Monographs* 75: 43–88.
Bremner, Robert H. (ed.)
    1970    *Children and Youth in America: A Documentary History.* Vol. I. Boston: Harvard University Press.
Bronfenbrenner, Urie
    1970    *Two Worlds of Childhood. U.S. and U.S.S.R.* New York: Russell Sage Foundation.
Campbell, Donald T. and H. Laurence Ross
    1968    "The Connecticut Crackdown on Speeding: Time Series Data in Quasi-Experimental Analysis." *Law and Society* 3 (August): 33–53.
Coles, Robert
    1970    *Uprooted Children.* New York: Harper and Row.
Gesell, Arnold
    1930    *The Guidance of Mental Growth in Infant and Child.* New York: Macmillan.
Getzels, Jacob W. and Philip W. Jackson
    1962    *Creativity and Intelligence.* New York: Wiley.
Gil, David G.
    1970    *Violence Against Children.* Boston: Harvard University Press.
Graham, Hugh Davis and Ted Robert Gurr
    1969    *Violence in America: Historical and Comparative Perspectives.* Vols. I and II. A Report to the National Commission on the Causes and Prevention of Violence. Washington, D.C.: U. S. Government Printing Office.
Kohn, Melvin L.
    1969    *Class and Conformity.* Homewood, Illinois: Dorsey Press.
Lambert, William W., Leigh Minturn Triandis and Margery Wolf
    1959    "Some Correlates of Beliefs in the Malevolence and Benevolence of Supernatural Beings: A Cross-Societal Study." *Journal of Abnormal and Social Psychology* 58 (March): 162–169.
Miller, Daniel R. and Guy E. Swanson
    1958    *The Changing American Parent.* New York: Wiley.
Paulsen, M. G.
    1968    "The Law and Abused Children." Pp. 175–200 in Ray E. Helfer and C. Henry Kempe (eds.), *The Battered Child.* Chicago: University of Chicago Press.
Stark, Rodney and James McEvoy III
    1970    "Middle Class Violence." *Psychology Today* 4 (November): 52–65.

# CHAPTER FIVE
# Physical Punishment

## 15. *When Parents Hit Out*
**MYRNA BLUMBERG**

The parents described in the following article live in Nottingham, England. However, we include this article rather than an excerpt from one of the American studies of physical punishment because it gives a more graphic and clear description than do any of the American research reports. We can use this British material because the available evidence suggests that situation is essentially the same in Nottingham, England; Nottingham, New Hampshire; or San Francisco, California. For example, the English research finds that 97 per cent of the children had been spanked by the time they were four years old. This is little different than the 94 per cent of Americans who reported having been spanked as children (see p. 6). But even if the percentages were to differ by larger amounts, the individual and family dynamics leading to physical punishment seem to be essentially the same in both countries—and perhaps in all Western societies. Thus, along with American studies, this research suggests that physical punishment tends to be as much a result of the stress experienced by parents as it is the result of the objective needs of the situation for controlling the child's behavior. In this respect, as in many others, the dynamics of physical punishment are comparable to the dynamics of child abuse analyzed by Richard J. Gelles (p. 190) and David G. Gil (p. 205).

When the doctors John and Elizabeth Newson, of Nottingham University psychology department, began their pioneering explorations seven years ago into the daily details of normal family upbringing in Nottingham, they did not set out to do a sort of time and motion study of how much, when and why parents hit their children; but this is what part of their newest research, to be published soon, amounts to. The doctors Newson (it's best to address them collectively) organized the interviewing of 700 "average families," a random cross-section of all classes except recent immigrants and mothers of illegitimate babies, and a chapter in their first remarkable book, *Infant Care in an Urban Community* (Allen & Unwin, 1963) showed that 62 per cent of Nottingham babies had been smacked by the time they were one year old—smacked for getting cross, or going near the fire, or twiddling television knobs, or not eating nicely, or not potting, or playing with their genitals, or just crying. (". . . I'd let her cry a good while," as one mother said about her baby, "until she got fed up herself, about a quarter of an hour; I'd leave her till she got tired of it, and if she didn't do she'd get a smacked bum.")

The Newsons have a horde of facts to come. By the time they're four, 97 per cent of Nottingham children are smacked, a few hit with canes, straps,

SOURCE: Reprinted with permission from *20th Century* (Winter, 1964–65): 39–41.

slippers or wooden spoons, but mostly with parental hands on their legs and backsides. The Newsons do not think the experiences of Nottingham children are very different from any others in Britain.

They obviously found it difficult to get an accurate estimate of how much smacking took place in any particular family, but decided they could reliably assess extremes of smacking—those who smacked a great deal and those who smacked very rarely: the vast majority of mothers smacked from about once a day to once a week. They found no class trend among the heavy smackers (6 per cent of all the mothers) but professional families predominated among the infrequent and non-smackers.

There were almost no class differences in physical punishment for defiance (67 per cent did this), but there were very marked differences in smacking for sex interests: 6 per cent of professional families punished genital play, compared with 52 per cent of unskilled labourers' families. The poorer the families on the whole, the more punitive were their attitudes to nakedness and sex (perhaps because they lived more on top of each other).

They found class differences, also, in alternatives to physical punishment: 12 per cent of professional parents threatened withdrawal of affection, compared with 42–43 per cent of skilled workers and semi- or unskilled; no professional parents threatened to leave the child or send him away, while for some reason 26 per cent of shop and clerical workers stood out for using this type of threat. The point, explain the Newsons in trying to discover under what circumstances some parents resort to physical or verbal violence, is that punitive acts themselves cannot be isolated from the complexity of attitudes, values and clashes of tension in families.

Is parental violence more easily accepted in Britain than in other European countries?

Dr. Elizabeth Newson, in an interview, said: "I don't think anyone has made any comparative studies. Indeed, there has been surprisingly little research into this subject generally. From our work here in Nottingham, we find that one of the most important things involved is the self-esteem between parent and child: parents can't bear being 'shown up' or 'let down,' especially *in public*. The mother decides, say, that she's got to show who's boss, both she and the child are afraid of losing face and in the end brute force settles it.

"We found rather a lot of mothers who were shocked at themselves. They didn't know they had these wells of violence until they had children. Some apologized to their children, or explained that they were in a 'low state'; some went through a bad phase, over a second baby or when they were overworked, and started hitting hard, perhaps for six months, and then stopped short, shocked at what they were doing when they saw their children becoming frightened of them. There's a lot of self-criticism, and they make resolutions not to do it again.

"Some say they feel violence 'coming on,' and occasionally at this point they will go out of the room, away from the child, to cool off; but others remain and then hit out. It's surprising, though, how many say that smacking doesn't seem to help much in practice but they hope it will work in the long run. When everything is getting on top of a mother she smacks more—

for instance, the mother who is coping with poor housing or a difficult marriage; if she has lots of children under her feet she is likely to smack, or if father is on shift work and she is afraid of waking him up or disturbing the neighbors. Sometimes when it's raining, and they're all cooped up, then, as one mother says, she 'moves into a smacking frame of mind.'

"A lot of mothers say, it does themselves more good than the children: 'it clears the air.' They feel a bit better afterwards, and making peace is very important. Smacking can very easily become a habit, and it tends to get worse. People say, well this hiding did no good, the next will have to be harder, and perhaps they move from the leg to the face. But there are many subtle permutations and in discussing smacking with parents it is quite clear from what they say that the degree of physical pain produced is only rarely a matter of primary importance. Normally the smack is just one element in a very complex social confrontation between parent and child. Being smacked is a threat to the child's self-esteem, and having her child disobey threatens the mother in a similar way. And both are fully aware of this. Thus the act of smacking the child is often just an emphatic gesture in a desperate attempt to communicate something to the child. It is usually accompanied by verbal reinforcement, but even if no actual word is spoken at the time, the mother intends and expects the child to know what the smack *means*. It may mean different things at different times: 'This is *wrong*, not just naughty'; 'I am just showing you what it feels like to be hit'; 'Stop ignoring me'; or 'I don't believe in smacking, but you're driving me mad.'

"Smacking isn't necessarily the worst, for it's very much a matter of what are the alternatives? I'm one of those people who don't believe in smacking, but still do it sometimes. What I've got against it is that the mother who smacks as a habit is passing on a habit of violence as the accepted way of dealing with situations. . . ."


# 16. Social Class Differences in
# Parents' Use of Physical Punishment
## HOWARD S. ERLANGER

The amount and frequency of physical punishment described in the previous article seems to be roughly similar for England and the United States, and so do the type of situations which lead to use of physical punishment. However, the review of American studies in the following article suggests that the tendency for physical punishment to increase as one goes down the socioeconomic status ladder is more marked in Britain than in the United States. This article, in fact, questions the conclusions which social scientists have tended to make about social class difference in physical punishment in the United States. Erlanger gives a more complete and systematic tabulation

SOURCE: Prepared for this book from part of a more detailed technical article by Howard S. Erlanger, "On the Incidence and Consequences of the Use of Corporal Punishment in Child Rearing—A Critique."

of the American studies than has been available up to now. On the basis of this careful analysis, he concludes that although there are class differences, they are not large. He particularly stresses the fact that it is not correct to conclude from these differences that lower class persons "typically" use physical punishment to control children, whereas middle class persons "typically" use other means. In short, Erlanger warns us of a tendency in social science to create and use misleading stereotypes about social classes.

Sociologists interested in an overview of social class variations in child rearing often turn to a comprehensive review article by Bronfenbrenner,[1] whose conclusion on methods of punishment is: "The most consistent finding documented is the more frequent use of physical punishment by working class parents. The middle class, in contrast, resort to reasoning, isolation, and . . . 'love oriented' discipline techniques" (1958: 419). This paper will critically examine the empirical evidence on this assertion.

Most statements on the relationship between social status (class or race) and techniques of punishment imply the existence of a *strong relationship* between those variables. At a minimum, spanking is thought to be a much more frequent occurrence in lower class and black families than in middle or upper class white families. But often something more fundamental is implied by these statements, and social groups are *characterized* as to methods of punishment. The task here is to move away from the stereotypes and attempt to estimate the actual extent of difference between social classes in the use of physical punishment. Unfortunately, this is not an easy task, since very few thorough studies have been carried out. These studies use divergent indicators of class and of punishment techniques, and all are limited by their reliance on some form of survey questionnaire. Many problems of comparability are discussed by Bronfenbrenner (1958: 404–406) and such discussion will not be repeated here; the limits of questionnaire data as compared to observational data are obvious. It is clear then, that no definitive answer to the question can be given. Nonetheless, it is worthwhile to assess whether the prevailing conclusions are consistent with the available data.

The chart on p. 152, "Findings of Major Studies of Punishment Techniques," displays representative findings from all readily accessible studies published between 1936 and 1970. The data in this chart suggests that the relationship between social class and the use of spanking is relatively weak. Bronfenbrenner's conclusion was based on an examination of the first six studies in the chart. But only three of those studies found significance at the .05 level, while at least two samples had a *reversed* relationship. The addition of two studies not available to Bronfenbrenner only serves to further cloud the issue.[2] Moreover, examination of the percentage differences shows

---

[1]Bronfenbrenner's article is reprinted in Lipset and Bendix's widely used reader on social stratification.

[2]In addition, Eron *et al.*—in a study done in Columbia County, New York in 1960— found that parents did not differ by occupational group in their use of psychological or physical punishment for direct aggression in their children (1971, 128). A North Carolina study by Bowerman and Elder (1963) is not shown in the chart because of its weak indicator of punishment technique. The study, primarily concerned with the effects of family size, found no clear relationship between father's occupation and the use of corporal punishment.

Findings of Major Studies of Punishment Techniques

| Study Reference | Study Sample and year of Field Work | % Favoring Physical Punishment ( ) = number on which % is based | | Significance Level | Percentage Point Difference |
|---|---|---|---|---|---|
| Anderson (1936) | National (1932) | upper/upper 61% (283) | lower/lower 78% (165) | <.001 | −17 |
| | | (Indicator: Was child spanked in last month?) | | | |
| Davis and Havighurst (1946) | Chicago (1943) | middle 53% (45) | lower 51% (47) | n.s. | +2 |
| | | (Indicator: What is the most successful way to get a child to obey?) | | | |
| Sears, et al. (1957) Maccoby and Gibbs (1954) | Newton/ Roxbury (1951–2) | upper middle 17% (198) | upper lower 33% (174) | <.001 | −16 |
| | | (Indicator: not specified) | | | |
| | | upper middle 3.9 (198) | upper lower 4.8 (174) | .01 | (0.9 point on scale of 9) |
| | | (Indicator is score, based on scale of 9, where 9 = physical punishment very often used) | | | |
| Miller and Swanson (1958, 1960) | Detroit (1953) (a) | upper middle 15% (33) | lower/lower 31% (65) | <.10 | −16 |
| | | (Indicator: Suppose your child of 10 were to do something you feel is very wrong, something you warned him against doing . . .) | | | |
| | (b) | middle 11% (38) | working 52% (77) | <.001 | −41 |
| | (c) | middle 16% (57) | working 34% (48) | <.05 | −18 |
| | | (Indicator: Here are some ways parents have of punishing their children. Which of these do you use most?) | | | |
| Littman, et al. (1957) | Eugene (1950) | father-child middle 19% (85) | lower 15% (121) | n.s. | +4 |
| | | mother-child middle 12% (85) | lower 13% (121) | n.s. | −1 |
| | | (Indicator: based on use of physical punishment as "primary mode" of punishment) | | | |

| Kahn (1969) | | | | | | |
|---|---|---|---|---|---|---|
| Washington D.C. (1956) | mother-son middle | 14% (79) | working | 16% (82) | n.s. | − 2 |
| | mother-daughter middle | 9% (75) | working | 16% (77) | n.s. | − 7 |
| | (Indicator: Report that physical punishment is used occasionally// frequently versus infrequently) | | | | | |
| Heinstein (n.d., ca 1956) | mother-son college educ. | 58% (80) | no college | 52% (352) | n.s. | + 6 |
| State of Calif. (1956) | mother-daughter college educ. | 44% (72) | no college | 51% (304) | n.s. | − 7 |
| Contra Costa County (1956) | mother-son college educ. | 49% (88) | no college | 53% (321) | n.s. | − 4 |
| | mother-daughter college educ. | 38% (96) | no college | 55% (288) | < .01 | − 17 |
| | (Indicator: physical punishment as usual method of punishment) | | | | | |
| McKinley (1964) | mother-child upper | 40% (62) | lower | 47% (92) | n.s. | − 7 |
| Boston Area (1959) | father-child upper | 33% (72) | lower | 49% (92) | < .05 | − 16 |
| | (Indicator: use of "relatively severe techniques of discipline") | | | | | |

(a) Reported in Miller and Swanson. (1958)

(b) Reported as "Sample I" in Miller and Swanson (1960).

(c) Reported as "Sample II" in Miller and Swanson (1960). In both samples, the proportion of respondents favoring a mixed approach of psychological and corporal was also greater for the working class.

(d) Among grade school educated mothers, the percent using corporal punishment was markedly *lower* than that shown for the non-college educated group as a whole.

N.B. Except for the California samples when data for more than two classes are reported, only those for the *two most extreme classes* are shown in the chart.

a range of + 6 (middle class *more* likely to use corporal punishment) to − 41 (working class more likely), with a mode around − 16 and a mean of about − 12 (mean and mode computed by sample, not by row). Given the number of samples and these findings, *the best conclusion is that there is indeed some relationship between class and punishment technique, but that is probably not strong enough to be of great theoretical or practical significance.*[3]

*Trend Over Time.* Looking over the data in this chart, it seems that the most consistent finding is *not* the difference between social classes, but rather that the relatively small difference appears in almost all the samples, independent of time. In addition, there *may* be evidence of a trend away from spanking at *all* social levels. Anderson found that in 1930 over 61 per cent of the parents in *all* classes had spanked their child in the previous month, while in the 1950's and 1960's the proportion of parents who consider spanking to be their usual or most effective method of punishment is considerably lower. Moreover, irrespective of the data at hand, there are good theoretical reasons to postulate a shift over time, as Miller and Swanson (1958) have done.[4] However, one should be very cautious about concluding that such a trend exists, since Anderson's indicator is not really comparable to the others. Heinstein's California data (1964), for instance, show a quite high use of spanking (albeit on young children); and in the data on self-reported socialization experiences discussed below, there is no evidence that the older respondents (i.e., those brought up at an earlier point in history) experienced more physical punishment.

SOME LIMITED NEW DATA

A 1968 survey which contained some limited items on corporal punishment is valuable because of its national sample. The survey instrument was designed for the National Commission on the Causes and Prevention of Violence by several sociologists and political scientists under the general supervision of Dr. Sandra Ball; the actual data collection was done by Louis Harris Associates.[5] The sample included 1176 adults (941 whites, 195 blacks, 40 other non-whites) over age 18, in 100 clusters in all parts of the United States.

*Personal Experiences.* Here as elsewhere, the analysis of the sample will be hindered by lack of adequate indicators. The respondent's experiences as a child are indicated by a single item, "As a child, were you spanked frequently, sometimes, or never?"; his class or origin is indicated by an even weaker item, "What (class) would you say your family was when you were

---

[3]On balance, perhaps 1 or 2 per cent of the variance is explained. On the other hand, the finding is not irrelevant, given that social class may still be one of the best predictors we have. The lack of clear relationships between class and child-rearing techniques is also evident with other aspects of child-rearing, such as feeding and toilet training. See, for example, Bronfenbrenner (1958, *passim*) or Heinstein (1964, *passim*).

[4]See also Bronfenbrenner (1958). For a critique of the conclusiveness of Miller and Swanson's findings on the cause of change, see Haber (1962).

[5]Permission to use the data was granted by James McEvoy III.

growing up—middle class or working class?" The difficulties with these items are many and obvious, and need not be outlined. What is surprising, however, is that when these items are cross-tabulated (Table 1), the resulting frequencies are quite compatible with those reported in the chart on p. 152.[6] Most important, the percentage-point differences between the classes are about the mean for the chart. Table 1 also presents some data for blacks; limited though they are, they are just about the only data available. Of the studies reviewed above, Davis and Havingshurst's (1946) is the only one which separates the findings by race. Their conclusion is compatible with the data shown here: insofar as there are differences between the races they seem to be at least in part related to class.[7]

*Table 1. Per Cent Who Were Spanked Frequently as a Child by Race and Parent's Class*

| | % who were spanked frequently for: | |
| --- | --- | --- |
| *Parent's Class* | *Whites* | *Blacks* |
| Middle class | 23 | 29[a] |
| | (N = 298) | (N = 17) |
| Working class | 34 | 44 |
| | (N = 603) | (N = 165) |
| Total | 30.0 | 42.6 |
| | (N = 941) | (N = 145) |
| Percentage-point difference between middle and working class | − 11 | − 15 |

[a]The stability of this percentage, based on such a small number of cases, is doubtful.

*Values.* In the Violence Commission survey, respondents were first asked whether they approved of spanking in general, and if they did, were then asked about four specific instances in which a parent might strike a child. The items are these: (a) Are there any situations that you can imagine in which you would approve of a parent spanking his or her child, assuming the child is healthy and over a year old? *If yes:* (b) Would you approve if the child (1) was noisy and getting on the parent's nerves; (2) had been disobedient all day; (3) had been expelled from school; (4) had broken a law? In each case, the respondent could reply "Yes," "No," or "Not sure."

[6]Virtually no respondents reported that they were never spanked, so these rates are not shown separately.

[7]Controls for sex and age did not affect the findings, and region of origin was not asked. However, there is evidence that *religion* may be a factor of importance. White Baptists (three-fourths of whom were raised in working-class homes) have a rate of 47 per cent, as compared to a rate of about 30 per cent for all other Christian groups. This is slightly higher than the rate for blacks (about one-half of whom were raised as Baptists), but the black rate is generally high for all religious groups.

*Table 2. Per Cent Who Would Approve of Spanking, by Education and Race, for Parents with Children Under 18*

| Score on Index | A. WHITES | | | | | |
|---|---|---|---|---|---|---|
| | Grade School | Some H.S. | H.S. Grad. | Some Coll. | Coll. Grad. | Post Grad. |
| 0 | 16 | 5 | 3 | 4 | 0 | 4 |
| 1–4 | 44 | 49 | 56 | 63 | 50 | 56 |
| 5–6 | 40 | 46 | 41 | 33 | 50 | 40 |
| N | (43) | (89) | (193) | (92) | (36) | (28) |

| Score on Index | B. BLACKS | | | |
|---|---|---|---|---|
| | Grade School[a] | Some H.S. | H.S. Grad. | All Coll.[a] |
| 0 | 0 | 0 | 3 | 23 |
| 1–4 | 21 | 37 | 50 | 46 |
| 5–6 | 79 | 63 | 47 | 31 |
| N | (14) | (41) | (30) | (13) |

[a]The stability of these percentages, based on such a small number of cases, is doubtful.

An index of approval of spanking was constructed by scoring item (a) and items (b-1) and (b-2) 0 for a reply of "No," 1 for "Not sure," [8] and 2 for "Yes." The resulting index has a range of 0–6.

Contrary to popular belief, poorly educated whites are the only group of parents with a high rate of outright rejection of spanking. Fifteen per cent of parents in this group, as compared to no more than 5 per cent of parents at any other level of education, score 0 on the index (see row 0 in Tables 2A and B). The distribution of index scores for adults without children (not shown) is similar. The highest rate of rejection of spanking for any college-educated subgroup is for those with postgraduate education, but even here the rate is only 9 per cent, and is based on less than 20 per cent of the college-educated respondents.[9]

## SPANKING AND CHILD ABUSE

One of the most unfortunate peripheral effects of the assertion that corporal punishment is rooted in "subcultural" differences is the notion that child

[8]The rate of "Not sure" is highest for item (b-1) at 6 per cent of the sample. Contrary to the usual pattern of "Don't know" responses, the rate is about constant for all social groups. The only exception is for the black *middle* class which has a rate of 15 per cent.

[9]One question which arises is whether the anti-spanking response reflects a new "permissive" trend. Two factors suggest that it does not. First, we would expect the better educated groups, rather than the poorly educated, to be the vanguard of "extreme Spock." Second, and most important, further analysis shows that when the relationship is controlled for age, it is *older.*

abuse is but an extreme instance of the emphasis on corporal punishment. Thus Gil (1970), in his important book on child abuse, argues that since both spanking and abuse are both predominantly found in families of low SES (socioeconomic status), the former is a major cause of the latter. In support of his statement that there is a strong association between low status and the use of physical means in disciplining children, Gil cites only Miller and Swanson's second 1953 sample. The chart on p. 152 shows that this particular sample had by far the most extreme finding in forty years of research.

Gil's comprehensive review of official data on abuse shows that nationwide, about 50 per cent of the families of abused children had income of less than $5,000, versus about 25 per cent of the U.S. population. About 60 per cent of the families had received some form of public aid during or prior to the year of abuse, and 40 per cent were on AFDC or other public assistance at the time of the abuse. The predominance of low-income families in the official data on abuse undoubtedly is in part related to their high visibility, but the extent of serious problems in families of reported offenders suggests that more than mere visibility is at work.

The data in Gil's study suggest that much serious abuse takes place *not* in the *lower* class, but in what might be described as an *underclass* of American society. Most of his findings are dramatic enough to suggest that child abuse takes place in families caught in a tangle of individual and social problems. Under these circumstances the occurrence of child abuse—although abhorrent—is not a particularly surprising outcome. The data indicate that eradication of corporal methods of child rearing would *not* have much effect on abuse, while social action to change life circumstances would probably have a significant effect.

There are no systematic data available on child abusers' usual punishment techniques, but Gil's data does indicate that mistreatment of children finds no support among the mass of low-status parents. In a nationwide survey of 1500 adults, he found that low-status persons are just as concerned about child abuse as high-status persons, and that low-status parents favor more strict measures to help abused children, such as removal from the home. Over 90 per cent of the respondents of all social classes indicated that they would take steps to remedy the situation if they knew of parents who abused their child. About 58 per cent of the respondents agreed that "almost anyone could at some time injure a child in his care, and 34 per cent of males under 55 thought that they could at some time intentionally injure a child." Given that the propensity to abuse is fairly evenly distributed in the population, while actual abuse is heavily skewed towards the very bottom of the social order, the most plausible explanation at this time seems to be a resource model of child abuse. Put briefly, when a middle class parent feels tense or quick tempered, he generally has access to medical or professional help, or the resources to take a break and "get away from it all"; it hardly seems necessary to add that unemployed parents of large families do not have these opportunities. Values, child-rearing practices, or parent's socialization experiences may play an ancillary role, but the root of the problem of child abuse seems to lie primarily in structural factors.[10] Emphasis on other factors serves only to individualize what is essentially a social problem.[11]

REFERENCES

Anderson, John E.
1936    *The Young Child in the Home.* White House Conference on Child Health and Protection, Committee on the Infant and Pre-school Child. New York: Appleton-Century.
Bowerman, Charles E. and Glen H. Elder, Jr.
1963    "Family Structure and Child-Rearing Patterns: The Effect of Family Size and Sex Composition." *American Sociological Review* 28: 891–905.
Bronfenbrenner, Urie
1958    "Socialization and Social Class Through Time and Space," in E. C. Maccoby, T. M. Newcomb, and E. L. Hartley (eds.), *Readings in Social Psychology,* third edition. New York: Holt, Rinehart, and Winston.
Davis, A. and R. J. Havingshurst
1946    "Social Class and Color Differences in Childrearing," *American Sociological Review* 11: 698–710.
Eron, Leonard D., Leopold O. Walder and Monroe M. Lefkowitz
1971    *Learning of Aggression in Children.* Boston: Little Brown.
Gil, David G.
1970    *Violence Against Children.* Cambridge: Harvard University Press.
Haber, Lawrence D.
1962    "Age and Integration Setting: A Reappraisal of The Changing American Parent," *American Sociological Review* 27: 682–689.
Heinstein, Martin
1964    *Childrearing in California.* California State Department of Public Health, Bureau of Maternal and Child Health. Berkeley.
Kohn, Melvin
1969    *Class and Conformity, A Study in Values.* Homewood, Ill.: Dorsey Press.
Littman, Richard A., Robert C. A. Moore and John Pierce-Jones
1957    "Social Class Differences in Childrearing: A Third Community for Comparison with Chicago and Newton," *American Sociological Review,* Vol. XXII, No. 6, pp. 694–704.
Maccoby, Eleanor E. and Patricia K. Gibbs
1964    "Methods of Childrearing in Two Social Classes," in Martin and Standler, pp. 380–96.
McKinley, Donald G.
1964    *Social Class and Family Life.* New York: The Free Press.
Miller, Daniel R. and Guy E. Swanson
1958    *The Changing American Parent.* New York: John Wiley.
Miller, Daniel R. and Guy E. Swanson
1960    *Inner Conflict and Defense.* New York: Henry Holt.
Sears, Robert R., Eleanor E. Maccoby and Harry Levin
1957    *Patterns of Child Rearing.* Evanston, Ill.: Row, Peterson and Co.

[10]The finding that child abuse breeds more child abuse would invalidate this statement only if one wishes to argue that abuse constitutes a form of child-rearing. I find it difficult to accept such reasoning; instead, I would see this pattern as part of a cycle of pathology, with it being largely the product of structural factors.

[11]Of course, this is not to say that treatment or immediate intervention should not be on an individual level.

# 17. Some Social Antecedents of Physical Punishment: A Linkage Theory Interpretation
## MURRAY A. STRAUS

A theme repeatedly emphasized in our choice of articles and in the introductions is the idea that violence between family members is influenced by social structural patterns which transcend individual differences. This idea is central to the system diagram on p. 18 ("System Model of Intra-Family Violence"). This article, and the article which follows by Suzanne Steinmetz, illustrate the way in which the use of violence in the family is influenced by the position of the family in the larger social system, specifically in the economic and occupational structure of society. The first of the articles concludes that the use of physical punishment is linked to the parents' perception of the kind of world the child will live in as an adult. Those parents who see the child as becoming a white collar rather than a blue collar worker will, according to this theory, tend to use the non-violent modes of social influence which are the norm for the white collar world.

The two studies are also of interest because they destroy the notion that physical punishment is restricted to young children. Both in the original study and in the two Steinmetz replications (see p. 166), just over half of the children were either hit or threatened with hitting during their senior year in high school!

Research on the issue of parental use of reward and punishment has focused almost entirely on the question of the consequences for the child of varying patterns and amounts of reward and punishment. A considerable body of research, for example, has found that children who have experienced large amounts of physical punishment tend to be highly aggressive. The irony of these findings is that these studies also find that the most frequent occasion for physical punishment is to control aggression on the part of the child (see the reviews of this literature in Becker, 1964, and Feshbach, 1970). Similarly, although the evidence is not as clear, there are indications that parental attempts to control excessive dependency by punishment tend to *increase* rather than decrease dependency by the child (Maccoby and Masters, 1970: 142–144). Finally, there is evidence that the use of punishment, especially physical punishment, tends to produce a child who is relatively low in internalized moral standards and self-directedness (Hoffman, 1970; Kohlberg, 1964).

Much remains to be done to establish such findings more firmly, and especially to test theories concerning the mediating processes which produce these effects. But even more needs to be done to determine the types of parents and the circumstances which lead to the use of corporal punishment. Such knowledge is, of course, needed to round out our theoretical understanding of the inner workings of the family. But, in addition, an understanding of the social and psychological antecedents of the use of corporal

SOURCE: Abridged with permission from *Journal of Marriage and the Family* 33 (November, 1971): 658–663.

punishment can have important practical applications. This would be the case if as the evidence seems to suggest, the predominant effects of corporal punishment on the child are negative. To the extent that this is the case, we would want to reduce or eliminate the use of physical punishment. One approach is to inform parents of these negative consequences. But if we do not understand the underlying social and psychological dynamics which lead to the use of physical punishment, such appeals are likely to have limited effectiveness. If, on the other hand, we have the knowledge to give parents an understanding of why physical punishment is used, the insight which such knowledge provides can aid parents in altering patterns of child rearing.

## SAMPLE AND METHOD

The study reported in this paper used data on a sample of 229 university students in undergraduate sociology classes at the University of Minnesota and the University of New Hampshire. The students completed an anonymous questionnaire to provide data for class research projects (Straus, 1969).

The questionnaire contained a short version of the Bronfenbrenner and Devereux "Parental Activity Index" (Devereux, 1970; Straus, 1969), including two items from their "physical punishment" score. These items were, "During your last year in high school, how often did your parents do each of the following? (a) Hit or slapped me, and (b) Threatened to hit or slap me." [1] The respondents answered separately for their father and for their mother, using response categories of never, sometimes, frequently, usually, and always or almost always, which were scored 0 to 4. The scores for the fathers were found to be highly correlated with those for the mothers (coefficient of contingency $C = .77$) and were therefore combined to form the physical punishment score used for this analysis.

As might be expected from the fact that the data refer to adolescents in the last year of high school, 47.8 per cent of the respondents reported no physical punishment or threats of physical punishment at all during their last year of high school. But the other side of the coin is more interesting: this is the fact that, even at this age, 52.3 per cent had experienced actual or threatened physical punishment. Moreover, almost one quarter of the 229 students (24.6 per cent) had scores of three or more.

We can see, then, that parental use of violence is by no means an isolated phenomenon. This fact, combined with the important consequences of phys-

[1] The last year of high school is rather late for the use of physical punishment. Had the data been gathered primarily for purposes of his analysis, an earlier age would undoubtedly have been selected. However, as previously noted, the physical punishment data are only a small part of a larger questionnaire. The time reference throughout this questionnaire for data on the family of orientation was standardized at the last year of high school. This choice was made because it is appropriate for most of the data in the questionnaire and because it was felt that an earlier time referent would pose more severe problems of recall.

It would have been desirable to consider the "actual" and "threatened" physical punishment scores separately. This was not possible because the questionnaires were no longer available and cards which were available already combined the data into a single index.

ical punishment noted in the introduction to this paper, suggested that the present data were worth pursuing despite the obvious limitations of the sample and measurement procedures.[2]

We will begin the analysis with a consideration of the extent to which physical punishment is related to the socioeconomic status of the parents and the sex of the child and then move on to data on role expectations.

## SOCIAL POSITION AND PHYSICAL PUNISHMENT

*Socioeconomic Status.* The only socialpsychological antecedent of physical punishment which has been investigated with any frequency is the socioeconomic status of the parents. Almost all of the studies we have located find that working class parents make more use of physical punishment than do middle class parents (see, for example, Bronfenbrenner, 1958; Eron *et al.*, 1963; Kohn, 1969). For the present sample, however, no significant relationship was found between socioeconomic status and use of physical punishment. The measures of socioeconomic status used for this purpose were the father's education, the mother's education, and father's occupation. None of these three cross tabulations showed important differences between socioeconomic levels, even when controls for the sex of the child were introduced. For example, the score distributions for the 122 children of nonmanual workers were 47.5 per cent scores of 0, 26.2 per cent scores of 1 or 2, and 26.2 per cent scores of 3 or more. For the 107 children of manual workers, the percentags were 48.1, 29.2 and 22.6.

We do not doubt the previous studies and, at the same time, we have sufficient confidence in the present data to preclude dismissing this finding as simply a measurement or other error.[3] Consequently, some explanation which fits both sets of findings seems necessary. We believe that what can be called a "linkage theory" of socialization subsumes both sets of findings.

The linkage theory hypothesizes that socialization practices will tend to be congruent with the type of personality needed to cope with the typical life circumstances which the child will face as an adult. This theory is exemplified in the work of Inkeles (1960) and Kohn (1963, 1969). Both Inkeles and Kohn hold that working class child rearing practices reflect the life conditions of the different social classes. It follows that if working class parents experience more physical violence and aggression and have less opportunity for self-directedness than do middle class parents, their child rearing patterns should be congruent with this fact. Moreover, to the extent that use of physical punishment produces a child who is relatively high in overt aggression and low in internalized moral standards and self-direction, and to the extent that these traits are characteristic of working class communi-

---

[2]A further caution for the reader to bear in mind is that this is a purely exploratory study. The selection of variables for analysis was, of course, guided by an informal judgment that the characteristic indexed by that variable was likely to be related to the use of physical punishment. However, no formal hypotheses were developed prior to the analysis, and all theoretical statements are in the form of *post factum* interpretations.

[3]Since this paper was written, Suzanne K. Steinmetz replicated part of this study on a sample at other universities and found almost identical percentages (see her article which follows this paper).

ties, it can be said that the use of physical punishment is an appropriate pattern of socialization for working class children.

Obviously, however, such a pattern is dysfunctional for working class children who will be upwardly mobile, such as those in the present sample. Consequently, it does not seem too far-fetched to suggest that working class parents who anticipate social mobility for their child, such as is occurring for the children in this sample, tend to adopt the socialization patterns characteristic of the class to which they aspire for their children. Such a phenomenon would be similar to the anticipatory socialization findings from other research. For example, the Kinsey data show that upwardly mobile individuals tend, prior to mobility, to have the sexual behavior patterns of the stratum into which they eventually move (Lindenfeld, 1960; Kinsey, 1948) and Turner (1964) has shown that adolescents who desire to move up the occupational ladder tend to take on the attitudes and values characteristic of their stratum of destination rather than those of the stratum from which they originated.[4]

*Sex of Child.* The linkage theory also fits the data on sex differences in the use of physical punishment. Specifically, the life conditions of women involve far less physical violence and aggression than is characteristic of men, and women are known to have stronger internaliped moral standards than men (seven of the eight studies reviewed by Maccoby, 1966: 347). Hence, to the extent that societies tend to evolve socialization practices which are linked to or congruent with the adult life conditions which will be faced by the child, we should expect that far less physical punishment would be used on girls than boys. The case of girls is especially appropriate because, in a sense, it is easier to use physical punishment on adolescent girls than boys since there is less danger of parental violence being met by violent resistance on the part of the child. The findings for the present sample show such a pattern of sex differences. In fact, the scores for the boys are roughly double those for the girls. The mean physical punishment score for the boys was 3.02 compared to only 1.85 for the girls.[5] Thus, the scores for boys were about double those for girls.

[4]It should be recognized that this interpretation depends on the *assumption* that a representative sample (as opposed to a college sample) would show physical punishment to be greater among the working class. Moreover, the interpretation would not be tenable if the middle class parents in this sample were *more* prone to use physical punishment than other middle class parents. The latter possibility seems unlikely in view of the Steinmetz data (see her commentary), but we cannot rule out the possibility that physical punishment at this age does not differ by class in more representative samples. Unfortunately, there are no data available to answer this question since the social class comparison studies I know of all refer to younger children and the differences they report might not apply at this age.

[5]As noted in footnote 2, this is an exploratory study for which no a priori hypotheses were formulated. Consequently, the meaning of tests of significance applied to these data is not clear. Nevertheless, statistical tests were computed for all the findings reported, and all produced p values of .05 or less. In view of the questions which can be raised about the appropriateness of such tests, and to save space, we will not report the actual chi-square and p values. However, for illustrative purposes, the 2 by 6 chi-square computed to compare the distributions of the boys parental punitiveness scores with those for the girls resulted in a chi-square of 17.758 which, with five degrees of freedom, gives a p of less than .003).

## ROLE EXPECTATIONS AND EXPLANATIONS

Although the data on the relationship of the socioeconomic status of the parents and the sex of the child are consistent with the linkage theory, by themselves they provide only weak support for the theory. This is because the linkage theory interpretation rests on two assumptions which have not been demonstrated. The first assumption is that the stratum of society which the parents hope the child will occupy as an adult, and the sex of the child, influence the traits parents visualize as desirable for a child.[6] The second assumption is that these conceptions of desired traits, in turn, influence the socialization practices employed by parents. In diagrammatic form, these assumptions are:

| A | | B | | C |
|---|---|---|---|---|
| Parent's perception of child's adult sex and social class roles | $\longrightarrow$ | Traits desired by parents in child | $\longrightarrow$ | Socialization practices |

The data available for this sample do not permit us to test the first of these assumptions (A to B). But fortunately, this is the more intuitively plausible of the two. We do have data which can be examined for consistency with the second assumption (B to C). We will do this by determining the extent to which differences in the personality traits parents value for their child are associated with the use of physical punishment.

*Traits Desired by Parents.* The respondents were presented with a list of seven characteristics and asked to rank them starting with the trait each parent felt was most important for the child to have when he or she was in high school.[7] Separate rankings were made for the father and the mother.

The results for the father and the mother are very similar. Those respondents who indicated that the most important trait for them to have was "That I obey my parents well," experienced the highest frequency of physical punishment. The mean physical punishment scores were 3.26 for the 30 fathers who considered this the most important characteristic, and 3.18 for the 35 mothers who considered this the most important characteristic.

At the other end of the scale, the lowest frequency of physical punishment was reported by those whose parents valued most "That I have self-control." The mean physical punishment score is 1.50 for the fathers who held this view and ·1.13 for the mothers. But these figures are tenuous because only four fathers and eight mothers were reported as viewing self-control as the most important trait for the child to have. However, similar conclusions can be drawn from the item "That I think for myself." Fifty-eight of the fathers and 46 of the mothers were reported as attaching

---

[6]The validity of this theory depends on working class parents having enough knowledge of middle class life styles and values to be able to envision traits which are appropriate for a child who will move into this stratum. There is considerable evidence that they do have this knowledge. See for example, Rodman, 1963, 1968.

[7]The items used were That I work hard, That I think for myself, That I be considerate of others, That I obey my parents well, That I be dependable, That I have self control, That I be popular with other children, and That I be able to defend myself.

greatest importance to this trait and these same parents also had the second lowest average physical punishment scores (1.88 for the fathers and 1.47 for the mothers).

These findings fill a gap in the chain of evidence because they show that family to family variation in the value placed on "thinking for oneself" and "self-control" is related to variation in the use of physical punishment as predicted by the linkage theory. Overall, then, these findings seem to be a remarkable example of the accuracy of "folk psychology" and pedogogy and of the functional linkage or consistency between the macro structure of society, the structure of the family, and family socialization practices.

## SUMMARY AND CONCLUSIONS

The linkage theory hypothesizes that socialization practices will tend to be congruent with the type of personality needed to cope with the typical life circumstances which the child will face as an adult. In the case of children who will occupy the same or similar positions in society as their parents, these life circumstances are, of course, those faced by the parents. But if the parents anticipate social mobility for the child, the socialization practices will be congruent with the conditions of life in the stratum of destination rather than the stratum into which the child is born. The findings which seem to fit the theory are the following:

1. Contrary to the large number of studies which have reported greater use of physical punishment by working class parents as compared to middle class parents, no such difference was found for this sample. This finding fits the linkage theory because all the children in the sample who are of working class origin are well on their way to upward mobility by virtue of being university students.

2. The physical punishment scores for the girls are only half those for the boys. This is consistent with the linkage theory because the life conditions of girls involves far less physical violence than is true of boys, while at the same time women have stronger internalized moral standards.

3. Parents who were reported as feeling that the most important behavioral characteristic for their child during his last year in high school is to "be obedient" to them used more physical punishment than parents holding any other trait as of primary importance. At the other end, parents who felt that either "self-control" or a child who "thinks for himself" is most important, used physical punishment least often. These findings support the linkage theory because the available evidence suggests that the use of physical punishment tends to produce a child who is low in self-directedness. Thus, the use of physical punishment by parents who value obedience in a child is, in fact, likely to produce a child who lacks internalized direction and hence is more amenable to external controls. '

Overall, the findings of this study are remarkably consistent with linkage theories of socialization such as those of Inkeles and Kohn. At the same time, the reader must bear in mind the limitations of the sample and the data. Even more important, data are needed to directly test the assumed linking mechanisms. Many questions can be raised about the plausibility of assuming that working class parents who anticipate upward mobility for a child will somehow use the kind of child rearing which will produce personality types appropriate for the stratum of destination, especially when many middle class parents do not use such techniques. Clearly, further research is needed on these issues using samples and data which are better suited to testing the theoretical issues which have been brought to the fore by the analysis of the present data.

## REFERENCES

Becker, Wesley C.
  1964    "Consequences of Different Kinds of Parental Discipline." Pp. 169–208 in
          Martin L. Hoffman and Lois Wladis Hoffman (eds.), *Review of Child Development Research*. New York: Russell Sage Foundation.
Bronfenbrenner, U.
  1958    "Socialization and Social Class Through Time and Space." Pp. 400–425 in
          E. E. Maccoby, T. M. Newcomb, and E. L. Hartley (eds.), *Readings in Social Psychology*, third edition. New York: Holt, Rinehart, and Winston.
Devereux, Edward C., Jr.
  1970    "Socialization in Cross-Cultural Perspective." Chapter 4 in Reuben Hill and
          Rene Konig (eds.), *Families in East and West*. Paris: Mouton.
Eron, L. D., L. O. Walder, R. Toigo, and M. M. Lefkowitz
  1963    "Social Class Parental Punishment for Aggression, and Child Aggression."
          *Child Development* 34 (4): 849–867.
Feshbach, Seymour
  1970    "Aggression." Chapter 22 in Paul H. Mussen (ed.), *Carmichael's Manual of Child Psychology*, third edition. New York: John Wiley and Sons.
Hoffman, Martin L.
  1970    "Moral Development." Chapter 28 in Paul H. Mussen (ed.), *Carmichael's Manual of Child Psychology*, third edition. New York: John Wiley and Sons.
Inkeles, Alex
  1960    "Industrial Man: The Relation of Status to Experience, Perception and
          Value." *American Journal of Sociology* 66 (July): 1–31.
Kinsey, A. C. *et al.*
  1948    *Sexual Behavior in the Human Male*. Philadelphia: W. B. Saunders.
Kohlberg, Lawrence
  1964    "Development of Moral Character and Moral Ideology." Pp. 383–432 in
          Martin L. Hoffman and Lois Wladis Hoffman (eds.), *Review of Child Development Research*. New York: Russell Sage Foundation.
Kohn, Melvin L.
  1963    "Social Class and Parent-Child Relationship: An Interpertation." *American Journal of Sociology* 68 (January): 471–480.
  1969    *Class and Conformity*. Homewood, Illinois: Dorsey Press.
Lindenfeld, Frank
  1960    "A Note on Social Mobility, Religiousity, and Students' Attitudes Toward
          Premarital Sexual Relations." *American Sociological Review* 25 (February):
          81–84.
Maccoby, Eleanor (ed.)
  1966    *The Development of Sex Differences*. Stanford, California: Stanford University Press.
Maccoby, Eleanor and John C. Masters
  1970    "Attachment and Dependency." Chapter 21 in Paul H. Mussen (ed.),
          *Carmichael's Manual of Child Psychology*, third edition. New York: John Wiley and Sons.
Rodman, Hyman
  1963    "The Lower-Class Value Stretch." *Social Forces* 42 (December): 205–215.
  1968    "Family and Social Pathology in the Ghetto." *Science* 161 (August 23):
          756–762.

Straus, Murray A.
  1969a    *Family Analysis.* Chicago: Rand McNally.
  1969b    *Family Measurement Techniques.* Minneapolis: University of Minnesota
           Press.
Turner, Ralph H.
  1964     *The Social Context of Ambition.* San Francisco: Chandler.

# 18. Occupational Environment in Relation to Physical Punishment and Dogmatism

## SUZANNE K. STEINMETZ

The study below, like the previous one, examines differences between occupational groups in the use of physical punishment. However, in this study Steinmetz goes beyond a simple dichotomy of working class versus middle class and looks at an aspect of occupation which seems to have more relevance for child rearing. The aspect she examines is what Holland (1959) calls the "occupational environment." This is the extent to which the father's occupation requires certain types of skills such as verbal ability, motor skills, or interpersonal skills. These characteristics of the father's occupation exert a pervasive influence on his behavior, including his family life. In particular, the study shows that the occupational environment a father is in makes a difference in the extent to which physical punishment is used. Steinmetz's study also found that the dogmatism (or closed mindedness) of children is significantly related to the father's occupational environment. The findings are particularly impressive because they held up in two different samples of students in two different regions of the country.

In one of the most important recent studies of the relationship between social structure and socialization, Kohn (1969) concludes that child-rearing techniques are congruent with the tasks which are required in the parents' occupation. He states: "Occupational experience helps structure men's view not only of the occupational world, but of social reality in general" (1969: 164). Thus, parents attempt to prepare their offspring to live within the social reality with which they are familiar, and the socialization techniques which they use are directly influenced by their occupational experiences.

Although Kohn found distinct social class differences, other studies seem to indicate that differences in socialization between the middle and working class are moderate (Litwak, 1960), and that the remaining gaps are rapidly narrowing (Bronfenbrenner, 1959).

In a recent study Straus (1971) found no differences between college students from middle and working class families in their parents' use of physical punishment. He developed a linkage theory which suggested that the working class parents of these upwardly mobile college students were using socialization techniques which were aimed at preparing their children for

SOURCE: This article is based on a paper presented at the 67th annual meeting of the American Sociological Association, August 28–31, 1972.

the class of destination (middle class) and therefore reflected the values of the middle class rather than those of the working class. This would seem logical in that the respondents were currently college students and therefore destined to middle class status.

There are two troublesome aspects to this study, however. First, although Straus found no social class differences between his two sample groups of college students, better than 50 per cent of *both* his middle class and working class sample reported use or threat of use of physical punishment. This finding cannot be taken as evidence of the prevalence of "middle class," love-oriented, non-physical punishment forms of discipline. Second, although anticipatory socialization may be an adequate explanation for working class parents who use middle class child-rearing techniques, it does not explain the over 50 per cent of the middle class sample who use physical punishment—a technique which is generally considered to be characteristic of the working class or lower class rather than the middle class.

The high level of reported physical punishment, plus the lack of a class difference in the use of physical punishment, raises questions about the emphasis in Straus's paper on social class differences. Consequently, in a comment on that paper (Steinmetz, 1971), it was suggested that the reason for these findings may be that the widely used classification of middle class versus working class may no longer be an important basis of differentiation in American society, particularly as it bears on socialization techniques. More specifically, it was suggested that:

. . . with the increased affluence and technological complexity of society, the dichotomy of manual versus non-manual may no longer validly serve as a basis for differentiating life styles and especially child rearing patterns. . . .

Even with education and occupational title held constant, there are differences inherent within the framework of one's occupation which may show a closer relationship to child rearing patterns. For example, consider three mechanical engineers, all with a M.S. degree. One engineer is a theoretically oriented college professor, another is in an executive administrative position, and the third is employed in a large factory installation and spends much of his time actually working with and redesigning machinery. . . .

On a traditional social class index such as Hollingshead-Redlich two factor index, all three engineers would be given the same social class. But the tasks required by their particular jobs, which (in line with Kohn's theory) are considered to influence the way they socialize their children, differ considerably.

These considerations led to a pilot study to test alternative ways of looking at linkages between the occupational system and socialization. This study was based on the assumption that the present nature of American society makes it essential to use a conceptualization which more accurately reflects what might be called the "demand" characteristics of an occupation. That is, rather than focusing on such factors as prestige and income (as does social class), what is needed is a set of categories which are based on the actual tasks or behaviors required for persons in a given occupation. One such conceptualization is the idea of "occupational environment" put forth by Holland (1959).

The results of the first pilot study replicated Straus's findings almost exactly (Steinmetz, 1971). For example, just over half of the respondents reported parental use or threat of use of physical punishment while in their last year of high school, and there were no social class differences in the mean physical punishment scores of the parents. Also consistent with the Straus study, parents who considered "obedience" to be the most important characteristic for their child had higher physical punishment scores than parents who felt that this characteristic was less important.

More important—in contrast to the lack of class differences discovered among respondents—when the pilot study used Holland's occupational-environment categories as the independent variable, it showed clear differences in the use of physical punishment reported. In addition, since dogmatism (i.e., closed mindedness) is also a variable which has been analyzed according to social class, 15 items from the Rokeach Dogmatism scale (1960) were included in the analysis. Again, no social class differences were found in the students' dogmatism, whereas meaningful differences emerged when the occupations of the parents were categorized using Holland's occupational environments.

The findings from the pilot study therefore suggest that both socialization techniques (as exemplified by physical punishment) and socialization outcomes (as exemplified by dogmatism) are related to the occupational environment of the parents, whereas (at least in these college-student samples) social class is unrelated. Although the results of this study were theoretically interesting, the small sample size (n = 17) and the exploratory nature of the study make any findings questionable. Therefore, a second replication, using a larger sample, was carried out. This replication attempted to assess the effect of occupational demands on the socialization techniques used by the parents and, in turn, to see how these techniques affected the degree of dogmatism displayed by the students.

METHOD

A questionnaire was administered to 79 students in an undergraduate sociology class.[1] The students responded to the following question for each of their parents: "How often did each parent do the following during your last year in high school: (a) Hit or slap you? (b) Threaten to hit or slap you?"[2] Students also ranked eight traits separately for their mother and father according to the importance they thought each parent placed on each trait.[3] A fifteen-item version of the Rokeach Dogmatism scale (form E) was also included in the questionnaire (Rokeach, 1960).

[1]Although this sample probably reflects more accurately the general population than is usual in a college sample, an "accidental" sample of this nature limits the generalizability of the results.

[2]The choices for responses were: never, sometimes, frequently, usually, and almost always.

[3]The eight traits were: That I work hard; That I think for myself; That I be considerate of others; That I obey my parents well; That I be dependable; That I be popular with other children; and That I be able to defend myself.

## CLASS AND OCCUPATIONAL-ENVIRONMENT DIFFERENCES

*Class Differences.* The data again showed over 50 per cent of both working and middle class students had experienced physical punishment or its threat during their last year in high school (53 per cent of middle class; 54 per cent of working class). Part A of Table 1 also shows no class differences in either mean physical punishment or dogmatism scores of students from working class and middle class families.

*Table 1. Mean Physical Punishment and Dogmatism Scores by Social Class and Occupational Environment*

| Occupational Classification | | Physical Punishment Scores[a] | Dogmatism Scores |
|---|---|---|---|
| A. *Social Class* | | | |
| Middle class | (n = 55) | 1.36 | 36.89 |
| Working class | (n = 24) | 1.42 | 38.69 |
| | | F = 1.108, p < .30 | F = 1.661, p < .20 |
| B. *Occupational Environment* | | | |
| Persuasive | (n = 29) | 2.28 | 35.62 |
| Motoric | (n = 27) | 1.30 | 41.63 |
| Supportive | (n = 5) | 0.40 | 32.88 |
| Conforming | (n = 18) | 0.33 | 35.33 |
| | | F = 5.806, p < .001 | F = 3.219, p < .02 |

[a]Combined mother's and father's scores.

However, when students were classified according to the "demand" characteristics of their fathers' job using Holland's "occupational environments" (part B of Table 1), a different situation is revealed. In contrast to the lack of social class differences, large differences in physical punishment and smaller, but significant, differences in students' dogmatism scores are found.

The *persuasive* category (business executives, salesmen) is described by Holland as containing individuals who identify with power and strength, and who utilize physical skills and control in interpersonal relationships. It is noteworthy that parents in this category were found to have significantly higher physical punishment scores. It is also pertinent that in a list of personality characteristics of students in each occupational environment, "punishing" appears only in the persuasive environment. Furthermore, it is listed for both boys and girls (Holland, 1963b: 20).

Those individuals who are categorized as belonging to the *motoric* environment (e.g., dentists, truck drivers) prefer concrete methods of problem solving, using physical skills and strengths, but are not dominating; and they avoid interpersonal relations. Thus, although they received the next highest physical punishment score, it is considerably lower than the mean score for parents in the persuasive category.

Individuals who are in the *supportive* (e.g., school teachers, social workers) and *conforming* (e.g., accountants, clerks) environments prefer concrete methods of problem solving, utilizing verbal skills rather than physical skills and strengths. Parents in both these environments have considerably lower punishment scores.[4] (See Holland, 1959; 1963a; 1963b; 1963c for further description of personality and occupational characteristics found within each environment.)

### "OBEDIENCE" AND SUPERVISORY EXPERIENCE

As in the previous two studies (Straus, 1971; Steinmetz, 1971), students who ranked "obedience" as the trait their parents considered to be most important had higher mean physical punishment scores (1.23) than students whose parents considered this trait to be less important (0.52).

In a review of the literature, Berelson and Steiner (1964: 259) note that severe disciplinary treatment by parents, unquestioning obedience, and harsh punishment tend to produce personalities which are described as rigid or inflexible (e.g., Rokeach's "close-mindedness"). This finding was supported by analysis of the present data, which showed that parents' punishment scores were correlated highly with their children's dogmatism scores ($r = .68$; $p < .001$). In addition, the findings previously reported show that the value parents place on obedience influences the amount of physical punishment they use. Since Kohn found that the values parents hold appear to be related to their occupational experiences, it would follow, then, that if a parent highly valued obedience and his occupational experience was that of having others "obey" him (i.e., supervisory position), he would be more likely to demand obedience at home.

To test this hypothesis, the sample was divided into a "high" (supervise 5 or more) and "low" supervisory category.[5] The data in Table 2 show that within the high supervisory group there are clear differences in both physical punishment and dogmatism, depending on the extent to which the father values obedience: fathers who rank obedience first use physical punishment more (1.08 vs. 0.27) and have more dogmatic children (41.85 vs. 35.00) than do those who rank obedience lower.

However, within the low supervisory category, these differences do not appear. Similarly, within the group of families in which the father ranks obedience first, there are large differences in both the use of physical punishment and dogmatism according to the supervisory position of the father's occupation. Those in high supervisory positions tend to use more physical punishment (1.08 vs. 0.50) and to have more dogmatic children (41.85 vs.

---

[4]No respondents were categorized as being in the *esthetic* (i.e., artists, musicians) environment or *intellectual* (e.g., basic research, or theoretically-orientated professor) environment. This is not seen as seriously limiting the interpretation of the data because both working class and middle class respondents were found in each of the other four environments. A second problem involves the retrospective nature of the responses. Although recall responses may not accurately reflect the actual behavior which occurred "during the student's last year in high school," no social class differences appeared in the use or threat of use of physical punishment; yet this same data produced significant differences according to the individual's occupational environment.

[5]Although each of the four cells contained both middle and working class respondents —or persuasive, supportive, motoric, conforming respondents when categorized by occupational environment—the small number of cases precludes meaningful analysis.

*Table 2. Fathers' Physical Punishment and Students' Dogmatism Scores by Rank-ing of "Obedience" and Supervisory Experience of the Father*[a]

| | Physical punishment scores for fathers who rank "obey" | | Dogmatism scores for fathers who rank "obey" | |
|---|---|---|---|---|
| | First[b] | Not First | First | Not First |
| High Supervisory | 1.08 | 0.27 | 41.85 | 35.00 |
| | (n = 13) | (n = 31) | (n = 13) | (n = 31) |
| Low Supervisory | 0.50 | 0.39 | 33.38 | 37.87 |
| | (n = 8) | (n = 24) | (n = 8) | (n = 24) |

[a]The table above is based on father's supervisory experience, his desired traits for his child, his supervisory experience, and his physical punishment scores. There was insuffi-cient data to accurately categorize mothers' supervisory experience.

[b]When supervisory and non-supervisory experience was not considered, the fathers' mean physical punishment scores were 0.76 and 0.30 for "obey" ranked first and not first respectively.

33.38) than those in the low supervisory positions. But these differences ac-cording to supervisory position are not present for children in families in which the father does not rank obedience first. Thus, higher physical pun-ishment and dogmatism scores are obtained when parents not only highly value obedience in their child, but receive reinforcement in the form of obedience from co-workers.[6]

The data presented appear to support the general hypothesis that occupa-tional environment influences the socialization techniques used by parents and that these techniques, in turn, affect the degree of dogmatism displayed by their children. The data also suggest that the traits parents consider im-portant for their children to possess (e.g., obedience)—especially if this trait is reflected in the parent's own occupational experiences (e.g., high super-visory position)—further intensifies the relationship between the occupa-tional structure, socialization techniques, and socialization outcomes.

## CONCLUSION

This paper finds support for the idea that a linkage exists between the occupational structure and socialization techniques of parents and the resul-tant dogmatism scores of their children. Although this linkage does not appear when fathers' occupations are categorized according to the tradi-tional working class/middle class dichotomy, it does appear when those occupations are categorized according to the occupational tasks fathers per-form in their jobs, appearing in significant differences in both physical pun-ishment and dogmatism scores. Furthermore, it was found that when fathers

[6]Scheffe test for difference of means was applied to select groups:
High supervisory category: Obey first and obey not first—significant at $p < .01$ for both dogmatism and physical punishment scores.
Obey ranked first category: High supervision and low supervision—significant at $p < .01$ for both dogmatism and physical punishment scores.

place a high value on "obedience," especially if they are used to expecting obedience from co-workers, then both their physical punishment scores and their children's dogmatism scores are higher.

It can be concluded that both this study and the previous pilot study indicate that the traditional dichotomy of working class vs. middle class (manual vs. nonmanual) may no longer discern differential socialization techniques; but when families are categorized directly by the occupational tasks required in the husband's job, the structure of their occupational realm is seen to influence the methods of discipline they use, and these methods, in turn, affect the degree of dogmatism in their child.

## REFERENCES

Berelson, Bernard and Gary A. Steiner
   1964    *Human Behavior: An Inventory of Scientific Findings.* New York: Harcourt, Brace and World.
Bronfenbrenner, Urie
   1961    "The Changing American Child: A Speculative Analysis." *Journal of Social Issues* 17 (January): 6–18. Also reprinted in Rose Coser (ed.), *Life Cycle and Achievement in America.* New York: Harper and Row, Harper Torchbooks, 1969.
Holland, John L.
   1959    "A Theory of Vocational Choice." *Journal of Counseling Psychology* 6 (1): 35–45.
   1963a    "Explorations of a Theory of Vocational Choice and Achievement." *Psychological Reports* 12: 547–594.
   1963b    "Explorations of a Theory of Vocational Choice: Part II, Self-Descriptions and Vocational Preference." *Vocational Guidance Quarterly* (Autumn): 17–23.
   1963c    "Explorations of a Theory of Vocational Choice: Vocational Images and Choice." *Vocational Guidance Quarterly* (Summer): 232–237.
Kohn, Melvin L.
   1969    *Class and Conformity.* Homewood, Illinois: Dorsey.
Litwak, Eugene
   1960    "Occupational Mobility and Extended Family Cohesion." *American Sociological Review* 25 (February): 9–22.
Rokeach, Milton
   1960    *The Open and Closed Mind.* New York: Basic Books.
Steinmetz, Suzanne K.
   1971    "Occupation and Physical Punishment: A Response to Straus." *Journal of Marriage and the Family* 33 (November): 664–666.
Straus, Murray A.
   1971    "Some Social Antecedents of Physical Punishment: A Linkage Theory Interpretation." *Journal of Marriage and the Family* 33 (November): 658–663.

# CHAPTER SIX
# Abusive Parents

## 19. *A History of Child Abuse and Infanticide*
### SAMUEL X. RADBILL

Before dealing with child abuse and extreme physical punishment in modern America, it is well to have an historical perspective on the issue. Without such a perspective, the contemporary statistics on the frequency of physical punishment and child abuse might lead one to conclude that ours is an era in which violence toward children is extremely high. In an absolute sense this is correct, as the figures in the last part of this article make clear. But relative to previous periods in Western history, Radbill suggests that children now are typically exposed to less violence from their parents than in the past. In fact, many of the customary punishments described in Radbill's article would today be defined as child abuse and would be the object of intervention by social agencies or legal authorities.

### MALTREATMENT OR DISCIPLINE

Maltreatment of children has been justified for many centuries by the belief that severe physical punishment was necessary either to maintain discipline, to transmit educational ideas, to please certain gods, or to expel evil spirits. Whipping children has always been the prerogative of teachers, as well as of parents. In the schools of Sumer, five thousand years ago, there was a "man in charge of the whip" to punish boys upon the slightest pretext (1, p. 11). Justification for maltreatment has also been based on religious beliefs and practices, and in ancient times boys were flogged by their parents before the altars of Diana (2, p. 195).

"Spare the rod and spoil the child" was a dictum backed by the Bible and expressed in 1633 in the *Bibliotheca Scholastica*. There was a time in most Christian countries when children were whipped on Innocents Day to make them remember the massacre of the innocents by Herod. Beatings to drive out the devil were a form of psychiatric treatment especially applicable to children, and where epilepsy was attributed to demoniacal possession, the sufferer was thrashed soundly to expel the demon. There was a sacred iron chain in India expressly for this purpose.

The ancient philosophers beat their pupils unmercifully. Parents, teachers, and ministers alike believed that the only cure for the "foolishness bound up

SOURCE: Reprinted with permission from Ray E. Helfer and Henry Kempe (eds.), *The Battered Child* (Chicago: University of Chicago Press, 1968), pp. 3–5 and 13–17. This paper was read at the Pediatric History Club, American Academy of Pediatrics, October 26, 1965.

in the heart of the child" was repression, especially by use of the rod, and the schoolmaster was proverbial for his severity. The ferule, a tough stalk of the giant fennel *(ferula)*, was used by Roman schoolmasters as the instrument of punishment. In England and America all pictures of pedagogues showed them armed with the birch. Michael Udall, headmaster at Eton during the reign of Elizabeth I, was noted for his addiction to the use of four apple twigs; his cruelty led Roger Ascham (sixteenth century) to write *The Schoolmaster* in which he advocated love instead of fear in teaching children. John Locke, a century later, pleaded for schoolmasters to reserve the rod for moral faults only. Severe forms of punishment were used; not only were they condoned and supported by law, but they were usually considered salutary, although occasionally parents did intercede on behalf of their children (3, pp. 191–210).

Throughout history there are accounts of the customary extremes in the chastisement of children. Pepys beat his boy until he (Pepys) was out of breath; John Wesley, Frederick the Great, Lady Jane Grey, and many others in adult life complained bitterly of their treatment in childhood. It always was taken for granted that the parents and guardians of children had every right to treat their children as they saw fit. When Henry VI, who was king when still in his cradle, grew old enough to put up an argument, his tutor had to appeal to council for assistance "in chastysing of him for his defaults." Thus regular flogging produced a most unhappy person in King Henry VI, even if it did make him a scholar and a gentleman (4, p. 119). Charles I was more fortunate for he had Mungo Murray available as a whipping boy to substitute for him when punishment was indicated.

History reveals that there were influential personages other than Henry VI to speak out against the maltreatment of children. Plato in 400 b.c. advised teachers to "train children not by compulsion but as if they were playing," and Plutarch, 500 years later, decried the use of the *scutica* (a whip made of leather thongs).

The beating of very young children, for a time, raised many objections which led to some mitigation. But then as the Calvinistic views that children were imps of darkness became popular, they were again whipped. In 1570, Thomas Ingeland became incensed by this practice and wrote a protest skit which he called *A Pretie and Merie New Interlude Called the Disobedient Child*. The climax came when a boy "through many stryppes was dead and cold" (4, p. 165).

Discipline oscillated between entire abandonment of the rod and its excessive use to the point of savagery. The German-born Queen Caroline complained that the English were not well bred because they were not whipped enough when they were young. The Lady Abergane is said to have severely beaten her own child of seven in a fit of passion. When the father complained, she threw the child so violently to the ground that his skull was fractured, and he was killed (4, p. 239).

Western education gradually began to yield to the demands of exemplars of modern thought, such as Erasmus, who although he brought up his own children with harsh formality, was greatly influenced by Sir Thomas More, who used peacock feathers to beat his daughters. There were others who protested vigorously against child abuse. During the reign of Henvy VIII there was a group of reformers in educational methods who urged gentleness; among them was John Colet, founder of St. Paul's School in London. When Richard Mulcaster, a schoolmaster, wrote his little book on education, he was criticized by Fuller who said "others have taught as much learning with fewer lashes" (5, p. 309). John Peter Frank, at the end of the eighteenth century, was a pioneer in the establishment of legal regulations curbing corporal punishment in the schools (6, pp. 257–68).

Pressure against child abuse was also exerted by those outside the educational system. In 1611, Roger L'Estrange published a book, *The Children's Petition*, begging for more leniency from parents toward their children. In 1698, another book appeared in England entitled *Lex Forcia, A Sensible Address to Parliament for an Act to Remedy the Foul Abuse of Children at Schools* (7, p. 297). Over 150 years passed before public opinion was aroused in the United States. In 1861, Samuel Halliday reported many instances of irrational child beating by sadistic parents in New York City (8, p. 102). . . .

## THE SOCIETY FOR THE PREVENTION OF CRUELTY TO CHILDREN

Even though the child stirs the most tender emotions in mankind, cruelty to children has always prevailed. Fontana (20, p. 8) reports the story of Mary Ellen, who was being maltreated by her adoptive parents. The child was being beaten regularly and was seriously malnourished. Interested church workers were unable to convince local authorities to take legal action against the parents. The right of parents to chastice their own children was still sacred, and there was no law under which any agency could interfere, to protect a child like her. The church workers were not discouraged; rather, they appealed to the Society for the Prevention of Cruelty to Animals (SPCA), which promptly took action. They were able to have Mary Ellen removed from her parents on the grounds that she was a member of the animal kingdom and that therefore her case could be included under the laws against animal cruelty.

As a direct result of this incident the Society for the Prevention of Cruelty to Children was founded in New York City in 1871. Following the example of the New York Society, many other societies with similar objectives were formed in different parts of this country. The Philadelphia Society to Protect Children from Cruelty was founded in 1877. In Great Britain in 1899 thirty-one such societies united to form the National Society for the Prevention of Cruelty to Children with Queen Victoria as patron, and Parliament passed an act for prevention of cruelty to children which was dubbed "The Children's Charter" (21, p. 30). In New York City, Samuel B. Halliday stirred the public consciousness with his work on behalf of destitute children (8), and in London Thomas John Barnardo, forcing upon the public conscience awareness of the existence of gangs of homeless children, succeeded in the establishment of the chain of homes and vocational schools that earned for him the title of "Father of Nobody's Children" (22).

## LAWS AGAINST CHILD ABUSE AND INFANTICIDE

The Code of Hammurabi about four thousand years ago provided that if a nurse allowed a suckling to die in her hands and substituted another, her breast should be amputated (23, p. 18). In ancient Egypt infanticide was common, but it was not legal. The Thebans made it a capital offense, and there is an Egyptian record of a child murderer who was ordered to carry the slain infant in her arms for three days and three nights. Even though the *Patria Potestas* gave a father supreme right to sell, mutilate, or even kill his offspring as far back as the reign of Numa Pompilius (about 700 B.C.), infanticide was relatively uncommon in ancient Rome. The Laws of the Twelve Tables (about 450 B.C.) modified the *Patria Potestas* so that a son could be sold only three times, and the *Lex Julia* and *Lex Papia* of Augustus Caesar in A.D. 4 checked the *Patria Potestas* and indirectly aided children; but the exposure of children, a common theme in the comedies of Plautus and of Terence, continued unabated. Child welfare laws and agitation on behalf of children were frequent under succeeding emperors. Tiberius ordered the death penalty for Carthaginian priests who sacrificed children in the fire to Moloch, but the practice continued in secret even in the lifetime of Tertullian, over a hundred years later. The empress Faustina, during the second century, established foundations to save female infants from destruction, but apparently her efforts were ephemeral because the next century proved to be an evil one for children (23, p. 42).

The Hebrews interdicted infanticide, and so did their religious offshoots, the Christians and the Mohammedans. God frequently exhorts all of them in their holy books, the Bible and Koran, against this sin. Philo Judaeus in the first century after Christ proclaimed it a crime, and in the next century, Tertullian, one of the fathers of the Christian Church, in speaking of infanticide, said "murder is murder in any shape" and a sin against the commandment, "Thou shalt not kill." Through the influence of Christianity, edicts against infanticide and the sale of children into slavery were issued by Constantine (A.D. 315 and 321), by Valentinian, Valens, and Gratian (A.D. 374), by Valentinian II, Theodosius, and Arcadius (A.D. 391), by Honorius and Theodosius (A.D. 409), by Theodosius II (A.D. 438), and by Valentinian III (A.D. 451). Infanticide by exposure or otherwise had been established as a crime by Barnabas in the time of the apostles; in A.D. 305 a sentence of excommunication for life was decreed, but in 314 this was reduced to ten years and in 524 to seven (23, p. 55).

The Council of Nicea (A.D. 325) ordered the establishment of a *xenodochion*, a hospital for the benefit of paupers, in each Christian village. Some of these institutions became *brephotrophia*, asylums for children. The Council of Vaison (A.D. 442) provided a means for the Church to receive abandoned children and care for them. This provision was reaffirmed ten years later at Arles and again at Agde. There a marble receptacle was set up to receive the children at the church door. At the Council of Toledo (A.D. 589), clergy and civil authorities were enjoined to unite their efforts to prevent infanticide. The Council of Constantinople the year before had compared infanticide to homicide, and the Theodosian Code prescribed the death penalty for this crime. Even though capital punishment was prescribed repeatedly thereafter, it was rarely carried out. Sixtus V and Gregory XIV in the sixteenth century and Frederick the Great in the eighteenth issued stern edicts against infanticide (23, p. 57), but as long as poverty, illegitimacy, and other social problems exist such laws will always be futile.

In 1556, Henry II of France decreed death to women who concealed the birth of a child; and not long after, James I, King of England, passed a similar law, but it subsequently had to be repealed. For "dropping" (abandoning) an infant in eighteenth-century England, a woman might have been sentenced to a month at hard labor, but many women still secretly murdered unwanted babies. "There is scarce an assizes," wrote Addison in 1773, "where some unhappy wretch is not executed for the murder of a child. And how many more of these monsters of inhumanity may we suppose to be wholly undiscovered or cleared for want of legal evidence?" (24, p. 38). An act of 1803 placed women tried for the murder of bastard children under the same laws as those pertaining to murder in general and with the same penalties. In this country, too, there has never been any legal distinction between the murder of adults and the killing of a newborn infant, or an infant at any age, legitimate or otherwise. As soon as the child is born it is a citizen with full protection of the law.

Other peoples and nations also had early infanticide laws. The Roman historian, Tacitus (A.D. 55–119), noted that the Germanic tribes considered infanticide a crime, and the Germanic law codes, the Salic law, and the Hispanic laws, contained penalties for this crime. The Visigothic King, Chindaswinth, who reigned A.D. 632–49, was the first monarch to set the death penalty; penalties were also severe under Charles V, and the Austrian Penal Code prescribed life imprisonment. It should be noted, however, that everywhere the penalty meted out for killing illegitimate infants was much less severe. Under Czar Alexis in 1647 the punishment for infanticide was extremely moderate (25, p. 822).

One of the vexing forensic problems in cases of infanticide has always been how to determine that the baby was born alive before it was killed. Obviously you cannot kill a dead child. For this reason Swammerdam's discovery in 1667 that fetal lungs will float on water after respiration has taken place was one of the most important medico-legal contributions of the seventeenth century. This was first put to practical application by Johann Schreyer in the case of a fifteen-year-old peasant girl accused of infanticide in 1681; the infant's sinking lungs dramatically secured the mother's acquittal. A letter by Schoepffer in 1684, published many years later in a book on infanticide based on eighty-eight autopsies, likewise corroborated this test (26, p. 45).

After the Franco-Prussian war Theophile Roussel (1816–1903) became an outstanding protagonist of the infant-welfare movement. The "loi Roussel," of December 23, 1874, for the protection of infants sent out to nurse and his law of July 25, 1889, for the protection of abandoned or maltreated children earned for him renown as "the advocate of abandoned children" and led to a long-continued social reform movement that extended well into the twentieth century (23, p. 155). In England the Infant Life Protection Act of the latter half of the nineteenth century regulated foster homes but was ineffectual because it did not provide for regular inspection. It was not until 1908, when a particularly lurid case of infanticide by an avaricious foster mother reached the front pages, that the Infant Life Protection Act required registration and inspection of foster homes, providing for the appointment of visitors to supervise the care received by foster children.

In the United States by this time state governments were entering the field of child welfare. In 1909, the first White House Conference was convened, and the American Association for Study and Prevention of Infant Mortality was founded. With the creation of the United States Children's Bureau, the trend for federal concern began. At the White House Conference on Child Health and Protection of 1930, an American "Children's Charter" was adopted, which among many other ambitions promised every child a home with love and security, plus full time public welfare services for protection from abuse, neglect, exploitation, or moral hazard.

## THE "BATTERED CHILD SYNDROME"

Abuse of children has excited periodic waves of sympathy, each rising to a high pitch, and then curiously subsiding until the next period of excitation. We owe the present wave of excitation to the relatively new discipline of pediatric radiology. Thomas Morgan Rotch as early as 1906 was presenting studies in infant X rays, ten years after Roentgen's original discovery. Twenty years later Ralph Bromer was to head the nation's first X-ray department in a children's hospital. It was not until 1946 that Caffey reported his original observations regarding the common association of subdural hematoma and abnormal X-ray changes in the long bones (27). A few years later Silverman (see chapter 4) reported similar findings and clearly defined the traumatic nature of the lesions (28). In 1955, Wooley brought out the startling fact that the trauma noted on the X rays was in many cases willfully inflicted (29). The news reached the radio, television, and press and electrified the public, as well as many social agencies.

Kempe was alarmed, in the early sixties, by the large number of children admitted to his pediatric service suffering from non-accidental injury. He contacted some eighty district attorneys in an effort to obtain a more accurate picture of the true incidence of the problem (30). In 1961, the American Academy of Pediatrics conducted a symposium on the problem of child abuse under Dr. Kempe's direction. To direct attention to the seriousness of the problem, he proposed the term "the battered child syndrome." This symposium, which attracted a large number of people, was the stimulus for the beginning of present-day interest. The Children's Bureau awarded grants for the study of child abuse, and the American Humane Society uncovered 662 cases in a single year. Every state and every social class was represented in this group. Twenty-seven per cent of these 662 cases represented fatalities; many more had permanent brain damage.

As a result of this recent surge of interest, the problems of the battered child are taking on a new phase in our history. It is one of the most serious concerns facing society. The progress made in the last decade is only a beginning of man's attempt to change the lot of these unfortunate children.

## REFERENCES

1. Kramer, Samuel Noah. 1956. *From the Tablets of Sumer: Twenty-five Firsts in Man's Recorded History.* Indian Hills, Colo.: Falcon's Wing.
2. Ryan, William Burke. 1862. *Infanticide: Its Law, Prevalence, Prevention and History.* London: J. Churchill.
3. Earle, Alice Morse. 1926. *Child Life in Colonial Days.* New York: Macmillan.
4. Godfrey, Elizabeth. 1907. *English Children in Olden Time.* London: Methuen & Co.
5. Still, George Frederic. 1965. *The History of Paediatrics. The Progress of the Study of Diseases of Children up to the End of the XVIIIth Century.* London: Dawsons of Pall Mall.
6. Aries, Philippe. 1962. *Centuries of Childhood. A Social History of Family Life.* New York: Alfred A. Knopf.
7. Dunn, Courtenay. 1920. *The Natural History of the Child.* New York: John Lane.
8. Halliday, Samuel B. 1861. *The Little Street Sweeper; Or, Life Among the Poor.* New York: Phinney, Blakeman & Mason.

\* \* \*

20. Fontana, Vincent J. 1964. *The Maltreated Child. The Maltreatment Syndrome in Children.* Springfield, Illinois: Charles C. Thomas.
21. Allen, Anne, and Morton, Arthur. 1961. *This Is Your Child. The Story of the National Society for the Prevention of Cruelty to Children.* London: Routledge & Kegan Paul.
22. Williams, A. E. 1966. *Barnardo of Stepney: The Father of Nobody's Children.* London: George Allen & Unwin, Ltd.
23. Garrison, Fielding H. 1965. *Abt-Garrison History of Pediatrics,* reprinted from *Pediatrics,* Volume I. Edited by Isaac A. Abt. Philadelphia: W. B. Saunders Co.
24. Caulfield, Ernest. 1931. *The Infant Welfare Movement in the Eighteenth Century.* New York: Paul B. Hoeber.
25. Gradewohl, R. B. H. 1954. *Legal Medicine.* Edited by T. A. Gonzales. New York: Appleton-Century-Crofts.
26. Buettner, Christoph Gottlieb. 1771. *Kindermord.* Koenigsberg and Leipzig.
27. Caffey, J. 1946. "Multiple Fractures in the Long Bones of Children Suffering from Chronic Subdural Hematoma." *Am. J. Roentgenol.* 56: 163.
28. Silverman, F. M. 1953. "The Roentgen Manifestations of Unrecognized Skeletal Trauma in Infants." *Am. J. Roentgenol Radium Therapy Nucl. Med.* 69: 413.
29. Wooley, P. V., Jr., and Evans, W. A., Jr. 1955. "Significance of Skeletal Lesions in Infants Resembling Those of Traumatic Origin." *J. Am. Med. Assoc.* 158: 539.
30. Kempe, C. Henry, Silverman, Frederic N., Steele, Brandt F., Droegemueller, William, and Silver, Henry K. 1962. "The Battered-Child Syndrome." *J. Am. Med. Assoc.* 181: 17.

# 20. *The Kent State Four/Should Have Studied More*
## JAMES A. MICHENER

It may seem strange to include an article on the anti-war disturbances at Kent State University in a chapter on "Abusive Parents." It was, after all, the students who set fire to buildings and the National Guard who killed four students. Our reason for including it here is because the important point is not the burning and the shooting. The part which speaks to violence be-tween family members is the public reaction to these events and to the life style of the students. Not only did many citizens feel that these were justified killings (and that perhaps it would have been better if a few more had been shot) but so did some parents. At the extreme is the mother of three stu-dents at Kent State who felt that hippie students "deserve to be shot." She went on to say that if *her sons* ". . . didn't do what the Guard told them, they should have been mowed down."

The article which follows, by Pulitzer-Prize winning author James A. Michener, is a condensation of the concluding section of his interpretation of the Kent State events, *Kent State: What Happened and Why.*

Harold Walker, the student photographer, had his compelling pictures of the Guard's action published in the *York Gazette and Daily,* of York, Pa. The *Gazette* editor asked Walker to accompany his photographs with an account of what happened, and the young newsman ended his essay with these words: "I think that when people look at the situation there will be sym-pathy across the nation. As for the city of Kent, the whole town seems in sympathy with the students." He concluded, "I believe the incident may bring the student and the adult communities together."

Never in his future career as a newspaperman will Harold C. Walker, Kent State '70, be more completely wrong, for even as the paper in York was printing these hopeful and constructive words, the *Record-Courier* in Kent was forced to find space for what will be remembered as one of the most virulent outpourings of community hatred in recent decades. Day after day for several weeks, the paper reserved a full page for this violent out-burst.

I stand behind the action of the National Guard! I want my property defended. Live ammunition? Well, really, what did they expect—spit balls?

Hooray! I shout for God and country, recourse to justice under laws, fifes, drums, martial music, parades, ice-cream cones—America, support it or leave it.

The volley of gunfire served its purpose. It broke up the riot, and I say the same method should be used again and again.

The sooner the students of this country learn that they are not running this country, that they are going to college to learn, *not teach,* the better. If those

SOURCE: Reprinted from *Kent State: What Happened and Why,* as condensed in the *Reader's Digest* (April 1971): 218, 263–276. Reprinted by permission of William Morris Agency, Inc., on behalf of the author. Copyright 1971 by Random House, Inc. and Reader's Digest Association, Inc.

students don't like our colleges, why don't they go to the country from which they are being indoctrinated?

I have one possible solution to the problem. Build a fence completely around KSU, put President White and his 550 faculty members inside along with all the agitators that they understand so well and let them do their thing. We could also change the name from KSU to "Idiot Hill." Then Dr. White and his faculty and students could assemble and throw rocks at each other and play with matches and burn things down.

The National Guard made only one mistake—they should have fired sooner and longer.

From time to time isolated writers would remind the public that four young people were dead, that something had gone fearfully wrong. They sounded like lost voices, except for the eloquence of their words.

Revolutionaries and SDSers don't frighten me, nor do squads of police or National Guards. I am afraid of the people who say, "Kill the demonstrators, because they destroyed our property." I am afraid of these who value property over human life. I am afraid not for my life, but for my soul, and for the sensitivity and humanity that is slowly being erased from our society.

Jesus said that no one can truly love God if he cannot love his fellow man. You people with the "mow 'em down" philosophy, can you love God without loving Jeffrey, Bill, Sandy and Allison?


"THE SCORE IS FOUR"

Many of the students who left Kent in their own cars offered rides to others. One of these was Daniel Gardner, a well-behaved, short-haired young junior with good manners, who got into his car with some friends at three o'clock on Monday afternoon and started the long drive back to his home on Cape Cod. Gardner had been in no way involved in either the shooting or the activities that led up to it. But the killings had made him think. "After all, 30.06-gauge bullets against a gang of unarmed kids," he says. "Too much, man, too much." He expected non-campus society to agree with him.

Gardner and his companions began to learn the facts of life when they left the Ohio Turnpike to enter the Pennsylvania. When the ticket-taker saw the Kent State sticker on Gardner's car, he snarled, "Those Guards shoulda shot all of you." When Gardner stopped at a bar on the outskirts of Buffalo, the men inside refused to allow the students entrance. "We don't want no commies in here." And when Gardner had dropped off his passengers and arrived on Cape Cod, his neighbors told him, "Anybody who defied the Guard should have been shot."

When Bob Hillegas, the ROTC student, reported to work at his part-time job at a factory in Akron, he was told: "Those damned kids got what was coming to them." The men were circulating a petition condoning the use of any weapons deemed necessary in future campus outbreaks and exonerating the Guard in advance if deaths resulted.

"I refused to sign," Hillegas says, "and now I'm regarded as an outsider. I tried arguing with them, but they said, 'If they were on the hill they were guilty. Next time if they don't do what the Guard says, they'll all get shot!' "

In various college towns in Ohio, memorial services were held for the dead students, but rarely without pickets. At the service in Toledo, women marched with signs reading:

> The Kent State Four
> Should have studied more.

In a newspaper interview, one Kent lawyer declared: "Frankly, if I'd been faced with the same situation and had a submachine gun, there would not have been 14 shot; there probably would have been 140 of them dead, and that's what they need."

Other citizens adopted the device of flashing their right hands in the air, thumb folded and four fingers extended. When a student asked what this meant, he was told, "This time we got four of you bastards. Next time we'll get more." A director of a Kent State residence hall was appalled when a policeman walked by him, raised four fingers and whispered, "The score is four."

It was difficult to find any student who escaped this harsh confrontation with public opinion, but those who bore a special burden of shock were the ones whose own parents said, "Everyone on the hill should have been shot."

The experience of one blond, saucy-eyed coed is typical. On Monday, as she was walking back to her dorm from class, she came in the direct line of fire when the rifles went off. She was not killed, but she might have been, and at her death no one could conceivably have said, "She had no right to be there." A top-notch scholar, she had every reason in the world to be where the bullets struck. That night when she returned to her home in a small town in rural Ohio, her parents said, "It would have been better for America if every student on that hill had been shot."

"Mother!" she cried in profound protest. "I was there. Only a miracle of some kind saved me. What about that?"

"You would have deserved it."

Of the 400 students who were interviewed during the research for this book, at least 25 per cent declared that they were told by their own parents that it might have been a good thing if they had been shot.

One of the strongest impressions that came from this emotional explosion was the virulence of the attitudes expressed by women. The most intransigent opposition to students came from them, and the harshest dismissal of the young.

Some believe that this resulted from a real sense of fear. There were numerous cases in which mothers on downtown shopping trips in Kent would clutch their children defensively if hippies wandered by. There was also the frightening experience of suddenly turning a corner and finding onself face-to-face with seven or eight totally disheveled members of a commune, the men dressed like Daniel Boone, the women barefoot and in long tattered dresses.

But there were other factors, too. It could not have been by accident that so many women referred with apparent hatred to the young girls who were appearing in town without bras. This became a fixation with many, and was apparently an intuitive reaction to a symbol. "If I've had to wear a bra all my life, why can't she?" This overreaction of women might be considered humorous, except that, in many cases, the depth of their bitterness and intensity of their rejection produced terrible consequences.

BEHIND THE VEIL

Perhaps no case of parental rejection equals that of a family living near Kent, with three good-looking, well-behaved, moderate sons at the university. The sons witnessed the shootings, although none had any previous record of participation in protest. When the mother spoke about her feelings, the conversation was so startling that pains were taken to get it exactly as spoken:

MOTHER: Anyone who appears on the streets of a city like Kent with long hair, dirty clothes or barefooted deserves to be shot.

MICHENER: Have I your permission to quote that?

MOTHER: You sure do. It would have been better if the Guard had shot the whole lot of them that morning.

MICHENER: But you had three sons there.

MOTHER: If they didn't do what the Guards told them, they should have been mowed down.

PROFESSOR OF PSYCHOLOGY, *listening in*: Is long hair a justification for shooting someone?

MOTHER: Yes. We have got to clean up this nation. And we'll start with the long-hairs.

PROFESSOR: Would you permit one of your sons to be shot simply because he went barefooted?

MOTHER: Yes.

PROFESSOR: Where do you get such ideas?

MOTHER: I teach at the local high school.

PROFESSOR: Do you mean that you are teaching your students such things?

MOTHER: Yes. I teach them the truth. That the lazy, the dirty, the ones you see walking the streets and doing nothing ought all to be shot.

Of course, as the summer progressed many of the parents retreated from their first harsh judgments. Communication with children was reopened, and in many cases an understanding was achieved. But in hundreds of other cases young students caught a terrifying glimpse of what their parents really thought. For a moment, the veil that properly exists between young and old was sundered and the former were shocked by what they saw. Reactions varied.

"I doubt that I'll ever bother to go home again," several students reported.

"I'm going to Canada," said others. "I've had it."

"I don't suppose I'll ever be able to talk with my parents again," was the most common reaction.

More frightening was the repeated admission that this sequence of events had alienated the students not only from their parents but from all society as they had known it.

"When I left home to return to school this fall, I was crying so hard my parents couldn't understand it. What they don't know is that I realized it was the last time I would ever be with them again. Everything I had said, they looked down on, resented and ridiculed. I just don't have it in me to fight them. So I've left for good, and I have left the kind of life they represent," says one petite coed.

And from a determined history major: "During the years of the sit-ins and peace rallies, my parents and I disagreed, but we respected each other's opinions. But after Kent, when I saw how so many people, including my parents, truly feared and hated students, I realized there was no middle ground. Now I'm working against everything my family has worked for, and I will fight as long as it is necessary."

## "HAVE THEY TAKEN OVER THE WORLD?"

When the flood of mail and speech had subsided, many people tried to decipher what the outburst had signified. The following conclusions seem in order.

The general population of middle America had become antagonized by its universities, the presidents who administered them, and the professors who taught in them. The average man had lost all comprehension of what a university ought to be in a time of change and was prepared to lash out at those who were allowing it to change from what it had been when he was young.

Many people were outraged that the university had allowed young radicals like Jerry Rubin, Mark Rudd and Bernardine Dohrn to speak on its campus. They were infuriated that students used profanity to college officials and campus policemen. They were deeply disturbed that young men—who in all past generations had marched off obediently to war—should now question the authority of the President of the United States to send them to war.

There was an honest longing for an old-fashioned college with old-fashioned problems. One citizen of Kent complains, "Why can't the kids come to college in the autumn the way they used to and worry about the things college kids always worried about? What fraternity to join? Where is the football rally going to be? Which of the coeds should I marry? That's the way it used to be. What's all this moratorium stuff and protesting the war? They can't do a damned thing about it."

No one could talk with a cross section of the local population without discovering that many people were truly frightened by the more disreputable young people they saw on the streets. One woman summarized the town's feeling: "My husband expects me to keep our house clean and myself neat. I take pride in it, just as I take pride in his advancement in his work. It's what we got married for. Then I go down-town and see these hippies barefooted, filthy, boasting about the ragged clothes they wear, elbowing me off my own streets, and using language I've never heard my husband speak.

What am I to think? Have they taken over the world? Have we got to surrender Kent to them?"

Sex plays a much larger role in the division between generations than was once apparent. Older townspeople both despise and envy the sexual freedom enjoyed by the young. A businessman will be saying, "The thing I can't stand is the way they dress." But he will add, "And it's disgusting the way the girls sleep around." Or a Kent housewife will explain, "I could tolerate them if they had any manners." But she will conclude in a lower voice, "And the way they sleep together in those dormitories!"

Numerous communes operated in Kent at the time of the shooting—not on campus—and rumors of the ebb and flow of partners infuriated the townspeople. Two reactions were customary: "The university should expel them all," and, "They ought to be horsewhipped." Sexual jealousy appears to be a very strong factor concerning how a citizen will react to the younger generation, which he sees enjoying itself in a manner forbidden to him when he was young.

## HUMILITY, LOVE, UNDERSTANDING

What can we learn from the tragedy at Kent State?

Among all types of students at Kent, and other universities, there is vigorous disgust with two aspects of American life: the war in Viet Nam and the draft. It is therefore tempting to conclude that if only the war were terminated, some kind of peace would return to America's campuses. For this hopeful belief there is scant justification. I believe that if the war ended tomorrow, students would remain as agitated and confused as they are today. Evidence of this can be found by looking at Japan, France and Venezuela.

In Japan, there is exactly the national commitment to peace and anti-militarism that American students demand. The Japanese constitution outlaws war. The military-industrial complex does not exist. Yet the students of Japan, in their assaults on society, are among the most determined of all young radicals.

The surging disturbances in France which came close to causing the collapse of de Gaulle's government occurred after de Gaulle had ended the Algerian war in accordance with the demands of students. French students had none of the American causes to protest against and none of the Japanese; yet the same types of protests occurred.

In Venezuela, students had none of the American causes, none of the Japanese and none of the French; yet their behavior has followed the same pattern, and their protests were perhaps the most violent of all.

What has caused this worldwide revolt? The single best explanation is that the young have rejected the life-styles of their parents and have committed themselves to a life-style they have been developing over the past two decades. If one fails to see that the revolts in Japan, France, Venezuela and the United States are identical in every aspect that matters, he misses the whole point of what is happening in the world.

Our age can best be understood if we compare it to European history in the year 1848. Then great revolutionary movements swept the continent with crucial disturbances in France, Germany and the Austro-Hungarian empire, and massive protest elsewhere. The old order established by Metternich and the Congress of Vienna was crumbling, and everyone knew this, but it still retained the power of self-defense. So one after another of the revolutions was crushed.

The United States profited spectacularly from this, because to our shores came thousands of the finest minds of Europe, seeking sanctuary from repression. Today, thousands of our young people are fleeing the United States to seek sanctuary in Canada, Sweden, Morocco, India and Australia. It was astonishing to find scores of students at Kent State who were seriously contemplating a life abroad. Case histories were compiled of at least 12 former students who had already taken the gamble and accepted permanent exile from their homeland.

It is obvious that a major responsibility of society today is the reconciliation of young people and old. The radical divergence between life-styles—the vast differences in dress, cleanliness, hair fashions, attitudes toward work, politics, music, religion, patriotism and sex—must not crystallize into permanent alienation. This does not mean that the older members of society have to surrender values which they have inherited and which they cherish. It does mean that there must be some understanding of what the young are trying to accomplish. It is crucial that older people not reject them automatically.

The older generation should acknowledge that the young have raised legitimate issues in their protests against war, in their concern about ecology, their determination to end racism and to find new, meaningful occupations. Dress, music, idiom, the length of hair and new dating practices are matters of style, which change from generation to generation. Older people should not allow themselves to become irritated by such trivial things. Drugs, delinquent sex habits and violence go much deeper than style and must be opposed where they are known to be destructive. But the older person ought to be able to distinguish between the two.

Unfortunately, this distinction is not often made. Many adults—parents, legislators, editorial writers—would like universities to outlaw the new lifestyles of the young entirely. This is a futile wish. The university must accept students as society delivers them to its door. It cannot revoke history.

If the confrontation between old and young comes to open warfare, as some radical leaders recommend, victory will surely rest with the older generation, for they have the police, the Army and the power. It is therefore obligatory that young people also make concessions. Specifically, they should:

*Act within the law.* The correction of legitimate grievances must be achieved in legitimate ways. The slow building of our democratic process required both moral commitment *and* patience. Society is going to demand that students comport themselves more responsibly. Arson and incitement to riot are crimes, and persons guilty of them should go to jail. The popular theory of the university as a sanctuary—where police and National Guardsmen should never be permitted—has never been acknowledged in our laws.

Already, strict new rules have been enacted for a number of universities, including Kent State. They impose no hardship on the young person who wants an education.

*Respect the moral convictions of others.* Young people are not obligated to pay allegiance to any church, but they ought not to ridicule those who do. Sex, it should be recognized, is a private occupation. Actually, many older people approve of the new sex mores, but they do not care to have them flagrantly promenaded in public.

*Reject obscenity as a weapon.* By their abusive language, young people have outraged sensibilities and made communication with others difficult, if not impossible. Nothing is gained when, in addition to pressure on such issues as the war and the draft, deliberate obscenity is offered as a challenge to the rest of society.

No wealth in this country is more valuable than the burgeoning talent of a new generation, and no expense is too great to cultivate it. The continuity of life is precious. The young need older people to argue with, to test their ideas. The old need to take hope from the young, to feel that civilization will continue to advance.

A few weeks before the shootings at Kent State, Jerry Rubin, radical leader of the American Youth International Party (Yippies), told a crowd of Kent students, "The first part of the Yippie program is to kill your parents." A few days after the shootings, the parents of hundreds of students who had escaped the bullets of the National Guard told their sons and daughters: "You should have been shot."

If we are not to commit national suicide, all of us, young and old, must condemn such extreme emotions. Then, with humility, love and understanding between the generations, we must begin to heal the wounds they have left.

## 21. *Parents Who Hate*
**LEONTINE YOUNG**

There are several things to be learned from this brief excerpt from Young's book on child abuse, *Wednesday's Children.* First, it provides a clear case example of a typical instance of child abuse so that we can vicariously experience something of what goes on in such families. Second, the author calls attention to the fact that the abusing father, Mr. Nolan, is a well-educated, solid, middle class citizen rather than a poverty-stricken slum resident. This is a healthy corrective to the tendency to see child abuse as occurring only among the disreputable segments of society. But it is an over-corrective. All the available statistical data show that child abuse, although far from absent in middle class families, is much more common as one goes down the status hierarchy of society. (In the article which follows this one,

SOURCE: Reprinted by permission of the author from *Wednesday's Children* (New York: McGraw-Hill, 1964), pp. 42–44. Copyright 1964 by Leontine Young.

Richard J. Gelles draws on these statistical studies and offers an explanation for the class difference that they show.) Probably the reason Miss Young stressed the middle class characteristics of child abusers was to call attention to the fact that child abuse *is* a problem among middle class families. Another reason may be that middle class persons have been the main clients of agencies such as the Family Service Association. Finally, this article is instructive because in the closing paragraphs it provides an example of the most widely accepted explanation for child abuse—what Gelles in the next article calls the "phychopathology model."

A tall, well-dressed man sits in the office of a social agency talking to a caseworker. She has called him because a neighbor has reluctantly complained that he beats his children with excessive brutality. Mr. Nolan speaks with quiet emphasis. His language and diction indicate an educated man.

He is explaining that he loves his children. His wife indulges them too much, but this is really the only problem. Of course, the children have to obey his commands, and when they don't he punishes them. One evening recently he told his four year old son to go into the basement and stay there. The little boy went down the stairs and ran quickly back. It was very dark, and he was frightened. "I spanked him and told him to go back," explains the smiling father. "He went down the stairs and again ran back to the light, frightened, so I spanked him again and sent him back. He returned four times and each time I spanked him harder. The last time he stayed down."

"And what did the little boy do that you punished him so severely?" asked the caseworker.

A look of blank surprise comes over Mr. Nolan's face. He stares at the caseworker, and when he speaks his voice is for the first time uncertain. "I don't remember. I can't think what he did." A wariness appears in his eyes, and he remarks that his time is short and he must leave shortly.

Mr. Nolan was a successful man and well educated. He was able to afford a comfortable home for his family, and there was no financial strain. His wife was a college graduate. There were four children, one still an infant. Mrs. Nolan looked older than her husband, and her face had a vague, uncertain expression that was reminiscent of a sleepwalker.

When she talked to the caseworker, she was worried and confused. Sometimes, she explained, she hated her husband for what he did to the children, and then again she thought perhaps she was wrong, perhaps it was all right to punish children like this. Only he beat them so terribly for nothing. One of them accidentally stepped on the kitchen floor which was still wet from washing, and his father beat him until he was a sodden, quivering bundle of pain. Still, her husband told her that she indulged the children too much. It was true she was not so strict with them as he was. He accused her of favoring Donald, the oldest child, and perhaps she did.

Lines of anxienty tightened her face as she told the caseworker, "He wants to break Donald. I know it. Donald is like me. He doesn't need outside recognition. He gets his security from inside himself. He only needs to know I care about him." Donald was a bed wetter, and this worried her. He was getting to be a big boy. Her husband told her enuresis is normal, and she had been reading too many books. She thought the family needed help and sometimes she wished the court would take the children away and protect them. Only she wouldn't want her husband punished. She loved him, and she would never want anyone but him.

A wistful look momentarily softened her face. When she was young, she told the caseworker, she was gay and loved to go out, to dance and join in parties. For a few moments she reminisced, and the memory of pleasure, perhaps greater in retrospect, glimmered in her expression. Then it was gone. Her shoulders drooped again, and she said wearily that perhaps her husband was right. He told her she had never grown up, that she remained a child with little sense of her true responsibilities. The trouble was she would get so confused. She would think sometimes that he was right and that she was a fool. Then again she would get so angry, and not be sure he was right. Sometimes she hated him, and sometimes she felt ashamed for feeling this way about her own husband. He provided a comfortable living for his family. He didn't drink or run around with other women. He was successful in his work and respected by his employer.

Mr. Nolan saw no further need to talk with the caseworker. There was no problem except for his wife's weakness and he was used to this.

Not long after this interview Donald went to the hospital with a broken leg, and his father explained he had accidentally fallen downstairs. The neighbors said they had heard the father beating him. Mrs. Nolan and the children said nothing. Donald refused to answer questions. His face was white and strained and his small body stiff with tension. At night he had frequent nightmares and screamed in his sleep. He jumped at unexpected noises; when someone approached him unexpectedly and without warning, he cried out and then was instantly silent.

A few months later Mrs. Nolan attempted to kill herself. Her husband said it was because she was subject to spells of depression. He had done all he could to give her strength and he would continue to care for her. He would take over more of the care of the children and relieve her of the strain and responsibility. He loved his children, he explained, although he observed in an unwary moment that he hated Donald because he was like his mother.

This is the outline of abuse. It is not the impetuous blow of the harassed parent nor even the transient brutality of an indifferent parent expressing with violence the immediate frustrations of his life. It is not the too severe discipline nor the physical roughness of ignorance. It is the perverse fascination with punishment as an entity in itself, divorced from discipline and even from the fury of revenge. It is the cold calculation of destruction which in itself requires neither provocation nor rationale. Mr. Nolan described in detail the agonizing pain and terror he inflicted upon his helpless son. He did not remember anything the boy had done to precipitate this punishment; in fact, it had not occurred to him that any precipitating act was necessary until the caseworker's pointed question caught him awkwardly unprepared.

## 22. Child Abuse as Psychopathology: A Sociological Critique and Reformulation
### RICHARD J. GELLES

The two previous articles in this chapter illustrate extreme poles in the explanations of child abuse. James Michener's article offers an implicit theory of child abuse: such actions grow out of the threat to parental authority and out of the moral outrage of parents over the rejection by children of values and standards of behavior which the parents hold dear. Michener, in effect, says that parents and adolescent children are engaged in a kind of class struggle and that a crisis such as Kent State can provoke abuse directly comparable to the beating of a young child by his parent. Leontine Young's article, on the other hand, is based on the premise that child abusers are outwardly normal people—often solid middle class citizens—who have inner psychological problems which lead them to abuse a child.

The following article takes a "social-psychological" stance. In it, Richard J. Gelles shows that the psychological explanation which dominates the literature on child abuse is inadequate. Instead, he suggests that an explanation of child abuse must include the social situation and the social characteristics of the parents and the child. His social psychological model of child abuse, therefore, includes both the psychological factors which have been the key concern of the social workers and psychiatrists dealing with the problem, and also the cultural and social situational factors which are largely ignored in the professional literature on child abuse but which figure prominently in historical and sociological studies of violence.

Each year in this country, thousands of children are brutally beaten, abused, and sometimes killed by their mothers and fathers. The dominant theme of research on this problem has stressed the use of a psychopathological model of child abuse—one demonstrating that the parent who abuses his or her child suffers from some psychological disease which must be cured in order to prevent future abuse.[1]

There are major deficiencies with the psychopathology theory of the cause of child abuse. In this paper, I will document these deficiencies and then go on to suggest an alternative social psychological model. The final section of the paper discusses some implications of this model for strategies of intervention in child abuse.

### THE PSYCHOPATHOLOGICAL MODEL

The major deficiencies of the psychopathology explanation of child abuse are that it is too narrow and is inconsistent. In addition, close examination of the

SOURCE: Reprinted with permission from the *American Journal of Orthopsychiatry*, 43 (July 1973): 611–621. Copyright 1973, the American Orthopsychiatric Association, Inc. A revised version of a paper presented at the 67th annual meeting of the American Sociological Association, August 28–31, 1972. The author wishes to express his appreciation to Murray Straus both for suggesting the need for a paper of this nature and for his comments on the drafts of the paper.

[1]It should be pointed out that *not all* students of child abuse subscribe to or support the "Psychopathological Model." Two notable exceptions who approach child abuse with a more multi-dimensional model are Gil (1971) and Blumberg (1964).

literature dealing with the theory shows that it is not based on research which meets even the minimal standards of evidence in social science (Spinetta and Rigler, 1972). The approach is too narrow to account for the majority of cases of child abuse because it posits a single causal variable (a presumed mental aberration or "disease") to account for child abuse and ignores other variables which this paper will show are equally or more important causal factors. The psychopathology theory is inconsistent in that while it states that abuse is caused by psychopathy, at the same time, many of the research reports state that not all abusers are psychopaths. Each of these problems with psychopathological models will be documented in the pages which follow.

*Overview of the Psychopathology Model.* An examination of the *Bibliography of the Battered Child* (1969) reveals that research on battering parents has been done chiefly by psychiatrists, clinical psychologists, social workers, and medical practitioners. The authors of this research generally examine two aspects of the problem. Most of the medical articles focus on how the practitioner can identify a "battered child," identify the psychological effects of the abuse on the child, and prescribe proper treatment. A primary focus of the psychiatric literature is to examine the parent to find the causes of parental abuse and to formulate strategies of intervention to prevent further attacks or abuse.

Throughout the literature there runs a common theme: "Anyone who would abuse or kill his child is sick." This theme has become synonymous with a cause-and-effect relationship: that is, it is suggested that there is a psychological pathology or sickness which accounts for child abuse. The notion of mental illness is the major explanatory tool of the psychopathological model of child abuse. Closely related is the assumption that child abusers tend to have distinctive personality traits which are typical of the psychopathic personality. The model assumes, furthermore, that the sickness is manifested in the form of a "transference psychosis." The final assumption of the model is that the cause of the psychopathy can be traced to the parent's early childhood, in which he or she was abused as a child. The following section of the paper will briefly discuss each of these assumptions of the model.

*The Child Abuser: A Psychopathic Portrait.* Articles on child abuse almost invariably open by asserting that a parent who would inflict serious abuse on a child is in some manner sick. This assertion ranges in form from the point-blank—occurring in the statement that the child-abusing parent is mentally ill (Coles, 1964: 12)—to the indirect—occurring in the statement that the abuser is the patient of the clinician (Bennie and Sclare, 1969: 975). In some cases, the sickness is traced to a flaw in the socialization process, where "something went haywire or was not touched in the humanization process" (Wasserman, 1967: 176). In others, the parents' behavior is compared to that of another "sick" deviant, such as a sexual psychopath. In many cases, the article or book begins with the assumption that the child abuser is a psychopath. Steele and Pollack almost gleefully announce that their first child abuse case was a "gold mine of psychopathology" (1968: 103); Kempe describes the abuser as the "psychopathological member of the family"

(1962: 22); while Galdston alludes to the fact that parents "illustrate their psychopathology" when discussing their relations with their children (1965: 442).

The psychopathological model goes on to focus on specific psychological characteristics of the parent. Steele and Pollack hold that child abusing parents have severe emotional problems (1968: 109), while Kempe locates the problem in a defect of the character structure (1962: 18). The parent who abuses is described as impulsive, immature, and depressed.[2] A link between sex and violence appears evident in the statement that abusive parents are sado-masochistic and that they abuse their children to displace aggression and sadism. Abusive parents are also described as having poor emotional control and being quick to react with poorly controlled aggression. Some authors describe the child abuser as inadequate, self-centered, hypersensitive, having pervasive anger, dependent, egocentric, narcissistic, demanding, and insecure. Abusive parents are also said to suffer from psychosomatic illnesses and have a perverse fascination with punishment of children.

Many other authors could be cited to illustrate the fact that those who use the psychopathological model view the abusing parent as having abnormal psychological traits. However, those works cited are sufficient to make clear the view that mental abnormality is viewed as the cause of child abuse.

*The Parent and Child: Revealing the Psychopathy.* The authors advancing the psychopathological model of child abuse find the disorder manifested in the parent's relationships with his child. One form of this manifestion is the "transference psychosis" (Galdston, 1965: 442). In this state, the parent acts as the child, looking at his own child as if he were an adult (Steele and Pollack, 1968: 109). Parents often speak of their child as if he were an adult; they perceive the child as a hostile persecuting adult, and often see former guilt in their own child. As a result of the "transference," the parental distortion of reality is said to cause a misinterpretation of the infant child. The child is perceived as the psychotic portion of the parent whom the parent wishes to destroy. The child is projected as the cause of the parent's troubles and becomes a "hostility sponge" for the parent.[3]

The psychopathy of the abusive parent is conceived as manifesting itself as a transference and distortion of reality on the part of the parent. In this state, the immature, impulsive, dependent (etc.) individual lashes out at a hostile world. More specifically, he lashes out at what he projects as the source of his troubles—his child.

*The Cause of the Psychopathy.* After identifying the abusive parent as sick, listing the traits or symptoms of the sickness, and illustrating how the sickness manifests itself in parent-child relations, the followers of the psychopathological model establish a causal explanation for the presence of the psychopathy. Steele and Pollack state that one cause is that the parent was raised in the same style (physical punishment and abuse) which he recre-

[2]The specific references to the psychopathological characteristics of abusing parents may be found in: Steele and Pollack, 1968: 109; Kempe, 1962: 18; Bennie and Sclare, 1969: 975–976; Zalba, 1971: 60; and Young, 1964: 44.

[3]References to material on the transference psychosis may be found in: Steele and Pollack, 1968: 109–110; Galdston, 1965: 442; Wasserman, 1967: 177.

ates in raising his own children (1968: 111). This position is elaborated by Reiner and Kaufman (1959), who find that an abusive parent is an imbedded depressive because he was emotionally or psychologically abandoned as a child. As a result of this, violent behavior becomes the child's means of communication. This establishes a life pattern of aggression and violence, which explains both the psychopathy and the abuse (Wasserman, 1967: 176). Thus, the cause of the pathology is the parent's early childhood experience, which included abuse and abandonment. The assumption is that the parent who was abused as a child will almost certainly pass this on to his own child.

The resulting psychopathological model can now be diagrammed: toward the child.

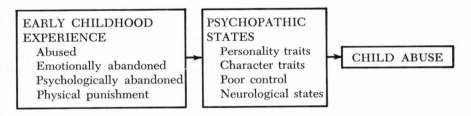

*Figure 1. Psychopathology Model of Child Abuse*

The model is an elementary linear model. Early childhood experience characterized by abuse creates psychological stress, which produces certain psychopathic states. These psychopathic states, in turn, cause abusive acts

*Social Factors*. It should be noted that the authors advancing the psychopathological model make a special effort to point out that social variables *do not* enter into the causal scheme of child abuse. Steele and Pollack, for instance, state that social, economic, and demographic factors are irrelevant to the actual act of child beating (1968: 108). Other researchers argue that their cases of child abuse make up a cross section of socioeconomic status, ethnicity, age, and education (Young, 1964: 42; Blumberg, 1964: 40; Galdston, 1964: 441; Zalba, 1971: 58). These authors often make a point of describing their cases—who were middle class, white-Anglo-Saxon-Protestants—as normal in every respect except the abuser psychology.

## SOME PROBLEMS WITH THE PSYCHOPATHOLOGICAL MODEL

An initial problem with the psychopathological approach is that most of the discussions of the causes of child abuse are clearly inconsistent and contradictory. Some authors blatantly contradict themselves by first stating that the abusing parent is a psychopath and then stating that the child abuser is no different from the rest of society. As already mentioned, Steele and Pollack state that their first patient was a "gold mine of psychopathology" (1968: 103) and then later state that their patients were a "random cross-section of the general population" who "would not seem much different than a group of people picked by stopping the first several dozen people one would meet on a downtown street" (1968: 106). Zalba states that child abusers do not fit easily into a psychiatric category (1971: 59), while Galdston states that, aside from the "transference psychosis," there are no other symptoms of psychotic disorder (1965: 442). Kempe, after describing the psychopathic personality of the child abuser, goes on to state that child beating is not confined to people with psychopathic disorders (1962: 18).

A second problem is an inability to pinpoint the personality traits which characterize the pathology. Of 19 traits listed by the authors of these studies, there was agreement by two or more authors concerning only four traits. Each remaining trait was mentioned by only a single author. Thus, there is little agreement as to the makeup of the psychopathy.

A third problem is that few studies attempt to test any hypothesis concerning the phenomenon. A recent comprehensive review of the literature found that most of the studies start and end with relatively untested commonsense assumptions (Spinetta and Rigler, 1972: 297). This, in turn, is due to the fact that most of the studies are *ex post facto* (Spinetta and Rigler, 1972: 297). When the analysis of the behavior takes place after the fact, little analytic understanding of the genesis of the behavior is offered. For instance, authors state that abusive parents have poor emotional control (Bennie and Sclare, 1969: 975), or that they react with poorly controlled aggression (Kempe, 1962: 18). Analyzed after the fact, it seems obvious that a parent who beats his child almost to the point of death has poor emotional control and reacts with uncontrolled aggression. This type of analysis does not distinguish the behavior in question from the explanation. The drawbacks of this type of labeling are pointed out by Szasz (1960, 1961, 1970) in his discussion of the myth of mental illness. Szasz argues that people who are labeled mentally ill are *then* thought to be suffering from mental illness. The types of after-the-fact explanation offered by the psychopathologic model offer little predictive power in the study of child abuse.

A final criticism of the psychopathological approach is the sampling technique used to gather the data. Most of the data are gathered from cases which medical or psychiatric practitioners have at hand. Thus, the sample cannot be considered truly representative of child abusers since many or most are not seen in clinics. More importantly, there is no attempt to compare samples of "patients" with any comparative group of non-child abusers. Without this comparison, we have no way of knowing whether, in fact, child abusers differ from the rest of the population in terms of the causal variables proposed by the psychopathological model.[4]

## A SOCIOLOGICAL APPROACH TO CHILD ABUSE

An alternative to the psychopathological approach to child abuse focuses on the sociological and contextual variables which are associated with the phe-

[4]Similar problems of the psychopathological approach to child abuse are also articulated in sociological analyses of other forms of deviancy. See, for example, Dunham, 1964: 13; Becker, 1963: 5; Hakeem, 1957: 201.

nomenon.[5] The first line of reasoning suggesting such an approach is reported but ignored in the studies just reviewed. Sociological patterns are evident in their data but are overlooked and ignored by the authors of these studies. This section reexamines the findings in terms of three aspects of child abuse: the social characteristics of the parents who abuse their children; the social characteristics of the victims, the children; and the situational or contextual properties of the act of child abuse.

*The Parent Who Abuses.* Even though the authors note that their case materials on child abuse evidence a large number of middle class parents, there is evidence that the working and lower classes are overrepresented among child abusers. In fact, all the articles which provide data on the socioeconomic class of each abuser show an association between social class and child abuse. Gil found that in most of his cases, the perpetrator of the abuse was of low socioeconomic status (1971: 641). Bennie and Sclare found that 80 per cent of their cases of child abuse (10 cases) were from the lower class (unskilled workers) (1968: 976). Factors related to socioeconomic status also support the notion of the low status of the abuser. Gil reports that education, occupation, and income of child abusers are lower than the general population (1971: 640). Galdston states that battering parents have limited education and financial means (1964: 441).

This evidence lends support to the claims that intra-family violence occurs more often in the lower class or the working class. Blumberg points out that the lower class uses "normal violence" more often than upper classes (1964: 40). Steinmetz and Straus (pp. 7–8), while arguing that the literature is not conclusive,[6] do concede that intra-family violence is more common among the working class. In explaining his findings, David Gil argues that the socioeconomic pressures on the lower class weakens the caretakers' psychological mechanisms of self-control (1971: 645). Thus, pressures cause weaknesses of self-control which eventually may lead to parental violence against children. Gil argues that the poverty of the lower classes produces frustration which is released in a physical attack on the child (1971: 645).

Another finding in the sociological analysis of child abuse is that the sex of the abuser is often female. Resnick's discussion of child filicide found that mothers kill more often than fathers (88–43) (1969: 327). Of Bennie and Sclare's 10 cases of abuse, 7 of the abusers were women. Steele and Pollack

[5]This multi-dimensional approach has been advocated by Gil (1971) in his research on child abuse. Much of the material in this section is drawn from Gil's empirical research and theoretical formulations which focus on social and economic factors related to child abuse.

[6]There are a wide range of interpretations which can be applied to statistical data on child abuse and intra-family violence (see footnotes 3 and 4 in the editors' introduction to this book for a discussion of the various interpretations). One problem in interpreting the data is that middle class children might be overrepresented in the case literature since their parents have more resources which they can draw from in getting medical and psychological attention for their children and themselves. On the other hand, middle class children might be underrepresented since the act of child abuse might be more shocking to a middle class family. Thus, middle class families might be likely to use their resources to "cover up" the abuse by seeking help from a private physician or clinic.

report that of their 57 cases of child abuse, the mother was the abuser 50 times (1968: 107). In Zalba's study, he found the sexes split 50–50 in terms of who was the actual abusing parent. Gil's analysis of cases found the mother abused children 50 per cent of the time while the father abused children 40 per cent of the time (1971: 641).[7]

Given the culturally defined male-aggressive/female-passive roles in our society and that men are usually more aggressive than women (Singer, 1971: 4), it might be surprising that females are so highly represented and overrepresented in cases of child abuse. There appears to be an aspect of the mother-child relationship producing stress and frustration which makes the mother more abusive-prone than the father. One explanation for this is that the child threatens or interferes with the mother's identity and esteem more than it does the father's. (This is true except when the father cannot fill the provider role. In that case, children can be a threat to his identity and esteem, which is so heavily tied to the provider role. See O'Brien, 1971: 693.) An illustration of this hypothesis is a case cited by Galdston in which a mother had to quit work as a result of a pregnancy and her husband's desire to return to work. Forced into closer contact with her ten-month-old child, she subsequently beat him because she found his cries "so demanding" (1965: 442). Other case studies indicate that it is the mother, who through close contact with the child, experiences the frustration of trying to rear and control the child. The child who is perceived by the mother as impinging on her freedom and desires seems to be vulnerable to abuse from the frustrated mother.

*The Child Who Is Abused.* The most dangerous period for the child is from three months to three years of age. The abused, battered, or murdered child is the most vulnerable during those years when he is the most defenseless and the least capable of meaningful social interaction. Resnick found that the first six months was the most dangerous time for the child (1969: 327). Bennie and Sclare report that in their sample, battered children were usually from two to four months old (1969: 977). Kempe stated that the "battered child syndrome" was most common in children under three years of age, while Galdston found that the most frequent cases of abuse were in children from three months to three-and-one-half years old. It is entirely possible that these data are somewhat misleading since the vulnerability of a child to physical damage is greater the younger he is. Gil found that 75 per cent of his cases of child abuse were over two years old; almost 50 per cent were over six years old; and 20 per cent of the cases were in their teens (1971: 640). The disparity between Gil's findings and the other findings may be a result of the type of data gathered. Gil gathered cases from a national survey, while Resnik, Bennie and Sclare, Kempe, and Galdston's cases were their own patients who were admitted into the hospital for treatment of serious injury resulting from parental abuse. Thus, while older children in

---

[7]Gil also determined that the reason for this might be the predominance of female-headed households. Gil states that in homes headed by fathers, the father was the abuser two-thirds of the time (1971: 641). Since the other authors did not standardize as did Gil, it is impossible to assume that their data would or would not support his findings.

Gil's survey are also subject to physical abuse, they do not appear in medical case studies because their age-produced physical durability makes them less vulnerable to serious physical damage caused by abuse.

There are two analytic directions which can be followed. The first is that there is something about parental relations with young, subsocial children which leads some parents to abuse them; while the second is that parental abuse of children is not a function of the child's age and that the data are misleading because of non-representative and selective gathering of cases. At this point, I would opt for the first direction. There seem to be three interrelated factors which result in the three-month to three-year-old child being particularly vulnerable to parental abuse. First, the small infant or toddler lacks the physical durability to withstand much physical punishment or force. While an older child might absorb a great deal of physical punishment, the three-month to three-year-old is likely to be severely damaged or even killed by the same type of force. Thus, since the younger child is more likely to be harmed, he is more easily abused. Secondly, the fact that the infant is not capable of much meaningful social interaction may create a great deal of frustration for the parent, who is trying to interact with the child. The case studies reveal that abusing parents often complain that they hit their child because they could not toilet-train him, get him to stop crying, or get him to obey their commands. Since the parent cannot "reason" with the infant, he may feel his only course of action is physical punishment. Thirdly, the new or infant child may create stress for the parent by his birth. The newborn child may create economic hardship for the family, or may interfere with professional, occupational, educational, or other plans of the parents. Thus, the new child may create structural stress for his parents, which is responded to by abuse. This proposal will be taken up in the next section, which discusses the social context of abuse.

*The Social Context of Child Abuse.* Perhaps the best example of the near-sightedness of the psychopathological approach to child abuse is the fact that it does not posit possible social causes of the psychological stress which it sees as leading to child abuse. This is indeed amazing considering the numerous mentions in the literature of stress-producing social situations which occur prior to the abuse or violent act.

One stress-producing condition is unemployment. O'Brien argues in his discussion of the causes of intra-family violence that one should find violence most common in families where the classically dominant member (male-adult-husband) fails to possess the superior skills, talents, or resources on which his preferred superior status is supposed to be legitimately based (1971: 693). O'Brien's theory would support the notion that unemployment of the husband would lead to intra-family violence. This assumption is supported in the child abuse literature. Gil found that nearly half of the fathers of abused children were not employed during the year preceding the abusive act, while 12 per cent were unemployed at the time of the abusive act (1971: 640). Galdston also found that in abusive families, the father of the abused child was unemployed or worked part-time while the wife worked part-time and cared for the child the rest of the time (1964: 442). While they do not have data to support their assumption, Steele and Pollack suspect that the low incidence of male attackers in their sample was, in part, a function of low unemployment among males in the group (1968: 108). However, Steele and Pollack go on to theorize that the reason why unemployed men would batter their children is that, as a result of unemployment, they would spend more time with the infant; thus, the male attacks rate would increase (1968: 108). Aside from supporting the notion that spending prolonged time with the infant would be frustrating, Steele and Pollack completely overlook the possible psychological stress that unemployment would create for the husband.

A second contextual factor is that the abused child is usually the product of an unwanted pregnancy. The Massachusetts Society for the Prevention of Cruelty to Children reports that in 50 per cent of 115 families studied, there was premarital conception (Zalba, 1971: 59). Wasserman found that in many of the child abuse cases, the child was conceived out of wedlock (1967: 177). Bennie and Sclare report that the abused child was often the product of an unwanted pregnancy (1969: 975)—the pregnancy was unwanted either because it was premarital or inconvenient. Kempe's Case #1 reveals that the battered child was an unwanted child which was born soon after marriage "before the parents were ready for it" (1962: 19). One of Resnick's cases of child murder reveals that a mother killed after she felt "labor pains" and was afraid she was pregnant again (1969: 327). The mother articulated the stress that another baby would cause by stating "how hard it is to raise even two children" (Resnick, 1969: 327).

The findings that the abused child is often the product of an unwanted pregnancy ties in with the finding that the abused child is both young and usually the youngest or only child (Bennie and Sclare, 1969: 977) and Gil's finding that there is more abuse in families of four or more children (1971: 640). These findings suggest that a newborn, unwanted child may create a tremendous amount of stress in family life. The child may be a financial burden, an emotional burden, or a psychological burden to the parent or parents who did not plan or want his arrival. Thus, the unwanted child can become the receiver of a parent's aggression, not because of some fantasy or "transference psychosis," but because the unwanted child is, in fact, a source of stress for the family. The abusive parent *is not* lashing out at a *projected* source of his troubles, he is beating a concrete source of family stress—an unwanted child.

The data about unemployment and unwanted children suggest that economic conditions producing stress and frustration are important factors in explaining parental abuse of children. This is a specific example of Goode's general proposition that a family that has little prestige, money, and power suffers greater frustration and bitterness and thus may resort to more violence (1971: 633).

Economic conditions are not the only source of stress which may lead to child abuse. Bennie and Sclare found that in four of seven cases of child abuse, women entered into marriage with men of different religions (1969: 979). The authors propose that intermarriage produced prolonged family stress, which eventually was a variable causing child abuse. Bennie and Sclare also found abusive families characterized by disrupted marital and family relationships (1969: 976). Zalba also found a great deal of marital and family conflicts in families where there were cases of child abuse (1971: 58).

*The Causes of Abuse: Toward a Social Psychological Model.* That stress is associated with child abuse is not a sufficient causal explanation of the phenomenon. It is insufficient because it does not explain why all families under similar structural stress do not abuse their children. It does not offer an explanation as to why one husband would hit his wife as an adaptation to stress while another would hit his child, and another not hit anyone. In order to develop a causal model of child abuse, one would have to explain the different adaptations to social conditions. A means of doing this is to reexamine the section on the causes of the psychopathy.

A review of the literature points out that abusive parents were raised in the same style which they have recreated in the pattern of rearing their own children (Steele and Pollack, 1968: 111). Kempe stated that attacking parents were subject to similar abuse as children and this pattern of child rearing is passed on in unchanged form (1962: 18). Gil's survey found that 11 per cent of parents who abuse their children were victims of abuse during childhood (1971: 641). Granted, as the authors articulating the psychopathological approach argue, that abuse as a child has psychological consequences, it also has sociological consequences. One factor which may determine what form of adaptation a parent will use in dealing with family stress is his own childhood socialization. A parent who was raised by parents who used physical force to train children and who grows up in a violent household has had as a role model the use of force and violence as a means of family problem solving. The parent who recreates the pattern of abusive child rearing may be doing this because this is the means of child rearing he learned while growing up. It is the way he knows of responding to stress and bringing up his child.

Considering this notion of child socialization and its effect on later patterns of child rearing, we may think of child abuse in terms of a social psychological model such as the one in Figure 2.

The purpose of presenting this model of factors influencing child abuse is not to suggest an exhaustive list of approaches nor to select one which is superior to the others. Instead, the purpose is to illustrate the complexity and the interrelationships of the factors which lead to child abuse.

This model assumes a certain amount of child abuse being a function of psychopathic states (bottom box). However, it goes beyond this unicausal approach by looking at other causes of child abuse. Thus, by imposing a social-psychological perspective, child abuse can be seen as a form of deviant behavior instead of being seen only as a result of individual pathology. The model assumes that frustration and stress are important variables associated with child abuse. Therefore, child abuse can be examined using a frustration-aggression approach (Miller, 1941). If the family stress is a result of certain structural conditions, such as social position or unemployment, a

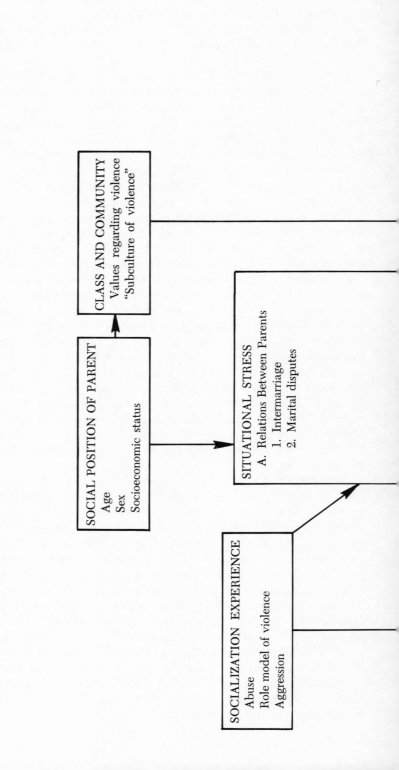

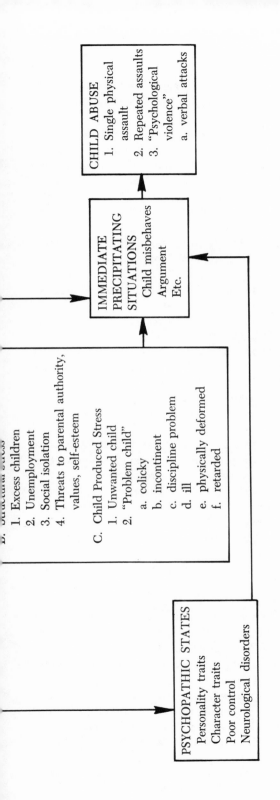

*Figure 2. A Social Psychological Model of the Causes of Child Abuse*

structural approach to deviance and aggressive behavior can be used (Merton, 1938). Conceptualizing child abuse as a form of violence, one can also look at it in terms of a subcultural approach (Wolfgang and Ferracuti, 1966).

*Conclusion: Implications for Strategies of Intervention and Future Research.* When a patient is diagnosed as sick, the treatment which is administered to him is designed to cure his illness. Consequently, when a child abuser is diagnosed as a psychopath, the treatment which is given him is designed to cure his disease and prevent future episodes which result from that disease. Basically, the cure prescribed is psychological counseling, psychotherapy, psychoanalysis, psychiatric aid, and other psychiatric mechanisms designed to rid the patient of his disorder. Galdston, for instance, advises telling the parents that their perception is erroneous and discolored by their own past experiences. In order to cure the "transference psychosis," the parent should be helped to review memories and ferret out sources of the psychosis (1965: 442). So far, the treatment of psychopathic disorders of abusive parents tends to be of limited effectiveness. Psychiatrists feel that treatment of the so-called sociopath or psychopath is rarely successful (Kempe, 1962: 20). With this treatment being of limited utility, the only remaining strategy of intervention is to remove the child from the parents. Even this strategy has little success since the state cannot keep the child from the parent indefinitely. Elmer (1967) reveals the case history of one family where the child was abused, removed from the family, thrived, returned, and was again beaten.

Thus far, it seems that the existing strategies of intervention in child abuse cases hold little promise for solving the problem. This paper suggests that one reason may be that the strategies are based on erroneous diagnoses of the problem. If one steps out of the psychopathological framework, it can be seen that the strategies are designed to cure symptoms which do not exist in many cases. If the parent is not a "psychopath" in any meaningful sense of the word, then how can treatment aimed at eliminating the psychopathy be of any consequence?

As far as developing new strategies of intervention, it is now necessary to stop thinking of child abuse as having a single cause: the mental aberrations of the parents. As Gil states, physical abuse of children is not a uniform phenomenon with one set of causal factors—but a multidimensional phenomenon (1971: 642). It is time to start thinking about the multiple social factors which influence child abuse. If unemployment and social class are important contextual variables, then strategies to prevent child abuse should aim at alleviating the disastrous effect of being poor in an affluent society. The fact that unwanted pregnancy appears so often in the cases indicates that programs ought to be designed to aid in planned parenthood, birth control devices, etc. Within this area is also a strong argument for the removal of the legal and social stigma of abortion so that unwanted children do not have to be born. And, finally, since there appears to be an association between child rearing and child abuse, programs should be developed to teach parents alternative means of bringing up their children.

The major flaw that exists in current programs and current strategies of intervention is that they amount to "an ambulance service at the bottom of the cliff." Child abuse programs now are after-the-fact treatment of parents and children. What needs to be done is to "fix the road on the cliff that causes the accidents." Strategies should be developed which can deal with the problem before the child is beaten or killed. These programs depend on a predictive theory of child abuse. The social psychological model of child abuse in this paper is a start in that direction.

## REFERENCES

Becker, Howard S.
1963    *Outsiders: Studies in the Sociology of Deviance.* New York: Free Press.
Bennie, E. H. and A. B. Sclare
1969    "The Battered Child Syndrome." *American Journal of Psychiatry* 125 (7): 975–979.
*Bibliography on the Battered Child*
1969    U. S. Department of Health, Education, and Welfare. Social and Rehabilitation Service, July.
Blumberg, Myrna
1964    "When Parents Hit Out." *Twentieth Century* 173 (Winter): 39–44.
Coles, Robert
1964    "Terror-Struck Children." *New Republic* 150 (May 30): 11–13.
Dunham, H. Warren
1964    "Anomie and Mental Disorder." Pp. 128–157 in Marshall B. Clinard (ed.), *Anomie and Deviant Behavior.* New York: Free Press.
Elmer, Elizabeth *et al.*
1967    *Children in Jeopardy: A Study of Abused Minors and their Families.* Pittsburgh: University of Pittsburgh Press.
Galdston, Richard
1965    "Observations of Children Who Have Been Physically Abused by Their Parents." *American Journal of Psychiatry* 122 (4): 440–443.
Gil, David G.
1971    "Violence Against Children." *Journal of Marriage and the Family* 33 (November): 637–657.
Goode, William J.
1971    "Force and Violence in the Family." *Journal of Marriage and the Family* 33 (November): 624–636.
Hakeem, Michael
1957    "A Critique of the Psychiatric Approach to the Prevention of Juvenile Delinquency." *Social Problems* 5 (Fall): 194–206.
Helfer, Ray E. and C. Henry Kempe (eds.)
1968    *The Battered Child.* Chicago: University of Chicago Press.
Kempe, C. Henry *et al.*
1962    "The Battered-Child Syndrome." *Journal of the American Medical Association* 181 (July 7): 17–24.
Merton, Robert K.
1938    "Social Structure and Anomie." *American Sociological Review* 3 (October): 672–682.
Miller, N. E.
1941    "The Frustration-Aggression Hypothesis." *Psychological Review* 48: 337–342.
O'Brien, John E.
1971    "Violence in Divorce Prone Families." *Journal of Marriage and the Family* 33 (November): 692–698.
Reiner, B. S. and I. Kaufman
1959    *Character Disorders in Parents of Delinquents.* New York: Family Service Association of America.

Resnick, Phillip J.
    1969    "Child Murder by Parents: A Psychiatric Review of Filicide." *American Journal of Psychiatry* 126 (3): 325–334.
Singer, Jerome
    1971    *The Control of Aggression and Violence.* New York: Academic Press.
Spinetta, John J., and David Rigler
    1972    "The Child Abusing Parent: A Psychological Review." *Psychological Bulletin* 77 (April): 296–304.
Steele, Brandt F. and Carl B. Pollack
    1968    "A Psychiatric Study of Parents Who Abuse Infants and Small Children." Pp. 103–147 in Ray E. Helfer and C. Henry Kempe (eds.), *The Battered Child.* Chicago: The University of Chicago Press.
Steinmetz, Suzanne K. and Murray A. Straus
    1973    "Five Myths About Violence in the Family." *Society,* Sept./Oct.
Szasz, Thomas S.
    1960    "The Myth of Mental Illness." *American Psychologist* 15 (February): 113–118.
    1961    *The Myth of Mental Illness: Foundations of a Theory of Personal Conduct.* New York: Delta.
    1970    *The Manufacture of Madness.* New York: Harper and Row.
Wasserman, Sidney
    1967    "The Abused Parent of the Abused Child." *Children* 14 (September-October): 175–179.
Wolfgang, Marvin E. and F. Ferracuti
    1967    *The Subculture of Violence.* London: Tavistock Publications.
Young, Leontine R.
    1964    *Wednesday's Children: A Study of Child Neglect and Abuse.* New York: McGraw-Hill.
Zalba, Serapio R.
    1971    "Battered Children." *Transaction* 8 (July–August): 58–61.

# CHAPTER SEVEN
# Helping Parents
# and Protecting Children

## 23. *A Conceptual Model of Child Abuse and its Implications for Social Policy*
### DAVID G. GIL

David Gil is the major figure among researchers and clinicians concerned with child abuse who rejects the psychopathology theory of the causes of child abuse. In the longer article from which the following selection was taken, Gil gives a summary of his studies. Among the findings of these studies are the following: (1) The rate for officially reported cases of child abuse is somewhere between six and ten thousand cases per year. However, these are only the most severe cases and the ones that get officially reported. Estimates based on sample surveys in which people were asked about cases they know suggest that the figure is over two *million* per year. (2) The families in which child abuse occurs are disproportionately poor, with low education, and are households headed by women. Nearly 60 per cent had received public assistance. (3) Stress due to difficulties in life circumstances were found to be present in 59 per cent of the cases in a special survey.

On the basis of findings such as these, it is no wonder that Gil puts primary emphasis on conditions in society which lead to child abuse rather than on abnormalities in the psychological makeup of the parents. In the following article, he first presents his interpretation of how these social factors bring about child abuse. Then, in the concluding section, he outlines the social policy implications, with emphasis on what needs to be changed in American society in order to reduce child abuse.

. . . *Culturally Sanctioned Use of Physical Force in Child Rearing.* One important conclusion of the nationwide surveys of child abuse (Gil, 1970a) was that physical abuse of children as defined here is not a rare and unusual occurrence in our society, and that by itself it should therefore not be considered as sufficient evidence of "deviance" of the perpetrator, the child, or the family. Physical abuse appears to be endemic in American society since our cultural norms of child rearing do not preclude the use of a certain measure of physical force toward children by adults caring for them. Rather, such use tends to be encouraged in subtle, and at times not so subtle, ways by "professional experts" in child rearing, education, and medicine; by the

SOURCE: Reprinted from David G. Gil, "Violence Against Children," *Journal of Marriage and the Family* 33 (November, 1971): 644–648.

press, radio and television; and by professional and popular publications. Furthermore, children are not infrequently subjected to physical abuse in the public domain in such settings as schools, child care faciles, foster homes, correctional and other children's institutions, and even in juvenile courts.

Strong support for considering child abuse as endemic in American society was provided by the public opinion survey, which revealed that nearly 60 per cent of adult Americans thought that "almost anybody could at some time injure a child in his care." That survey also indicated that several millions of children may be subjected every year to a wide range of physical abuse, though only several thousands suffer serious physical injury and a few hundred die as a consequence of abusive attacks. Against the background of public sanction of the use of violence against children, and the endemic scope of the prevalence of such cases, it should surprise no one that extreme incidents will occur from time to time in the course of "normal" child rearing practices.

It should be noted that in most incidents of child abuse the caretakers involved are "normal" individuals exercising their prerogative of disciplining a child whose behavior they find in need of correction. While some of these adults may often go farther than they intended because of anger and temporary loss of self-control, and/or because of chance events, their behavior does, nevertheless, not exceed the normative range of disciplining children as defined by the existing culture. Moreover, their acts are usually not in conflict with any law since parents, as well as teachers and other child care personnel, are in many American jurisdictions permitted to use a "reasonable" amount of corporal punishment. For children are not protected by law against bodily attack in the same way as are adults and, consequently, do not enjoy "equal protection under the law" as guaranteed by the XIVth Amendment to the U.S. Constitution.

While, then culturally sanctioned and patterned use of physical force in child rearing seems to constitute the basic causal dimension of all violence against children in American society, it does not explain many specific aspects of this phenomenon, especially its differential incidence rates among different population segments. Several additional causal dimensions need therefore be considered in interpreting the complex dynamics of physical child abuse.

*Difference in Child Rearing Patterns Among Social Strata and Ethnic Groups.* Different social and economic strata of society, and different ethnic and nationality groups tend to differ for various environmental and cultural reasons in their child rearing philosophies and practices, and consequently in the extent to which they approve of corporal punishment of children. These variations in child rearing styles among social and economic strata and ethnic groups constitute a second set of causal dimensions of child abuse, and are reflected in significant variations in incidence rates among these strata and groups. Thus, for instance, incidence rates tend to be negatively correlated with education and income. Also, certain ethnic groups reveal characteristic incidence patterns. Some American Indian tribes will never use physical force in disciplining their children while the incidence rates of child abuse are relatively high among American blacks and Puerto Ricans.

Lest the higher incidence rates among black and Puerto Rican minority groups be misinterpreted, it should be remembered that as a result of centuries of discrimination, non-white ethnic minority status tends to be associated in American society with low educational achievement and low income. The incidence rates of child abuse among these minority groups are likely to reflect this fact, as much as their specific cultural patterns. Furthermore, exposure of these minority groups to various forms of external societal violence to which they could not respond in kind, is likely to have contributed over time to an increase in the level of frustration-generated violence directed against their own members. Relatively high rates of homicide among members of these minority groups seem to support this interpretation.

Higher reporting rates of physical child abuse, and especially of more serious incidents, among the poor and among non-white minority groups may reflect biased reporting procedures. It may be true that the poor and non-whites are more likely to be reported than middle class and white population groups for anything they do or fail to do. At the same time there may also be considerable under-reporting of reportable transgressions not only among middle class and white population groups but also among the poor and the non-white minorities. The net effect of reporting bias and of overall and specific under-reporting with respect to child abuse can, at this time, not be estimated.

It should not be overlooked, however, that life in poverty and in minority group ghettoes tends to generate many stressful experiences which are likely to become precipitating factors of child abuse by weakening a caretaker's psychological mechanisms of self-control and contributing, thus, to the uninhibited discharge of his aggressive and destructive impulses toward physically powerless children. The poor and members of ethnic minority groups seem to be subject to many of the conditions and forces which may lead to abusive behavior toward children in other groups of the population and, in addition to this, they seem to be subject to the special environmental stresses and strains associated with socioeconomic deprivation and discrimination. This would suggest that the significantly higher reporting rates for poor and non-white segments of the population reflect a real underlying higher incidence rate among these groups.

It should also be noted that the poor and non-whites tend to have more children per family unit and less living space. They also tend to have fewer alternatives than other population groups for avoiding or dealing with aggressive impulses toward their children. The poor tend to discharge aggressive impulses more directly as they seem less inhibited in expressing feelings through action. These tendencies are apparently learned through lower class and ghetto socialization, which tends to differ in this respect from middle class socialization and mores.

Middle class parents, apparently as a result of exposure to modern psychological theories of child rearing, tend to engage more than lower class parents in verbal interaction with their children, and to use psychological approaches in disciplining them. It may be noted, parenthetically, that verbal and psychological interaction with children may at times be as violent and abusive in its effects, or even more so, than the use of physical force in disciplining them. Life in middle class families tends to generate tensions and pressures characteristic of the dominant individualistic and competitive value orientations of American society, and these pressures may also precipitate violence against children. However, middle class families are spared the more devastating daily tensions and pressures of life in poverty. They also tend to have fewer children, more living space, and more options to relax, at times, without their children. All this would suggest a lower real incidence rate of physical child abuse among middle class families.

*Deviance and Pathology in Bio-Psycho-Social Functioning of Individuals and Families.* A further set of causal dimensions of violence against children involves a broad range of deviance in biological, psychological, and social functioning of caretakers, children in their care, and of entire family units. This is the causal context which had been identified and stressed by most clinical investigators of child abuse. It is important to note that this dimension of child abuse is by no means independent of the basic cultural dimension discussed above. The choice of symptoms through which intra-psychic conflicts are expressed by members of a society tends to be influenced by the culture of that society. Symptoms of personality deviance involve often exaggerated levels of culturally sanctioned trends. It would thus seem that violent acts against children would less likely be symptoms of personality disorders in a society which did not sanction the use of physical force in rearing its young.

The presence of this third dimension of child abuse was reflected in findings from our surveys, which revealed relatively high rates of deviance in bio-psycho-social circumstances and functioning of children and adults involved in many reported incidents. Often manifestations of such deviance had been observed during the year preceding an incident. Deviance in functioning of individuals was also matched by high rates of deviance in family structure reflected in a high proportion of female-headed households, and of households from which the biological fathers of the abused children were absent.

*Environmental Chance Events.* A final, but not insignificant causal dimension of child abuse is environmental chance events which may transform "acceptable" disciplinary measures into serious and "unacceptable" outcomes. It is thus obvious that physical abuse of children, like so many other social problems, is a multidimensional phenomenon rather than a unidimensional one with a single set of causal factors. This multidimensional conception of child abuse and its dynamics suggests a corresponding multidimensional approach to the prevention or reduction of the incidence rate of this destructive phenomenon.

IMPLICATIONS FOR SOCIAL POLICY

Violence against children constitutes a severe infringement of their rights as members of society. Since distribution of rights in a society is a key aspect of its social policies, modifications of these policies are necessary if the rights of children to physical safety are to be assured (Gil, 1970). For social policies to be effective they must be based on a causal theory concerning the etiology of the condition which is to be corrected or prevented. Accordingly, social policies aimed at protecting the rights of children to bodily safety should be designed around the causal dimensions of child abuse presented in the conceptual model of this phenomenon.

Since cultural sanctions of the use of physical force in child rearing constitute the common core of all physical abuse of children in American society, efforts aimed at gradually changing this aspect of the prevailing child rearing philosophy, and developing clear-cut cultural prohibitions and legal sanctions against such use of physical force, are likely to produce over time the strongest possible reduction of the incidence and prevalence of physical abuse of children.

Suggesting to forego the use of physical force in rearing children does not mean that inherently non-social traits of children need not be modified in the course of socialization. It merely means that non-violent, constructive, educational measures would have to replace physical force. It needs to be recognized that giving up the use of physical force against children may not be easy for adults who were subjected to physical force and violence in their own childhood and who have integrated the existing value system of American society. Moreover, children can sometimes be very irritating and provocative in their behavior and may strain the tolerance of adults to the limit. Yet, in spite of these realities, which must be acknowledged and faced openly, society needs to work toward the gradual reduction, and eventual complete elimination, of the use of physical force against children if it intends to protect their basic right of security from physical attack.

As a first, concrete step toward developing eventually comprehensive legal sanctions against the use of physical force in rearing children, the Congress and legislatures of the states could outlaw corporal punishment in schools, juvenile courts, correctional institutions and other child care facilities. Such legislation would assure children the same constitutional protection against physical attack outside their homes as the law provides for adult members of society. Moreover, such legislation is likely to affect child rearing attitudes and practices in American homes, for it would symbolize society's growing rejection of violence against children.

To avoid misinterpretations it should be noted here that rejecting corporal punishment does not imply favoring unlimited permissiveness in rearing children. To grow up successfully, children require a sense of security which is inherent in non-arbitrary structures and limits. Understanding adults can establish such structures and limits through love, patience, firmness, consistency, and rational authority. Corporal punishment seems devoid of constructive educational value since it cannot provide that sense of security and nonarbitrary authority. Rarely, if ever, is corporal punishment administered for the benefit of an attacked child, for usually it serves the immediate needs of the attacking adult who is seeking relief from his uncontrollable anger and stress.

The multiple links between poverty and racial discrimination and physical abuse of children suggest that one essential route toward reducing the incidence and prevalence of child abuse is the elimination of poverty and of structural social inequalities. This objective could be approached through the establishment of a guaranteed decent annual income for all, at least at the level of the Bureau of Labor Statistics "low" standard of living. No doubt this is only a partial answer to the complex issue of preventing violence toward children, but perhaps a very important part of the total answer, and certainly that part without which other preventive efforts may be utterly futile. Eliminating poverty by equalizing opportunities and rights, and by opening up access for all to all levels of the social status system, also happens to be that part of the answer for which this nation possesses the necessary know-how and resources, provided we were willing to introduce changes in our priorities of resource development, and to redistribute national wealth more equitably.

Deviance and pathology in biological, psychological, and social functioning of individuals and of family units were identified as a third set of forces which contribute to the incidence and prevalence of physical abuse of children. These conditions tend to be strongly associated with poverty and racial discrimination, and, therefore, eliminating poverty and discrimination are likely to reduce, though by no means to eliminate, the incidence and prevalence of these various dysfunctional phenomena. The following measures, aimed at the secondary and tertiary prevention and amelioration of these conditions and their consequences, and at the strengthening of individual and family functioning, should be available in every community as components of a comprehensive program for reducing the incidence of physical abuse of children, and also for helping individuals and families once abuse has occurred:

a. Comprehensive family planning programs including the repeal of all legislation concerning medical abortions: The availability of family planning resources and medical abortions are likely to reduce the number of unwanted and rejected children, who are known to be frequently victims of severe physical abuse and even infanticide. It is important to recall in this context that families with many children, and female-headed households, are overrepresented among families involved in physical abuse of children.

b. Family life education and counseling programs for adolescents and adults in preparation for, and after marriage: Such programs should be developed in accordance with the assumption that there is much to learn about married life and parenthood which one does not know merely on the basis of sexual and chronological maturity.

c. A comprehensive, high quality, neighborhood based, national health service, financed through general tax revenue, and geared not only to the treatment of acute and chronic illness, but also the promotion and maintenance of maximum feasible physical and mental health for everyone.

d. A range of high quality, neighborhood based social services geared to the reduction of environmental stresses on family life and especially on mothers who carry major responsibility for the child rearing function. Any measure which would reduce these stresses would also indirectly reduce the incidence rate of child abuse. Homemaker and housekeeping services, mothers' helpers and baby-sitting services, family and group day-care facilities for pre-school and school age children are all examples of such services. It should be recognized, however, that unless a decent income is assured to all families, these social services are unlikely to achieve their objectives.

e. Every community needs also a system of social services and child care facilities geared to assisting families and children who cannot live together because of severe relationship and/or reality problems. Physically abused children belong frequently to this category.

The measures proposed herewith are aimed at different causal dimensions of violence against children. The first set would attack the culturally determined core of the phenomenon; the second set would attack and eliminate major conditions to which child abuse is linked in many ways; the third set approaches the causes of child abuse indirectly. It would be futile to argue the relative merits of these approaches as all three are important. The basic question seems to be, not which measure to select for combating child abuse, but whether American society is indeed committed to assuring equal rights to all its children, and to eradicate child abuse in any form, abuse perpetrated by individual caretakers, as well as abuse perpetrated collectively by society. Our affluent society certainly seems to possess the resources and the skills to eradicate the massive forms of abuse committed by society collectively as well as the physical violence perpetrated by individuals and societal institutions against children in their care.

## REFERENCES

Gil, David G.
  1970a    "A Systematic Approach to Social Policy Analysis." *The Social Service Review* 44 (December).
Gil, David G.
  1970b    *Violence Against Children: Physical Abuse in the United States.* Cambridge, Mass.: Harvard University Press.
Kempe, C. Henry *et al.*
  1962    "The Battered Child Syndrome." *Journal American Medical Association* 181 (17).
U.S. Children's Bureau
  1962    *The Abused Child: Principles and Suggested Language on Reporting the Physically Abused Child.* Washington, D.C.: U.S. Government Printing Office.
  1966    *The Child Abuse Reporting Laws—A Tabular View.* Washington, D.C.: U.S. Government Printing Office.
  1969    *Bibliography on the Battered Child.* Washington, D.C.: Clearinghouse for Research in Child Life, U.S. Government Printing Office.

## 24. *Treatment of Child Abuse*
### SERAPIO R. ZALBA

Although our main emphasis is on the social conditions which lead to child abuse, this does not deny the importance of treating individual cases. The larger social changes called for by the analyses of Gelles and Gil will take a long time to be implemented and an even longer time to be effective. Moreover, it is by no means sure that such policies will be implemented or that, if implemented, they will be effective. Finally, even those who are most convinced of the greater importance of social causes of child abuse compared to psychological causes, do not deny that some cases occur because of defects in the personality of the parent. For these reasons individual casework treatment of child-abusing parents will always be desirable. Zalba has long been concerned with methods of treating such cases and has written widely on the topic. This article presents a summary of some of the specific steps which can be taken to deal with instances of child abuse, not the least of which are techniques for locating cases before the child ends up in the hospital.

. . . There seems to be agreement about the general strategy in protective service with cases of child abuse. The first step is to verify the actual existence of abuse, then determine the imminent danger of harm to the children if they remain in the home. These are extremely difficult tasks for a variety of reasons.

*Identification.* As Kempe and others have pointed out, a number of factors militate against the recognition and reporting or referral of cases of child abuse. Medical personnel do not always recognize that traumatic injuries may be inflicted rather than accidental or owing to physiological factors. When they do recognize that injury was inflicted, they are reluctant to risk involving themselves in court appearances and the like by reporting the incidents to the authorities (3, 16, 17, 28).

Inadequacies exist as well in case-finding and referral for protective services from other social welfare institutions in the community. While this is partly owing to the factors mentioned above, it is also related to the general lack of communication and co-ordination of community welfare services (9, 38, 39, 40, 41).[1] Law enforcement personnel tell of having identified cases in need of protective treatment, but not having local resources to which to refer them.[2] Developing a community program of protective services requires a balance of both community co-operation in case-finding and the provision of adequate resources for treatment once cases are identified.

*Evidence.* In cases where abuse or neglect are suspected it is difficult to get conclusive evidence for the following reasons: the abusers tend to deny their actions, marital partners tend to protect the abusing ones, the children are often too young to give credible testimony, often there are no witnesses.

SOURCE: Reprinted with permission of the author and The National Association of Social Workers, from *Social Work*, Vol. 11, No. 4 (October, 1966), pp. 8–16.

[1]For a study on the difficulties in the co-ordination and co-operation of services for a similar clientele *see* Zalba (49).

[2]Personal communications to the writer.

Consequently the task of establishing the fact of serious child abuse is difficult, especially since time is of the essence in the protection against further, sometimes fatal, injury (3, 18). When imminent danger is believed to exist, it may be necessary to petition the courts for removal of the child or children, or the abusive adult, from the home. Protection against unwarranted infringement of the adult's rights requires that sufficient evidence be presented to the court that danger of serious abuse does exist. The dual demands of sufficient and immediate evidence thus contribute to the difficulty of the protective workers' task.

*Diagnosis.* The next step in providing protective services is to determine in greater depth and detail the dynamics of the case and the diagnosis and prognosis. When it is consistent with the safety of the children, it is considered preferable to keep the children in the home and proceed with treatment on that basis (6, 14, 38, 41). When removal becomes necessary, care must be exercised to avoid returning the child home until there is some assurance that significant and stable change has been accomplished that makes it safe to return him. The hospital studies and the Philadelphia study are very careful to make this point (3, 14, 18, 28).

*Removal.* While the physical safety of the children must be the primary criterion in deciding whether their removal is absolutely necessary, there are other important considerations. Despite or perhaps because of the disturbed relationship with the abusing parent, the victimized child may not be able to tolerate losing the only security he knows, namely, his home, his other parent, and his siblings (7, 21, 26, 38). Because of the abuse he has experienced he may also have emotional and behavioral disorders (e.g., bedwetting, truanting, fire-setting, or withdrawing) that make him extremely hard to place in foster home care (14, 26). Keeping him in placement may require moving him as he aborts a number of placements. Such a pattern is very trying for the agency and worker and devastating for the child (38, 49).

Yet if children remain in homes where there is repeated abuse they are likely to internalize the behavioral models to which they are exposed. As Reiner and Kaufman say:

Having experienced loss of love or inconsistent care themselves, they are unable as adults to provide a mature and consistent type of parental care for their children, but pass on these elements to them. . . . Such parents have a tendency to subject their own children to similar losses and to experiences that will engender the same attitudes. (41)

There are other considerations when removal of an abused child is contemplated. What about the children who remain behind? It may be that removal of the abused child will result in the choice of a new scapegoat. Also, while in some cases one specific child is the target of abuse, this is by no means always true. Often two, three, or all of the children are abused, and this happens in some of the most serious and dangerous cases (14).

*Casework Treatment.* Perhaps the issue to be faced is that we are dealing with disturbed families—that even in cases when all the children are removed from the home a seriously disturbed individual (the abusing parent), who may need treatment or supervision, remains behind. The parents we are considering are among the core group of the "hard-to-reach" families, well known to all social welfare agencies. Reiner and Kaufman state, "It is probably safe to say that families with members suffering from severe character disorders represent the most serious social problem in our country" (41). They are a difficult group of clients to work with because of their demanding, hostile, inconsistent behavior (41). When treatment is provided, a long-term, consistent, relationship-oriented approach is indicated; there appears to be general consensus on the inadvisability of short-term, emergency-oriented treatment (6, 14, 38, 41).

The specifics of casework treatment with child-abusing parents cannot be dealt with adequately in a paper of this length. The reader should refer to the Reiner and Kaufman book, which deals with the treatment of character-disordered parents, who make up the majority of child-battering parents (41). There are, however, a number of treatment problems indigenous to protective treatment that it might be useful to enumerate here:

1. Massive denial of abusive behavior or other personal problems.

2. Provocative behavior toward the worker, such as demandingness, rage, hostility, and acting out.

3. Fear of closeness in relationships; preference for authority-based relationships.

4. Little guilt over abusive or other hostile behavior.

The basic treatment objectives are to work closely with the clients and perform certain ego functions for them, such as setting limits on behavior, making realistic judgments for and with them, and helping them develop their own reality perception by pointing out distorted perceptions and consequences of their choices and acts. In effect the worker is lending his ego abilities to his client in the hope that his positive relationship with the client and the effectiveness of his ego behavior will lead the client to incorporate some of the worker's "ego strengths." As a consequence he would then be able to face the depressive nucleus of his personality and express his underlying feelings of fear and hurt, instead of defending against depression and anxiety through flight and denial. In this way he would come to realize and accept the finality of his childhood losses, begin to incorporate the attitudes of the worker, and evolve a new ego ideal and sense of identity. The foregoing description of Reiner and Kaufman's formulation of the treatment process provides some sense of why the client in such cases is so fearful of investing in a positive meaningful relationship with the worker; he needs to assure himself that he will not suffer another significant interpersonal loss, which he is so poorly equipped to handle. Part of his basic malady is an uncertain sense of identity.[3] Thus he is also handicapped in dealing with changes in workers or referrals from one agency to another.[4]

---

[3]Bernard L. Diamond provides a succinct statement of this problem (15).

[4]Those who have worked with correctional clients will recognize many of the client attributes described here. Character-disordered people make up the bulk of correctional case loads. This is true for county jail and probation clients as well as prison inmates and parolees.

*Group Methods.* There is some indication that group methods of treatment are desirable, perhaps even preferable, in the treatment of many abusive parents. Such parents have been described earlier as typically isolated and socially unskilled. They tend to deny their difficulties, have problems of control over impulses, and have difficulties with authority. These characteristics make them prime candidates for ego-oriented group treatment. Reiner and Kaufman do, in fact, say that group techniques may be indicated with parents who have character disorders (41). McFerran reports on a successful program of group counseling with parents in child neglect cases in Kentucky (31). There has been extensive correctional experience with group treatment methods in New Jersey (30), California (25), and with county jail clientele similar to the abusive parents under consideration.[5]

*The Children.* The discussion of treatment up to this point has dealt primarily with the parents. The child-battering literature has little to say on treatment of the children. When the children are very young and remain in the home, it is likely that the main course of treatment *for* (rather than *of*) children is change of the malignant environment, either by removal from it or by changing it through treatment of the parents or removal of the abusive one. When the children are old enough and disturbed enough to need direct treatment, some guidance is provided by Kaufman, who outlines three phases of treatment:

1. Management of the reality situation and achievement of environmental stability (preferably in the child's own home).

2. With regression and expression of direct hostility by the child (i.e., testing) the worker needs to be firm and consistent; it is helpful to use activity programs such as trips, ball games, and so on.

3. Psychotherapy when needed.

Another possible treatment approach would be to treat the whole family conjointly. This has been done successfully with schizophrenics by Don D. Jackson and Virginia Satir (24). Both probation officers and parole officers with training in the conjoint family therapy method have treated juvenile delinquents and their families.[6]

*Treatment Personnel.* In discussing the question of who should provide the protective treatment services, Kaufman has stated repeatedly that relationship therapy is indicated—i.e., the presentation of a reality situation—and that social workers are good at this kind of treatment (26, 27, 41). He feels that some social workers perceive relationship therapy as having low status; they would prefer doing "psychotherapy." This is an unfortunate assessment, in his view, because of the efficacy of the treatment; the choice of

[5]The writer has visited group-oriented programs in the California county jail systems of San Diego and Santa Clara counties, and conducted group counseling programs in San Francisco and San Mateo counties.

[6]The writer was acquainted with a number of probation officers in San Mateo County's family-centered unit who used conjoint family therapy. Some of the Youth Authority parole officers in California's Community Treatment Project have also used this technique (22).

technique should be in terms of its efficacy, not its status (26). An important qualification for effective work with this client group is the proper temperament. There are tremendous emotional, as well as technical and intellectual, demands in the work (41). The worker must communicate on both a verbal *and* nonverbal level with clients whose behavior is bizarre, asocial, aggressive, childish, and provocative. The clients are extremely sensitive to artificiality or insincerity. The worker must therefore be alert to his own feelings and honest and forthright, yet in control of his hostility.

The problem, as Reiner and Kaufman point out, is not so much one of cross-cultural conflict between worker and client, but of psychosexual developmental conflict; it is difficult to be tolerant of an oral or anal character who is messy, demanding, or who cannot hold onto money or a job (41). Such demands on a worker necessitate that he receive support and assistance from his peers, supervisor, and agency, and the agency must make provision to meet those needs.

In addition to the difficulties and demands that inhere in relationships with such clients, the worker must cope with the complexity of the medical and legal matters involved. He will need consultation—medical, legal, and psychological (22)—and, as any correctional or protective worker can testify, he will need tact and patience in dealing with the courts.

## TREATMENT PROGNOSES AND RESULTS

Little can be said about the efficacy of treatment efforts reported by the studies reviewed in this paper. The Massachusetts group indicated that 66 per cent of the 115 families included in their study were structurally intact at the time of their report, children had been placed outside the home in 27 per cent of the cases, and the family structure had been changed (i.e., removal of an adult) in 12 per cent (14). It does not seem wise to infer that the figures given are indices of treatment outcomes. If the structurally intact homes are taken to be indicative of successful treatment, what must be said about the splintered homes? Common sense tells us that the removal of a seriously battered child from a dangerous situation at home in time to avoid his destruction or permanent injury must be counted as successful intervention.

Delsordo, by specifying categories of parents with poor prognoses for treatment, implied that favorable results were achieved (or could have been achieved) with the other categories. He gives the following prognostic assessments of treatability (14):

1. *Battered child.* "I know of no case of classical child battering in which the child has been able to remain safely with the abusive parent." Even after separation and treatment, extreme care should be taken not to reunite the abused child and the abusive parent precipitously. (Delsordo reports on one case of precipitous reunion in which the child was killed.)

2. *Disciplinary abuse.* While the parents may comply temporarily with the worker's standards, he should continue his services until real progress is made (implied treatability).

3. *Misplaced abuse.* Prognosis is good. Children are rarely in danger of death, and parents manifest some guilt and are able to control their behavior. While this group is amenable to casework treatment, they are not easy to treat.

4. *Mentally ill* (this category is the same as the "psychotic attitudes" category of Reiner and Kaufman). Prognosis is poor. These parents need psychiatric treatment; they should be separated from the children until substantially improved through treatment.

McFerran and Reiner and Kaufman indicate that favorable results are achieved by use of group techniques, but they do not specify *which* parents would be most amenable to *which* group techniques. In a report on the treatment of delinquents in the community, a California group indicated that conjoint family therapy was most successful with the families of high maturity delinquents, and family re-education (counseling and discussion) with the families of middle maturity cases (22).[7]

## COMMUNITY CONSIDERATIONS

Because of the extremely serious consequences of child battering it is imperative that it be recognized and reported when it is encountered. Physicians are an especially crucial group in this respect, yet, as Kempe (28), Dodge (16), and others have pointed out, many of them are not aware of the phenomenon and some prefer to do nothing when they do recognize it. This points to the need for educational efforts directed to the medical profession and to other groups that are likely to have frequent contact with serious cases of child abuse, e.g., law enforcement personnel, schools, public health nurses, social agencies, and the like. Some states have specific laws that make it mandatory to report cases of verified or suspected child battering.[8] Even in states where protection against physical injury derives from the more general statutes pertaining to mayhem, assault and battery, and so on, the physician, as Schoepfer (42) points out, may make himself an accessory to a crime by accepting a fee from the offender (abusive parent) for treating the victim (abused child) and then not reporting the crime. Some writers recommend the passage of specific anti-child-battering laws (in all states) as a way of clarifying the societal sanction for reporting cases of child abuse (16, 32).

*Resources.* Part of the dilemma in protective services is that the resources for dealing with the cases identified and reported are rather limited. The study of protective service needs and resources in California makes this clear (39). Moreover, while authorities in the field point out the specialized nature

[7]The Community Treatment Project of the California Youth Authority uses a typology of delinquents based on interpersonal maturity levels (1 through 4) and delinquent subtypes associated with specific levels (e.g., middle maturity, $I_s$; Subtype: Manipulator, $M_p$) (22).

[8]Fontana cites the following states as having such laws as of 1964: California, Colorado, Florida, Minnesota, Ohio, Pennsylvania, Tennessee, Wisconsin, and Wyoming (20). De Francis adds Idaho and Oregon to the list of states with such laws in 1963, but omits Tennessee (13).

of the technical and emotional demands inherent in protective work (26, 38), Reiner and Kaufman (41) report that during the past few years case loads in a variety of social work agencies appear to contain more and more character disorder cases. If this is true, then the techniques and problems associated with protective cases will become the same as those found in the other agencies, and protective *services,* rather than protective *agencies,* should be the goal.

It was noted earlier that there is a polarization of private agency auspices for protective services in the East and public agency auspices in the West. Nevertheless, it has been pointed out that in *all* states it is a public responsibility to assure the provision of such services (40). Arguments can be made for both patterns of auspices—the *right to services* is associated with public programs, and *flexibility to experiment* is associated with private programs—but if private agencies are to prosper, the financial realities of increasing difficulty in private fund-raising would seem to indicate a pattern of public purchase of the private service (38). Ultimately, however, there is public responsibility for the availability and provision of protective services.

While public welfare programs are generally organized along state lines (sometimes with county administration), a number of federally financed projects to demonstrate the efficacy of protective services have been conducted on the local level. But despite the general agreement that the utility and effectiveness of such programs has been satisfactorily demonstrated, once the project funds have been exhausted the services tend to be dropped (39). What seems necessary is a federally supported ongoing program of such services, and it appears that the efforts continually being made to strengthen the AFDC and child welfare programs under the Social Security Act have this objective partly in mind. A major requirement in accomplishing this is the upgrading of the skills of the public assistance worker, which involves vastly improved and intensified in-service training of personnel. It is crucial that graduate schools of social work participate and provide some leadership in this important task.

Agencies attempting to give increased emphasis to protection or prevention-focused services are faced with the need to modify some of the typical features of social agency practice. Protective case needs cannot generally be met by a worker during prescribed office hours at the agency. A great deal of field work and investigation are required, often in the evening. Accommodations must be made to the availability of the clients and ancillary resources. Stereotypes about law enforcement and correctional personnel must be discarded, and contacts must be individualized. Community organization is every worker's job, and in protective cases this will become especially apparent.

Descriptions of other hard-to-reach clients (36, 47, 49) give an indication of their essential similarity to the clients in protective cases. Consideration thus might be given to following the pattern set by the Family-centered Project in St. Paul, where an interagency pool of skilled, well-trained workers was created to provide treatment for the most critical cases identified in the community (37).

## DISCUSSION AND CONCLUSIONS

Child-battering and serious child abuse are inflicted by parents with a variety of problems ranging from violent and episodic schizophrenia to immature and impulse-ridden character disorder, who displace and act out their anger over marital conflicts onto their children. The common element among them is that children are used as targets of abuse and injury in the process of projecting, displacing, and denying intra-psychic and other-object-oriented hostility and aggression.

The children are the injured parties, and the term "battered child syndrome" may be of use in hospitals where it is important to identify the external source of the injuries. But insofar as the term does not identify the etiological problems involved—i.e., the psychosocial dynamics and problems of the parents and the family that result in the battering of the child—it is of little use to those involved in providing protective services. A more appropriate label would be "families with child-battering adults"—without the term "syndrome," since there is no *clearly defined entity* that can be identified.

The family environment plays a crucial role in the development of the child's personality, character, and social style of life. Life in an unfavorable family environment can result in a dependent, unstable, impulse-ridden, delinquent adult who will, in turn, be a poor parent, generating in this way an epidemiological chain of inadequate, destructive parenting. Many of the studies cited in this paper have reported on the histories of childhood abuse, neglect, and deprivation typical of the abusive parent.

Early identification and intervention are thus indicated. While the schools are good at identification, it would be preferable to identify the still earlier, preschool instances of neglect and abuse. The National Study Service's report on California observes that many of the protective cases coming to the attention of the authorities had histories of prior mistreatment; thus the difficulties had continued without identification or remedy for some time (39). Class comments on the more recent tendency in this country to "play it safe," to not get involved in the personal affairs of others (9). He cites a case in which three children had been chained to a bed for days, yet neighbors were not aware that the children lived in the house, although they had been there for six months! In the past few years a number of incidents have been reported prominently in the national press in which citizens stood by without taking action while some innocent person was beaten or stabbed. (This is, perhaps, another of the unfortunate consequences of industrialization and the movement from rural openness and co-operation to urban privacy and isolation.) Hopefully, help will come to the abused child and his family before it is too late. Abuse, like other behavior, becomes habitual; children learn from the behavior they witness and they internalize conceptions of themselves communicated to them by others.

Beginning attempts have been made at a typology of child abuse. Typological systems have been hypothesized and given preliminary tests. Treatment models have been proposed. What is needed now is a more precisely formulated typological system, replete with predictive indicators of the danger to the children and the probabilities of various outcomes for specifically prescribed treatment.

An American Public Welfare Association report calls for the statutory assignment of responsibility for protective services in each state (40). Only then is there any accountability and ultimate assurance of at least a minimum acceptable level of service. In the report of the National Study Service the recommendation is made that protective services in California be a function of public child welfare services in a new division to be called "Child Care and Protection" (39). Class argues that probation departments are already overloaded and that public welfare agencies are identified with public assistance; he proposes that protective services be located in "child welfare agencies" (9). (Many public welfare departments would resent the implication that they are not, at least partly, child welfare agencies, but Class seems to be referring to the private "family" agencies.)

As the APWA report states, ultimately there is public responsibility to see that protective services are available when needed (40). The problems of many public assistance families require treatment similar to that considered efficacious for protective service cases. There appears to be a significant similarity of purpose, technique, and public responsibility that makes public welfare auspices a natural environment for protective services.

Any agency carrying the responsibility for protective casework services will have to work out viable relationships with a number of agencies that share responsibility for aspects of protective work other than the primary casework with the parents. Law enforcement personnel are extremely important and crucial. They generally have responsibility for answering emergency calls, especially during evenings, weekends, and holidays. Often they have to make immediate decisions about whether to remove a child from his home. When there is no specified emergency child shelter care, the task of the juvenile police officer is even more difficult. Often juvenile detention homes, hospitals, and jails are utilized for emergency care. In some cases police officers will even take children to their own homes, even though this may not be legally authorized.[9] It can be seen that the police officer is an extremely important ally and colleague in protective work. So are the probation officer, the doctor, the judge, and school personnel. The logical necessity for interagency co-operation belies the extreme difficulty of accomplishing it (49).

A number of ancillary services are required for an effective program of community protective services. Included are emergency shelter care, homemaker services, day care, foster homes, financial assistance, and psychiatric treatment.

. . . This paper has attempted to bring some perspective to the extremely serious problem of child battering and abuse. The recent interest and concern with the problem is, it is hoped, a harbinger of increased services and research activity.

[9]Personal communication to the writer.

# REFERENCES

1. Adelson, Lester. "Slaughter of the Innocents," *New England Journal of Medicine*, Vol. 264 (1961), pp. 1345–1349.
2. Allen, A., and Morton, A. *This is Your Child: The Story of the National Society for the Prevention of Cruelty to Children*. London, Eng.: Routledge & Kegan Paul, 1961.
3. Boardman, Helen E. "A Project to Rescue Children from Inflicted Injuries," *Social Work*, Vol. 7, No. 1 (January, 1962). pp. 43–51.
4. Bossard, James H. S. *The Sociology of Child Development*. New York: Harper & Bros., 1948.
5. Bowlby, John. *Child Care and the Growth of Love*. London, Eng.: Whitefriars Press, 1953.
6. Bryant, Harold D., *et al.* "Physical Abuse of Children in an Agency Study," *Child Welfare*, Vol. 42, No. 3 (March, 1963), pp. 125–130.
7. Burlington, Dorothy, and Freud, Anna. *Infants Without Families*. New York: International Universities Press, 1944.
8. Chesser, Eustace. *Cruelty to Children*. New York: Philosophical Library, 1952.
9. Class, Norris E. "Neglect, Social Deviance, Community Action," *NPPA Journal*, Vol. 6, No. 1 (January, 1960), pp. 17–23.
10. Cohen, Nathan E. *Social Work in the American Tradition*. New York: Dryden Press, 1958.
11. DeFrancis, Vincent. *Child Protective Services in the U.S.* Denver: Children's Division, American Humane Association, 1956.
12. ———. *The Fundamentals of Child Protection*. Denver: Children's Division, American Humane Association, 1955.
13. ———. *Review of Legislation to Protect the Battered Child*. Denver: American Humane Association, undated.
14. Delsordo, James D. "Protective Casework for Abused Children," *Children*, Vol. 10, No. 6 (November–December, 1963), pp. 213–218.
15. Diamond, Bernard L. "Newsletter of the Northern California Service League." San Francisco, January, 1959. Mimeographed.
16. Dodge, Philip R. "Medical Implications of Physical Abuse of Children," in *Protecting the Battered Child*. Denver: American Humane Association, 1962. Pp. 23–25.
17. Elmer, Elizabeth. "Abused Young Children Seen in Hospitals," *Social Work*, Vol. 5, No. 4 (October, 1960), pp. 98–102.
18. ———. "Identification of Abused Children," *Children*, Vol. 10, No. 5 (September–October, 1963), pp. 180–184.
19. Erikson, Erik H. *Childhood and Society*. New York: W. W: Norton & Co., 1950.
20. Fontana, Vincent J. *The Maltreated Child*. Springfield, Ill.: Charles C. Thomas, 1964.
21. Freud, Anna. "Special Experiences of Children—Especially in Times of Social Disturbance," in Kenneth Soddy, ed., *Mental Health and Infant Development*. New York: Basic Books, 1956.
22. Grant, Marguerite Q., Warren, Martin, and Turner, James K. "Community Treatment Project Report No. 3." Sacramento: California Youth Authority, 1963.
23. Housden, Leslie G. *The Prevention of Cruelty to Children*. London, Eng.: Cape, 1955.
24. Jackson, Don D., and Weakland, J. H. "Conjoint Family Therapy: Some Considerations in Theory, Technique, and Results," *Psychiatry*, Vol. 24 (1961), pp. 30–45.
25. Kassebaum, Gene G., Ward David A., and Wilner, Daniel M. *Group Treatment by Correctional Personnel*. Sacramento: California Department of Corrections, 1963.
26. Kaufman, Irving. "The Contribution of Protective Services," *Child Welfare*, Vol. 36, No. 2 (February, 1957).
27. ———. "Psychiatric Implications of Physical Abuse of Children," in *Protecting the Battered Child*. Denver: American Humane Association, 1962. Pp. 17–22.
28. Kempe, Henry C., *et al.* "The Battered Child Syndrome," *Journal of the American Medical Association*, Vol. 181, No. 1 (July 7, 1962), p. 17.
29. Maas, Henry S., *et al. Children in Need of Parents*. New York: Columbia University Press, 1959.
30. McCorkle, L. W., Elias, A., and Bixby, F. L. *The Highfields Story: A Unique Experiment in the Treatment of Juvenile Delinquents*. New York: Henry Holt & Co., 1958.

31. McFerran, Jane. "Parents' Groups in Protective Services," *Children*, Vol. 5, No. 6 (November–December, 1958), pp. 223–228.
32. Merrill, Edgar J. "Physical Abuse of Children—An Agency Study," in *Protecting the Battered Child*. Denver: American Humane Association, 1962. Pp. 1–16.
33. Morris, Marian G., and Gould, Robert W. "Role Reversal: A Concept in Dealing with the Neglected/Battered-Child Syndrome," in *The Neglected Battered-Child Syndrome*. New York: Child Welfare League of America, 1963.
34. ———, Gold, Robert W., and Matthews, Patricia J. "Toward Prevention of Child Abuse," *Children*, Vol. 11, No. 2 (March–April, 1964).
35. Nurse, Shirley M. "Parents Who Abuse Their Children," *Smith College Studies in Social Work*, Vol. 35, No. 4 (October, 1964), pp. 11–25.
36. Overton, Alice. "Aggressive Casework," *Social Work Journal*, Vol. 33, No. 3 (July, 1952), pp. 149–151.
37. ———, and Tinker, Katharine H. *Casework Notebook*. St. Paul: Family-centered Project, 1957.
38. Philbrick, Elizabeth Barry. *Treating Parental Pathology Through Child Protective Services*. Denver: Children's Division, American Humane Association, 1960.
39. *Planning for the Protection and Care of Neglected Children in California*. Sacramento: National Study Service, 1964.
40. *Preventive and Protective Services to Children, A Responsibility of the Public Welfare Agency*. Chicago: American Public Welfare Association, 1958.
41. Reiner, Beatrice Simcox, and Kaufman, Irving. *Character Disorders in Parents of Delinquents*. New York: Family Service Association of America, 1959.
42. Schoepfer, Arthur E. "Legal Implications in Connection with Physical Abuse of Children," in *Protecting the Battered Child*. Denver: American Humane Association, 1962. P. 26.
43. Studt, Elliot. "Worker-Client Authority Relationships in Social Work," *Social Work*, Vol. 4, No. 1 (January, 1959), pp. 18–28.
44. U.S. Bureau of the Census, *Statistical Abstract of the United States 1964*. Washington, D.C.: U.S. Government Printing Office, 1964.
45. U.S. Children's Bureau, "Bibliography on the Battered Child." Washington, D.C.: U.S. Government Printing Office, October, 1963. Mimeographed.
46. U.S. Department of Health, Education, and Welfare. *The Abused Child: Principles and Suggested Language by Legislation on Reporting of the Physically Abused Child*. Washington, D.C.: U.S. Government Printing Office, 1963.
47. Wiltse, Kermit T. "Social Casework Services in the ADC Program," *Social Service Review*, Vol. 28, No. 2 (June, 1954).
48. Young, Leontine. *Wednesday's Children*. New York: McGraw-Hill Book Co., 1964.
49. Zalba, Serapio R. *Women Prisoners and Their Families*. Los Angeles: Delmar Publishing Co., 1964.

# 25. *The Abused Parent of the Abused Child*

### SIDNEY WASSERMAN

The psychopathology theory is the dominant approach to the problem of child abuse. We therefore feel it is important for readers to be able to examine an example of this approach at first hand. However, the value of this article does not depend entirely on accepting psychopathology as the causal factor since the article contains a number of suggestions which concern ways of helping child-abusing parents and which are, for the most part, as consistent with other theories as they are with the psychopathology theory. For example, Wasserman states that abusing parents ". . . require long-term help

SOURCE: Reprinted with permission from *Children* 14 (September–October, 1967): 175–179.

from a consistent relationship with one person only." He makes this recommendation on the assumption that the pathological personality of the abusing parent will take it as a sign of rejection if the caseworker is changed. Our own view is that abusing parents have long-term and continuing stresses to surmount and that it takes a long-term and continuing relationship for the caseworker to understand the situation of the family, to secure their trust, and thereby be in position to help restructure the life circumstances. This is necessary to prevent the stresses which lead to child abuse. Examples of such preventative actions include helping the husband to get and hold a job and providing contraceptive information and materials which will prevent another pregnancy.

Willful intent in parents to injure their own children is an "unthinkable thought" for most of us. Even physicians, persons who seem to be in a position to judge whether violence has been done to a child, are often unwilling to accept the "reality of willful child abuse," according to a recent survey among physicians in the Washington metropolitan area conducted by a group of psychiatrists.[1] A fifth of the nearly 200 physicians questioned said they rarely or never considered the "battered child syndrome" when seeing an injured child, and a fourth said they would not report a suspected case even if protected by law against legal action by the parents. Apparently, they did not believe the evidence would stand up in court.

To accept as fact that some parents intentionally injure their children is difficult and upsetting. Thus, we all tend, like the physicians studied, to give the parent "the benefit of the doubt." There may be many reasons for our reluctance, but one is certainly this—when we accept willful intent as a fact, we must face our anger at such parents and our desire to protect the child, even if we harm the parent. But we cannot effectively intervene to protect an abused child and prevent abuse from recurring unless we understand what it is like to be a "battering parent."

One of the dangers of using the label "battering parent" is the possibility of increasing bias and prejudice against the parent. Labeling a particular person as a "battering parent" can release us from the responsibility of making our response to and attitude toward his actions sensitive to his needs. The temptation is great to think of him as being far removed from those of us who do not batter our children. In so thinking, we keep intact our image of ourselves as righteous.

How easy it is to deny that within all of us lies a potential for violence and that any of us could be unreachable! What is more repugnant to our rational, "mature" minds than the thought of committing impulsive, violent acts against a helpless child? We tell ourselves that the primitive, untempered instincts responsible for such acts could not erupt in us. But stripped of our defenses against such instincts and placed in a social and psychological climate conducive to violent behavior, any of us could do the "un-

[1]Silver, L. B.; Barton, W.; Dublin, C. C.: "Child Abuse Laws—Are They Enough?" *The Journal of the American Medical Association*, January 9, 1967.

thinkable." This thought should humble us: perhaps we are not battering parents only because conditions do not lead us to commit "unnatural" acts.


## NO CLASS MONOPOLY

Writers on social phenomenon, lawyers, social scientists, and others interested in social problems have long recognized that the phenomenon of parents physically abusing their children has been with us since the beginnings of mankind. Only since World War II, however, has much been written on the subject of· unexplained, shocking, and traumatic injuries to children. Since then, too, much has been said and written about the legal confusion surrounding the use of authority and sanctions in instances of apparent abuse of children by their parents.

Historically, the helping professions have viewed physical abuse of children by their parents as the result of poverty, life in the slums, ignorance, and the hardships produced by immigration, war, industrialization, and urbanization. No one can deny that these conditions can be a cause of child abuse. Nevertheless, we are finding that the phenomenon can be found anywhere in society. Once we regarded violence against a child as characteristic of parents in the lower socioeconomic classes. Now we are finding that such behavior is not exclusive with any particular social class but that "better" families can more easily conceal the problem than poor ones. In other words, a sociological explanation by itself is inadequate and simplistic.

Through sometimes frustrating and bitter experience, the professions, and particularly that of social work, have come to see that prosecuting the battering parent solves the problems of neither the child nor the parent. Helping the abused child leads us inevitably to the need to help the battering parent and family. As pointed out by Delsordo,[2] Boardman,[3] Nurse,[4] and others in studies of child abuse, practically all cases of abuse involve longstanding, severe interpersonal conflict either between the parents themselves or between one parent and another member of the family.

Because we are dealing with a complex subject involving many social, psychological, medical, and legal elements, we must narrow our scope and take first things first. Nothing precedes understanding who the battering parent is and what he is. Studies point out that battering parents and families, regardless of class, have certain psychological and social characteristics in common; for example, we are learning more all the time about the severe damage to personality these people suffer. Few are psychotic, but all have marked inability to set up a genuine relationship with another human being. Absorbed by their own hurt feelings, they cannot sympathize with the feelings of others. The nonpsychotic battering parent seldom shows remorse for

---

[2]Delsordo, J. D.: "Protective Casework for Abused Children." *Children*, November–December, 1963.

[3]Boardman, H. E.: "A Project to Rescue Children From Inflicted Injuries." *Social Work*, January, 1962.

[4]Nurse, S. M.: "Familial Patterns of Parents Who Abuse Their Children." *Smith College Studies in Social Work*, October, 1964.

having hurt his child, but he can be very much concerned about the harm a person in authority might inflict on his own person. When facing a person in authority, he cries out: "What are you going to do to me?"

## "DONE TO"

Obviously, something went haywire or was not touched in the humanization process when such persons were growing up. Apparently, they never had the kind of relations with other people that offers incentives for delaying pleasure or gratification or the feeling that it is worthwhile to yield an immediate, antisocial pleasure for the love and acceptance of another. They have been "done to" both socially and psychologically. A battering adult goes about his daily life with the gnawing, unfulfilled feeling of having been unloved or not having been loved as much as he should have been as a child. His life is focused on his own needs, and he cannot tolerate any frustration to the gratification of those needs. What else can he feel but his own hurt, his own hunger for love? He is anesthetized against feeling compassion for others.

This kind of person, according to Reiner and Kaufman,[5] is unaware that he has a buried feeling of "imbedded depression" because he was emotionally or psychologically abandoned by his parent as a child, an act he interpreted as rejection of himself. Unable to understand such a distressing emotional event and not psychologically strong enough to bear it, as a child he buried the feeling of rejection deep within himself and with it the accompanying depression. Because his use of language was not developed, he expressed his feelings by the only means he had—his behavior. Explosive, violent behavior became his means of communicating with those around him. When he was violent, he was unable to feel his hurt, his sense of worthlessness, his depression. Denied a consistent, supportive relationship with an adult, he set up a life pattern of aggression and violence—and is now inflicting on others what was inflicted on him. For him the world is hostile and dangerous; it is a place where one attacks or is attacked.

Studies also suggest that the battering parent feels his parents were punishing him when they rejected him and that he is longing for a mother. He wants to be loved, yet does everything to prevent another from loving him. Instead, he is caught in a cycle of violence and rejection. When speaking of his physical attacks on his child, the battering parent strongly defends his right to act as he has. He seems unable to feel love for and protectiveness toward his child. He can be extremely compulsive in his behavior and make unreasonable demands on his child. Cleanliness, for instance, may be an obsession with some. I have heard of a child being mercilessly beaten for putting chicken bones on a clean tablecloth and of an 18-month-old baby being seated with his buttocks uncovered on a hotplate whenever he soiled himself. Such people are way over their heads when they become parents.

[5]Reiner, B. S.; Kaufman, I.: *Character Disorders in Parents of Delinquents.* Family Service Association of America, New York. 1959.

How can they give a child what they have never had themselves—security, safety, and love?

## THE HOSTILITY SPONGE

This description is supported by a growing amount of evidence that when a battering parent becomes violent, he apparently is releasing his rage on a particular child, selected to act as the "hostility sponge" for that rage. The parent views the child as a competitor, as someone taking and getting what belongs to him. The child is an unconscious symbol of someone or something that once caused him pain—a competitive brother or sister, a distrusted parent, his rejected self. Sometimes the parent is reliving a childhood experience that left him traumatized. Some of these parents talk about being rejected by their own parents in favor of a brother or sister.

In many instances the abused child has been conceived out of wedlock. The parent is now punishing him for being the cause of an unwanted marriage. Sometimes a stepfather is the offender. He beats the child for reminding him of his wife's "badness." Or the mother may beat the child because he reminds her of her "badness" or of that "bad" man, his father, who deserted her when she was pregnant. By beating out the "badness" in the child, the parent beats out his own badness or that of another person who has injured him. In other words, the parent is reacting to his own inner feelings, not to the behavior of the child. The child is the provoker by being what he is—an infant or a child demanding attention. It is this demand that provokes the parent.

The use of the child as a hostility sponge may be absolutely essential to the mental balance of the parent, and, thus, the child is sacrificed to that mental balance. Removing the child from the home without a well thought-out plan to help the parent and the family may only invite the parent to shift his rage to another child. We can easily get caught up in symptom-shifting without getting to the bottom of the problem—the parent's need to be protected from himself.

To really help such a parent, we must break the chains he has inherited. To do that, we must clearly understand that intervention should act as a brake on the parent's behavior and that the injuries he inflicts on the child, injuries that bring the attention of the community to join them, are his way of saying—"Stop me!" The act of rushing a child to a hospital or of beating him in front of neighbors or strangers carries a message to the community—"Please save me from going out of control. Stop me from going out of my mind. Keep me from—killing!"

We are gradually realizing that in such cases we are dealing not only with a seriously disturbed person but also with a disturbed family. Once the existence of abuse is ascertained and the degree of imminent danger determined, the parent and the family must be dealt with whether or not the child is removed from the home. Even in cases where law enforcement has been effective and community services have been well coordinated, problems in helping the battering parent and the family remain.

According to Zalba,[6] battering parents tend to deny their actions, the husband or wife of the battering parent protects the other, or the children are too young to explain to outsiders what has occurred in the home. The parents also tend to deny the existence of personal or family problems and to provoke judges, lawyers, and social workers by making impossible demands on them; or they rage at everyone in authority and, sometimes, physically attack them.

## FIRMNESS ABOVE ALL

In reaching out to the battering parent, we must keep in mind an important key to his behavior—his fear of a close relationship. Because he suffered rejection in early life, he wards off human relationships.[7] He has emotionally divorced himself from the significant people in his life. He feels safer with and responds more readily to a relationship that clearly offers authority—firm but not punitive. In other words, the battering parent can often be reached by setting firm limits and controls on his behavior. Whatever he may say, he needs firm control—and wants it. In the early stages of trying to reach the battering parent and family, the social caseworker or other helper must make realistic judgments and decisions for and with the parents and family to gradually help them develop a sense of reality.

To provide this basic treatment requires long-term help from a consistent relationship with one person only. Shifting the parent from one worker to another only stirs up his basic, deep-seated belief that to get close to another human being is to expose one's self to hurt and abandonment. Deep within, he sees himself as the kiss of death in personal relations. He wants to get close to another person, but he thinks that if he does the person will learn to dislike him and will break off the relationship. For a long, indefinite period, the helping person must stand by and support the parent by setting limits and by providing services through community resources. He must not try to get too close to or expect such a person to unload his innermost feelings, especially feelings he is hardly aware of. For such a person, having limits set on explosive, violent behavior provides the kind of protection a good parent would give. The battering parent must be constantly assured that he will not be allowed to get out of control. At the same time, he must be assured that the worker believes that he does not want to hurt his child, that he is capable of change, and that he wants to be a better parent. He needs to learn what the community expects of him and what choices he has. He needs to be helped to understand clearly that consequences will follow his violent act and what those consequences will be.

## A LONG PROCESS

In this long and trying process, such a parent will continually test the patience of the helping person and will use every means to provoke rejection

---

[6]Zalba, S. R.: "The Abused Child: II. A Typology for Classification and Treatment." *Social Work*, January, 1967.
[7]Reiner and Kaufman.

to reassure himself that he will not be rejected. For a long time he will reveal only his unlikeable side. When he is reassured, he will make feeble attempts to plant the seeds of a relationship. Reaching out to such a person makes a very great emotional and intellectual demand on the helping person. The battering parent is very perceptive and can immediately sense insincerity. Actually, the helping person must become the "hostility sponge" instead of the child by letting the parent test him, yet he must never let the parent get out of control.

Psychiatrists, psychologists, social caseworkers, and other persons trained for this work have observed that as treatment progresses and a basic trust is established the battering parent gradually faces up to the depression within himself. With extreme caution, he talks about his deep-seated fear that he is a loser and that people always desert him. Only when his need for violence abandons him and he stops expressing himself through it can he talk about his childhood and begin to come to grips with his problems. Though he improves, he continues to try to provoke the helping person, for he is never convinced that he will not be rejected. However, he does move cautiously toward having a relationship with the helping person, gives up or modifies his violent outbursts, and lets himself be guided toward patterning his actions after the standards of the helping person. In time, the pattern becomes a part of him and a new self appears.

To start and set in motion such a long, painstaking process requires a firm commitment by the community to providing excellent service, a goal not easily attained. To obtain qualified staff members and to train persons specifically as workers are expensive and time-consuming. Often efforts to reach the battering parent are obstructed because workers—nurses, social workers, volunteers—come and go frequently on the staffs of agencies. For the battering parent is likely to regard a change in workers as another experience in rejection. The helping person may leave the staff at the most critical moment —just as the parent is testing the worker to find out if rejection will follow his actions. The parent takes the worker's leaving the agency as proof that it never pays to get close to another person. If only a community or agency could insure permanent service for such troubled human beings!

But life affords few opportunities for permanency. We are all only temporary to each other. That is a human condition, and most people accept it. The battering parent cannot. Plans for helping him must include ways to help him accept this truth. We must be ready to test various methods of working with him, always keeping in mind his deep fear of involvement and loss. We must continue to direct efforts to alert the medical, legal, and social work professions, and all groups who might come in contact with the battering person to the need for continuity in helping him. The challenge is not a small one; social workers are finding that cases involving battering parents as well as other hard-to-reach families are making up more and more of their caseloads.

In addition to individual treatment, working with groups of battering parents and their spouses is also proving effective. Many of these parents are isolated from the community. Having an opportunity to socialize in a group of similarly troubled parents tends to lower their resistance to facing and discussing their problems. Working with such families as family groups has also proved effective.[8]

## THE COMMUNITY MUST LEARN

Beyond the abused child, his parents, and his family is the community around them. Battering parents and their families suffer from a not uncommon malaise often called "community exclusion." In various ways, whether economically, politically, psychologically, or socially, these families frequently suffer exclusion. Unfortunately, when such persons vent their rage on their children and the shocked community retaliates immediately, the family's sense of rejection is increased. A cycle of reciprocal aggression is set in motion and, once set in motion, is difficult to halt. The battering parent often succeeds in provoking hospitals, the police, the courts, and social agencies into treating him as his parents once treated him—the opposite of what he needs. Communities must constantly reexamine ways to set up controls and limits while bringing all families into the community life. When a battering parent has only known "community exclusion," he desperately needs "inclusion" to break the cycle.

Finally, we cannot examine our attitude as a community toward the battering parent without examining what it means to be part of a whole—a State, a nation, or the world. Like it or not, we are bound each to the other and our destinies are interwoven. As we try to understand the battering parent, we must look into ourselves to find out what there is in each of us, in our community, our Nation, and the world that the battering parent takes as a sign that what he is doing is permissible.

To answer this question we must face up to the paradoxes in our moral code that condemn violence in one form, permit it in another. Many Americans seem to persistently dismiss from their thoughts and acts a basic truth —there is nothing more precious than human life, or so it seems to me.

The people of the United States have yet to learn how to convert their tendency to violence into compassion and tenderness. We are in danger of losing sight of one of this Nation's major social goals, one on which it was founded, that is, to tap the humanity and creative potential of all citizens and to provide the environment and resources necessary for the individual citizen to realize his creative potential. We possess the potential both for violence and for humaneness, and are capable of acting in brotherhood and with understanding. If this were not so, we would not now be seeking new and different ways of helping our less fortunate citizens. By seeking to tap the humanity and potential for growth of the battering parent and family, we are tapping our own potential for personal, community, national, and international growth. We must ever encourage the tapping of this potential.

[8]Zalba.

# PART FOUR
# The Family as Training Ground for Societal Violence

As a result of political assassinations, urban riots, atrocities in Viet Nam, and a rapid increase in crimes involving personal injuries, violence is now much on the minds of the American people. The concern with violence has revived one of the great controversies of human history, one which has manifested itself in great debates over the centuries in religion, in secular philosophy, and in early and contemporary biological and social science. This controversy concerns the basic nature of man. Is the human animal inherently aggressive and violent, kept in bounds by the rules of society, which are all that stand between him and the war of all against all; or is he inherently cooperative and peaceful, but led to violent acts by the distortions of human nature imposed by an increasingly brutal civilization?

It is a controversy which, if accepted on its own terms, will never be resolved. It is like the heredity vs. environment debate over intelligence. We believe that progress in understanding human violence will be greatest if, for purposes of advancing knowledge, one simply assumes that human beings have built into their biological heritage *both* aggressive and benevolent potentials. Furthermore, the actual development of behaviors based on such biological programming is heavily dependent on the social setting in which the human infant is reared. Thus, the aggressive and violent behaviors of mankind can be fully understood only if we take into account the way in which social learning and social pressures interact with biological capacities and dispositions. On the basis of these assumptions, Part Four is intended to show some of the ways in which violence is learned and controlled in the family context. Chapter VIII considers ways in which the family experiences of children can create an aggressive and violence-prone person—one who will commit *individual* acts of violence. Chapter IX considers the family as the agent for creating or maintaining a society which commits violence for socially defined purposes, such as punishment of criminals, bringing about needed social change, or waging war. Chapter X looks at the other side of the coin. It is concerned with how the family can be a force for non-violence. Finally, Chapter XI speculates about the family and violence in the future.[1]

DIRECT TRAINING IN VIOLENCE

How does the family serve as a training group for the violent society? The ways are almost infinite. Some are direct and some indirect. By "direct" means, we mean explicitly teaching toughness and violence to children. Two vivid examples of such direct training are included in our selections. One is

[1]We have omitted treatment of the effects of mass media, particularly television, on the learning of violence by children. In part this is because it is an issue which is covered in full detail in other books. Primarily, however, it is because our focus is on the family: on violence between family members and on the family factors which produce violent versus non-violent individuals. To a limited extent the family can control the TV-viewing patterns of at least young children and hence can limit exposure to television violence. But given the saturation of American television with violence, such attempts will have limited success, even at the ages when it is possible. Consequently, we view the relationship of mass media violence to individual violence as a problem which is related to, but outside the scope of, this book.

Claude Brown's vivid account of the systematic encouragement of violence he received from his peers and his father (p. 262). Here we see the slum "subculture of violence" being transmitted to the next generation.

Among groups who, at least on the surface, reject violence, the process is harder to see. That is why we included Jules Henry's description of Pete Portman and his father (p. 238). If most of us were to meet the Portmans, we would find little to distinguish them from millions of other middle class Americans. Henry had to actually live with families such as the Portmans before he could discover the hidden agenda by which "peace-loving" parents train boys for violence under the guise of teaching them to be men.

Families such as the Browns and the Portmans *explicitly* teach toughness and violence as an appropriate mode of dealing with the world. Some of these families train their children to use violence in their day-to-day lives. Others would reject the teaching of such immediate interpersonal violence, but at the same time teach violence as an instrument of public policy, international relations, punishment of criminals, and control of social deviants.

What proportion of American families engage in such direct training for violence? Perhaps it is only a minority since the rhetoric of peace and non-violence is also a part of American values. As in the case of so many other aspects of violence, however, the proportion is probably greater than most Americans think it is. For example, the survey conducted for the National Commission on the Causes and Prevention of Violence (Stark and McEvoy, 1970) reveals that 70 per cent of the 1176 respondents in that survey agreed with the statement: "When a boy is growing up it is very important for him to have a few fistfights." The Portmans; the Browns; the authoritarian parents in T. W. Adorno *et al.*'s study, *The Authoritarian Personality* (p. 268); the families of 574 college students in Robert A. Lewis' study, "The Family Life of Hawkish Students" (p. 275); and the seven out of ten Americans who feel it is important to have fistfights—all illustrate the way in which the culture of violence is directly transmitted from generation to generation.

## INDIRECT TRAINING

Far more is involved, however, than a *culture* of violence which gives explicit approval to the use of violence. Even if violence were not part of the cultural heritage transmitted by the family, the family would still play a key role in training for violence since family experiences are such powerful molders of personality. A family can be opposed to violence in principle and still produce a violence-prone child because the structure of relationships within the family provides many opportunities to *indirectly* train children to be violent.

Probably one of the most efficient of these indirect means of training for violence is in the way the parents control the child. If they use violence (i.e., spanking and slapping) as a means of controlling the child's behavior, it should be no surprise that the child learns that violence is an effective means of dealing with others. A description of just how this works in a sample of pre-school children is given in the article on "The Sources of Aggression in the Home" by Robert R. Sears *et al.* (p .240).

It would be tremendously valuable to have data on what kind of people the children studied by Sears *et al.* are *now* as young adults. Are those whose parents used non-violent means of child rearing also less aggressive as adults? Are those who were subject to frequent physical punishment now, as adults, the young men and women who engage in physical fights with their husbands or wives; and are they among those who believe in capital punishment and the rightness of the Viet Nam war? Perhaps so, but many things happen between the temper-tantrum stage and adulthood. Consequently, only a follow-up study can provide a definite answer. Nonetheless, there is evidence suggesting a "yes" answer. One can get a feeling for this from sixteen-year-old Willie A.*:

> My story is all about my life.
>
> When I was a little boy my father was always beating on me and my brothers for just about anything we would do. We was living in Brooklyn then. And then one day he and my mother had a fight and my father had a very bad heart and he taked a over dose of pills and die in Brooklyn.
>
> I didn't know what the youth house was.
>
> And then we move to the Bronx were I met some new friends and start getting in a lot of gangs and start robbing places. And then I was lock up on May 6, 1966.
>
> I went home and came back May 25, 1966, and stayed until June 30, 1966. And then they send me to a Star Camp and I get into two fights. And they send me back to the Youth House.
>
> But when I go home the next time you can believe that I'am not coming back know more. *

By age sixteen, Willie has been in jail twice. He ends his story by resolving not to go back but one has a gut-level feeling that he will be back. He faces a life of poverty, discrimination, and frustration; and the roles he learned in the family provided him with few modes of coping with these problems other than striking out violently. Perhaps he will be an exception, but the evidence from Robert A. Lewis' study of attitudes towards the war in Viet Nam (p. 275) and from Stuart Palmer's study of murderers (p. 91) suggests not. In his study, Palmer compared a sample of murderers with their brothers. Both his statistical data and his examples show that from birth on, the murderers experienced far more violence than did their brothers. Since both the murderers and their brothers shared the same family culture, it is likely that differences in the violent behavior of the two groups reflects the indirect effects of their violent childhood experiences rather than the direct learning of a violent culture.

It would seem, then, that the prescription used by families to produce violent individuals contains one or more of the following ingredients: placing a high value on toughness and teaching children to fight; using physical punishment to increase frustration and to provide an appropriate role model in the use of violence; and—if an extremely violent individual is to be produced—using extremely violent methods of dealing with the child, especially severe and senseless beatings. These steps *are* likely to produce the "desired" effects. However, they are not the only ways to do it. Parents could avoid all the steps just outlined and, under certain circumstances, still produce a violence-prone child. Part of the reason for this is that we simply do not know all the family factors which make men violent or non-violent. Another part of the explanation is that what goes on inside the family can have different consequences depending on what goes on in the society at large and on the place of the family in that society. That is illustrated by research on student revolutionaries, such as the Columbia University group studied by Herbert Hendin (p. 287).

None of the studies of violence-prone radical students shows evidence that they come from families with authoritarian, punitive parents who believe in violence. In fact, the opposite tends to be the case. What, then, turned these students toward violence? No one knows for sure; but a theme which occurs in most of these studies is moral outrage over the social and economic injustices of American society, combined with a feeling of being unable to do anything about either these injustices or to engage in any other activity which is important for the society. This situation is directly parallel to our interpretation of husband-wife violence in Part Three. Our conclusion then was that violence between husband and wife tends to be a mode of problem solving—a mode which is called into play for dealing with problems which are intense but for which the violent husband or wife has no other solution. Similarly, political violence for these students is a mode of dealing with problems which are intense but which they perceive as unsolvable because they have no part in the decision making of society.

For a group of young people whose family experiences impressed on them the importance of doing something—of being an active, creative, positive force in society—"being 20 and utterly dispensable" (Novak, 1971) represents a combination of family experience and social position which leads to violence. More generally, it is indicative of one of the most fundamental problems of modern society: the lack of a meaningful *and needed* contribution from adolescents. This void in social integration is a source of immense frustration to millions of youth.

Deplorable as is the violence which this frustration has helped to provoke, it is also an example of one of the "social functions of violence" described by Coser (1968). It has forced us to pay attention to the problems of youth. It may even have served as the stimulus for a profound set of changes in the educational and occupational system of society. If we are to have a world with minimal violence, we must also have a world which provides non-violent avenues for such functions of violence as providing warning signals and providing an impetus to social change. William James's idea of "the moral equivalent of war" must somehow be provided if we are to have society which is both non-violent and non-stagnant.

NON-VIOLENCE AND THE FAMILY

The discussion up to now in this introduction has been concerned with how the family creates and transmits the conditions which result in violence—both interpersonal violence and violence as an instrument of public policy. We know far less about the other side of the coin: what the role of the family is in creating and maintaining a non-violent society. Social scientists have some major disagreements on this issue.

One of the most important such controversies is between those who take a biological deterministic view of violence and those who take a social learning view. The biological determinists include the psychoanalysts (Freud, of course, and contemporary figures such as Bruno Bettelheim) and the ethologists such as Robert Ardrey, Konrad Lorenz, and Desmond Morris. Both the psychoanalysts' and the ethologists' points of view enjoy wide public support, but scientific evidence for the existence of *innate* aggressive behavior patterns *in man* is minimal or non-existent (Allard, 1972).

Bruno Bettelheim's article "Children Should Learn About Violence" (p. 299) is representative of the psychoanalytic perspective as applied to child rearing in relation to violence. We agree with Bettelheim when he urges parents to recognize the fact that they and their children live in a violent world. This being the case, he urges parents to help their children to face the issue directly, preparing them to control violence rather than to ignore it and hope that it will not enter their lives—as we once did with sex. But we question Bettelheim and the ethologists when they assert that human beings are *inherently* violent, especially when they go on from this assumption to say that opportunities must therefore be provided for the non-destructive discharge of this violence. The critique of the "catharsis myth" in our general introduction (p. 14) has already indicated that we are skeptical of both the biological argument and especially of the catharsis theory, which holds that by allowing mild violence to occur, or by engaging in vicarious violence, pent-up aggression is drained off and destructive violence is thereby avoided.

Our skepticism is partly based on the work of Albert Bandura and Richard H. Walters. Their classic book, *Social Learning and Personality Development* (1963), summarizes a great deal of their own research and the work of others on how children learn to be members of society, including learning to be violent. The section of their book which we reprint under the title "Catharsis—A Questionable Mode of Coping with Violence" (p. 303) indicates that neither their own experiments, nor previous research, support the catharsis or "drainage" view.

The last article in Chapter Ten, G. R. Patterson *et al.*'s "Training Parents to Control an Aggressive Child" (p. 308), presents a still different approach to the role of the family in controlling violence. This article describes an experiment carried out with parents of highly aggressive and destructive children. The methods of structuring parent-child interaction used in this experiment employ the principles of "operant conditioning" and "behavioral therapy" (Bergin and Garfield, 1971), as well as the social learning approach of Bandura and Walters.

But what about the parents of normal children? Are behavioral modification techniques also relevant for them? A growing number of specialists in child rearing seem to think so, judging from the number of books which have taken this stance in the last two years. G. R. Patterson is the author of one of these books (Patterson and Gullion, 1971), and there are others, for example, Fitzhugh Dodson (1970) and Thomas Gordon (1971). As we pointed out in the introduction to Part Three (p. 141), if these techniques are as effective as their proponents suggest, they offer the promise of an escape from the problems of previously available models of child rearing. At one extreme is the old authoritarian parent model, planting the seeds of violence by the example set for children and by the frustrations generated by physical punishment and arbitrary controls. At the other extreme is the model of the permissive parent, leaving children to be brought up by their peers and planting the seeds of alienation and despair—the model of child rearing which Urie Bronfenbrenner (1970) calls "affluent neglect." There have, of course, been many calls to parents to avoid either of these extremes, but little has been provided in the way of specific techniques to accomplish this. Whether the new approach to child rearing provides the needed methods is really unknown at this point. There is also the possibility of unforeseen negative side effects. Results based on carefully controlled experiments such as Patterson's study do not prove the general applicability of these techniques. It seems as though we will have to wait at least a generation for an answer.

Unfortunately, even if we are willing to wait a generation, social change will not permit it. In a modern society, the forces of social change will not stand still for a controlled experiment. Therefore, what may seem to be positive effects of a new child rearing technique may simply be the result of the changed structure of society in the intervening years. The same problem applies to what may seem to be negative effects.

Another problem is that it is difficult to make even an informed guess about what changes will take place in society. However, it is possible to systematically examine one or more of the *possible* changes and to explore their implications for the level of violence in the family. That is what Robert N. Whitehurst does in Chapter XI of Part Four, "The Family and Violence in the Future" (p. 315). Whitehurst focuses on changes in the structure of the family itself—what he calls "alternative" family structures. Supposing such alternatives to the present family system were to become widespread, he attempts to answer the question of whether this change would reduce violence between members of such groups and would reduce violence in the society at large. Whitehurst's answer is a qualified "yes."

In a final article (No. 38) we deal briefly with other possible changes. In considering these possibilities, it is important to remember that the family is a system embedded within the larger system of society. This system perspective alerts us to important limitations on what changes in any one segment is likely to accomplish. But it is a positive rather than just a cautionary view because it points to what needs to be done to more fully understand the future pattern of relationships between the family and violence.

REFERENCES

Alland, Alexander, Jr.
1972    *The Human Imperative.* New York: Columbia University Press.
Bergin, Allen E. and Sol L. Garfield (eds.)
1971    *Handbook of Psychotherapy and Behavior Change: An Empirical Analysis.*
        Part III: "Analysis of Behavioral Therapies." Pp. 543–750. New York: John
        Wiley.
Bronfenbrenner, Urie
1970    *Two Worlds of Childhood. U.S. and U.S.S.R.* New York: Russell Sage
        Foundation.
Coser, Lewis A.
1966    "Some Social Functions of Violence." Pp. 8–18 in Marvin E. Wolfgang
        (ed.), *Patterns of Violence: The Annals of the American Academy of Polit-
        ical and Social Science,* Vol. 364 (Philadelphia: American Academy of Po-
        litical and Social Science, March, 1966).
Dodson, Fitzhugh
1970    *How to Parent.* New York: New American Library.
Gordon, Thomas
1970    *Parent Effectiveness Training.* New York: Peter H. Wyden.
Novak, Michael
1971    "Battles of Old Westbury," *New York Times* (July 17): 23.
Patterson, Gerald R. and M. Elizabeth Gullion
1971    *Living with Children. New Methods for Parents and Teachers.* Champaign,
        Illinois: Research Press.
Stark, Rodney and James McEvoy III
1970    "Middle Class Violence." *Psychology Today* 4 (November): 52–65.

# CHAPTER EIGHT
# The Family
# and Individual Violence

## 26. *Making Pete Tough*
### JULES HENRY

Henry was one of America's leading anthropologists. He started his career with studies of a fierce and aggressive South American tribe. Perhaps that is one of the things which led him to be perceptive about aggressiveness in American families in his later research. Henry's method of gathering the data on these American families is typical of the approach of anthropologists: he lived with each of the families in his study so that he could directly observe their interaction. Here is his report (including sections of his field notes) on one of these families. It shows the subtle but powerful way in which a father can train a son in being tough and violent.

A great many fathers use similar techniques. What is different about the Portman family (as Henry hints in this excerpt but shows in detail in other parts of his book) is the combination of the violent father, who shows affection for his son through roughness and the "icy" mother. The training in violent social roles coupled with the lack of training in interpersonally close and supportive roles is literally deadly. Training in violence can be counterbalanced by warm human attachments which inhibit acting out the violent roles. But when, as in the case of Pete, training in violence occurs in a family context which prevents the child from learning how to be loving and supportive of other human beings, the stage is set for Pete to act out the violent roles learned on his father's knee.

. . . He liked to keep Pete beside him at the table and played with the child before leaving for work in the morning and at night when he came home. With the goal of making Pete tough and athletic, his play was always more or less of a rough-house: Mr. Portman would growl (like a monster!) and roll and heave Pete around. Sometimes he would give the child a kind of tigerish, devouring kiss with yawning mouth. Extracts from the record follow:

2:48:1

Stretched out in the big leather chair in the living room, with Pete on top of him, Mr. Portman "ate Pete up," opening his mouth wide and pressing it against the child's face. Pete loved it. Then Mr. Portman played a little ball with him. Next he swung him around like a dumbbell, like a barbell, and like a pendulum. Mr.

SOURCE: From Jules Henry, *Culture Against Man.* Copyright © 1963 by Random House, Inc. Reprinted by permission of the publisher.

Portman rolled Pete up on his own (Mr. Portman's) back and, on all fours, rode Pete around. Then he rolled Pete over on Pete's back, held him tight, and rubbed his fist hard into the child's belly several times. He exercised Pete's legs; he crawled on all fours and growled fiercely at him. It went on and on and the child loved it, got terrifically excited, smiled and laughed. It was obvious that Mr. Portman was intentionally giving the child a work-out, toughening him, etc. Mr. Portman said to me that one must be careful with Pete because he is so big for his age people expect him to behave like a three-year-old.

3:62:10

Before Mr. Portman left this morning he was not so rushed that he did not have time to punch Pete twice in the belly. This was too much for Pete, who, though he smiled, went away from his father.

6:116:3

This morning at 7:10 I went into the living room where Mr. Portman was playing with Pete. He held him on his lap; he crawled around on the floor with him. He growled at him; he made playful biting movements at his arm, putting the child's arm in his mouth. He held him on his lap. Pete enjoyed this very much, as evidenced by his smiling and cooing.

The difference between Pete's experiences with his mother and father could hardly be more dramatic: joyless (funless), detached acquiescence alternating in the mother with icy boredom and humiliation; intense, interested bodily collision in the relations between imp-of-fun father and son. Here roughness and toughness do the work of love: Mr. Portman expresses his love for his son through throwing him around, punching him in the belly, and imitating a devouring animal. Pete cannot fail, therefore, to associate love with physical violence: to love a person is to throw him around, wallop him, and symbolically chew him up—in other words, to have fun. Pete tries a baby version of this on Elaine, his little playmate next door. Thus the toughness-love-violence combination, so common in our movies, is here built into the child's flesh and bone through the basic biological mammalian function of play. My impression of Mr. Portman was that only through violent play could this rather withdrawn man bring himself into contact with Pete. But he is not interested merely in enjoying and having fun with his son; he wants also, he says, to toughen him, strengthen him, make him a man. So, while father fires him, mother freezes him, and Pete is caught in the cultural paradoxes expressed through his parents.

Mr. Portman's roughhousing probably makes Pete more difficult for his mother to handle; and Mr. Portman's coolness to her contrasts so with his involvement in Pete that she might take out her resentment on the child. Thus emotional illness is the result of what is done to the child by his parents, motivated by their relationship to each other; and, if the child does not become psychotic very early, the outcome of its experiences with its parents is heavily affected for health or illness by school and play group.

When Pete is a little bigger he will probably have toy pistols and cowboy chaps; his father will be proud, when Pete is about eight years old, to buy him his first real football togs. His toy box, mostly a collection of odds and ends now, will probably sprout soldiers, tanks, and artillery, and he may have a toy missile that actually goes off. As he matures he will enjoy guns, prize fights, football, hockey, Western movies, movies of gangsters and war, and stories of murder and robbery in the "funnies." So he will make his contribution to the gross national product. *Violence is a natural resource.* More valuable than the iron of Mesabi (which is nearly exhausted) or lead and zinc (which are drugs on the market), violence is inexhaustible and constantly increases in price—a better investment by far than diamonds!

## 27. *The Sources of Aggression in the Home*
### ROBERT R. SEARS, ELEANOR E. MACCOBY, AND HARRY LEVIN

A trait such as the tendency to be aggressive or violent can be acquired in many different ways. It has multiple causes rather than a single cause. In the previous selection we saw two of these causal factors operating: explicit role practice in violence and parental inability to show warmth to the child. In this selection from one of the classic studies of child rearing in America, Sears, Maccoby, and Levin provide evidence on another of the causal factors: the use of physical punishment by parents. The use of physical punishment as a causal factor in producing aggressiveness is particularly interesting because it is so often used with the intent of *controlling* the child's aggressiveness and teaching him *not* to be aggressive. Just how this paradoxical result comes about is shown by the data which Sears, *et al.*, present for a sample of 379 five-year-olds and their mothers.

What makes a child aggressive and quarrelsome? Among these youngsters, there were a few whose mothers could recall almost no angry behavior around home, but this was not the case for most of them. In spite of the general aura of prohibition, the majority of the youngsters had displayed many varieties and combinations of angry emotional response. Some children were more aggressive toward one parent than the other, some quarreled mainly with siblings and were pleasant toward the parents, some expressed themselves openly, and some relied chiefly on non-co-operation for their expression.

Nearly all the mothers gave fairly detailed reports of the typical forms of aggression their children displayed. It was thus possible to make a rating of *amount of aggression exhibited in the home* (excluding that toward siblings). The scale-point descriptions and the percentage of children rated at each level are shown in Table VII:7.

These ratings can be compared with the mothers' reports of child-rearing practices to discover what characteristics of the latter were associated with high or low degree of reported aggression by the child.

SOURCE: Reprinted with permission from Robert R. Sears, Eleanor E. Maccoby, and Harry Levin, *Patterns of Child Rearing* (New York: Harper & Row, 1957), pp. 255–263, 266–268. Copyright © 1957 by Harper & Row, Publishers, Inc.

*Table VII:7. Amount of Aggression Exhibited by Child in the Home, Excluding That Toward Siblings*

| | |
|---|---|
| 1. None. Child has never shown any aggression toward parents, and mother does not mention any other displays of temper | 4% |
| 2. Mild. Occasional minor outbursts, but generally even-tempered | 29 |
| 3. Some | 49 |
| 4. Quite a bit of aggression | 16 |
| 5. A great deal. Often screams, hits. "I have had a real problem with tantrums" | 1 |
| Not ascertained | 1 |
| Total | 100% |

Again, as was the case with dependency, the measures of the mothers' practices and the children's reactions were not independent. Both came from the mother herself. We cannot be certain in any particular case, therefore, that we have secured an unbiased report of the child's actual behavior. It is possible that some quality in a given mother—for instance, a sense of despair about her effectiveness as a child rearer—might lead her to give an exaggerated report about her child's aggressiveness. If we find, as we do, that mothers who felt little confidence in themselves had more (reportedly) aggressive children, we cannot tell whether this finding results from exaggerated reports by these mothers, or whether there was actually something about their behavior toward children that evoked more child aggressiveness. It would not be surprising if both were true, for the same qualities of her personality that influence her perception of the child may also induce a characteristic set of responses in him. . . .

*Permissiveness and punishment.* There is a constant tug of war in a child's behavior between the instigation and the inhibition of aggression. On one hand there are frustrations, threats, or other stimulating situations that tend to evoke aggressive action; on the other, there are warnings that inhibit aggression, and there are instigators to competing responses that the mother finds more desirable than aggression. One of the major research problems in the investigation of the socialization process is the discovery of just what kinds of maternal behavior fall into these classifications. What does the mother do that excites aggression in her child? What does she do that inhibits it?

The two scales of *permissiveness for aggression* and *severity of punishment for aggression* are the most obviously relevant dimensions to examine first. What should we expect of their relation to the reported amount of aggression the child shows in the home? Permissiveness, by definition, is an expression of the mother's willingness to have the child perform such acts. A simple and straightforward prediction is that children with permissive mothers will be more aggressive than children with non-permissive mothers. Similarly with punishment: if we assume that this method of discipline establishes in the child a fear of behaving aggressively, then the more punitive the mother is, the more the child should avoid being aggressive. These two predictions fit together nicely. The scales for *permissiveness* and *punishment* are correlated − .46; that is, to some degree the more permissive mothers tended to be less severe in their punishment.

In point of fact, however, one of the predictions is right and the other is wrong. It is true that high *permissiveness* is associated with high aggression. The correlation is + .23. But *punishment* works just the other way: the more severe the punishment, the more aggression the child showed. The correlation is + .16. Both these correlations are small, but they are significant, and they are artificially reduced by the negative correlation between the permissiveness and punitiveness scales. Their true importance is substantially greater, as will be seen in the next section. . . .

We interpret these findings in this way. When a mother adopts a permissive point of view about aggression, she is saying to her child, in effect, "Go ahead and express your angry emotions; don't worry about me." She gives few signals in advance that would lead the child to fear to be aggressive. On the contrary, her attitude is one of expectancy that he *will* be, and that such behavior is acceptable. It is scarcely surprising that the child tends to fulfill her expectations. The non-permissive mother, however, does something quite different. She has an attitude that aggression is wrong, that it is not to be tolerated, and an expectancy (often very subtly expressed) that the child will not behave in such undesirable ways. When he is aggressive, she does something to try to stop it—sometimes by punishment, sometimes by other means. He, also, fulfills his mother's expectations. This dimension of permissiveness, then, is a measure of the extent to which the mother prevents or stops aggression, the non-permissive extreme being the most common.

Punishment is apparently a somewhat different matter. It is a kind of maternal behavior that occurs *after* the child's aggression has been displayed. The child has already enjoyed the satisfaction of hurting or of expressing anger—and so has had a reinforcement for aggressive action. But then he gets hurt in turn. He suffers further frustration. This should, and on the average does, incite him to more aggression. If the punishment is very severe, he may gradually learn to fear the consequences of his own actions, and the particular acts that get most repeatedly punished may be inhibited. But the total frustration is increased, and hence the total amount of aggression displayed in the home is higher. The dimension called *severity of punishment for aggression toward parents*, then, is one measure of the amount of painful frustration that is imposed on the child without direct guidance as to what would be a more acceptable form of behavior.

It is evident from this analysis that the mothers who were most permissive but also most severely punitive would have the most aggressive children; those who were most non-permissive but least punitive would have the least aggressive ones. As may be seen in Table VII:8, this was the case for both sexes. The children of mothers in the other two groups were in between.

These findings are similar to those of an earlier study (Sears *et al.*, 1953) in one respect. In that research, 40 children were observed in nursery school. The amount of aggression they showed there was compared with their mothers' reports of the severity of punishment for aggression that they suffered at home. In that study, too, high aggression was found to be associated with severe punishment, especially in the boys. There was some indication

*Table VII:8. Percentage of Highly Aggressive Children in Subgroups Divided According to Whether Mother Was in Upper or Lower Half of the Distribution on Permissiveness and Severity of Punishment for Aggression Toward Parents*

| | Highly Aggressive* | | | |
| | Boys | | Girls | |
| Subgroup | Per Cent | N† | Per Cent | N |
|---|---|---|---|---|
| Low permissiveness and low punishment | 3.7 | 27 | 13.3 | 30 |
| Low permissiveness and high punishment | 20.4 | 51 | 19.1 | 47 |
| High permissiveness and low punishment | 25.3 | 81 | 20.6 | 63 |
| High permissiveness and high punishment | 41.7 | 36 | 38.1 | 22 |

*By "highly aggressive" is meant that the child was rated by one or both raters as being in one of the two highest levels of aggression; these are scale points 4 and 5 in Table VII:7.
†Number of cases.

that the *most* severely punished girls had become quite passive and inhibited. They displayed little activity of any kind, including aggression. When activity level was taken into consideration, they tended to be more like the boys, i.e., the more severely punished girls were *relatively* more aggressive than the less severely punished. It is interesting to note the similarity between the present findings and the earlier study, because in that research the measure of child aggression was entirely independent of the measures of child-rearing practices.

A word of caution must be said here about the interpretation of our results. We have shown that the mothers who punished their children most severely for aggression tended to report that their children displayed more than the average amount of aggression toward their parents. We have implied in our discussion that the maternal behavior *caused* the child behavior. It is entirely possible, of course, that the correlation could be explained as a parental response to the child's pre-existing temperament. That is, some children may have been born with a higher level of aggressive impulses than others, and the more aggressive the child naturally was, the more his parents were forced to punish him for aggression. We have chosen to interpret the matter the other way around: that punishment by the mother bred counter-aggression in the child. Our reason is that permissiveness was also associated with aggression, and we cannot see why aggression in the child should elicit permissiveness in the mother.

Our interpretation must be tentative, however, for the other explanation of the results cannot be ruled out without further research. It is quite possible, of course, that a circular process develops: the parent's punishment makes the child aggressive, this aggression leads to further punishment, and so on. Which came first, to set the whole thing in motion, is a problem we cannot solve with our existing information.

We can look now at some of the other possible sources of excitation and inhibition of aggression, for it is clear that permissiveness and severity of punishment are not the only influences.

*Physical punishment.* There have been a number of studies during the past three decades that have suggested some rather untoward effects of this disciplinary technique. One of the most important is that of the Gluecks (1950), which indicated that the use of severe physical punishment was one of five major factors associated with the development of delinquency in young boys.

In the present study, we have found that those mothers who punished aggression most severely also tended to use physical punishment more ($r = .44$). Not surprisingly, therefore, physical punishment was related to mothers' reports of high aggression in their children ($r = .23$). However, it had an important positive effect only when it occurred in association with quite severe punishment for aggression. That is, if a child was being severely punished for aggression, the high use of *physical punishment* (as distinct from other kinds of punishment) increased his aggression markedly. If his parents did not punish aggression severely, the use of physical punishment for other kinds of misdeeds had no effect on the amount of aggression the child showed.

Our present data do not tell why, but one can speculate a little on the reasons. Physical punishment is itself a form of attack—perhaps often perceived as aggression by the child. If parents serve as models, then it is not surprising that the children adopt similar ways of behaving. Too, physical punishment is like punishing for aggression in general—it is a form of frustration. This is particularly true for the very young child, who is helpless before the physical power of adults and must accept their control whenever it is displayed in physical form. We have no way of telling whether the most physically punished children in this study had learned to avoid certain specific actions that were most often followed by spankings, but it is evident that even if they did, they expressed more aggression in other ways. Whatever the mechanism, we may conclude that strong physical punishment produced high aggression when it was used as a technique on children who were being severely punished for aggression in general. . . .

Our findings suggest that the way for parents to produce a non-aggressive child is to make abundantly clear that aggression is frowned upon, and to stop aggression when it occurs, but to avoid punishing the child for his aggression. Punishment seems to have complex effects. While undoubtedly it often stops a particular form of aggression, at least momentarily, it appears to generate more hostility in the child and lead to further aggressive outbursts at some other time or place. Furthermore, when the parents punish —particularly when they employ physical punishment—they are providing a living example of the use of aggression at the very moment they are trying to teach the child not to be aggressive. The child, who copies his parents in many ways, is likely to learn as much from this example of successful aggression on his parents' part as he is from the pain of punishment. Thus, the most peaceful home is one in which the mother believes aggression is not desirable and under no circumstances is ever to be expressed toward her, but who relies mainly on non-punitive forms of control. The homes where the children show angry, aggressive outbursts frequently are likely to be homes in which the mother has a relatively tolerant (or careless!) attitude toward such behavior, or where she administers severe punishment for it, or both.

These conclusions will certainly not astonish anyone who has worked professionally with children and their parents. Social workers, psychologists, teachers, psychiatrists, and probation officers have seen the twin effects of permissiveness and punishment many times in their own experience. What is important in the present report is the demonstration with this group of families. When one works with a few cases, particularly when most of them are quite deviant from the general population, one often has some uncertainty as to whether the relationships he sees would apply to a more normal group. Here is as normal a group of American mothers and their children as one could want for these purposes. The principles hold good.

There is another aspect to the matter worth emphasizing, however. The effects of these two aspects of control may already be known by professionals, but, even with a demonstration of this sort, they will not find ready acceptance by many others. There are two reasons.

First, *punishment is satisfying* to the parent. When a child aggresses toward his mother, he angers her, interferes with what she is doing, with her peace of mind, with her dignity and self-respect. Aggression hurts. It is meant to. And it produces in the mother the appropriate stimulation to retaliate in kind. Combined with her sense of obligation to rear her child properly, this retaliation comes out in a way she thinks of as "punishment"—that is, a form of aggression designed to have a good *training* effect on its recipient. As will be seen in a later chapter, many mothers have developed strong beliefs that punishment is a helpful method of control. (Sometimes it is, too.) These beliefs are essential to the peace of mind of such mothers. Without the conviction that "punishment is *good* for my child," these mothers would be forced to view their own behavior as retaliatory, aggressive, childish—in short, contemptible. This would not long provide a tolerable self-image. It is to be expected, then, that our demonstration of the deleterious effect of severe punishment of aggression will not be an easy finding for many people to swallow.

A second matter has to do with permissiveness. The difficulty grows out of the problem of punishment. During the last three decades there has developed, among the more literate and sensitive part of the American people, an uneasy recognition that punishment sometimes eliminates a few specific responses, but leaves a strongly hostile drive bottled up within the child. There is evidence to support this belief. With this consideration in mind, and an urgent desire to provide better mental hygiene for their children, not a few parents have developed what almost amounts to a cult of being permissive about aggression. Their aim is to avoid repression, to permit the child easier and freer expression of his impulses, and thus to prevent the development of aggression-anxiety, with its accompanying displacements, projections, and sometimes uncontrollable fantasies.

This aim is good, both for the children and the society they will compose, but whether it can be achieved by a high degree of permissiveness for expression of aggression toward the parents is a question. Does a permissive attitude, with the consequent freer expression of aggression, decrease the strength of projective fantasies? There is no indication in our own data that it does. Each of the children in the present study was tested with two 20-minute sessions of doll play. The children of the more non-permissive half of the group of mothers showed little if any more fantasy aggression under these circumstances than the children of the more permissive half. This finding is in sharp contrast to that with respect to punishment; the children of the more severely punishing mothers displayed quite significantly more fantasy aggression than the children of the less severely punishing ones (Levin and Sears, 1956). Permissiveness does not seem to decrease fantasy indications of aggressive impulses.

Permissiveness does increase the amount of aggression in the home, however, and it is worth considering what this does to the child himself. An angry child is not usually a happy child, nor is he one who receives affection and willing companionship from others. He is a source of discomfort to family and peers, and probably receives a certain amount of retaliation. He upsets his siblings, raises the level of frustration imposed on his parents, and inevitably has an increase, to some extent, of his own aggression-anxiety. There seems little advantage in all this, either to the child himself or to his parents.

These comments may seem to encourage a conclusion that parents will find it to their advantage to be somewhat non-permissive of aggression that is directed toward themselves. This can be a dangerous conclusion if the kind of permissiveness we mean is not clearly understood.

Therefore, let us be as clear as possible about the aspect of permissiveness we have in mind. A child is more likely to be non-aggressive if his parents hold the value that aggression is undesirable and should not occur. He is more likely to be non-aggressive if his parents prevent or stop the occurrence of aggressive outbursts instead of passively letting them go on, but prevent them by other means than punishment or threats of retaliation. If the parents' non-permissiveness takes the form of punishing the child (and thus leading the child to *expect* punishment) for aggressive behavior, then non-permissiveness will not have the effect of reducing the child's aggression. On the contrary, the instant that punishment enters, all the consequences of punishment that have been discussed earlier may be anticipated, including that of increasing the child's level of aggression.

REFERENCES

Glueck, S. and E. Glueck
   1950     *Unraveling Juvenile Delinquency.* Cambridge, Massachusetts: Harvard University Press.
Levin, H. and Robert Sears
   1957     "Identification with Parents as a Determinant of Doll-Play Aggression." *Journal of Abnormal and Social Psychology* 55: 304–308.
Sears, R. R., J. W. M. Whiting, W. Nowlis, and P. S. Sears
   1953     "Some Child-Rearing Antecedents of Aggression and Dependency in Young Children." *Genetic Psychology Monographs* 47: 135–236.

# 28. *Physical Frustration and Murder*
## STUART PALMER

The findings reported in the previous article show that parents who use physical punishment tend to have children who are more aggressive than do those parents who rarely use such punishment. This conclusion has been confirmed by many other studies using a wide variety of methods. But there is a big difference between the minor aggressiveness of a five-year-old and "real violence." Our guess is that the effects of physical punishment on producing tendencies towards violence are in direct proportion to the severity of the punishment. The more violent the experiences of the child at the hands of his parents, the more violent he is likely to be to others as an adult. Such a relationship is suggested by the studies of child-abusing parents, which show that such parents frequently come from families in which they were abused. Although some children exposed to abuse may have learned how terrible it is *and* therefore become inhibited from doing the same thing to their own children, more apparently learn how terrible it is *and* internalize beating as a mode of dealing with their own children. The same process is dramatically demonstrated in relation to men who commit murder. Palmer shows that his sample of murderers experienced tremendously more violence as children than did their brothers. Frequently, they were almost beaten to death as children. As adults, many actually did beat another person to death.

This is a study of fifty-one men convicted of murder, of their early life experiences, and of how those experiences led each of them to kill one or more of their fellow human beings. The study was carried out in New England over a period of three years, 1956 to 1959. During that time, and following a careful plan, I interviewed murderers, their relatives and friends, and correctional officials.

A control group of fifty-one men who had not committed murder was used in order to have a standard with which to compare the murderers. This control group was composed of the nearest-in-age brother of each murderer. In the research, special emphasis was placed on finding out whether there was a connection between severe frustration experienced in infancy and childhood and murder committed in adolescence or adulthood. However, many other aspects of the total problem of murder were also investigated and will be reported on here. . . .

The mothers were asked questions concerning whether they or their husbands struck hard or beat severely the murderers and control brothers. (Spanking is not included here.) They were also asked how old the children were when first beaten and how frequently the beatings occurred. It is of course possible that the mothers de-emphasized instances where they themselves beat their children. However, a number of the mothers were quick to admit they had beaten their sons severely.

SOURCE: Reprinted with permission of the publisher from Stuart Palmer, *The Psychology of Murder* (New York: Thomas Y. Crowell, 1960), pp. 1, 76–80. Copyright © 1960 by Stuart Palmer.

As one mother said, "He was was always getting into trouble. I shouldn't have done it, I suppose, but I'd get so mad at him I'd pick up a stick or anything I could get my hands on and lay into him. Once I beat him real bad."

Another mother said, "I remember one time I got so upset with him I took this poker we had for the stove and I hit him with that. I kind of lost control of myself and I couldn't stop."

A slightly greater number of murderers than control brothers were beaten by the mothers: twenty-two murderers as compared to sixteen brothers. But the beatings began at approximately the same ages in the cases of both murderers and brothers: usually between the ages three and six. There were no important differences in the frequency with which mothers beat the murderers and the brothers. On the average, they beat the twenty-two murderers, and the sixteen brothers as well, about once every six months. However, four of the murderers and two of the brothers were beaten once a week or more often.

The fathers (and stepfathers) struck hard or beat severely twenty-three of the murderers and fourteen of the brothers. The murderers were slightly younger than the brothers when the fathers first beat them. The fathers beat the murderers and the brothers about once every three months, somewhat more frequently than did the mothers. According to the mothers, therefore, neither they nor the fathers generally beat the sons to what could be termed a tremendous extent. However, when they did beat them, the beatings were often extremely severe. This was especially true with respect to the fathers.

A spry little old woman said in talking about her husband and her murderer son, "He beat him once, I thought the boy was done for. Oh, I'd hit them pretty hard on occasion but nothing like that. This time his father just lost his head. He knocked that boy from one end of the house to the other. Beating him. Beating him. He was like a man gone insane, my husband."

"Before that," I asked, "had your husband seemed to like the other children better than John?" John was the murderer.

"Liked? Well, I don't know how he liked them. But John was the one he got mad at the most. Of course, John was always—well, he was a peculiar child. Always getting into trouble and yet you'd never know it until he'd done it. But that was no excuse for the way his father beat him that time.

"I can still remember it to this day, the way he beat him. There was blood on the wall, I can see it now."

"How did John act toward his father after that?"

The mother drew herself up, in a sense proudly. "Never spoke to him again. Never. Except as he had to. If his father asked him something, he'd answer. But that was all."

"How old was John when this happened?"

"He was—he was six. He'd just started school."

Perhaps it was coincidence, perhaps it was not. But when he was twenty-four years old, John beat to death a man thirty years older than himself.

About three times as many murderers as control brothers were beaten severely once or more by people other than their parents: nineteen murderers and six brothers. These other people included uncles, older brothers, unrelated men, or adolescent boys in the neighborhood. The remaining thirty-two murderers and forty-five brothers were not beaten in this way, to the best of the mothers' knowledge. These differences are statistically significant at the one per cent level. ($X^2 = 8.954$; two-by-two table used.)

During the course of the research, an Index of Physical Frustration was developed. This index utilizes most of the more or less specific types of presumed physical frustration which have previously been enumerated in this chapter. The index pertains only to physical frustrations which the individual has experienced during the first twelve years of life.

One point is allotted for:

1. A difficult birth.
2. Serious effects of forceps at birth.
3. Each serious operation.
4. Each serious illness.
5. Each serious accident.
6. Each serious beating by someone other than a parent or stepparent.
7. One or more serious beatings by the mother.
8. One or more serious beatings by the father or stepfather.

The higher the index score, the greater the physical frustration in early life is taken to be. The minimum score is zero but there is no maximum limit. The reader may ask, why assign the equal weight of one point to each serious operation, illness, accident, beating, and the like when it is obvious that differing degrees of frustration were involved? The reason for assigning one point to each is that there is no especially reliable way to distinguish systematically among the amounts of resultant frustration. In the behavioral sciences at present, we usually have to employ broad-gauge, rough-and-ready measures. But those measures are far better than none at all.

The Index of Physical Frustration scores are significantly higher for the fifty-one murderers than for the fifty-one control brothers. (See Table 3.) In fact, the differences are strikingly great: twenty-five of the murderers have scores of four or less, while fifty of the brothers have scores of four or less. Conversely, twenty-six of the murderers have scores of five or more, while only one brother has a score that high. The mean score for the fifty-one murderers is 4.53; for the fifty-one brothers the mean score is 1.65, indicating a tremendous difference.

The index scores of the pairs of murderers and their brothers were analyzed. Forty of the murderers had scores higher than their brothers. In the cases of seven pairs, the scores of the murderers and their brothers were equal. And in the remaining four pairs the scores of the murderers were lower than those of their brothers. There were, then, eleven murderers who did not have index scores higher than those of their respective control brothers. In some of these cases, the murderer had experienced much greater *psychological* frustrations than his brother, thus causing the over-all amount of his frustration to outweigh that of the brother.

However, if the mothers were reporting accurately, there can be little

*Table 3. Scores of Murderers and Control Brothers on Index of Physical Frustration*

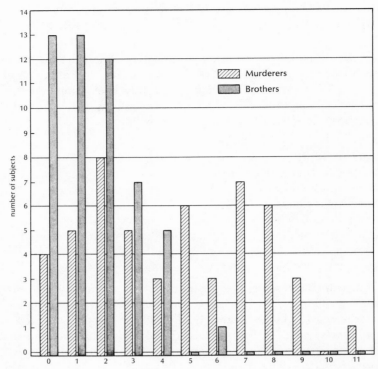

*Total number of murderers $= 51$. Total number of brothers $= 51$. Using a two-by-six table (scores 5 through 11 combined for the calculation), $X^2 = 33.102$; $P < 0.01$.

doubt that, in the cases of the fifty-one murderers and fifty-one control brothers studied here, the murderers were *as a group* subjected in childhood and adolescence to an overwhelmingly greater amount of physical frustration than were the brothers. In the next chapter, the psychological frustrations experienced by the murderers and their brothers will be enumerated. An Index of Psychological Frustration will be employed to provide a measure of the differences between the two groups. Then, an Index of General Frustration, which combines physical and psychological frustration, will be used to distinguish still further between the murderers and the control brothers.

# 29. *The Family and Violence*
## JAMES S. CAMPBELL

The United States is a society with a high rate of violence of all types. The best available evidence suggests that this has been true since colonial days. No doubt part of the explanation can be traced to the harsh conditions of the frontier and the fact that a sizeable proportion of the colonists came from the lowest and most violent sections of British society. Many in fact were convicted criminals, whose punishment was banishment to the American colonies. Against such a background, it has taken a series of violent dramatic events—in particular, the assassinations of an extremely popular president, senator, and civil rights leader—to arouse public awareness and concern with the high level of violence. The National Commission on the Causes and Prevention of Violence, which was established as a result of this newly awakened concern with violence, consequently carried out intensive investigations for sixteen months and issued thirteen volumes of reports. On the basis of these reports, a double conclusion becomes inescapable: the United States is the world leader in violence among advanced industrial societies and this level of violence is not a recent development. The Commission furthermore makes clear that many of the roots of this violence are to be found in the family. The following section from one of the Commission reports summarizes much of what is known about the family and violence. It also shows that the relationship of the family to violence is, in turn, interwoven with the relation of the family to other aspects of society.

. . . During our lifetime, we ordinarily belong to two families—the first when we are children, the second when we are parents. One we are born into; the other we establish ourselves. These two experiences represent life's major activity from birth to death.

The American family has clearly lost some of its solidarity, however. Once it was the source of cohesion and security, the unit of economic activity, the means of recreation and education. Today it is increasingly disrupted. Divorce rates rise, but are outrun by the incidence of marital conflicts. Parents, especially working mothers, spend more time outside the home, and television changes the character of family recreation. A generation gap widens, as young people identify more with peer groups in colleges, dropout communities, and street cultures than with their own families.

These changes do not necessarily signify a decline in the importance of the family. They do reflect the increasing pressures which the family is under —but these stresses frequently stem precisely from the fact that more is being demanded of family life than ever before. Thus, as urbanization depersonalizes human relationships, husbands and wives become more dependent upon each other for the satisfaction of emotional needs that were

SOURCE: This selection was prepared by James S. Campbell on the basis of a paper submitted by Shlomo Shoham, Director of the Institute of Criminal Law and Criminology, Tel-Aviv University, Israel, and on materials made available to the Task Force by Commissioner W. Walter Menninger, M.D. It is reprinted here from James S. Campbell, Joseph R. Sahid, and David P. Stang, *Law and Order Reconsidered* (Washington, D.C.: U.S. Government Printing Office, 1969), pp. 177–189.

previously met outside of the family. And, despite the impact of television, the family manifestly retains its central role in the upbringing of children.

The family is, after all, the primary channel through which human culture is transmitted to the young of the species. The family and the home are the first molding cast for a child's behavior and the basic unit for the child's "socialization." Values are inculcated by example, teaching and interaction.[1] It is the function of the family to transmit to the children what the prescribed, permitted and proscribed values of the society are, as well as to indicate what are acceptable and unacceptable means of achievement. In a culture, for instance, where violence is a commendable pattern of masculine behavior, the education of children in the family will include a permissive attitude toward violence. Conversely, if a society or distinct class within it prohibits over-aggression, the family experience will direct the children toward the solution of conflicts by other than violent means.

The crucial role of the family in disposing a child to violence or nonviolence is generally accepted. Whatever be the hereditary predisposition and the biological factors contributing to a child's development, the patterns of behavior of the child are largely established by his early life experiences. Any observation of young children reveals the potential for aggressive behavior, destructive behavior, temper tantrums, and the like. It is the challenge to the family to orient or socialize these creatures to a principle of operation whereby their impulses of a socially unacceptable nature are controlled.

Of course, the ultimate development of any individual and his ultimate violence-proneness are the result of many factors. Crime and violence are the result of a complex interaction of individuals' biologies and life experiences. Criminologists have identified specific characteristics often associated with crime and violence, including social disorganization, cultural conflict resulting from migration, highly packed urban living, poverty, and other important elements. Nevertheless, despite the importance of these other factors, the family remains the first socializing agency to which the human being is exposed in the crucial formative years of his life. What, then is the ability of the family unit to instill a restraining, normative barrier against violence within the personality framework of the child?

## FORMATION OF THE CHILD'S MORAL PERSONALITY

Personality growth and development is a complex process. The infant in the beginning does not have any conception of the values as expressed by society. The infant after birth is motivated by some basic drives to survive and to achieve satisfaction and relief of tension through the satisfaction of bodily needs. In addition, there are some basic psychological needs which include mothering, without which the infant will waste away. but the infant has no

---

[1]Lyman C. Wynne, Irving M. Ryckoff, Juliana Day and Stanley I. Hirsch, "Pseudo-Mutuality in the Family Relations of Schizophrenics," in *The Family*, ed. by Norman W. Bell and Ezra F. Vogel (Glencoe, Ill.: The Free Press, 1960), at 573.

real conception or understanding, or capacity to understand in adult logic what is happening about him, or what the consequences are of his behavior.

The early years of life are occupied with the maturation and growth of all the organ systems and the beginning mastery of body skills; i.e., learning to grasp, sit, walk, talk, control body processes. The discipline and control of children as they first develop these skills of body control and locomotion depend entirely upon the parents. The child of two or three has no specific moral controls, no sense of right or wrong except in terms of a self-related reference. Something is right if it provides for his satisfaction and pleasure or relief of tension; something is wrong if it hurts him or causes pain. His response to something wrong is to attempt to retaliate or protest mightily. The basic moral law of the young child might be expressed in terms of the *lex talionis,* or an eye for an eye: "When I hurt, I want you to know I hurt, and I want you to hurt like I hurt. Therefore, if you hit me, I'll hit you back."

Self-centered behavior of this character makes for anarchy, and increasingly, as the child grows, parental discipline sets certain limits. Gradually, the child learns that he cannot always have what he wants when he wants it, and that there must be respect for other people—if only for the reality that he is going to be hurt when he transgresses acceptable limits. The child tends to absorb within his personality the standards of those about him, with their "norms" (rules) for violence as well as other kinds of behavior. This process of socialization, incorporating the parental and social values, is a process that evolves in varying degrees over the period of childhood. The initial absorption is in a concrete and mechanical sense; the child complies with parental rules because the parents have the authority to back up those rules. In due course the child achieves an autonomous ethical system, tested through a process of trial and error, by which he weighs his conduct according to his own inner standards.[2]

Sigmund Freud, from his clinical observations, noted a crucial period in the incorporation of an inner value system in the child around the age of 5 or 6. This he related to the process of the child's forming a more specific sense of identity as a boy or a girl, a process which also involves the child's developing a sense of his role in the family. Freud also related this development to his observation of a process he characterized as the oedipal complex. Simply stated, the boy who has up to this point selfishly wanted to have the mother all to himself, is forced to recognize that father has the inside track. Father is too big to be conquered in this competition, and therefore the young boy in effect operates on the principle that "if he can't beat 'em, join 'em." In other words, he gives up competing with the father for mother, and instead identifies with father *and makes father's values a part of himself.* A comparable process takes place in the young girl. Essentially, it is at this period of time that the child does develop an inner sense of rules, a conscience, a sense of right and wrong, and will then manifest some inner control which is not just related to parental correction.

---

[2]Lawrence Kohlberg, *Stage and Sequence: The Developmental Approach to Moralization* (New York: Holt, Rinehart & Winston, 1969).

This is a continuing process that is refined as the child grows older, and it reoccurs significantly during adolescence as the young person retests society's rights and wrongs, and through social-role experimentation works toward establishing an identity as an adult.

In adolescence, sometimes, the adult values have to be challenged and tested in order for the individual to prove that he has separate identity and is capable of independent action. This challenge to adult values may be done by an individual adolescent, but it is more commonly experienced as adolescents join together in groups or gangs. The gang membership provides a sense of security and strength in numbers which permits a youth to act in a way that he could not act on his own.[3] The gang in this sense, or the "street culture" as it has been called, provides a challenge to the family unit, but does so while replacing the family security with gang security and in establishing simple and consistent norms where values are sharply defined in black and white, without ambiguities.

Adolescence, then, is a period of development crises, which if not overcome may result in a predisposition to crime, violence, or deviance. This is not unlike the childhood diseases which everyone has to pass through but from which serious complications can arise. If the socialization in the family prior to or within this critical period has been faulty, there will not be any strong and clear normative barriers against delinquent solutions to life problems.

Jean Genet, the thief, playwright and philosopher, depicts with devastating sincerity the development of a criminal. Genet was born out of wedlock. His mother abandoned him in his cradle, and he was cared for in his formative years by an orphanage, which in due course entrusted him to a foster home, a peasant family in Le Morvan. He soon realized that he was not like the other village youngsters. He was a foundling, with no mother, no father, and therefore no clear identity to internalize. The village was a close community, and he soon found out that in the peasant family he was "Jean, the little bastard," the receptacle for all the residuary, unwanted and despised attributes of the family and the small peasant community.

When Genet commits a crime, he complies with the expectations of his immediate environment. This in itself is satisfying. He is no more Jean the nameless bastard, he is Jean the thief. Moreover, the newly found criminal self-image is a course of strength and achievement: compliance with the image of a criminal gives Jean an individual identity. Further, it makes him eligible for the group of other thieves and homosexuals, affording thus the opportunity for identification with a group and a sense of belonging.

## SOCIALIZATION IN THE FAMILY.

The general scheme of socialization in the family may be presented as a "norm-sending" process by which the father, for example, transmits the rules of behavior to the family members. This process may be divided for clarity's sake into three phases:

[3]Sophia M. Robison, *Juvenile Delinquency* (New York: Holt, Rinehart & Winston, 1960), at 81.

(1) *Statement of rules:* the father in our case states the desired behavior, verbally, by gestures, by some other mode of communication, or by his own behavior as a model for imitation.

(2) *Surveillance:* by the father (or other members of the family) to ensure compliance to the rules.

(3) *Sanctions:* applied for the infringement of the rules or for noncompliance to them.

The sanctions may be either negative in the form of punishment for noncompliance with the rules, or positive in the form of rewards for conformity to the rules. The child on the receiving end may conform to the norm for fear of punishment (sanction orientation); he may be induced to conform by the rewarding sanction (identification); or he may absorb the norm very deeply within his personality structure so that conformity becomes "the right thing to do" (moral orientation). At this deep level of internalization, where the norm becomes a personality element, surveillance and sanctions are essentially superfluous.[4]

The efficacy of the family norm-sending process and the depth to which the child absorbs these controls can be the crucial factor which tips the scale for or against violent behavior by the child. It determines the degree to which the child has internalized the restraining norm as a personality element and hence the force of the pressures which would be necessary to overcome or "neutralize" the restraining force of the norm in order to commit an act of violence. Without taking into account the factor of socialization within the family (or family surrogate), any explanation of violence (or any criminal, deviant or rebellious behavior) is bound to remain incomplete.

The starving Hindu has all the reasons (and all the pressures) in the world to slay one of the holy cows that roam the streets and fry himself a steak, but he would not dream of doing it because of the deeply internalized religious norm forbidding it.[5] The same idea is even more apparent in the actions of religious dissenters, "freedom fighters," and rebels throughout the ages who have undergone extreme torture and death but have not acted contrary to their deeply internalized sets of norms. Research carried out in Israel on delinquent and violent gangs sought to discover why some boys, not distinguishable from the rest by socio-economic background, did not participate in the gangs' delinquent and violent activities but only in its nondelinquent ones. The most significant differences between the two groups of boys was the degree to which the norms concerning the sanctity of private property and the nonuse of aggression were internalized to form an initial barrier against criminal and violent behavior. Similar differences arising from different family socialization patterns help explain why even in the worst of slums plagued by poverty, bad living conditions, criminal gangs, prostitutes, and dope peddlers, only some boys become delinquent, whereas a far greater number remain law abiding.

[4]John W. Thibaut and Harold M. Kelley, *The Social Psychology of Groups* (New York: John Wiley & Sons, Inc., 1959).

[5]Edwin H. Sutherland and Donald R. Cressey, *Principles of Criminology*, 6th ed. (Philadelphia: Lippincott, 1960), at 195.

Conflict situations, however, may make the whole process of norm-sending ineffective, so that the norm is internalized by the individual at a very shallow level or even not at all. Continuing conflicts in the norm-sending process may also injure a set of norms that has already been previously internalized by the individual. The greater the intensity and extent of conflict situations in the socialization process, the greater will be the shift away from moral orientation toward sanction orientation, and from fully internalized rules to rules which are followed only out of fear of being caught. At this state the normative barrier against a given crime or violent behavior is completely shattered, and the crime then is only in being caught and not in committing the offense.

Adolescence—the crucial stage in the norm-receiving process—is characterized by, among other things, a yen for absolute values and a desire for sharply defined roles. As described by countless works of literature, youth is not only a seething cauldron of idealism, but also passionately in favor of unequivocal statements of facts and rules—otherwise known, by the young themselves, as plain honesty.

Gobesque, Balzac's stingy old scoundrel, sits before the fireplace with his teen-aged friend and promises him a loan without guarantees, because up to twenty a person's best guarantee is his age and "because you, my young friend, are idealistic, you visualize great ideas, basic truths and beautiful Utopias while staring at the dancing flames. At my age, however, we see in the fireplace plain burning coal."

Those youths whose socialization is most riddled with conflict situations are most liable to reject the offered adjustment to contradictory, hypocritical, and confused sets of norms. If this is adulthood, he prefers the more direct behavior and clearly defined normative system of the delinquent subculture. Because of his inability to internalize the contradictory norms of the adult world, he may be branded as "infantile," "rigid," "a permanent adolescent," "a troublemaker," and thereby be pushed further toward the values of his delinquent peers.

## CONFLICTS IN THE SOCIALIZATION PROCESS

What are the kinds of conflict situations in the socialization process within the family which can have harmful effects on the creation of a normative barrier against violence?

The family "broken" by divorce, death, or prolonged or permanent incapacitation of one or both parents was once considered a major cause of delinquency, but research has revealed that the broken home as such may not have the crucial significance that was attributed to it.

Instead, continuous family tension and discord is a far more important factor in delinquency than the actual divorce of the parents. The rates of delinquency are significantly higher in unbroken but unhappy and conflict-ridden homes than in broken ones.[6] Divorce may even lessen the chances of children

[6]Francis I. Nye, *Family Relationships and Delinquent Behavior* (New York: John Wiley & Sons, Inc., 1958), at 47.

in a tension-laden family from becoming delinquent or violent.[7] A recent study published in Israel reveals that the most significant factor linked with delinquency was *lack of value consensus among family members*.[8]

Lidz observes that a child properly requires two parents: a parent of the same sex with whom to identify and who provides a model to follow into adulthood, and a parent of the opposite sex who becomes a love object and whose love and approval the child seeks in return by identifying with the parent of the same sex. But, he notes, a parent can fill neither of his roles effectively if he is despised or treated contemptuously by the other parent. The child internalizes directives from both parents and identifies to a greater or lesser extent with both; if the parent's personalities cannot be reconciled, a split may occur in the child's personality as he attempts to relate to both parents but finds that efforts to satisfy one may elicit rebuff and rejection from the other.[9]

Another kind of conflict that impairs socialization in the family is that which arises from an external source and which injures the prestige of the norm-sender. Families in communities that undergo rapid or sudden social change, especially immigrant families whose cultural tradition in their countries of origin is markedly divergent from the culture of the absorbing community, may suffer socio-economic injuries which harm or even shatter the status of the head of the family. These types of conflict stem basically from "external" sources such as industrialization, urbanization, mass immigration, and social change, and they create conflict situations within the family between parents and the offspring, with a high probability of injuring the prestige of the norm-source and thus hampering and injuring the norm-sending process. In Israel, for instance, this type of conflict has been proved a factor in weakening the cohesion of the family unit and thus shattering family control over the young.

In the United States, the impact of slavery and segregation on the Negro family has often had a similarly debilitating effect on its ability to socialize its children. The shattering of family control typically results in the "street-culture" replacing the family as the primary norm-sender. The Kerner Commission Report has described the process well:

The high rates of unemployment and underemployment in racial ghettos are evidence, in part, that many men living in these areas are seeking, but cannot obtain, jobs which will support a family. Perhaps equally important, most jobs they can get are at the low end of the occupational scale, and often lack the necessary status to sustain a worker's self-respect, or the respect of his family and friends.

Wives of these men are forced to work and usually produce more money. If the men stay at home without working, their inadequacies constantly confront them

[7]C. R. Shaw and H. D. McKay, "Social Factors of Juvenile Delinquency," National Commission on Law Observance and Enforcement, *Report on the Causes of Crime, II* (Washington, D.C.: Government Printing Office, 1931), at 276 *et seq.*

[8]L. D. Jaffe, "Delinquency Proneness and Family Anomie," *Megamot*, March, 1962.

[9]Theodore Lidz, *The Person: His Development Throughout the Life Cycle* (New York: Basic Books, 1968).

and tensions arise between them and their wives and children. Under these pressures, it is not surprising that many of these men flee their responsibilities as husbands and fathers, leaving home, and drifting from city to city, or adopting the style of "street corner men."

With the father absent and the mother working, many ghetto children spend the bulk of their time on the streets—the streets of a crime-ridden, violence-prone, and poverty-stricken world. The image of success in this world is not that of the "solid citizen," the responsible husband and father, but rather that of the "hustler" who promotes his own interests by exploiting others. The dope sellers and the numbers runners are the "successful" men because their earnings far outstrip those men who try to climb the economic ladder in honest ways.

. . . Under these circumstances, many adopt exploitation and the "hustle" as a way of life, disclaiming both work and marriage in favor of casual and temporary liaisons. This pattern reinforces itself from one generation to the next, creating a "culture of poverty" and an ingrained cynicism about society and its institutions.

A third kind of conflict situation is conflict between verbally transmitted rules and the actual behavior of parents. When parents pay lip-service to legitimate behavior but act contrary to these same norms, conflict situations are created. This phenomenon may help to explain some middle- and upper-class juvenile delinquency—the so-called "good home delinquents." On deeper analysis these homes may not be all that good, for conflict of this kind may have entirely destroyed the legitimate norm-sending capacity of the family.

Thus the parents may preach idealistic achievement, Christian love and spiritual values, but their actual behavior may be directed solely toward material achievement. Parents may *preach* law observance, but children may *see* their parents push their way up in the "rat race" or in the cutthroat competition for upward social mobility without being particularly scrupulous about the means used to achieve their coveted goals. The verbal rule may state that one's interests should be sacrificed to help others, but the way the parents behave reveals that their actual belief is "everyone for himself." Even if the children do not identify themselves with their parents' *acts* instead of with their verbally phrased norms, the norm-sending process is still hampered by the conflict situations created by the parents' preaching and teaching one set of norms and behaving according to another.

Another and deeper kind of conflict between verbally transmitted rules and actual behavior of parents stems from the fact that adults, as grown children, still have within them some of the unresolved struggle of growing up which gets played up in relationships to others in ways of which they may be unaware. Thus there can be unconscious communications by adults which are perhaps in absolute contrast to their conscious intent. Some dramatic work by investigators Johnson and Szurek demonstrated the degree to which children can present problems in behavior and be extremely difficult to manage due to a vicarious psychological participation on the part of the parent who consciously decries the behavior of the child. It is this kind of conflict between the consciously stated standards of the parents and their unresolved, underlying feelings about behavior such as violence and aggression that may prompt the youngster to act out the behavior as part of his relationship to the parent.

A fourth kind of conflict which impairs socialization is inconsistent or crudely punitive disciplining of children. Where sanctions are sporadic, erratic, and inconsistent, social conditioning does not take place and consequently the normative barrier against violent behavior is not formed. Too severe punitive sanctions are also detrimental to norm internalization. Some findings have indicated that unusually severe or harsh child-rearing practices are linked with poor and fragmentary norm internalization.[10] In like manner, too intense punishment is ineffective in suppressing undesired behavior.[11] A research finding which is directly related to violence indicates that children who have experienced rejection or extreme punitiveness from their parents are likely to show weak internalization of a sense of duty and responsibility and have bad control over their tendencies for aggressive behavior.[12]

A survey of delinquent group members revealed consistently that their parents were usually punitive and rejecting.[13] Professor Kohlberg also finds parents of delinquents tend to be more punitive than parents of nondelinquents, although they do not differ in extent of "firmness" of socialization and home demands. They are less warm and affectionate and more inconsistent and neglectful than parents of nondelinquents.[14] Conversely, the parents', and especially the mothers', warm and affectionate treatment of the infant enhance greatly the efficacy of socialization. Consequently, withdrawal of affection or the threat of it is the most durable and effective sanction.[15] Delay of reward is also found to be effective in suppressing undesirable behavior.[16]

Middle class families resort more to withdrawal of affection as sanctions in socializing their children, whereas the lower classes inflict more repressive punishment.[17] This difference may help explain the lower incidence of violence among middle-class youth whose socialization is presumably more effective. As a rule-of-thumb conclusion, then, aggressive parents breed aggressive children, whereas the subtle manipulation of rewards may help create an effective barrier against violence.

## WHAT CAN BE DONE?

In theory, we have many methods to prevent or to correct the effects of faulty, conflict-ridden socialization on delinquent and violent children. In

[10]Justin Aronfreed, *Conduct and Conscience; the Socialization of Internalized Control over Behavior* (New York: Academic Press, 1968), at 305.

[11]*Id.*, at 203.

[12]W. McCord *et al.*, "Familial Correlates of Aggression in Nondelinquent Male Children," 62 *Journal of Abnormal and Social Psychology* 79–83 (1961).

[13]Albert Bandura and Richard Walters, *Adolescent Aggression* (New York: Ronald Press Co., 1959).

[14]Lawrence Kohlberg, "Development of Moral Character and Moral Ideology," in *Review of Child Development Research*, Vol. 1, ed. by Lois W. Hoffman and Martin L. Hoffman (New York: Russell Sage Foundation, 1964), at 383–433.

[15]Aronfreed, *supra* note 10, at 316.

[16]C. B. Ferster and J. B. Appel, "Punishment of S Responding in Matching-to-Sample by Time-Out from Positive Reinforcement," 4 *Journal of the Experimental Analysis of Behavior* 45–46 (1961).

[17]Aronfreed, *supra* note 10, at 318.

practice, the effectiveness of most of these methods is limited by a number of factors.

Child-guidance clinics and family counseling bureaus may advise parents on desirable methods of child rearing and socialization, but those who most need help are not the ones who seek out such services even where they are available and of high quality. Sometimes an influential aunt or grandmother, or even a teacher or priest, may succeed in socializing children with whom parents have failed. But the "extended family," with a large network of relatives surrounding the nuclear family and participating in the raising of its children, is increasingly disrupted by social and geographic mobility, and teachers and clergymen have less and less personal contact with families in today's society.

It is a sad fact, but a fact nonetheless, that today for the most part we are taught how to be parents by our first-born children (and by occasional desperate forays into Dr. Spock). We go through a process of trial and error, and we don't really have much in the way of social institutions that help parents effectively learn how to be parents. This vital skill is not generally taught in the course of formal schooling, and this is one area where there could be a major step—by building some effective training for parents into the formal educational process.

Many institutions report some success in efforts to correct the faulty socialization of delinquents and criminals. The Highfield Institution for Delinquents and the Boys Industrial School of Kansas, which has an association with the Menninger Clinic in Topeka, Kans., exemplify such intensive treatment programs. Professor Ernst Popanek, who directed the Wiltwyck School in New York, tried to counter aggression by friendship, permissiveness, and understanding which permeated the violence-prone boys' "total environment." Similar attempts have been carried out by Prof. Fritz Redl to ease the aggressivity of "children who hate" [18] at Pioneer House in Detroit, and by Professor Bruno Bettelheim at the Orthogenic School of the University of Chicago. In all these cases, aggressive and guiltless psychopathic children gained a fair measure of internalized guilt and their aggressivity declined.

The crucial question, however, is whether society is prepared to foot the immense bill for this kind of psychiatric treatment of every violent child. Intensive psychotherapy is expensive and, when successful, may take years to achieve positive results. How many children may be accepted in the select and experimental institutions which offer this complex, elaborate, and costly "milieu therapy"? Shouldn't the focus be on preventive strategies aimed at problem groups, rather than on corrective programs of this type?

A bewildering multiplicity of factors are involved in any preventive strategies, however. The ghetto Negro family, for instance, has tended to become matriarchal because of social influences that can be traced all the way back to the practice of slave owners to break up families by selling their individual

---

[18]Fritz Fedl and David Wineman, *Controls from Within: Techniques for the Treatment of the Aggressive Child* (New York: The Free Press, 1954).

members.[19] Prevention of the deleterious effects that this family structure has on socialization entails nothing less than a virtual revolution in American attitudes, mores, and race relations. This revolution is probably taking place right now, but before it is carried through many more cohorts of violence-prone Negro children will be born into the slums of our cities.

At the level of preventive individual treatment, the most severe difficulties are encountered. How can outside agencies detect violence-breeding socialization processes? Conflict-ridden socialization leaves its scars on the personality of the child at a very early age, and it often manifests itself only in quite subtle modes of familial interaction. The aggressivity or violence may not erupt until years later. Moreover, assuming detection were possible, how would we intervene? In America, even the rudest home is a castle, and even the most miserable family is a shrine. What agency would we dare let to trespass into this sanctuary when no law has been broken?

Neither government nor any other institution of society can make a husband and wife create a relationship of love among themselves and their children; they must do that on their own, as individuals. But government can at least try to create the conditions under which stable families can thrive.[20] It can make it possible for fathers to have jobs, and hense to have the self-respect that comes from being able to support a family. Government can act against hunger, disease, poor housing, and urban decay, thereby creating a humane environment in which humane personal relationships can develop. Schools can give hope to the young, and to the parents whose hope is in their children. Churches can awaken men and women to the moral and spiritual dimensions of family life.

Given the velocity of change in our society, it is inevitable that family structures will come under increasing pressures. These pressures are likely to underscore the family's importance even more than at present; for the stability of man, and his ability to respond nonviolently to his life experiences, depend on the stability of the family in which he is raised. The family, the central institution of human society, whose failure undermines all, can and must be strengthened by the operations of the other institutions of society.

[19]*Report of the National Advisory Commission on Civil Disorders* (Washington, D.C.: Government Printing Office, 1968), at 144–45.

[20]See discussion and recommendations concerning the family in *The Challenge of Crime In a Free Society*, at 63–66 (Washington, D.C.: Government Printing Office, 1967); see generally the comprehensive review and bibliography in Rodman & Grams, "Juvenile Delinquency and the Family: A Review and Discussion," Appendix L of the *Task Force Report on Juvenile Delinquency* (President's Commission on Law Enforcement and Administration of Justice) (Washington, D.C.: Government Printing Office, 1967).

# CHAPTER NINE
# The Family and Socially
# Patterned Violence

## 30. *The Family and the Subculture of Violence*
**CLAUDE BROWN**

There are some important similarities as well as some important differences between Jules Henry's account of the training in violence experienced by Pete Portman (p. 238) and Claude Brown's account of his childhood training in violence. Both describe the way in which a father systematically trains his son to use violence. However, they differ in a number of ways. First is the fact that the Portmans were middle class and did not live in the atmosphere of poverty and violence which typified the slum in which Brown grew up. Second, it follows from this difference that Brown's father was teaching him to behave in accord with community-recognized standards of behavior in respect to violence: the "subculture of violence"; Mr. Portman, on the other hand, was teaching his son a pattern of behavior which is contrary to at least the professed values of most middle class persons. One father was teaching his son to follow the socially approved (within his own subculture) pattern of violence; the other was teaching his son a pattern which conflicted with the norms of his community. Perhaps that is part of the reason why the later life of these two boys became so different: Claude Brown found himself in jail and Pete Portman in a mental hospital.

If anyone had asked me around the latter part of 1957 just what I thought had made the greatest impression on my generation in Harlem, I would have said, "Drugs." I don't think too many people would have contested this. About ten years earlier, in 1947, or just eight years earlier, in 1949, this wouldn't have been true.

In 1949, I would have answered the same question with the answer, "The knife." Perhaps all this could have been summed up in saying, "The bad mother-fucker." Throughout my childhood in Harlem, nothing was more strongly impressed upon me than the fact that you had to fight and that you should fight. Everybody would accept it if a person was scared to fight, but not if he was so scared that he didn't fight.

As I saw it in my childhood, most of the cats I swung with were more afraid of not fighting than they were of fighting. This was how it was supposed to be, because this was what we had come up under. The adults in the

SOURCE: Reprinted with permission from Claude Brown, *Manchild in the Promised Land* (New York: The Macmillan Company, 1965), pp. 263–271. Copyright © 1965 by Claude Brown.

neighborhood practiced this. They lived by the concept that a man was supposed to fight. When two little boys got into a fight in the neighborhood, the men around would encourage them and egg them on. They'd never think about stopping the fight.

There were some little boys, like myself, who when we got into a fight even though we weren't ten years old yet—all the young men, the street-corner cats, they would come out of the bars or the numbers joints or anyplace they were and watch. Somebody would say, "Little Sonny Boy is on the street fightin' again," and everybody had to see this.

Down on 146th Street, they'd put money on street fights. If there were two little boys on one block who were good with their hands, or one around the corner and one on Eighth Avenue, men on the corner would try and egg them into a fight.

I remember Big Bill, one of the street-corner hustlers before he went to jail for killing a bartender. When I was about seven or eight years old, I remember being on the street and Bill telling me one day, "Sonny Boy, I know you can kick this little boy's ass on 146th Street, and I'll give you a dollar to do it."

I knew I couldn't say no, couldn't be afraid. He was telling all these other men around there on the street that I could beat this boy's ass. There was another man, a numbers hustler, who said, "No. They ain't got no boy here on Eighth Avenue who could beat little Rip's ass on 146th Street."

Bill said, "Sonny Boy, can you do it?" And he'd already promised me the dollar.

I said, "Yeah." I was scared, because I'd seen Rip and heard of him.

He was a mean-looking little boy. He was real dark-skinned, had big lips and bulgy eyes, and looked like he was always mad. One time I had seen him go at somebody with a knife. A woman had taken the knife out of his hands, but she cut her hand getting it. I knew he would have messed up the cat if he could have held on to that knife.

He knew me too, and he had never messed with me. I remember one time he told me that he was going to kick my ass. I said, "Well, here it is. Start kickin'." He never did. I don't think he was too anxious to mess with me. I didn't want to mess with him either, but since Big Bill had given me this dollar and kept pushing me, I couldn't have said no. They would have said I was scared of him, and if that had gotten back to him, I know he would have messed with me.

I fought him for three days. I beat him one day, and he beat me the next day. On the third day, we fought three fights. I had a black eye, and he had a bloody lip. He had a bloody nose, and I had a bloody nose. By the end of the day, we had become good friends. Somebody took us to the candy store and bought us ice-cream cones.

Rip and I got real tight. If anybody messed with him and I heard about it, I wanted to fight them. And it was the same with him if anybody messed with me.

This was something that took place in all the poor colored neighborhoods throughout New York City. Every place I went, it was the same way, at least with the colored guys. You had to fight, and everybody respected people for fighting. I guess if you were used to it and were good at it, there was nothing else you could do. I guess that was why Turk became a fighter. He had fought so long and had been so preoccupied with fighting that he couldn't do anything else. He had to get this fighting out of his system.

With cats like Turk and many others who came up on the Harlem streets, the first day they came out of the house by themselves, at about five or six years old, the prizefight ring beckoned to them. It beckoned to them in the form of the cat around the corner who had the reputation or the cat who wanted to mess with your little brother or your little sister. If you went to school and somebody said, "I'm gon kick your ass if you don't bring me some money tomorrow to buy my lunch," it was the prizefight ring beckoning to you.

I remember they used to say on the streets, "Don't mess with a man's money, his woman, or his manhood." This was the thing when I was about twelve or thirteen. This was what the gang fights were all about. If somebody messed with your brother, you could just punch him in his mouth, and this was all right. But if anybody was to mess with your sister, you had to really fuck him up—break his leg or stab him in the eye with an ice pick, something vicious.

I suppose the main things were the women in the family and the money. This was something we learned very early. If you went to the store and lost some money or if you let somebody gorilla you out of some money that your mother or your father had given you, you got your ass beaten when you came back home. You couldn't go upstairs and say, "Well, Daddy, that big boy down there took the money that you gave me to buy some cigars." Shit, you didn't have any business letting anybody take your money. You got your ass whipped for that, and you were supposed to.

You were supposed to go to war about your money. Maybe this was why the cats on the corner were killing each other over a two-dollar crap game or a petty debt. People were always shooting, cutting, or killing somebody over three dollars.

I remember going to the store for my father on a Sunday morning. He'd given me a quarter to get him some chewing tobacco. I had to walk up to 149th Street, because no place else was open. I went up to this drugstore on 149th Street, and there were some cats standing around there. I was about eight, and they were about ten or eleven.

One of them said, "Hey, boy, come here," one of those things. I was scared to run, because I knew I wouldn't be able to outrun them all. I figured that if I acted kind of bad, they might not be so quick to mess with me. So I walked right up to them. One cat said, "You got any money?"

I said, "No, I ain't got no money."

I guess I shouldn't have said that. He kept looking at me real mean, trying to scare me. He said, "Jump up and down." I knew what this was all about, because I used to do it myself. If you jumped up and down and the cat who was shaking you down heard some change jingling, he was supposed to try to beat your ass and take the money.

I said, "No, man. I ain't jumpin' up and down."

He grabbed me by my collar. Somebody said, "He's got something in his hand." That was Dad's quarter. One cat grabbed my hand. I'd forgotten all about the guy who had my collar. I hit the boy who had my hand. Then the cat who had me by the collar started punching me in the jaw. I wasn't even thinking about him. I was still fighting the other cat to keep the quarter.

A woman came out a door and said, "You all stop beatin' that boy!"

I had a bloody nose; they'd kicked my ass good, but I didn't mind, because they hadn't taken my quarter. It wasn't the value of money. It couldn't have been. It was just that these things symbolized a man's manhood or principles. That's what Johnny Wilkes used to like to call it, a man's principles. You don't mess with a man's money; you don't mess with a man's woman; you don't mess with a man's family or his manhood—these were a man's principles, according to Johnny Wilkes.

Most girls in Harlem could fight pretty well themselves, and if other girls bothered them, they could take care of themselves. You couldn't let other cats bother your sisters. In the bebopping days in Harlem, if the girls had brothers who were scared to fight, everybody would mess with them and treat them like they wanted to. Cats would come up and say things like, "You better meet me up on the roof," or "You better meet me in the park."

It went deep. It went very deep—until drugs came. Fighting was the thing that people concentrated on. In our childhood, we all had to make our reputations in the neighborhood. Then we'd spend the rest of our lives living up to them. A man was respected on the basis of his reputation. The people in the neighborhood whom everybody looked up to were the cats who'd killed somebody. The little boys in the neighborhood whom the adults respected were the little boys who didn't let anybody mess with them.

Dad once saw me run away from a fight. He was looking out the window one day, and the Morris brothers were messing with me. I didn't think I could beat both of them, so I ran in the house. Dad was at the door when I got there. He said, "Where are you runnin' to, boy?"

I said, "Dad, these boys are out there, and they messin' with me."

He said, "Well, if you come in here, I'm gon mess with you too. You ain't got no business runnin' from nobody."

I said, "Yeah, Dad, I know that. But there's two of 'em, and they're both bigger than me. They can hit harder than I can hit."

Dad said, "You think they can hit harder than I can hit?"

I said, "No, Dad. I know they can't hit harder than you." I was wondering what was behind this remark, because I knew he wasn't going to go out there on the street and fight some boys for me. He wasn't going to fight anybody for me.

He said, "Well, damn right I can hit harder than they can. And if you come in here you got to get hit by me."

He stood on the side of the door and held on to the knob with one hand. I knew I couldn't go in there. If I went downstairs, the Morris brothers were going to kick my ass. I just stood there looking at Dad, and he stood there for a while looking at me and mumbling about me running from somebody like some little girl, all that kind of shit.

Dad had a complex about his size, I think. He was real short. Maybe that's why he played that bad mother-fucker part so strong. That's probably why he always had his knife. This was what used to scare me about him more than anything—the scar on the neck and his knife. I used to associate the two of them together.

Every night when Dad went to bed, he'd put his watch, his money, his wallet, and his knife under his pillow. When he got up, he would wind his watch, but he would take more time with his knife. He had a switchblade, and he would try it a couple of times. Sometimes he would oil it. He never went out without his knife. He never went to church, but I don't think Dad would have even gone to church without his knife. I guess it was because of that scar on his neck; he never was going to get caught without it again.

The Morris brothers were hollering, "Sonny, you ain't comin' down? Man, you better not come down here any more, 'cause I'm gon kick your ass."

They would take turns hollering up and telling me all this. Dad was standing there in the doorway, and I had a headache. I had a real bad headache, but I knew that wasn't going to help. Dad started telling me about running from somebody who was bigger than me. He said, "You'll probably be short all your life, and little too. But that don't mean you got to run from anybody. If you gon start runnin' this early, you better be good at it, 'cause you probably gon be runnin' all your life."

I just sat down there on the cold hallway tile, my head hurting.

Dad said, "Get up off that floor, boy."

Mama came to the door and said, "Boy, what's wrong with you?"

Dad said, "There ain't nothin' wrong with him. He just scared, that's all. That's what's wrong with him. The thing that's wrong is you try and pamper him too much. You stay away from that boy."

Mama said, "That boy looks like he sick. Don't be botherin' him now. What you gettin' ready to beat him for?"

Dad said, "Ain't nobody gettin' ready to beat him. I'm just gon beat him if he come in this house."

Mama came in the hallway and put her arms around me and said, "Come on in the house and lay down."

I went in and I laid down. I just got sicker until I went downstairs. They really did kick my ass. But it was all right. I didn't feel sick any more.

I remember one time I hit a boy in the face with a bottle of Pepsi-Cola. I did it because I knew the older cats on 146th Street were watching me. The boy had messed with Carole. He had taken her candy from her and thrown it on the ground.

I came up to him and said, "Man, what you mess with my sister for?"

All the older guys were saying, "That's that little boy who lives on Eighth Avenue. They call him Sonny Boy. We gon see somethin' good out here now."

There was a Pepsi-Cola truck there; they were unloading some crates. They were stacking up the crates to roll them inside. The boy who had hit Carole was kind of big and acted kind of mean. He had a stick in his hand, and he said, "Yeah, I did it, so what you gon do about it?"

I looked at him for a while, and he looked big. He was holding that stick like he meant to use it, so I snatched a Pepsi-Cola bottle and hit him right in the face. He grabbed his face and started crying. He fell down, and I started to hit him again, but the man who was unloading the Pepsi-Cola bottles grabbed me. He took the bottle away from me and shook me. He asked me if I was crazy or something.

All the guys on the corner started saying, "You better leave that boy alone," and "Let go of that kid." I guess he got kind of scared. He was white, and here were all these mean-looking colored cats talking about "Let go that kid" and looking at him. They weren't asking him to let me go; they were telling him. He let me go.

Afterward, if I came by, they'd start saying, "Hey, Sonny Boy, how you doin'?" They'd ask me, "You kick anybody's ass today?" I knew that they admired me for this, and I knew that I had to keep on doing it. This was the reputation I was making, and I had to keep living up to it every day that I came out of the house. Every day, there was a greater demand on me. I couldn't beat the same little boys every day. They got bigger and bigger. I had to get more vicious as the cats got bigger. When the bigger guys started messing with you, you couldn't hit them or give them a black eye or a bloody nose. You had to get a bottle or a stick or a knife. All the other cats out there on the streets expected this of me, and they gave me encouragement.

When I was about ten years old, the Forty Thieves—part of the Buccaneers—adopted me. Danny and Butch and Kid were already in it. Johnny Wilkes was older than Butch, and Butch was older than Danny and Kid. Johnny was an old Buccaneer. He had to be. When he came out on the streets in the early forties, it must have been twice as hard as it was a few years later. Harlem became less vicious from year to year, and it was hard when I first started coming out of the house, in 1944 and 1945, and raising all kinds of hell. It was something terrible out there on the streets.

Being one of the older Buccaneers, Johnny took Butch, Danny, and Kid as his fellows. He adopted them. I guess he liked the fact that they all admired him. They adopted me because I was a thief. I don't know why or how I first started stealing. I remember it was Danny and Butch who were the first ones who took me up on the hill to the white stores and downtown. I had already started stealing in Harlem. It was before I started going to school, so it must have been about 1943. Danny used to steal money, and he used to take me to the show with him and buy me popcorn and potato chips. After a while, I stole money too. Stealing became something good. It was exciting. I don't know what made it so exciting, but I liked it. I liked stealing more than I liked fighting.

I didn't like fighting at first. But after a while, it got me a lot of praise and respect in the street. It was the fighting and the stealing that made me somebody. If I hadn't fought or stolen, I would have been just another kid in the street. I put bandages on cats, and people would ask, "Who did that?" The older cats didn't believe that a little boy had broke somebody's arm by hitting him with a pipe or had hit somebody in the face with a bottle or had hit somebody in the head with a door hinge and put that big patch on his head. They didn't believe things like this at first, but my name got around and they believed it.

I became the mascot of the Buccaneers. They adopted me, and they started teaching me things. At that time, they were just the street-corner hoodlums, the delinquents, the little teen-age gangsters of the future. They were outside of things, but they knew the people who were into things, all the older hustlers and the prostitutes, the bootleggers, the pimps, the numbers runners. They knew the professional thieves, the people who dealt the guns, the stickup artists, the people who sold reefers. I was learning how to make homemades and how to steal things and what reefers were. I was learning all the things that you needed to know in the streets. The main thing I was learning was our code.

We looked upon ourselves as the aristocracy of the community. We felt that we were the hippest people and that the other people didn't know anything. When I was in the street with these people, we all had to live for one another. We had to live in a way that we would be respected by one another. We couldn't let our friends think anything terrible of us, and we didn't want to think bad about our friends.

# 31. *Repressive Parents and Violent Social Controls*
## T. W. ADORNO, ELSE FRENKEL-BRUNSWIK, DANIEL J. LEVINSON, AND NEVITT SANFORD

The articles in Part Four up to this point have dealt with the question of what makes *individuals* violent. In the following article, the focus is on one aspect of what makes a *society* approve of and use violence. It is taken from a social science classic—*The Authoritarian Personality*. In this pioneering research, Adorno and his colleagues tried to identify what makes people favor the legal use of violence, ranging from physical punishment of children and criminals to the death penalty and war. The test they developed to identify such authoritarian and punitive persons, the "F Scale," has been widely used in social science. People who get high scores on this test, for example, feel that "an insult to our honor should always be punished," that "homosexuals are nothing but degenerates and ought to be severely punished," and that sex criminals should both be imprisoned and ". . . publicly whipped, or worse." In short, one component of the authoritarian personality is a tendency to use violence as a means of social control. People with authoritarian personalities believe in an eye for an eye, a tooth for a tooth; they are the supporters of violence as an

SOURCE: From pp. 373–375, 384–386, 386–389 in *The Authoritarian Personality* by T. W. Adorno, Else Frenkel-Brunswik, Daniel J. Levinson, and R. Nevitt Sanford. Copyright, 1950, by The American Jewish Committee. By permission of Harper & Row, Publishers, Inc.

instrument of national policy, ranging from whipping sex criminals, to executing capital offenders, to bombing in Viet Nam.

How did these people get to be this way? No doubt many factors are involved. Violence as a means of social control is a part of our cultural heritage going back to the code of Hammurabi. But not everyone favors violent methods of maintaining public order. There are probably also genetic differences between individuals with respect to aggressive tendencies. In addition to these factors, the research on authoritarian personalities done by Adorno, *et al.*, shows that the home environment also plays an important part.

The following excerpt from *The Authoritarian Personality* gives examples of the type of violent and insensitive social controls experienced by the high-authoritarian group when they were children. This is followed by a summary describing disciplinary practices and other ways in which the parents of the low- and high-authoritarian groups differ in bringing up their children—differences which Adorno, *et al.*, feel are part of the explanation of why the high-scoring group has come to endorse violence as the most appropriate way of securing conformity to the moral standards of society.

Since discipline is of particular importance for our general theory concerning the genesis of the prejudiced personality, a series of examples from the records of high-scoring men is given herewith:

*M 45* reports that his father "did not believe in sparing the rod for stealing candy or someone's peaches off the tree."

*M 51*: "My father spanked me on rare occasions, did it solemnly and it didn't hurt; and when he did it everybody cried. . . . But mother had a way of punishing me—lock me in a closet—or threaten to give me to a neighborhood woman who she said was a witch. . . . I think that's why I was afraid of the dark."

A similar psychologically cruel way of punishment is reported by *M 44*: "Father picked upon things and threatened to put me in an orphanage."

*M 52* who, as quoted above, was struck on the finger with a knife at the table for being a bit too hungry, also reports that he "got a whipping (with a razor strop) that I thought was a little unreasonable." He tells a story about a friend who at the friend's home, in playing around, accidentally shoved subject through a window. When his father learned about it the same day, subject "got a whipping without a chance to explain. . . ."

*M 58*, asked which parent he was closest to, answers: "I think my father. Although he beat the life out of me." He continues to emphasize that his father always gave everyone, including himself, "a square deal."

A good example of how some men in this group were frightened into obedience and submission is the following:

*M 57*, asked about spanking, reports, "Not after 17. . . . Father had to give us one look and we knew what he meant."

An example of delayed punishment experienced as meaningless and cruel is given in the following quotation:

*M 20*: (Nature of discipline?) "She would hold me back in. Never let me play if I'd done something wrong. . . . If I did anything wrong during the day, they couldn't spank me in public, in the hotel; they would spank me at night when I had maybe forgotten what it was for and resented it. Too delayed." Subject says he usually cried when he was spanked in order to get it over sooner, because when he started to cry, his grandmother would usually stop shortly. "It hurt my pride. . . . Just another restriction. . . . Or, sometimes, they would take away a movie." Subject says he resented this particularly since movies were few and far between for him anyway. "Grandfather never spanked me. . . ." About 10 or 12, subject says, he started running around more . . . "and they sort of lost their grip on me. I just stayed away from home. More school activities and work. . . .'"

Another high-scoring man expresses his own ideas about the necessity for harsh punishment as follows:

M 41: "If they have to whip them, I believe in whipping them. I don't believe in sparing the rod and spoiling the child, though I don't believe in abusing them. . . . Go down the street and hear a mother (threaten a spanking), the child says, 'Oh, mother, you know you don't mean that.' If I'd have said that to my mother, I wouldn't be able to sit down."

Further examples of the "High" type of discipline, taken from the records of high-scoring men and containing, among other things, deference to the emphasis on "being told" in terms of "petty" rules or "laws" lacking sufficient explanations, are the following:

M 43: (Who gave the discipline?) "Uncle. (What kind?) Whip us. (How often?) Two or three times a month. (What for?) Going off without asking, not doing things we were told. (Was he always fair?) Well, after you'd think it over, you had it coming. (Ever question whether he was right about it?) No."

To the question whether he has been often punished, M 45 answers: "Often, and the hard part about it was that my stepmother would tell him (father) that my brother or I had done things and he wouldn't give us a chance to explain. . . . (What was your reaction?) Well, I ran off twice. . . . It didn't cause me to hate him. I held it mostly against her. (Did he exercise most of the discipline?) He did. (Did she sometimes punish you?) Yes, but not often. (For what?) Oh, things that seemed so trivial, like getting home late from school to do my chores."

M 47: (What was the usual nature of the discipline?) ". . . . just bawl us out. (Q) She made it seem like it was hurting her more than it did us. . . . I think I'd rather have a licking than a good bawling out. (Q) She'd look hurt. (What were your feelings?) . . . Make me feel hurt . . . ashamed of myself. (Example?) One time I stayed out pretty late one night. When I got home, why she bawled me out, just little things like that. . . . Or going some place where she told me not to go . . . like some kid's house she told me not to play with."

Similarly, to the question, for what sort of things have you been punished, M 51 answers, "Usually something petty, stealing fudge off a shelf or something like that."

M 58: "Well, my father was a very strict man. He wasn't religious, but strict in raising the youngsters. His word was law, and whenever he was disobeyed, there was punishment. When I was 12, my father beat me practically every day for getting into the tool chest in the backyard, and not putting everything away . . . finally he explained that those things cost money, and I must learn to put it back."

Another high-scoring man, M 6, reports: "My father left the discipline to my mother, though he was the law when you came right down to it. I don't mean to say that either of them dominated us, but they kept us on the right track. I always had more respect for my mother than most. It was just the idea that she wanted me to do things that kept me on the right path. She spanked me sometimes. Father laid the strap on rarely; the last time was when I was 12 or 13 for talking back to my mother."

There is much reference to cruel punishment such as "whipping," "not sparing the rod," or "beating the life out of me" in the records of high-scoring subjects. Furthermore, the above quotations show that the discipline in the home is experienced as something arbitrary. Often it is implied that the punishment was unjust or "unreasonable" and that the subject had to submit to it without being given a "chance to explain" the situation. This is especially evident in the use, without further comment, of delayed punishment, an example of which was given above: "They would spank me at night, when I had maybe forgotten what it was for and resented it."

Furthermore, there is in these records a great deal of stress upon the fact that punishment was administered for something which seemed petty to the subject, for the violation of an external rule rather than of a basic principle.

Quite different are the reports of low-scoring men about the type of discipline they received:

Asked as to how discipline was enforced, *M 16* relates: "Father lectured a good deal about honesty and integrity, etc."

A relaxed type of discipline with few restrictions is clearly indicated in the protocols of the following two low-scoring women:

*F 75*: (Family training?) "Mother was in charge although they handled us well, I think. We were good, almost too good—and we were punished only rarely. Then it was a little spanking or scolding. There were never problems about going out. We could have had more freedom than we took."

*F 70*: (What kind of things did she stress in your upbringing?) "She seems to me thoroughly liberal; there were not many restrictions anywhere. She accepted practically anything I did." . . .

## SUMMARY AND CONCLUDING REMARKS ON FAMILY PATTERNS

The quantitative data just presented give evidence that presence or absence of extreme ethnic prejudice in individuals of our culture tends to be related to a complex network of attitudes within, and relating to, the family. Lasswell in his pioneer study (66), found that the interrelationships of his subjects with their parents and siblings were of paramount importance in determining their future political activities.

In the following summary a composite picture of the prejudiced and unprejudiced trends as based on our material is presented.[1] As stated before, most of the high-scoring and low-scoring individuals exhibit "High" as well as "Low" personality traits in varying proportions. In fact, single individuals

---

[1] Although the results discussed in this summary are primarily based on the statements of our subjects about their families, direct evidence gathered in a separate study on social discrimination in children and their parents substantiate our inferences about the differences in the family constellation of high scorers and low scorers (see Else Frenkel-Brunswik, 30).

may display any kind of configuration of traits. What is attempted in the present context is no more than a schematic outline of prevalent group trends. Such a picture must of necessity do injustice to all the many existing exceptions.

It also must be reiterated that our composite picture deals with groups scoring *extremely* high or low on the prejudice questionnaire rather than with groups that are more average in this respect.

Prejudiced subjects tend to report a relatively harsh and more threatening type of home discipline which was experienced as arbitrary by the child. Related to this is a tendency apparent in families of prejudiced subjects to base interrelations on rather clearly defined roles of dominance and submission in contradistinction to equalitarian policies. In consequence, the images of the parents seem to acquire for the child a forbidding or at least a distant quality. Family relationships are characterized by fearful subservience to the demands of the parents and by an early suppression of impulses not acceptable to them.

The goals which such parents have in mind in rearing and training their children tend to be highly conventional. The status-anxiety so often found in families of prejudiced subjects is reflected in the adoption of a rigid and externalized set of values: what is socially accepted and what is helpful in climbing the social ladder is considered "good," and what deviates, what is different, and what is socially inferior is considered "bad." With this narrow path in mind, the parents are likely to be intolerant of any manifestation of impulses on the part of the child which seems to distract from, or to oppose, the desired goal. The more urgent the "social needs" of the parents, the more they are apt to view the child's behavior in terms of their own instead of the child's needs.

Since the values of the parents are outside the child's scope, yet are rigorously imposed upon him, conduct not in conformity with the behavior, or with the behaviorial façade, required by the parents has to be rendered ego-alien and "split off" from the rest of the personality . . . , with a resultant loss of integration. Much of the submission to parental authority in the prejudiced subject seems to be induced by impatience on the part of the parents and by the child's fear of displeasing them.

It is in the area of social and political attitudes that the suppressed yet unmodified impulses find one of their distorted outlets and emerge with particular intensity. In particular, moral indignation first experienced in the attitude of one's parents toward oneself is being redirected against weaker outgroups.

The lack of an internalized and individualized approach to the child, on the part of the parents, as well as a tendency to transmit mainly a set of conventional rules and customs, may be considered as interfering with the development of a clear-cut personal identity in the growing child. Instead, we find surface conformity without integration, expressing itself in a stereotyped approach devoid of genuine affect in almost all areas of life. The general, pervasive character of the tendency, on the part of prejudiced individuals, toward a conventional, externalized, shallow type of relation will be demonstrated further in subsequent chapters. Even in the purely cognitive domain, ready-made clichés tend to take the place of spontaneous reactions. Whatever the topic may be, statements made by the prejudiced as contrasted with the unprejudiced are apt to stand out by their comparative lack of imagination, of spontaneity, and of originality and by a certain constrictive character.

Faithful execution of prescribed roles and the exchange of duties and obligations is, in the families of the prejudiced, often given preference over the exchange of free-flowing affection. We are led to assume that an authoritarian home régime, which induces a relative lack of mutuality in the area of emotion and shifts emphasis onto the exchange of "goods" and of material benefits without adequate development of underlying self-reliance, forms the basis for the opportunistic type of dependence of children on their parents, described in the present chapter.

This kind of dependence on the parents, the wish to be taken care of by them, coupled with the fear ensuing from the same general pattern, seems firmly to establish the self-negating submission to parents just described. There are, however, certain cues which seem to indicate the presence, at the same time, of underlying resentment against, and feelings of victimization by, the parents. Occasionally such attitudes manage to break through to the overt level in the interview material. But they are seen more directly, more consistently, and in more intense form in the fantasy material gathered from the same individuals.

Resentment, be it open or disguised, may readily be understood in view of the strong parental pressures to enforce "good" behavior together with the meagerness of the rewards offered. As a reaction against the underlying hostility, there is often rigid glorification and idealization of the parents. The artificiality of this attitude may be recognized from the description of the parents in exaggerated, superlative (and at the same time stereotypical and externalized) terms.

Usually it is only this admiration which is admitted and ego-accepted. The resentment, rendered ego-alien, is the more active through the operation of mechanisms of displacement. The larger social implications of this displaced hostility are discussed in various contexts throughout the present volume.

The superficial character of the identification with the parents and the consequent underlying resentment against them recurs in the attitudes to authority and social institutions in general. As will be seen, we often find in our high-scoring subjects both overconformity and underlying destructiveness toward established authority, customs, and institutions. A person possessed by such ambivalence may easily be kept in check and may even behave in an exemplary fashion in following those external authorities who take over the function of the superego—and partly even those of the ego. On the other hand, if permitted to do so by outside authority, the same person may be induced very easily to uncontrolled release of his instinctual tendencies, especially those of destructiveness. Under certain conditions he will even join forces with the delinquent, a fusion in Nazism.

The orientation toward power and the contempt for the allegedly inferior and weak, found in our typical prejudiced subjects, must likewise be considered as having been taken over from the parents' attitude toward the child. The fact that his helplessness as a child was exploited by the parents and that he was forced into submission must have reinforced any existing antiweakness attitude. Prejudiced individuals thus tend to display "negative identification" with the weak along with their positive though superficial identification with the strong.

This orientation toward the strong is often expressed in conscious identification with the more powerful parent. Above all, the men among our prejudiced subjects tend to report having a "stern and distant" father who seems to have been domineering within the family. It is this type of father who elicits in his son tendencies toward passive submission, as well as the ideal of aggressive and rugged masculinity and a compensatory striving for independence. Furthermore, the son's inadequate relation to his mother prevents him from adopting some of the "softer" values.

In line with the fact that the families of the prejudiced, especially those of our male subjects, tend to be father-dominated, there is a tendency in such families toward a dichotomous conception of the sex roles and a relative separation of the sexes within the family. . . .

In the case of the individuals extremely low on ethnic prejudice the pattern of family relationships differs at least in the degree of emphasis that is placed upon the various factors just listed. One of the most important differences as compared with the family of the typical high scorer is that less obedience is expected of the children. Parents are less status-ridden and thus show less anxiety with respect to conformity and are less intolerant toward manifestations of socially unaccepted behavior. Instead of condemning they tend to provide more guidance and support, thus helping the child to work out his instinctual problems. This makes possible a better development of socialization and of the sublimation of instinctual tendencies.

Comparatively less pronounced status-concern often goes hand in hand with greater richness and liberation of emotional life. There is, on the whole, more affection, or more unconditional affection, in the families of unprejudiced subjects. There is less surrender to conventional rules, and therefore relations within the family tend to be more internalized and individualized. To be sure, this sometimes goes to the extreme of falling short of the acceptance of normal standards and customs.

Additional evidence will be offered in the next chapter for the fact that unprejudiced individuals often manifest an unrealistic search for love in an attempt to restore the type of early relations they enjoyed within their family. Exaggerated cravings in this direction are often a source of dissatisfaction and open ambivalence.

The unprejudiced man, especially, seems oriented toward his mother and tends to retain a love-dependent nurturance-succorance attitude toward women in general which is not easily satisfied. Such an orientation toward the mother, together with the conception of the father as "mild and relaxed," makes it possible for the unprejudiced man to absorb a measure of passivity in his ideal of masculinity. No compensation through pseudo-toughness and antiweakness attitudes is thus necessary. The humanitarian approach can then be adopted on the basis of identification both with the mother and with the father.

The unprejudiced woman, on the other hand, seems to have more often a genuine liking and admiration for the father, for, say, his intellectual-aesthetic abilities. This often leads to conscious identification with him.

Since the unprejudiced subjects on the whole received more love and feel more basically secure in relation to their parents, they more easily express disagreement with them without fear of retaliation or of a complete loss of love. As is to be expected, such expressions of disagreement will nonetheless often lead to internal conflict, guilt, and anxieties. This is the more to be understood since in this group the relations to the parents tend to be intensive and often highly gratifying. There is certainly a great deal of ambivalence in this type of love-oriented family attachment. Ambivalence is here more openly faced, however, than in the case of the prejudiced.

In spite of the conflicts just mentioned, unprejudiced subjects often succeed in attaining a considerable degree of independence from their parents, and of freedom in making their own decisions. Since hostility toward the parents, when present, tends to be more open, it often takes the form of rebellion against other authorities or, more generally, against objects nearer to the original objects of aggression than are the really, or presumably, weak which serve as favorite objects of aggression in the case of the prejudiced. It is often in this form that the unprejudiced man expresses his hostility against his father.

On the whole, this type of independence recurs in the unprejudiced subjects' attitude toward social institutions and authorities in general. At the same time, the existing identification with the parents is often accompanied by a more basic identification with mankind and society in general.

## 32. *The Family Life of Hawkish Students*
### ROBERT A. LEWIS

The authoritarian personality research described in the previous selection was carried out in the closing days of the second world war. It was stimulated in part by a desire to understand how the people of a great and civilized nation such as Germany could come to commit such unspeakable violence. Much the same motivation underlies the work of Lewis. But a quarter of a century later the unspeakable violence and aggression against

SOURCE: Reprinted with the permission of the author and the publisher from Robert A. Lewis, "Socialization into National Violence: Familial Correlates of Hawkish Attitudes toward War," *Journal of Marriage and the Family* 33 (November, 1971): 699–708. The article has been shortened and edited slightly by the author for the present volume.

innocent people is that committed by an entirely different great and civilized nation: the United States of America.

There is an even closer tie between these two studies, and one which indirectly validates the conclusions of the first study: the parents of the college students studied by Lewis are the generation studied (as children of punitive parents) by T. W. Adorno, et. al. Moreover, Lewis used the same F-Scale to measure the authoritarianism as that used by Adorno. It is particularly noteworthy that one of the largest correlations found by Lewis is between the authoritarianism score and the approval of the Viet Nam war. This suggests how the pattern of violence cycles through generations: the punitive parents studied by Adorno produce a generation of authoritarian parents who in turn produce citizens willing to drop napalm on innocent villagers, presumably for their own good. Of course, this is not conclusive evidence. But even this level of evidence takes on importance when we consider what is involved.

As agents of socialization, families play a major part in transmitting to the young of every generation certain values toward national violence, i.e., the acceptance or rejection of war as a viable means for settling international disputes. In this nuclear age, where peaceful coexistence of nations has assumed a critical priority, it is difficult to understand why so little study has been directed to the patterns of familial socialization which produce youth who are willing to accept warlike options.

A few studies of college student attitudes toward war have been reported by Suchman et al. (1953); Putney and Middleton (1962); and Chesler and Schmuck (1964). These studies, however, have not focused primarily on familial origins of attitudes toward war. This omission is regrettable in light of the impact that primary groups, such as the family, have upon the molding of attitudes (Maccoby et al., 1954 and W. I. Thomas, 1966).

Nevertheless, Putney and Middleton (1962), investigating the social status of their respondents, did report finding no consistent relationship between students' acceptance of war and their fathers' occupational status. However, they did find an empirical association between the acceptance of warlike options and students' concern for social status. Likewise, Verba et al. (1967) also discovered that social status variables such as occupation, income and education did not relate to policy preferences on the Viet Nam war. In contrast, Chesler and Schmuck (1964) had reported for a more limited sample of college students that the higher the father's education, the more aggressive (hawklike) the student's reactions to the Cuban Crisis. This finding has been corroborated by Hamilton's (1968) research which was based on the 1952 and 1964 Election Studies conducted by the Survey Research Center at the University of Michigan. Hamilton found that military commitment to both the Korean and Vietnam wars was associated for nonstudents with high status occupations, high educational backgrounds and high income levels. Generally, these studies reveal little about the relationship between familial socialization patterns and militant attitudes toward war.

A larger number of current studies have probed into the familial socialization of student activists (dovish protesters). Flacks (1967) has reported family backgrounds of student activists at the University of Chicago to be more frequently urban, highly educated, affluent, professional in occupation, and disproportionately Jewish or irreligious. Parent-child relationships, rather than being colored by alienation and rebellion, were marked by warmth and mutual respect. The parents were also not only characterized as permissive in child-raising and less interventional in the personal affairs of their children, but as those who also deemphasized personal achievement, conventional morality and religiosity. Similar configurations have been reported by Westby and Braungart (1966); Cavalli and Martinelli (1967) and Watts *et al.* (1969). The latter of these writers have also identified higher status occupations and higher educational backgrounds for the parents of a group of Berkeley activists than for a comparative random sample of nonstudent protesters. In addition, these researchers cited more frequent discussions and greater agreement in intellectual ideas and politics for activists and their parents than for nonprotesters, a finding which suggests effective socialization and family climates in which there is parental support for the questioning of arbitrary authority.

In view of the paucity of research on the familial socialization of hawkish students, it is tempting to assume that patterns must have existed in their family life which are antithetical to those in families which have produced dovish youth. However, there is little empirical support for this assumption. This dearth of information was one impetus for this research report, the central goal of which was the identification of familial factors which in part would account for some students' greater acceptance of warlike alternatives.

## METHODOLOGY

*The Sample.* Measures of student attitudes toward war were obtained during 1968–1969 from 574 students. Four hundred eighteen (418) were undergraduates at an urban university; 126 were from a small, church-related college; and 30 were first-year students at a protestant theological seminary. All three schools were located in the same midwestern geographical area. The data were gathered by means of 13-page questionnaires, which were distributed but not always completed during class sessions at the three schools.[1] These particular institutions of higher learning were chosen to provide the greatest possible range for variables, such as social class, rural-urban residence, religiosity, and various liberal-conservative family values.

The final sample for the study was composed of 412 males (72 per cent) and 162 females. Although these individuals were predominantly Caucasian, they presented a diversity in respect to marital status, college classification,

---

[1]This unavoidable restriction upon the data collection and the length of the questionnaires limited the overall response rate to 64 per cent of those distributed. It should be noted that the students were not randomly selected from their respective institutions but were chosen primarily on the basis of their academic major, so that a wide range of disciplines would be represented. This strategy is most appropriate for studies which focus on the associations between variables rather than on the characteristics of a particular population.

social class and religion. Seventy-seven per cent of the respondents were single while 22 per cent were married students. Of the 574 students, 14 per cent were freshmen; 11 per cent, sophomores; 35 per cent, juniors; 34 per cent, seniors; and six per cent were first-year theological students. The students were grouped on Hollingshead's Index of Social Position as follows: Social Class I, 15 per cent; Social Class II, 14 per cent; Social Class III, 30 per cent; Social Class IV, 25 per cent; and Social Class V, 13 per cent. The remaining three per cent could not be classified, due to a lack of information. On religious preference 18 per cent of the respondents indicated Roman Catholic; 63 per cent, Protestant; four per cent, Jewish; 13 per cent, no preference; and the remainder (two per cent), other. The average age of the students was 21.7 years; the range in ages extended from 17 to 45 years.

*Instruments.* Attitudes of acceptance and rejection of war were ascertained by four indices; two indices were measures of dovishness (a pacifism scale[2] and a de-escalation scale[3]), while two were measures of hawkishness (an involvement scale[4] and an escalation scale[5]). All four instruments met the criteria of Guttman scaling needed for the assumption of unidimensionality, e.g., the coefficients of reproducibility ranged from .92 to .99. Furthermore, the two measures of dovishness were found to be positively correlated with each other and negatively correlated with the two measures of hawkishness.[6] A variety of other scales and questions was utilized for measurement

[2]Six items formed the Pacifism Scale, which measured respondents' unwillingness to accept war as a national policy. A representative item of this agree-disagree test was the following statement: "It is contrary to my moral principles to participate in war and in the killing of other people." This scale was a reduced version of the seven-item pacifism scale used by Putney and Middleton (1962).

[3]The other measure of dovishness, the Deescalation Scale, was an eight-item instrument taken from the study of Verba *et al.* (1967). This scale assessed the degree to which one would approve the withdrawal of American troops from Vietnam. For example, respondents were asked: "Would you approve withdrawal from Vietnam, even if it meant a communist take-over in Laos as well as in Vietnam?"

[4]Forty-two items in six separate indices formed the Involvement Scale, a measure of hawkishness. This scale assessed the degree of provocation it would take for a subject to justify various degrees of involvement, such as the use of nuclear weapons. These indices described six situations, such as "a direct attack launched on the United States" and "communists attack an ally of the United States with whom we have a treaty." For each situation respondents were given the following seven military options (in order of increasing seriousness): diplomatic channels, military advisors, ground-troops, bombing of enemy troops and supply lines, bombing of military targets in enemy territory, sending troops in a major military effort, and engaging in the use of nuclear weapons. These indices were expanded versions of a seven-item provocation scale used by Putney and Middleton (1962).

[5]Hawkishness in regard to the Vietnam War was also measured by means of an Escalation Scale, patterned after that used by Verba *et al.* (1967). This scale was used to determine the extent to which a subject was willing to continue the present war in Vietnam. Six options, such as "saturation bombing of Hanoi and Haiphong" and "fighting the Chinese in Vietnam" formed the items of this yes-no test.

[6]Associations between these four indices, as judged by the gamma statistic, were consistently high (.63–.71) but not so high as to indicate that the measures were tapping identical dimensions. Therefore, all four measures were utilized in the cross tabulations. All four of the indices were ordinal scales, which correctly reflect the "more or less" nature of the attitudes being measured. The research design of this study has thus attempted to avoid the watertight, nominal concepts of "dove" and "hawk," since few persons can be placed simply in one or the other category (Lipset 1966, 38, and Verba *et al.*, 1967, 330).

of the independent variables, i.e., familial factors that were suspected to have had some influence in molding student attitudes toward war.[7]

*Data Analysis.* Wherever possible in the data analysis Goodman and Kruskal gamma was used to assess the degree of association between the four dependent variables and various independent variables. Most variables were thus dichotomized on the basis of median scores, in order that two by two contingency tables might be set up for the calculation of gammas and chi-squares.

## FINDINGS

In this study hawkishness (i.e., students' greater willingness for their country to become involved in war and greater willingness to escalate the Viet Nam War) was shown to be significantly associated with several familial factors.

*Family Backgrounds and Values.* In their studies of student attitudes toward war both Putney and Middleton (1962) and Verba *et al.* (1967) reported no marked relationships between students' socioeconomic background and their acceptance or rejection of war. This was attributed partly to the alleged relative homogeneity of college students. Other studies, however, have suggested that student activists on the political right (hawks) are more likely to be from the lower-middle and working-classes, while activists on the political left (doves) have higher social status origins (Westby and Braungart, 1966; Watts and Whittaker, 1966; Cavalli and Martinelli, 1967; Flacks, 1967; Block *et al.*, 1968).

The data in Table 1 appear to support the findings of the latter studies, i.e., hawkish attitudes of students were positively associated (while dovish attitudes were negatively associated) with family origins characterized by lower family income, lower education of the father and lower social status. Although these associations were not large, all were consistent with the hypotheses and nearly half of them (five) were judged to be statistically significant.[8]

Residence in rural communities has been linked in many national polls with politically conservative (pro-war) sympathies. In the present study

[7]For instance, doctrinal orthodoxy was determined by means of a five-item Likert scale, drawn from items suggested by Glock (1962) and Marx (1967). An example of these items is the question, "How sure are you that there is a life beyond death?" Social status concern was measured by four items taken from a scale used by Kaufman (1957). One item of this scale asks for agreement or disagreement on five degrees to the statement: "One should always try to live in a highly respectable residential area even though it entails sacrifices." Local-cosmopolitan orientations were assessed by items suggested by Thielbar (1966), such as "I prefer a newspaper that has good international and national coverage than lots of local news items." Assessment of authoritarian personality traits was made by means of the F-scale of Adorno *et al.* (1950). Determination of social class was made via Hollingshead's Two-factor Index of Social Position (1957). Other variables related to family relationships, values, authority patterns, and contact with war were assessed by one-item self report questions, such as : "When your parents disagreed about something important, who generally would have the final say?"

[8]Some sex differences were also noted, when partial gammas for each sex were computed for these relationships. For instance, more consistent and somewhat stronger associations between lower social status variables and pro-war attitudes were noted for males (Lewis, 1971).

Table 1. Familial Correlates of Attitudes Toward War[a]

| | Dovish Attitudes | | Hawkish Attitudes | |
|---|---|---|---|---|
| | Pacifism scale | De-escala-tion scale | Involve-ment scale | Escalation scale |
| **Family Background Characteristics** | | | | |
| Lower family income | − .08 | − .13 | + .07 | + .17[*] |
| Lower education of father | − .17[*] | − .05 | + .06 | + .16[*] |
| Lower social class | − .09 | − .16[*] | + .03 | + .17[*] |
| Rural residence | − .18[*] | − .24[**] | + .08 | + .14 |
| Higher social status concern | − .26[**] | − .29[***] | + .36[***] | + .29[***] |
| Local orientation | − .47[***] | − .55[***] | + .38[***] | + .40[***] |
| Political right | − .43[***] | − .32[***] | + .24[**] | + .41[***] |
| Doctrinal orthodoxy | − .40[***] | − .43[***] | + .36[***] | + .32[***] |
| **Family Relationships** | | | | |
| Closeness to parental family | − .16[*] | − .15 | + .04 | + .02 |
| Priority of parental family | − .21[**] | − .28[***] | + .20[**] | + .30[***] |
| Childhood happiness | − .13 | − .11 | + .13 | − .11 |
| Family stability | + .01 | − .14 | + .02 | + .03 |
| One dominant parent | .00 | + .10 | + .12 | + .13 |
| Authoritarian personality | − .42[***] | − .50[***] | + .35[***] | + .40[***] |
| **Family Contact with War** | | | | |
| Father had military service | + .08 | + .02 | − .04 | + .04 |
| Father had combat experience | + .02 | − .11 | + .05 | + .04 |

[a]The measure of association was gamma.
  [*]Chi-square significant p < .05, df 1.
 [**]Chi-square significant p < .01, df 1.
[***]Chi-square significant p < .001, df 1.

also rural residence was found to be somewhat associated with respondents' attitudes toward war. Consonant with the hypothesis, students' residence in rural areas during their adolescent years was positively related to pro-war sentiments and negatively related to anti-war sentiments. For females these relationships seemed to be somewhat stronger than for males. This was true in three out of the four comparisons of partial gammas, which were set up to control for the sex of the respondent. In summary, the data indicate low order but consistent associations between pro-war attitudes and parental family backgrounds which were characterized as rural, and lower in each of the following: income, education of the father, and social class.

Even stronger associations than those for actual social status, however, were found between pro-war attitudes and higher scores on Kaufman's Index of Social-Status Concern. This finding corroborates a similar finding by Putney and Middleton (1962). Other data in Table 1 further suggest that those students who were more hawklike tended to be more conservative on another social, a political, and a religious index, namely, pro-war attitudes were positively associated with local (rather than cosmopolitan) orientations and political attitudes which inclined to the right and doctrinal orthodoxy. (All of these relationships reached at least the .01 level of statistical significance.) Thus, these data further imply for the more hawklike students familial backgrounds which were sharply outlined by strong inclinations toward conservatism and conformity, in that they tended not only to have come from working-class and rural origins but also were more desirous of the respect of others, and had adopted socially, politically and religiously conservative value systems.[9]

*Parental Family Relationships.* Further investigation into the family relationships of students who were more accepting of war continued to confirm these earmarks of conformity behavior. Table 1 exhibits unexpected, low but consistent associations between respondents' reported closeness to their families of orientation and their attitudes toward war. Students had been asked: "Do you feel that in the last year you have been growing closer to your family or further away?" Drawing upon the literature on the Authoritarian Personality and punative childraising patterns which accompany it, it had been hypothesized that hawkish attitudes would be associated for students with less closeness to their parents. This expectation was not confirmed by the data. In fact, the opposite was significantly demonstrated in two of the four tests for females alone. In addition, strong associations are evident in Table 1 between attitudes toward war and priority given by students to their families of orientation. Students had been asked: "Would you agree that a person should generally consider the needs of his parental family as a whole more important than his own needs?" The cross tabulations resulting from responses to this question and the four measures of the dependent variable yielded substantial, consistent evidence that pro-war respondents were substantially more often those who gave loyalty and priority to their families. (These relationships were all statistically significant.) In short, contrary to the hypotheses, students who were more accepting of warlike options and more willing for their country to escalate the war in Viet Nam appeared to be those who felt closer to and still gave priority to their families of orientation.[10]

[9]Unfortunately, no direct measures on these social, political, and religious indices were obtained from parents of the respondents. Although one can assume that parental values are similar to those of their children (Maccoby *et al.*, 1954), extrapolations from these data to the parental families should be tenuously and guardedly made.

Considerable sex differences, however, were also evident. In general the associations were stronger for females than for males. This was somewhat surprising, in light of the findings that female scores were lower on both of the hawkish scales and higher on the pacifism scale. However, these stronger associations for females suggest that they are more thoroughly socialized in relation to war through these values (Lewis, 1971; 1972).

[10]As in the previous comparisons the partial gammas for these two family correlates were substantially larger for females than for males. These data imply that the acceptance of warlike options for females was more closely related to their acceptance of (conformity to) familial values than for males. These findings are certainly in accord with general socialization theory, which holds that American females internalize familial norms and values to a greater degree than males do.

However, the fact that these relationships hold for both males and females is even more colorful, when it is noted that the students who were more conforming to parents and more accepting of warlike options also tended to be the older students. Three out of four tests confirmed this relationship at the .05 level of significance.

In setting up the hypotheses for this study it had also been anticipated that respondents whose childhood had been marked by personal unhappiness or the dissolution of the family in divorce or parental separation would tend to act out the resultant hostility through generalized warlike sentiments. Data derived from such questions, however, were less consistent and thus unclear. The associations between the four dependent variables and self-reports of childhood happiness and family stability were mixed and negligible.[11]

One of the better known explanations for the development of pro-war sentiments is one which focuses on authoritarian personality correlates, and the familial relationships which allegedly produce that type of personality structure. In particular, efforts have been made during the past few decades of social research to draw closure for a causal relationship between the "authoritarian personality structure" and numerous social ills, including the development of pro-war sentiments, e.g., Adorno *et al.* (1950); Chesler and Schmuck (1964). Supportive of this thesis were four of the most compelling associations in Table 1, i.e., those calculated between the four war related indices and the traditional assessment of the authoritarian personality structure, as measured by the F-scale. Not only were all of the resultant associations large, but all were statistically significant at the .001 level. As such, these associations gave strong confirmation to the hypothesis that the authoritarian personality would be more evident for those who had adopted hawklike attitudes toward the use of war.[12]

*Familial Contact with War.* Notions following the theory of cognitive dissonance likewise suggested some hypotheses for this study. For instance, it was reasoned that students whose fathers had served in the military would have resolved to some degree the dissonance between any personal rejection of war and their fathers' military service or combat experience with the rationale: "He did not live (or die) in vain." Therefore, it was assumed that members of a family which had direct contact with the realities of war, e.g., combat experience, would evidence more accepting attitutes toward the "rightness" of a necessary war.

Surprisingly, the two hypotheses concerning familial contact with war were not supported; the data yielded low and mixed associations, none of which was statistically significant. See Table 1.

[11]Although none of the relationships was statistically significant, partial gammas for the females alone were all consistent with the hypotheses and one (between childhood happiness and pacifism) was statistically significant. The lower associations for the correlate of childhood happiness are thus due in part to large sex differences.

[12]Measures of the authoritarian personality and authoritarian decision-making structures in families did not evidence similar relationships with militaristic attitudes. In contrast to the large associations on the F-scale, the gammas were small and mixed for the relationships between respondents' war attitudes and their having had either a mother or father who was a dominant parent. Disconfirmation of the hypothesis was surprising, since Flacks (1967) found that a sample of liberal (dovish) student protesters more often than a group of non-protesting students had been raised in equalitarian homes. Flacks has suggested that, upon leaving their democratic homes for college, these youth rebel against the authoritarian structures and policies which in contrast seem arbitrary and undemocratic.

DISCUSSION

Several familial correlates of pro-war sentiments were identified in this study of students' attitudes toward war. Family background correlates included low family income, low education for the father, low social class, rural residence, and high concern for social status and respectability. Although these associations were of a low order, their consistency supports a class-based model of socialization, in that these students' attitudes toward national violence appeared to be in part a function of the stratification system.

The findings that hawklike attitudes were more highly associated with lower-middle, working class and rural backgrounds and with higher status concerns fits the "status politics" theory of Hofstadter (1962) and Lipset (1962). This theory suggests that extreme "right" activists are most often found in status threatened groups, such as the above. It is these groups which lack economic security and feel most threatened by the rising minorities. Thus, it is also within these economic groups that concern for social status and respectability is maintained at a high level and thereby conformity to traditional social conventions becomes for their members the mainspring of motivation in many spheres, including the seeking of solutions to international problems.

Social research has long focused on value differences which have been noted in the child-raising practices of middle-class and lower-class parents (Kohn and Carroll, 1960; Bronfenbrenner, 1961; Straus, 1967; and Kohn, 1968). Kohn (1968) has particularly underlined the role that conformity plays in working-class families, i.e., while middle-class parents promote internal qualities such as happiness, self control and curiosity in their children, working-class parents seek obedience, cleanliness and neatness. Likewise, in another study Pearlin and Kohn (1966) have shown that, while both American and Italian middle-class parents value their children's self direction, working-class parents in both cultures value their children's conformity to external proscriptions.

However, conformity to societal means and goals in contemporary America often entails the acceptance of violence. According to Slater (1970) and Sanford and Comstock (1971) it is only within the last few years that Americans have become fully aware of the violence which continues to permeate American institutions and interpersonal relationships. If this analysis is true, then it may be further reasoned that those individuals who have been strongly socialized to conform to societal conventions will therefore opt for the more warlike solutions to international problems, since these have been the traditional means by which nations have settled their most serious problems. Nuclear warfare for those of lower-class and rural backgrounds would thus seem to be only a new form for a most traditional and conventional solution to international problems.

Yinger (1970: 417), in examining the cultural, structural, and personality sources of pacifism, has suggested that a non-pacifist may be even ". . . a person brought up in a community rich in pacifist values and supportive groups, but who, as a result of the accidents of his socialization, places high priority on conformity to the larger society or on success." The data from the present study appear to fit Yinger's contention. Not only did hawkish students register themselves higher on several measures of conservatism (local orientation, political right, and religious orthodoxy) but also on other indices of conformity: 1) to the larger society (social status concern) and 2) to their families of orientation (closeness to their families and priority given to their parental families).

Nevertheless, conformity is also one of the earmarks of the "authoritarian personality," a two-decade old theory for which there was substantial support in the data of the present study. Thus, not only was there direct support in the form of higher scores for "hawkish" students on the F-scale, the traditional index of the authoritarian personality, but there was also considerable indirect support. First, the more hawklike students gave evidence of rigid adherence to conservative and conventional values, such as those which largely composed the localism, political right, and doctrinal orthodoxy scales; secondly, they still evidenced conformity, submission and allegiance to their parental family relationships. All of these characteristics are in accord with the authoritarian personality (Sanford and Comstock, 1971: 136–154).

It must be noted, however, that one premise of the authoritarian personality theory is the assumption that this complex personality type is an outcome, due in part to repressed hostility toward a parent whose behavior had spelled extreme rejection of the child. The finding that hawklike students (especially females) felt closer to their families and reported happier childhoods than their counterparts strikes some discordant notes. At first glance these correlates are not consonant with the model of parental rejection which is demanded by the theory.

However, could it be that the female students who reported closeness to their parental families and happy childhoods were mainly reporting a lack of overt conflict? Perhaps these were children in whose homes primary value had been placed on "getting along," on minimizing and ignoring interpersonal conflict (note the value placed on the priority of the parental family), so that conflict had to find other outlets. Such patterns of tension management, rather than denying the authoritarian personality theory, would appear to confirm its dynamics.

Slater (1970) has suggested a similar rationale for the genocidal activities of some American troops in Viet Nam. Slater points to the elaborate mechanisms that Americans create to avoid close interpersonal conflict, only to drain their hostility and violence at a distance upon unknown others who have been defined as "less than human." The theoretical model of the authoritarian personality suggests precisely this configuration, the character structure of one who, not able to admit or direct hostility to parental figures, must direct it to a less threatening "enemy" who cannot reciprocate in kind. This would be the counterpart of the "dovish" activists, reported by Watts *et al.* (1969), who apparently had sufficient familial outlets for their hostilities, i.e., parents who provided climates conducive to discussion and disagreement. Further research, however, is needed to further clarify these speculations.

## CONCLUSIONS

In summary, on the basis of the data it seems reasonable to assume that some families, as socialization agents, transmit to their young attitudes which are more accepting of national violence. The data intimate that students from these families more frequently have somewhat lower-class and rural origins and evidence greater concern for social status and respectability than their counterparts. The more "hawklike" students likewise revealed both conservative values in terms of social relations, politics and religion and also conformity in parent-child relationships. This configuration suggested support for the "status politics" theory, namely, low status families, threatened by new minorities, adopt conformity behavior as a means of attaining respectability. In terms of holding attitudes toward war, these families apparently adopt more conventional and traditional approaches for dealing with international disputes, i.e., pro-war attitudes and dispositions.

Generally speaking, the findings of this study also seemed to be consonant with the literature on the "authoritarian personality." Not only did "hawkish" students score significantly higher on the F-scale, but they revealed other indirect evidence of authoritarianism: rigid conformity and allegiance to their family.

Even though a causal connection is unclear between the students' attitudes toward war and the childraising patterns in their homes of orientation, the data are certainly suggestive of some relationships between lower social status, controlled childraising and conformity responses in terms of the use of national violence.

If, as some proponents hold, the authoritarian personality structure and punitive childraising techniques allegedly associated with its production are responsible for the hawklike attitudes of some Americans, a future extension of this research might well probe family careers by means of more developmental techniques. For instance, by means of panels familial correlates might be explored in the early childhood of those who would in later years be judged on their dispositions and attitudes toward war.

In conclusion, the data seem to support both the theories of "status politics" and the "authoritarian personality." However, although these may be competing theories to some, in this problem area they need not be mutually exclusive since the former is macroscopic in its focus, while the latter is microscopic. The one seeks answers from structures and relationships between major social groups, the other, from relationships between members in a family unit and the formation of personality. Social groups and personalities are both complex organizations within social systems. It is impossible to understand one without understanding the other, since changes in one part often result in changes in other parts. It therefore is incumbent for one who would understand the processual intricacies of familial socialization into national violence to seek answers from all the complex interrelations between various societal strata, family units and personalities.

## REFERENCES

Adorno, T. W., E. Frenkel-Brunswik, D. J. Levinson, and N. Sanford
1950    *The Authoritarian Personality.* New York: Harper and Row.
Block, J., N. Haan, and M. Smith
1968    "Activism and Apathy in ContemporaryAdolescents." In J. F. Adams (ed.), *Contributions to the Understanding of Adolescence.* Boston: Allyn and Bacon.
Bronfenbrenner, Urie
1961    "The Changing American Child: A Speculative Analysis." *Journal of Social Issues* 17: 6–18.
Cavalli, A. and A. Martinelli
1967    "Il profilo sociale dell'attivista di Berkeley." (The Social Profile of the Activist of Berkeley), *Quaderni di Sociologia* 16: 429–440.
Chesler, Mark and Richard Schmuck
1964    "Student Reactions to the Cuban Crisis and Public Dissent." *The Public Opinion Quarterly* 28: 467–482.
Flacks, Richard
1967    "The Liberated Generation: An Exploration of the Roots of Student Protest." *Journal of Social Issues* 23: 52–75.
Glock, Charles Y.
1962    "On the Study of Religious Commitment." *Religious Education Research Supplement* 57 (July–August): 98–100.
Goodman, Leo A. and William H. Kruskal
1954    "Measures of Association for Cross Classifications." *Journal of the American Statistical Association* 49 (December): 732–764.
Hamilton, Richard F.
1968    "A Research Note on the Mass Support for 'Tough' Military Initiatives." *American Sociological Review* 33 (June): 439–445.
Hofstadter, Richard
1962    "The Pseudo-Conservative Revolt—1955." In Daniel Bell (ed.), *The Radical Right.* New York: Doubleday.
Hollingshead, August B.
1957    *Two Factor Index of Social Position.* New Haven, Connecticut (mimeographed by the author).
Kaufman, Walter C.
1957    "Status, Authoritarianism, and Anti-Semitism." *American Journal of Sociology* 62: 381.
Kohn, Melvin L. and Eleanor E. Carroll
1960    "Social Class and the Allocation of Parental Responsibilities." *Sociometry* 23: 372–392.
Kohn, Melvin L.
1963    "Social Class and Parent-Child Relationships: An Interpretation." *American Journal of Sociology* 68: 471–480.
Lewis, Robert A.
1971    "Socialization into National Violence: Familial Correlates of Hawkish Attitudes Toward War." *Journal of Marriage and the Family* 33 (November): 699–708.
Lewis, Robert A.
1972    "A Contemporary Religious Enigma: Churches as Socializing Agents for War." A paper presented at the annual meetings of the Society for the Study of Social Problems, New Orleans, Louisiana, August 26, 1972.
Lipset, Seymour M.
1962    "The Sources of the 'Radical Right'." In Daniel Bell (ed.), *The Radical Right.* New York: Doubleday.
Lipset, Seymour M.
1966    "Doves, Hawks, and Polls." *Encounter* 27 (October): 38–45.

Maccoby, Eleanor, Richard Matthews, and Anton Morton
   1954     "Youth and Political Change." *Public Opinion Quarterly* 18 (Spring): 23–39.
Marx, Gary T.
   1967     "Religion: Opiate or Inspiration of Civil Rights Militancy Among Negroes?"
           *American Sociological Review* 32: 64–72.
Pearlin, Leonard I. and Melvin L. Kohn
   1966     "Social Class, Occupation, and Parental Values: A Cross-National Study."
           *American Sociological Review* 31 (August): 466–479.
Putney, Snell and Russell Middleton
   1962     "Some Factors Associated With Student Acceptance or Rejection of War."
           *American Sociological Review* 27 (October): 655–667.
Sanford, Nevitt and Craig Comstock
   1971     *Sanctions for Evil.* San Francisco: Jossey Bass.
Slater, Philip E.
   1970     *The Pursuit of Loneliness.* Boston: Beacon.
Straus, Murray A.
   1967     "The Influence of Sex of Children and Social Class on Instrumental and
           Expressive Family Roles in a Laboratory Setting." *Sociology and Social Re-
           search* 52: 7–21.
Suchman, Edward A., Rose K. Goldsen and Robin M. Williams, Jr.
   1953     "Attitudes Toward the Korean War." *Public Opinion Quarterly* 17: 171–184.
Thielbar, Gerald W.
   1966     *Localism-Cosmopolitanism: Social Differentiation in Mass Society.* University
           of Minnesota. Unpublished Ph.D. Dissertation.
Thomas, W. I.
   1966     *On Social Organization and Social Personality.* Selected papers in Morris
           Janowitz (ed.), The Heritage of Sociology Series. The University of Chicago
           Press.
Verba, Sidney, Richard A. Brody, Edwin B. Parker, Norman H. Nie, Nelson W. Polsby,
Paul Ekman, and Gordon S. Black
   1967     "Public Opinion and the War in Vietnam." *The American Political Science
           Review* 61 (June): 317–330.
Watts, William, Steve Lynch, and David Whittaker
   1969     "Alienation and Activism in Today's College-Age Youth: Socialization Pat-
           terns and Current Family Relationships." *Journal of Counseling Psychology*
           16: 1–7.
Westby, David L. and Richard G. Braungart
   1966     "Class and Politics in the Family Backgrounds of Student Political Activists."
           *American Sociological Review* 31: 690–692.
Yinger, J. Milton
   1970     *The Scientific Study of Religion.* London: The Macmillan Company.

# 33. *A Psychoanalyst Looks at Student Revolutionaries*
## HERBERT HENDIN

The findings on the causes and correlates of violence presented so far are complex but they are a long way from providing a complete explanation of why so many people favor the use of violence to achieve what they think of as socially desirable ends. Some indication that these findings have only scratched the surface of what needs to be known about the causes of violence is given in Hendin's study of violently radical students at Columbia

SOURCE: Reprinted from *The New York Times Magazine* (January 17, 1971): 16–17, 19, 22–24, with permission of the author. Copyright © 1971 by Herbert Hendin.

University. Hendin does not mention presence or absence of physical punishment, but the family information which he does provide suggests that punishment was rare. Instead, the childhood experiences of these young revolutionaries were probably as far from the authoritarian-punitive pole as one is likely to find in American society. The parents of these students went to such great lengths to allow them maximum autonomy that the parents' behavior was perceived as emotional withdrawal by the child. We are given a picture of young people enraged over lack of personal intimacy and engagement with their parents.[1] As a result, they are desperate for close interpersonal ties and total acceptance. They find it in the "revolutionary family" of the SDS and similar organizations, where the one sure way of getting this total acceptance is to excel in revolutionary rhetoric and violent antiestablishment acts. The revolutionary group is one way of dealing with the problem of "being 20 and utterly dispensable."

*"The tactical police try to knock us down and bust us. The campus police were trying to hurt us in the spine or kidneys."*

*"Trashing is no use. We have to work for political action and prepare with guns for real revolution."*

*"If Bobby Seale is convicted, it would be O.K. for us to kill a couple of police."*

The fervor of revolutionary students describing the violence they experience and expect has shocked even those who take refuge in agreeing with their aims but not their methods. Yet these students, however fervid, however forceful, have remained essentially anonymous.

Radical students have told us they believe that America is too unjust to reform or to be worth reforming, that it exploits many in the interests of few, that it cares for nothing but power and money. They have told us that they wish to bring about the end of American life as we know it, and that the revolution they desire will be achieved only through violence. Their commitment to the violent implementation of their beliefs distinguishes the revolutionary students I am discussing from other young people who share their feelings about society. And we have seen that the translation of their beliefs into action leads them into ever fiercer encounters with their colleges, municipal police and Federal authorities. We have listened to their speeches, seen their actions, argued their politics. But have we any idea of what these revolutionary students are like?

So exclusively have we responded to their political activity and political violence that the people behind the politics have remained hidden. Even distinguished psychologists, psychiatrists and social scientists have so concerned themselves with the politics of these students that they have done little more than reflect sophisticated ways of disapproving or approving. For example, in one view, articulately advocated by Bruno Bettelheim, radical

---

[1]Since Hendin did not interview their parents, his data are subject to many different and sometimes opposite interpretations. For example, the parents, rather than being the cold fish depicted by their children, may be the opposite: in providing unlimited love and support early in childhood, the parents may have created a set of expectations for intimacy and total acceptance which are not possible once the standards of the real world come into play in adolescence.

students are the product of overpermissive families: the students are violent because they have never had sufficient control exerted over them and consequently have never learned how to control themselves.

An opposing view, most identified with Kenneth Keniston, holds that radical students tend to be "healthier" than nonradicals. They have come from close, supportive families who have encouraged their individuality, and with whom they are not in conflict. Their radical action is the outgrowth of what is best in them, and their outrage is the product of a sound awareness of the American social, cultural and political wrongs of today.

But to understand student revolutionaries it is necessary to move beyond sympathy or antipathy for their politics to explore their inner lives and those internal forces which give their protest its distinctive shape.

Using psychoanalytic interviewing techniques involving free associations, dreams and fantasies, I am interviewing radical undergraduates at Columbia and Barnard as part of an over-all study of the problems of college students. . . .

The radical students I have seen are in many ways the successors at Columbia of Mark Rudd—often they are leaders in Students for a Democratic Society, the December 4th Movement (named after the date of the shooting by police of Fred Hampton, Black Panther leader, in 1969) and the Revolutionary Youth Movement (Weathermen). These students are paid $50 for completing a series of five interviews and a battery of psychological tests. Interviews with 15 such students have now been completed. They are white, from middle-class or affluent families and have a variety of religious backgrounds. They all believe in the necessity for a violent revolution and they work actively to radicalize groups ranging from high-school students to soldiers at Army bases.

On campus they have been involved in the use of physical intimidation and actual force against individuals who oppose them, in seizures of buildings and in the destruction of property. Both on and off campus they have been involved in fights with the police. Although none had yet participated in bombings or assaults that might destroy life as well as property, many advocated and all defended such acts as necessary to the cause. Some appeared likely to join a revolutionary underground committed to guerrilla warfare.

I gradually got a picture of the inner lives of these revolutionary students, of the relation between their inner feelings and their outer revolt. Their actual lives were strikingly different from widespread conceptions about them, particularly the ideas that they are the products either of overpermissive families, or of healthy "superior" families with whom they are not in conflict.

James (all names have been changed), an intense and articulate young man, spoke animatedly of the revolution he feels will come to America through violence. He is sure it is inevitable but is uncertain whether it will take the form of a race war or of a broad-based battle between all the oppressed and all of those in power. He spent his first year at Columbia organizing in high schools, at the college, at Army bases, and becoming involved in the violent disruption of university life—all of which he sees as preparation for the revolution to come.

When I first saw him, James was depressed and discouraged about the lack of progress of the revolutionary movement during this, his second, year at college. Political activity had been minimal on campus and S.D.S. had found organizing difficult and interest almost impossible to arouse in the majority of students. He wistfully described the mixture of fear and exhilaration he felt in past confrontations with the police. As the interviews progressed, the Panther trial in New York and the conspiracy trial in Chicago had revived the movement on campus and he became part of a group that disrupted a meeting of the faculty senate and took over the platform to demand that Columbia provide bail for the Panthers. The success of the takeover made him outwardly more optimistic about the movement and also seemed to make him come alive.

But James has far more conflict over the use of violent tactics than he realizes. He dreamed that he was leading some dangerous and violent political maneuver that he had managed to pull off successfully. He began to run. He was caught in a barbed-wire fence and badly cut. Blood flowed. He was captured and put in a preventive-detention camp. James called this a "political dream" and enjoyed talking about it in political terms. He spoke of the possibility of going to prison for his radical activity and predicted a right-wing reaction in which revolutionary students throughout the country would be placed in "preventive-detention camps." He believes that would be the only way to stop left-wing violence. He almost seems to need and want some forceful outside reaction to control his behavior.

In talking of his "political dream," James came close to the personal origins of the anguish he feels when there is no preventive-detention camp to stop him from doing what he says he wants to do. He recalled an incident that occurred when he was home visiting his parents over Christmas vacation. Both his parents were anxious about his taking the car out after a blizzard, but his father said nothing and let him have it, although he knew driving was next to impossible. "Fifteen times," James said furiously, "I nearly killed myself or someone else." After he returned home he criticized his father for letting him use the car, knowing the conditions as he did. His father said that he had not wanted him to take it, but that he felt James would think he was overprotective if he refused and would get angry.

James is certainly indicating here that he needs outside control from his father to prevent him from becoming involved in destructive or self-destructive activity. But emotional withdrawal, not permissiveness, would be a more accurate description of his father's behavior. In this instance, his father wants to avoid having to deal with James's anger. James not only is furious at his father's withdrawal but he has learned how to use his father's difficulty in expressing his feelings as a weapon against him. While James began our sessions claiming that his parents supported his aims if not all of his tactics, he eventually admitted with a satisfied smile that he sensed his father was inwardly seething at the things he was doing, but was unable to say anything about them.

These students generally had parents with little ability or desire to see their children as they are, or to confront their actual feelings. This kind of emotional abandonment is anything but "permissive."

Amy, a bright, militant and successful radical leader, was, like most of the radical students, more at ease discussing politics than her personal life. She tried to see her personal feelings in political terms—for example, attributing the loneliness she felt in high school to the fact that all the other kids had more middle-class values than she.

She came to Barnard hoping that it would reflect the diversity of social classes in New York. But she soon came to feel that Barnard was insulated from city life. Although politically sympathetic to S.D.S., she attended only one meeting in her first year. She tended to be cynical and skeptical about what could be accomplished by radical action.

All this changed when the building occupation and strike of 1968 made her feel she had to take some stand. On the second day of the strike, she went into a building and stayed there until the "bust," when she was arrested. This was a crucial point in her political life; she became increasingly active. At first she was shy and held back at meetings, but she gradually got to be known and liked and she became part of the hard-core leadership of both S.D.S. and the December 4th Movement.

Amy in our first sessions emphasized the closeness of her family, claiming that she discussed her political activities with her parents, even though they were "only creeping Socialists" and she is a "violent revolutionary." As our talks progressed, she began to suggest that although it was possible to discuss politics with her family, non-political, personal matters were avoided. But both politically and personally her parents withdrew from her whenever she needed them most. When she called her father for advice before participating in her first occupation of a campus building, he refused to give an opinion other than to say he was sure she would do the right thing.

But whenever they disapproved of what she did, her parents would say that it was not really Amy who occupied a building or got arrested. They implied that she was led or influenced by others and would say that if she thought about it, or was really "herself," she would see things their way.

Commenting that they had always behaved like this, she told of buying a bedspread for her room when she lived with her parents. Her mother said she didn't think it was good for her room and insisted that when Amy thought about it, she would see that it was not really her taste.

Amy's parents repeatedly tried to avoid direct conflict with her by insisting that it was not really Amy who was seeing or feeling or behaving whenever she saw, felt or did anything they did not like. The means they chose for avoiding conflict with her maintained the illusion of closeness without much of the content; they preserved the outward form of discussion without any acceptance of Amy's tastes or character. The only Amy who existed for them was the non-Amy they wished to see.

Nonrecognition or intolerance of her feelings enabled Amy's family to create an illusion of harmony, but left Amy with the problem of coping with the very tastes, feelings and character her parents denied she had. She has partly adopted her parents' way of dealing with her and is not now in touch with her feelings, particularly toward them. She speaks of them in a detached, objective way as being well-meaning but as having a life style that she would not choose for herself.

Kenneth Keniston writes that radical students have achieved a detached, objective view of their parents. But the use of psychoanalytic interviewing techniques makes clear that such detachment, as in Amy's case, usually conceals pain too difficult for the students to face. Their acute ability to see and feel the flaws of society is in striking contrast to their need not to see or know the often devastating effects their family life has had on them.

If Amy is pained by not being seen, Carl's experience with an even more painful family situation has made him want to be invisible. At 22 he has been "busted" six times and convicted twice for his political activity and he is increasingly attracted to the revolutionary underground. He came to his first interview last fall in shorts and sneakers and wore large, dark sunglasses throughout the session. He sank so deeply into his chair that he seemed to be lying rather than sitting. He spoke in a soft, almost faint voice and seemed generally quite depressed. He began the hour by talking about a conflict he feels over leaving the political group he's involved with, a conflict that illustrates the degree to which he conceals his feelings from others.

Carl lives in a commune of radical students who share several Manhattan apartments. He has had the urge to leave them to join a group of activists who are not college-educated and who live and work in a working-class neighborhood where he grew up. He feels they have taught him about people and life and that he is more comfortable with them than with the affluent kids in his commune whom he envies and resents. His bitterest complaints center on Kenny, whom he calls his closest friend. He's been hurt by Kenny's possessiveness toward Ellie, a girl in the commune, and by how intensely he resents any interest she shows in him.

The situation has become worse since Arlene, a girl Carl fell in love with some time ago, has returned from Cuba and joined their group. She told Carl she did not want a serious sexual involvement with anyone and he consequently tried to control or hide his sexual feeling for her. Kenny, however, did become sexually involved with Arlene. He comes to Carl for sympathy, help and advice because he feels "caught" between the two women. When Carl, suppressing his anger, merely replies that he does not want to be bothered with his problem, Kenny acts hurt and has even cried. Carl tries to hide his rage from him much as he tries to conceal his sexual desire for Arlene.

Carl finds it far easier to express his anger with the Establishment than with Kenny. The night of his most intense frustration and rage with Kenny, he dreamed of having a gun battle with the police. His passivity with Kenny and Arlene goes hand in hand with his extreme political activism, a commitment that includes becoming skillful with firearms in preparation for guerrilla warfare. He says he is "very turned on by Weathermen" and he believes he will become part of the revolutionary underground. When I asked whether he felt he'd be able to kill anyone, he answered, "Yes." He thought it might be difficult for him at first, but he expected that some of his friends would be killed and that their deaths would make it easier for him to kill.

Carl's retreat from competition and his need to hide his anger have operated to give him a peculiar role in his political life. While not himself a leader (his old friends jokingly ask him why he hasn't made the big time, like Mark Rudd or Bernadine Dohrn), he is often a catalyst for more violent political protest than the actual leaders have planned. When a friend who had become prominent in S.D.S. was leading an outdoor protest (permitted by college rules) against recruiting on campus by a company involved in military production, Carl took over the group, succeeded in getting it to enter and forcibly occupy the building and physically disrupt the recruiting. Once inside, however, he turned to his friend and said, "It's your group. Now it's your baby."

Carl linked his difficulties in competition and his retreat from the limelight to a lifelong reluctance to show his emotions. "If you show your feelings, you get your legs cut off," was his way of putting it. He was one of the few radicals interviewed who came from families in which there was an actual breakup: his mother and father were divorced when he was 8. His father, whom he saw occasionally through the years, belittled any feelings Carl expressed. Forced to support the family, his mother was bitter about her situation and exhausted from work. Carl describes her as withdrawn and unaffectionate.

Carl learned to keep his feelings to himself and to stay out of his mother's sight. That he somehow knew the degree to which he was supposed to be neither seen nor heard is rather movingly suggested by his behavior as a child: he slept under his bed. He recalls a recurring nightmare during this period in which he came home from school and rang the bell to his house. He was told by his mother that she didn't know him and that he didn't belong there. He went to his cousin's house and they told him the same thing. Finally, he walked across the country to his father's house in California and was told by his father that he didn't know him and that he didn't belong there. The dream ended with him disappearing into the Pacific Ocean.

If Carl is able to conceal his feelings in silence, Nancy, an attractive, witty radical leader, conceals them in vivacity. "I was a nice girl from a nice family and everything in my life moved a certain way until a year and a half ago [the time she entered college] when everything changed," she said. Her current life, which is a series of encounters with the authorities, would seem to have changed from her outwardly tranquil high-school life in her home town.

While she was away during Easter recess at Barnard, the F.B.I. came twice to search her room and she was really "freaked out" about it. She describes being in trouble with the "pigs" almost every day because she won't pay her subway fare (in protest against a fare increase), which results in her being chased through subway stations. She has been in trouble for taking food from the larger chain stores. She feels there is nothing wrong in taking food from the large, impersonal supermarkets since her stealing is less of a crime than she believes the stores are committing against society.

When she came to Barnard, Nancy explained, she realized that there was nothing worthwhile in this society to be part of and the only worthwhile thing was to be opposed to everything in the society. She is active in S.D.S., was one of the organizers of the December 4th Movement, and when I saw her she was under indictment and awaiting trial for her political activities.

Nancy believes that people "aren't interested in your feelings," and that "really, you should take care of these things yourself." "These things" seemed to refer to some inner turmoil. Her accounts of her childhood suggest how she came to think that people aren't interested in what she feels.

Nancy's parents are both professional people with active careers. As the oldest of the children, she had to care for her two younger siblings. She seems to have been disturbed not so much by her duties as by the feeling that she was forced to be independent at too early an age and was deprived of a childhood. She describes her parents as "nice, pleasure-loving people" who are "sort of like camp counselors." She added that she "sort of liked" some of her counselors even though she was miserable at camp. She says, "My parents aren't the sort who feel the family has to do something on a Sunday, so if they are together they get along fine because they are doing things that independently they want to do. If it happens that two of them want to do something at the same time, then it's O.K. If they all had to go to the zoo together, they'd probably kill each other. They're better than families who feel they have to be together. My parents aren't the type who sacrifice themselves for their children. I don't think parents should."

Nancy defends her family's lack of contact by contrasting it with a constricting, self-sacrificing "straw" family in which everyone is bound together through some overwhelming sense of obligation. She talks as though these are the only possible alternatives. She adopts a tragicomic, humorous tone in describing her frustrations with her parents. For example, while she has dropped out of college, is devoting all her time to her political activities, and is scheduled for trial in a few weeks, her last letter from her mother suggests that she take a course in marine biology which her mother enjoyed 20 years ago. Needless to say, Nancy has no interest in marine biology. In a light ironic way, which does not conceal the sadness in her eyes, she told me that her parents were persuaded that her brother stays home from school to study with his friends when actually he spent his time with them "tripping on acid."

Although she alternates between irony and defensiveness in describing her parents' lack of contact with her, it is clear she has experienced this as a profound rejection. That "lack of contact" was her euphemism for emotional abandonment was most movingly suggested in an event she related that occurred after a tonsillectomy when she was 11. She was left alone in the house. She developed a severe hemorrhage and became panicky. Her mother had gone out for several hours and told her to call a neighbor if something like that happened. But she knew that the neighbor was a hysterical woman who would be of no help. Nancy recalls standing by a window for two hours choking on the blood in her throat, waiting for her mother to come home, feeling that her mother had no right to expect her to take care of herself in that kind of situation. She is still figuratively drowning in her own juices and unable to trust anyone enough to ask for help.

James, Nancy, Carl and Amy were typical of the revolutionary students in describing parents who withdrew from them when they needed them most, or were simply unavailable. Obviously many other students have had similar experiences without becoming revolutionaries. But it is striking how pervasive the impact of emotional abandonment was on the lives of all these revolutionary students.

Although most of the students interviewed did have parents with a left-wing or at least liberal background, their ideology proved to be less important than the fact that political discussions were the closest thing to personal exchanges that took place in the family—a circumstance that may have some bearing on the use of politics to express feelings that are personal. An atmosphere of polite estrangement seemed to prevail between these parents who got along well with each other on the surface but who were not deeply involved with each other.

All the students felt their parents had not been physically affectionate toward them or each other, and described their fathers as especially repressed and emotionally tight. Most saw their fathers as successful at work, but as failures as fathers and husbands. Although they felt their parents were capable of compassion and pity for the weak, the oppressed or the handicapped, they did not see them as able to experience genuine passion.

Most of them felt that they too would have difficulty in sustaining personal passion in the intense and powerful way they can experience their political commitment. Their feelings of abandonment and parental withdrawal have left them with a pervasive depression and a diminished self-confidence. Considering their vulnerability and despair, it is not surprising that they feared both closeness and loneliness. They have an unusually great fear of losing out to other men or women in competition for the opposite sex, and in competition for various kinds of achievement. One student described how insecure he felt in high school competing with the ambitious, aggressive, athletic boys who were popular. Although they accepted him, he felt comfortable only when he left them to join the school's "counter-culture"—i.e., a group that made fun of the "jocks" and was active in drug-taking and politics.

The idea that student revolutionaries are able to go the straight and affluent way but choose to do otherwise, turned out not to be true. Although they are all intelligent and articulate men and women, most will not finish college. Their frustration, their anger and their increasingly exclusive interest in violent political action deprive them of the necessary patience to finish— even though they realize that education, such as in law, would enable them to contribute more to the radical cause.

Some of the students said they took part in their first serious radical action at college "to see how it felt." They discovered that it "felt" better than almost anything they had felt before, that the exhilaration and excitement of a building-occupation or a confrontation with the police elevated them to a pitch of emotion they did not normally experience. They came to need the exhilaration of a violent political action to such an extent that far from choosing radical politics freely out of a wealth of possible choices, it became the only possible life for them.

The radical involvement, however, does more for these students than give them the thrill of becoming "action freaks." In the revolutionary culture many have found a "family" which understands their emotional needs better than their real families ever did. Since the radical movement discourages exclusive monogamous relationships, it does much to soften these students' anxiety over not being able to form deep attachments. The same young men who complain of passivity in their personal relations find that they can be forceful and aggressive in behalf of the radical cause. Many who suffer from a lack of direction find that the radical involvement brings them to life and focuses their energies. The prospect of each new violent protest provides an outlet for their anger and gives some relief to their depression.

Danger from outside—from college, police and Federal authorities—cements the closeness that comes from shared values and beliefs and tightens the bonds within the revolutionary "family." While their own parents, like Amy's or Nancy's, refuse to realize that their daughters are young revolutionaries—not marine biologists, "nice" girls or moderate Socialists—these students find in the reaction of the authorities some adequate response to themselves. They have a need for enemies that transcends their realistic suspicion that their phones have been tapped, their ranks infiltrated, or their rooms searched by Federal authorities. . . .

To attempt to understand the politics of radical students without first gaining an understanding of their inner lives is to invite confusion or bewilderment. The fervor with which these students attack property, the intensity with which they scorn America's concern for money, and the force they bring to their agreement with most militant blacks must be seen in the context of their backgrounds. These young radicals have suffered in families which more than provided for their material needs but which ignored and frustrated their personal needs and continue to be blind to them as people. In rejecting the life style of their parents as too involved with property, wealth and economic security, they are saying that their parents were never concerned in any meaningful way with them.

Identification with the poor and the oppressed permits these radical students to react to poverty and oppression without having to face how personally impoverished, victimized and enraged they feel. Their acute sense of injustice derives from their personal, if often unrecognized, experience as victims. To insist that these students are products of overprivilege, the spoiled sons and daughters of the affluent, is to insist that the only hunger is for food and the only deprivation is material and economic. . . .

Whether or not these students directly attack their parents, they do say they are "irrelevant." But it is the pain that can be inflicted by treating someone as irrelevant, by seeing their needs and character as having no *raison d'être,* that these students have learned so effectively at the feet of their parents. There could be no more satisfying revenge.

Student revolutionaries are accused of not providing any alternative plan for a future society. But these students are hardly interested in their own future, let alone in the future of the rest of us. The future will "take care of itself" or "the future as an idea is vastly overrated" are typical of their comments. They predict they will die young either in the revolution or in some nuclear or ecological disaster that will end the world. The prediction of cataclysm for the world must be seen partly as a projection of their inner world, since the inner revolution that may consume them is already under way, their personal environment has already been poisoned, and the bomb that may destroy them may well be of their own making.

(Of course, not all student violence can be attributed to student revolutionaries. Angry, "turned-off" students with no more political goals than the disruption of classes and the cancellation of final exams appear to have been responsible for the bombing of Columbia's Alma Mater statue last spring. Such students at times participate in violent actions initiated by radical students, but their role in the revolutionary group which I am discussing is only peripheral.)

In dealing with radical students, college administrators have tended to see the problem as one of permissiveness vs. discipline. If in the past college administrators have acted toward students with a kind of rigid aloofness, they have now under student pressure adopted a more permissive aloofness. Rigidity and permissiveness, however, are often opposite sides of the same coin. They are designed to enable adult authorities, be they parents or administrators, to avoid confronting the students as people—not merely to avoid student anger but to avoid facing the students' feelings in any significant way.

Student demands are often specifically designed to provoke rejection and subsequent confrontation. When college administrators accede to them, radical students often rightly feel they have yielded through fear. But to be yielded to through fear is as dehumanizing and infuriating to them as having their demands ignored. By treating these students as non-people, as an impersonal force to be managed through ignoring them when possible, through placation when afraid of them, or through force when all else fails, administrators touch some very sensitive chords in many students, arousing feelings of outrage that make it possible for revolutionary students to gain wide support.

The existence of inner turmoil in these students does not invalidate their critique of society. Such turmoil may even suggest a deeper and more subtle indictment of American life. Nor can psychological forces alone explain why students become revolutionaries at a particular time and place in history. But to discuss the historical and social forces that produce revolutionaries without knowing who student revolutionaries are or what they feel is misguided. However, even analysts and social scientists have ignored this inner dimension because of their involvement in the politics of the students. Agreeing with many of the students' criticisms of society, many psychoanalysts and social scientists try to become the students' advocates and allies. They desire to show through compassion that they are not out of touch with the aspirations of the radical young (and, perhaps, not growing old and "irrelevant").

But the students see through a sympathy based on lack of understanding and a compassion that has its source in fear or sentimentality. All this arouses only their benign contempt and further estranges them. As one student said of a judge who gave a sympathetic talk on the problem of students today before suspending sentence: "He means well, but with fools like that running the system, how can the revolution help but succeed?"

# CHAPTER TEN
## Learning Non-Violence in the Family Context

### 34. *Children Should Learn About Violence*
**BRUNO BETTELHEIM**

Although much psychoanalytic theory is being questioned today, part of the psychoanalytic perspective has remained popular and has, in fact, received a new lease on life as a result of the popularity of the work of ethologists such as Robert Ardrey and Konrad Lorenz. This is the part based on Freud's assertion that there is a human instinct for aggression and self-destruction. Since they assume that aggression is basic to human nature, Freud and his followers (including Bettelheim) hold that aggression cannot be eliminated. Instead, it must be accepted as a part of human nature and then channeled into non-destructive outlets.

The following article, by one of the most widely known writers on psychoanalysis, provides a forceful statement of the psychoanalytic explanation of violence and the catharsis theory for dealing with violence. However, a growing body of literature seriously questions the catharsis approach (see Bandura and Walters, p. 303) and there is much evidence that situational forces (e.g., poverty and frustrated life goals) are a more central cause of violence than instincts. Nevertheless, Bettelheim's article offers parents some practical advice which would be valid under both the psychoanalytic and other approaches: since life from earliest childhood to old age is full of frustrations which tend to produce aggression and violence, we must teach children to recognize this potential, to realize that these feelings are normal, and to deal with them effectively. This advice is also consistent with our view that a more fundamental approach to controlling violence might be to find ways to alter the social structure which forces its people into these situations instead of just finding ways of either containing or allowing for "the safe discharge of aggression." As Bettelheim himself says, "Whether or not we use violence or avoid it depends entirely on what alternatives are known to a person facing a problem."

We delight in watching violence at the movies or on TV, and reading about it in the spy stories, and talking about it so that even the plight of the Negro is often a thin disguise for telling violent stories. Yet we fear nothing more than the violence rampant in some of our big-city schools, and many of us live in dread of violence as we go home at night, and even in broad daylight. Despite the fascination and the dread, we try to pretend to our children that

SOURCE: Reprinted with permission from *Saturday Evening Post* 240 (March 11, 1967): 10–12.

violence is to be ignored or treated with contempt. This makes no sense. Children must be taught about violence so that they can learn to master it.

As long ago as the *Iliad,* the first great epic of the western world, the Greeks won one day, the Trojans the next, and in the end practically all perished. And since Homer, in this book, introduced the spirit that violence is the central problem to be dealt with in a world striving to be civilized, we were warned to think seriously of what our attitude toward violence should be. Today, the gunfighter has taken hold of our imagination as a moral "hero" (to use the term of literary critic Robert Warshow) because the man with the gun on his thigh believes in violence—but also in self-restraint: ". . . he suggests that even in killing or being killed we are not freed from the necessity of establishing satisfactory modes of behavior. . . ." We deceive ourselves and our children by failing to recognize this openly, at home and in our schools.

Nowadays parents get a great deal of help in accepting *some* of their children's instinctual behavior—even sex. But as far as violence is concerned, we overlook the fact that it is an ineradicable part of human nature. As Freud wrote in summing his views about the future, "The fateful question for the human species seems to me to be whether and to what extent [they] will succeed in mastering the disturbance of their communal life by the human instinct of aggression and self-destruction."

Long before our children have reached the age of reason, we expect them neither to hit nor to swear, not to yell back at us or their playmates. They are supposed to refrain from destroying property, even their own toy. Sure, they have to learn to control themselves. But what outlets for the human instinct of violence *do* we provide? And more important, what learning do we provide that would teach them how to deal with their violent feelings? We are so unreasonable about violence that it is apt to make us violent ourselves. Few children of the educated middle classes are slapped for masturbating any more, though they are not exactly raised in sexual freedom. But let the same parents meet with violence in their youngsters, and as likely as not they will slap the children or give them hell. Thus they demonstrate that violence without restraint is all right if one is older and stronger. We end up using violence to suppress it, and in doing so we teach our children that we believe there is just no other reasonable or intelligent way to deal with it. Yet the same parents, in another situation, would agree that suppression is the worst way to deal with instincts.

When I was a young man of good intentions, I objected to legalized prostitution. But my Victorian father told me, "It is these girls who protect nice women like your mother from the danger of being raped."

I still do not favor prostitution, because these girls should not have to serve as protection for the rest of the population. But by declaring there is no place for sex outside of marriage, just as we declare there is none for violence in our society, we force each person to suppress his violent tendencies till they build up to a pitch where he can no longer deny or control them. Then they suddenly erupt in the isolated act of explosive violence—whether against eight Chicago nurses or against the President of our country.

These outbursts are conspicuous. By their spectacular nature they even give the impression that ours is an age of violence. So we clamor for still greater suppression of even small eruptions of violence, as in the present outcry by some against children playing with guns. At their age such play provides the safety valve that drains off small amounts of violence, leaving a balance that can be managed.

I am convinced that neither comics, nor TV, nor even James Bond corrupts children, despite all the warnings that these media are "seducing the innocent." It is high time that the myth of original innocence be dispatched to the land of the unicorns along with its opposite, the myth of original sin. Most of the time innocence is little more than an anxious clinging to ignorance, and against violence there is no protection in ignorance. Violence exists, all right, and each of us is born with his potential for it. We are also born with opposite tendencies, and these must be carefully nurtured if they are to offset the violence. To do this one must know the nature of the enemy.

Recently there has been much talk about the "revolt" of the "young generation." This worries us because for most of man's existence there was no adolescent revolt. When boys had to be self-supporting by 12 or 14, when girls married at a similar age, youthful revolt was hardly possible. Nor will adolescents revolt where the social attitude is that man has always lived the same God-ordered existence from which any change is inconceivable.

But today society is affluent enough to dispense with child labor and keep the young economically dependent; and society also wishes to keep its youth sexually inactive beyond the age when sexual maturity is reached. Youngsters are asked to obey customs their parents have only recently created. Many youngsters submit, or grind out a boring existence, or opt out of society and become beats. But others explode and resort to violence.

For them, of course, violence seems a shortcut toward gaining an objective. And by their very revolt they show that they do not know what they are doing—they have not been taught what violence is. It is so primitive in nature that it is generically unsuitable to get for us those subtler satisfactions we want. That is why its examination marks the very beginning of man's becoming a socialized human being.

Whether or not we will use violence or avoid it depends entirely on what alternative solutions are known to a person facing a problem. This shows up most clearly in gang warfare. It is also the reaction of a bewildered dropout. Far from seeing school the way most of us do—as a ladder to success—he views it as the enemy that demands the impossible and thereby prevents success. The frustrated student's violence is not directed against learning as such; it is directed against a system that forces you to return again and again to a place where you have met nothing but defeat. He naturally becomes violent, or bands with similar youths in a violent gang for mutual protection.

Today we are bombarded by images of a life of consuming and owning. But for an awful lot of people the means to such a life are slim. This is especially true of many young people, before they find a sure place in our economic system, if they ever do. Yet they are told that they cannot have a satisfying life without owning things. So they see no alternative to violence, even though their whole education has denied the existence of any such thing. Violence, for the gang member, has precisely the same goals as the ones approved by respectable society: competitive success and prestige in the eyes of one's peers. The social scientist L. Yablonsky quotes one homicidal youngster: "I'm not going to let anybody be better than me and steal my 'reputation' . . . when I go to a gang fight I punch, stomp and stab harder than anyone." Senseless violence—not premeditated violence—seems a quick, almost magical way to prestige for a person who despairs of any alternatives.

Despite our persistent anxieties, ours is definitely not an age of increased violence—we do not even burn witches publicly, or use hanging as a popular spectacle. But we also must recognize that the chances for safe discharge of aggression are now severely curbed. Rural life, for instance, used to give the child some vicarious experience with the "delights" that violence can provide. In my native Austria, slaughtering the pig was a distinct highlight in the lives of peasant children. There was wood to be chopped. There was the power of horses or oxen that needed to be harnessed, not to speak of the problem of how to deal with the ferocity of a bull. These were not violent pursuits as such, but they nevertheless permitted, often demanded, a great deal of well-controlled violence. Moreover, they were safe outlets; they aroused no counter-violence in their target.

Today we try to achieve the same results with sports. But they are no substitute, for they raise the aggressive feelings of competition to the boiling point, and for every game we win, we are likely to lose one. And we confuse children by pushing the competitive spirit to a pitch while denying them acquaintance with aggression. Even while we send our children into these games, we expect them to keep their clothes and hands clean, to sit too still for too long stretches of time, to play "nicely" years before they have reached the age where playing by the rules of the game makes any sense to them. All this repression builds up an anger that will press for violent release. Even the few approved outlets for violence that existed until recently have been closed. No more Roman candles on the Fourth of July, no more turning over of garbage cans on Halloween.

If we would just listen to the children we would hear how much they want to learn about aggression. Almost as if they had all studied Freud, they somehow sense, in our pushing them, that we are teaching them only about half of themselves. Children know how great is their wish to get even, to take advantage, to grab things, to yell. Yet our nice teaching materials never hint that even the slightest difference can arise among the people in the picture books. We teach the child that either these stories are not true, which means that learning has no merit, or that something is wrong with their parents because sometimes they argue. We can tell children through stories that people are sometimes angry at each other and quarrel, but can still live successfully together—and that this is better, though harder, than to deny that one's parents ever differ.

In my school, children who for years have resisted learning even the simplest words from the primers that picture only sweetness and light learn to recognize, read, and spell a hundred words in a couple of weeks' time once it is admitted to them that violence is a fact. To begin with, we have to introduce the idea that what is hardest to do is to master one's own scary ideas, and that what we do or what happens to us can be destructive and overpowering. After such an explanation a group of these children once picked, as the first words they wanted to learn, the words "scary," "fire" and "hit." To me these children had outlined a course on how to learn about violence: "Hit" deals with human violence; "fire" with inanimate destruction; and "scary" with the outcome of violence and destruction. Words that such children can learn to read after seeing them only once are words like *fire, knife, cut, crash, shoot, kill, hit, bite, teeth, cry, fight, jail, scream, yell*. Compare them with words like *look* and *see*, which are generally considered easy to learn.

Unfortunately the stories we now teach from in class never include any incidents of aggression. No child ever hits, becomes angry, or destroys things in an outburst. The worst they ever do is to tease or to pout. All of them live on Pleasant Street, in Friendly Town. But none of us really live there, and it is time to confess this to our children so that they can learn to deal with the violent potential we all have—the potential to hit, knife, shoot, kill. Maybe there was some wisdom to the old-fashioned readers where the child was told what cruel fate befalls the evildoer. These stories scared children, but there was also the lesson that those who savor violent delights come to violent ends.

# 35. Catharsis—A Questionable
# Mode of Coping with Violence
## ALBERT BANDURA AND RICHARD H. WALTERS

The Freudian view of man as instinctively aggressive has many practical implications, including implications for child rearing. An example is Bettelheim's recommendation in the previous article that children be allowed to experience violence under controlled conditions so as to avoid bottling up the aggressive potential and risking an explosive outbreak. This recommendation is an example of what we called the "catharsis myth" in our general introduction (p. 3). The catharsis theory (or myth) is one of the aspects of psychoanalytic theory on which there has been a reasonable amount of scientifically valid research. The following article summarizes and integrates much of this evidence. The authors conclude that the evidence, far from supporting the catharsis theory, suggests that participation in violent activities may actually increase violence.

The opposing "social learning" theory holds that violence is a technique

SOURCE: *Social Learning and Personality Development* by Albert Bandura and Richard H. Walters, pp. 254–258. Copyright © 1963 by Holt, Rinehart and Winston, Inc. Reprinted by permission of Holt, Rinehart and Winston, Inc., New York.

of adaptation which is systematically learned by the child through inter-action with and observation of parents and others using violence. When the child becomes involved in stressful or problematic situations for which he has learned no other mode of coping, the stage is set for the use of violence to solve the problem (see boxes C and D in the system diagram, p. 18).

As used by Aristotle, catharsis referred to the purging of the passions or suf-ferings of spectators through vicarious participation in the suffering of a tragic hero as this is portrayed on the stage. In contrast, in psychoanalytic writings (Breuer and Freud, 1955 [1895]; Fenichel, 1945; Freud, 1924 [1914]) catharsis referred to the "liberation of affect" through the re-experi-encing of blocked or inhibited emotions, which is supposedly an essential phase in the resolution of unconscious conflicts. In applying this principle to aggressive behavior, Dollard *et al.* (1939) state that "the occurrence of any act of aggression is assumed to reduce the instigation to aggression" (p. 50). So stated, the catharsis hypothesis is not essentially different from the psy-choanalytic displacement and projection hypotheses, since all three imply that in some way one aggressive response can serve as a substitute for another in reducing an instinct, urge, or drive of aggression. Whereas the Aris-totelian principle of catharsis emphasized the *vicarious* experience of emo-tional reactions exhibited by social models, the Freudian (and neo-Hullian) hypothesis focused primarily on permitting persons *themselves* to express emotional behavior in fantasy, play, or real life.

Although Freud (1924 [1914]) discarded the belief that cathartic dis-charge of emotion could by itself serve to produce therapeutic change, never-theless free expression of affect is widely accepted as an important ingredient in therapy (Menninger, 1948) and in the management of behavior problems (Baruch, 1949). Guided by the catharsis hypothesis, parents and mental-health workers frequently provide hyperaggressive children with opportuni-ties to participate in aggressive recreational activities, encourage them to view aggressive televised programs, and subtly or openly instigate the ex-pression of aggressive behavior in psychotherapeutic playrooms, through the provision of aggressive play materials, in the hope of reducing aggressive im-pulses that are presumably maintaining the troublesome behavior.

The hydraulic model of personality, the interpretation of deviant behavior as disguised forms of energy discharge, and the therapeutic effects of cathar-tic drainage are dramatically portrayed in a popular book on discipline widely circulated among parents and teachers.

Another possibility is that the pressure of the unwelcome feelings becomes too great and springs a leak, in the same way that boiling water may spring a leak in a kettle if the steam it generates has no proper channel for release.

Meanwhile, our child is still trying to hide the unwanted feelings from sight. If they were to leak out in their original form, he would recognize them. But this he must not do, so he finds a device for letting them reappear in such a way that he won't recognize them. He *masks* them. He *lets them out in disguises only* and he keeps them disguised in two ways. By changing their form. And by changing their target (Baruch, 1949, p. 35).

When pus accumulates and forms an abscess, the abscess must be opened and drained. If it isn't done the infection spreads. In the end, it may destroy the individual. Just so with feelings. The "badness" must come out. The hurts and fears and anger must be released and drained. Otherwise, these too may destroy the individual (pp. 38–39).

Many times this is the way it happens. When enough of the hurt and fear and anger have been released, they diminish. They stop pushing from within. They stop springing out in compulsive ways, disguising what lies underneath so that it can not be dealt with. After enough of the "badness" has come out, the "goodness" appears (p. 44).

For, curious as it may seem, this has been observed many times over:
When unwanted NEGATIVE FEELINGS
have been emptied out sufficiently
then—
warm and good POSITIVE FEELINGS
flow in
When muddy water, which has dammed up, drains out from a pool, then fresh, clear water can flow in. So it is with these feelings. But the change does not happen quickly. It often takes a long time (p. 45).[1]

While the encouragement of expressive behavior may be of value in the treatment of overinhibited children, this procedure is quite evidently inappropriate for overexpressive clients. Indeed, consistent with the social-learning theory presented in this book, evidence from controlled research studies of children indicates that far from producing a cathartic reduction of aggression, direct or vicarious participation in aggressive activities within a permissive setting maintains the behavior at its original level and may actually increase it.

Kenny (1952) tested the hypothesis that participation in doll-play sessions of the "release-therapy" type would lead to a reduction of aggression. The aggressive responses of young children to the first half of a story-completion test formed the pretest measure. Two "therapy" sessions in which physical and verbal aggression were fostered provided the fifteen children in the experimental group with opportunities for catharsis. Control children were instead given two sessions of nonaggressive play. Following the play sessions, the second half of the story-completion test, which supplied the posttest measure of aggression, was administered to both experimental and control subjects. The control group showed a significantly greater decrease in aggression than the experimental therapy group, a finding that provides no support at all for the catharsis hypothesis.

Feshbach (1956) used both high-aggressive and low-aggressive children in a study of the extent to which play with aggressive toys modified aggression in school situations. Children under the aggressive-toy condition listened to stories and records with aggressive themes and played with objects, such

---

[1]Reprinted by permission from Dorothy W. Baruch, *New Ways in Discipline.* New York, McGraw-Hill, 1949.

as guns, selected to stimulate the expression of aggression. Another group of children participated in play sessions in which nonaggressive themes and objects were introduced, while a third group followed their regular classroom schedule. Pretest-to-posttest changes in aggression, based on ratings made by observers, failed to reveal any significant decrease in aggression in the group that had been encouraged to exhibit aggressive behavior in play. This study, like Kenny's, therefore fails to supply evidence for cathartic drive-reduction.

Studies in which children have vicariously participated in the aggressive activities of models have invariably shown that this kind of participation results in an increase in aggression, provided the model's behavior brings rewarding consequences or goes unpunished (Bandura, Ross, and Ross, 1961, 1963a, 1963b; Lövaas, 1961; Mussen and Rutherford, 1961; Siegel, 1956; Walters, Leat, and Mezei, 1963; Walters and Llewellyn Thomas, 1963; Walters, Llewellyn Thomas, and Acker, 1962). If, in treating hyperaggressive children, a therapist were to use procedures based on the catharsis energy-reduction principle, it is highly probable that the behavior the treatment was designed to eliminate would be inadvertently reinforced.

Findings from adult studies are less clear-cut than those obtained with children. Generally speaking, participation, direct or vicarious, by nonangered adults seems to increase the incidence of subsequent aggression, both in the same and different stimulus situations (Buss, 1961; Walters and Llewellyn Thomas, 1963). Feshbach (1956, 1961) has reported that adults who have initially been angered and then are permitted to express aggression through fantasy or are exposed to aggressive models show a subsequent decrease in aggression. In contrast, Kahn (1960) reported an increase in aggression in angered subjects, following a display of anger in a social situation in which hostile remarks were permitted and accepted. This study is especially relevant since the subjects' expressions of anger were addressed to a sympathetic "physician" in an interview, thus making the interaction similar to many that occur in therapy sessions. Moreover, the effects reported by Feshbach may reflect guilt-motivated inhibition following open aggressive displays (Berkowitz, 1958, 1962), while similar outcomes in other studies are certainly not interpretable as due to the reduction of anger (Rosenbaum and deCharms, 1960; Thibaut and Coules, 1952).

The persistence of the "drainage" hypothesis, in spite of criticism (Allport, 1954; McClelland, 1956) and largely negative experimental findings, reflects the resilience of the hydraulic model of personality popularized through psychoanalytic writings. Its application is nevertheless by no means consistent. While therapists, educators, and parents are frequently heard to defend the exposure of children to violent television and movie material, as well as children's participation in highly aggressive body-contact sports, on the grounds that aggressive impulses will thereby be reduced, few adults in North American society are likely to argue that vicarious participation in sexual activities will bring about a decrease in the observers' sexual responses. Indeed, considerable care is taken to exclude adolescents from "restricted admission" movies, presumably on the grounds that such exposure may generate sexual excitation and premature imitative sexual behavior.

# REFERENCES

Allport, G. W.
1954    *The Nature of Prejudice*. Reading, Massachusetts: Addison-Wesley.
Bandura, A., Dorothea Ross, and Shiela A. Ross
1961    "Transmission of Aggression Through Imitation of Aggressive Models." *Journal of Abnormal and Social Psychology* 63: 757–582.
1963a   "Imitation of Film-Mediated Aggressive Models." *Journal of Abnormal and Social Psychology* 66: 3–11.
1963b   "Vicarious Reinforcement and Imitative Learning." *Journal of Abnormal and Social Psychology* 67: 601–607.
Baruch, Dorothy W.
1949    *New Ways in Discipline*. New York: McGraw-Hill. P. 35.
Berkowitz, L.
1958    "The Expression and Reduction of Hostility." *Psychological Bulletin* 55: 257–283.
1962    *Aggression: A Social Psychological Analysis*. New York: McGraw-Hill.
Breuer, J. and S. Freud
1955    "Studies on Hysteria." In J. Strachey (ed.), Standard Edition, Vol. II. London: Hogarth. (First German edition, 1895.)
Buss, A. H.
1961    *The Psychology of Aggression*. New York: Wiley.
Dollard, J., L. W. Doob, N. E. Miller, O. H. Mowrer, and R. R. Sears
1939    *Frustration and Aggression*. New Haven: Yale University Press.
Fenichel, O.
1945    *The Psychoanalytic Theory of Neurosis*. New York: Norton.
Feshbach, S.
1956    "The Catharsis Hypothesis and Some Consequences of Interaction with Aggressive and Neutral Play Objects." *Journal of Personality* 24: 449–462.
1961    "The Stimulating Versus Cathartic Effects of a Vicarious Aggressive Activity." *Journal of Abnormal and Social Psychology* 63: 381–385.
Freud, S.
1924    "On the History of the Psychoanalytic Movement." Pp. 284–389 in E. Jones (ed.), *Collected Papers*, Vol. I. London: Hogarth. (First published in the *Hahrbuch der Psychoanalyses*, bd. VI, 1914.)
Kahn, M.
1960    "A Polygraph Study of the Catharsis of Aggression." Unpublished doctoral dissertation, University of Washington.
Kenny, D. T.
1952    "An Experimental Test of the Catharsis Theory of Aggression." Unpublished doctoral dissertation, University of Washington.
Lövaas, O. I.
1961    "Interaction Between Verbal and Nonverbal Behavior." *Child Development* 32: 37–44.
McClelland, D. C.
1956    "Personality." Pp. 39–62 in P. R. Fransworth and Q. McNemar (eds.), *Annual Review of Psychology*. Stanford: Annual Reviews, Inc.
Menninger, W. C.
1948    "Recreation and Mental Health." *Recreation* 42: 340–346.
Mussen, P. H. and E. Rutherford
1961    "Effects of Aggressive Cartoons on Children's Aggressive Play." *Journal of Abnormal and Social Psychology* 62: 461–464.
Rosenbaum, M. E. and R. deCharms
1960    "Direct and Vicarious Reduction of Hostility." *Journal of Abnormal and Social Psychology* 60: 105–111.
Siegel, Alberta E.
1956    "Film-mediated Fantasy Aggression and Strength of Aggressive Drive." *Child Development* 27: 365–378.
Thibaut, J. W. and J. Coules
1952    "The Role of Communication in the Reduction of Interpersonal Hostility." *Journal of Abnormal and Social Psychology* 47: 770–777.

# 36. Training Parents to Control an Aggressive Child
## G. R. PATTERSON, J. A. COBB, AND ROBERTA S. RAY

One of the most important developments in psychotherapy in the last decade has been the rapid spread of behavior modification techniques. These techniques are based on the principles of operant conditioning pioneered by B. F. Skinner. The essence of operant conditioning lies in the fact that dependable patterns of behavior can be established by rewarding the individual every time he happens to perform the desired act. This is known as "reinforcement." Each time an act occurs and is reinforced, the probability of its occurring again is greatly increased. The reward or reinforcement, of course, can be the elimination of something which is unpleasant (or, in the technical language of psychology, "aversive"). Similarly, behavior patterns which are not desired can gradually be eliminated by being careful not to directly or indirectly reward them.

The contrast between behavior modification techniques and other methods of psychological therapy is very great. Most other therapeutic techniques are based on reconstructing the life history of the client, finding out what may have caused the difficulty, and then helping the client to achieve insight into his problem so that he is in a better position to overcome the difficulty. In contrast to such insight and self-understanding approaches, the behavior modification approach concentrates on the current behavior of the person and simply applies the principles of operant conditioning to change that behavior.

An important development in behavior modification work is the use of laymen rather than psychotherapists for the treatment—but under the direction of trained therapists. The following article illustrates the application of these principles to the problem of extremely aggressive and destructive children, a type of problem which has rarely been overcome with traditional psychotherapy.

The analysis of sequences of family interaction by Patterson and Cobb (1970) showed that unpleasant or aversive behaviors of the younger children in the family significantly increased the probability of occurrence of similar behaviors by another family member. Aggression is a social behavior whose occurrence is largely controlled by aversive stimuli presented by another person. Analysis of sequential observation data among older children by Rausch (1965) showed that aversive or unpleasant social behaviors were the most likely antecedent for unfriendly behaviors. Kopfstein (1970) showed that for retarded preadolescents, behaviors such as Disapproval, Hit, and Noncompliance accounted for a large share of the antecedent events for aggressive behaviors.

If the coercive behavior, such as Hit, produces a withdrawal of the unpleasant antecedent stimulus, then there is an increase in the probability that

SOURCE: This article is abridged with permission of the authors and the publisher, from G. R. Patterson, J. A. Cobb, and Roberta S. Ray, "A Social Engineering Technology for Retraining Families of Aggressive Boys," in H. E. Adams and I. P. Unikel (eds.), *Issues and Trends in Behavior Therapy* (Springfield, Illinois: Chas. C. Thomas, 1973), pp. 139-224. Courtesy of Charles C. Thomas, Publisher, Springfield, Illinois.

a Hit will occur in the future. However, if the coercive behavior is not followed by a removal of the unpleasant stimulus, then it is likely to recur immediately, and with a possible increase in amplitude. In effect, the behavior of both the victim and the aggressor is under the control of negative reinforcement. Termination of the aversive behavior by either member constitutes a withdrawal of aversive stimuli for the other. If the initiator of the chain, or the "victim," withdraws his aversive behavior first, then the Hitter is reinforced. If the aggressor terminates his hitting and it is followed by yet more aversive behavior from the initiator, then the initiator is reinforced. Whichever member stops first reinforces the other party.

The data from these studies suggest that some aggressive behaviors displayed by children are under the control of aversive behaviors presented by another child or by family members. These aversive behaviors set the occasion for the attack; if they occur again as a consequence for the attack, they function as accelerators for that behavior, increasing the rate and/or amplitude of the attack (Patterson & Cobb, 1971).

It is hypothesized that aggressive child behaviors are under the control of both positive and negative reinforcement (Patterson & Cobb, 1971).

METHODOLOGY

Thirteen consecutive families participated in a relatively standardized training program in which the parents were trained as behavior managers. The families were referred to the project because one or more of the boys displayed high rate aggressive behaviors. Following six to ten baseline observation sessions in the home, the parents were trained in observation techniques, social learning concepts, and participated in a series of group training sessions with other parents having similar difficulties. The parents were supervised by daily telephone calls, and when necessary, by visits to the home.

Systematic observations were carried out during intervention after four and eight weeks of training, at termination, and at regular intervals during a 12-month follow-up. These data constitute the main criterion for evaluating the success of the training program. Parent report data obtained from daily telephone calls provided a secondary source of data.

It was predicted that there would be a significant decrease by termination in rates of behaviors for which the parents received specific training and this would generalize to deviant behaviors for which the parents had not been specifically trained. The generalization should also be found in decreased rates of deviant behavior for the siblings. This latter effect had been obtained in a previous attempt to intervene in the homes of six problem families (Patterson *et al.*, 1968).

Finally, it was predicted that the changes in deviant child behavior observed in the home would be accompanied by changes in the parents' global descriptions of the child provided prior to and following intervention.

During the first 10 to 12 weeks of intervention all families participate in essentially the same training program. Each stage of the training involves a contingency, such that the parent(s) must make an accurate response before being exposed to the next set of material. In effect, the parents must "earn" each step in the training program.

The first contingency requires that the parents learn the basic social learning framework from which our intervention procedures emerge. This involves their responding to a programmed textbook on child management (Patterson & Gullion, 1968). Then the staff responds by teaching the parents to pinpoint behavior and supervises the parents while they collect observation data. When the parents have collected sufficient data, they are invited to join the parents' group, where they are supervised as they alter a series of child and/or parent behaviors.

After a 10- to 12-week period, if the data show that the problems still persist, home visits are initiated and procedures developed to fit the individual needs of the family.

The parents are trained to apply two general sets of procedures for altering deviant behaviors. One set is designed to strengthen socially adaptive behaviors, which already exist in the repertoires of most of these children. The other procedures are designed to weaken the deviant behaviors.

While it might seem that the most reasonable course of action is simply to train the parents to apply richer schedules of social reinforcers contingent upon socially adaptive behaviors, there are several lines of evidence which suggest that for many families, such a procedure would be ineffective. First, a substantial proportion of the parents report feeling intense anger and while they may dispense social reinforcers for some members of the family, they often indicate their unwillingness to supply them for the identified deviant child. In addition, the laboratory data strongly suggest that deviant boys are less responsive to social reinforcers dispensed by adults (Levine & Simons, 1962; Patterson, 1965; Perkins, 1967; Patterson *et al.*, 1967; Wahler, 1967; Walker & Buckley, 1970). Thus, if the parents were trained solely to use social reinforcers, they might initially obtain little effect. Many of these parents are already concerned that they cannot control the child's behavior; such an initial failure would tend to confirm their low estimation of their abilities as child managers. Therefore, token point systems are introduced *early* in the training series, accompanied by parent-dispensed reinforcers. Every effort is made to arrange a program or contract such that the child is reinforced for performance that is well within his reach. Thus, he almost always earns many points or tokens on the first day the program is introduced. Interestingly enough, the greatest problem is that of seeing to it that the parent *actually delivers* the back-up reinforcer which the child has earned with his points; many parents seem to "forget" this part of the procedure.

The first program may last only a few days. Both the child and the parent are fully aware of the target behaviors, the reinforcing contingencies, and the back-up reinforcers. These points are carefully discussed with the child and with all the other family members. Typically, the points are written down in the form of a "contract" and actually signed by all the participants. Often this written agreement is typed to the bottom of the data sheet upon which the daily observations are recorded. For example, the contract for Noncompliance might list the specific behaviors that define the problem behavior and the specific behaviors that would produce a point (and a social reinforcer). The child negotiates with the parents to determine what will be "bought" with his points. Most children seem delighted with this arrangement and enthusiastically enter into negotiations for additional TV time, an extra dessert, or small amounts of money. Later, the time periods covered by a contract may be lengthened to a week or two; and he now may work for "grander things" such as bowling, fishing, and hiking, with one or both of the parents. He might, for example, earn the right to decide what the whole family will have for dinner, or which movie they will see.

The general effect of these contracts is to teach both parent and child to be clear about what behaviors are desired and which are not, as well as specifying consequences for both pro-social behaviors and for transgressions. The child learns that his parents are not only tracking him, but also that they are reacting to him in a *predictable* fashion. Many of these parents have come to rely almost completely upon aversive consequences in controlling child behaviors. One of the important outcomes of the training program should be that of significantly increasing overall levels of reinforcers for the whole family and, at the same time, increasing the child's responsiveness to the social reinforcers which are supplied.

*Time Out.* The very first program instituted to strengthen adaptive behaviors is accompanied by training the parents to follow procedures which will reduce the rate of occurrence of the deviant response. *Each time* the deviant response occurs, the child is removed from the reinforcing environment and is placed in "Time Out" (TO). The review of the laboratory studies by Leitenberg (1965) suggests that TO functions as an aversive stimulus in that its removal reinforces avoidance behaviors. The effect of repeated applications of TO is to produce rapid decreases in rate of deviant social behaviors in children, as shown in most of the studies reviewed by Patterson and White (1969).

While the writers have some reservations about the use of even mildly aversive stimuli for behavioral control, there is some empirical evidence to suggest that it is a significant, and perhaps even necessary, adjunct to intervention procedures for out-of-control boys. In a multiple baseline designed study the data showed that when TO was removed, rates of deviant behavior in the classroom were significantly increased (Walker, Mattson, & Buckley, 1969). In another study, before TO was introduced, parents were unable to obtain control of their "oppositional" children in a laboratory situation even though they had previously been using both social and nonsocial contingencies (Wahler, 1968).

There is yet another reason for its application; it is our impression that about a third of the parents beat their children. Typically, they seem to ignore the early components of the child's behavioral chains which lead to the high amplitude behaviors. It is the latter which are so aversive to the parent. As the end of the chain is reached and all bedlam ensues, the father emerges from his parental slumbers to do the one thing that will immediately reduce the noise level; he beats the child and is almost invariably reinforced for doing so.

It is our purpose to not only train the parent to track the earlier components of these chains, but to train them to introduce a procedure for controlling behavior at all points in the chain. The parent learns to observe, to apply TO, and to reinforce pro-social behaviors as alternatives to beating the child. One father was unconvinced by our expositions and beat his son after putting him in TO. It was only as he could see that the general program worked that he gave up his "theory of child raising."

The parent is trained to use TO *every* time the target behavior is observed. Usually the bathroom, sans all towels and toilet articles, serves as the locale. In the group, the parents usually role-play the process by which they "calmly" tell the child to go into TO. Because of the ubiquitous "parent debater" syndrome, the parents are instructed *not to talk* to the child while he is in Time Out nor to debate with him prior to or following its use. If the child debates, argues, yells, screams, kicks, or refuses to comply with the request to go to TO, each infraction costs an additional five minutes of TO. Most aggressive children will test out the situation the first time; some practiced monsters have "earned" up to an hour and a half of TO on their first trial. Many of them retaliate by messing up the room. For this episode, there is a "scrub" contingency in which the child cleans up the room.

The parents are monitored each day by telephone to see that the procedures are not used inappropriately. Generally a few days of bitter struggle

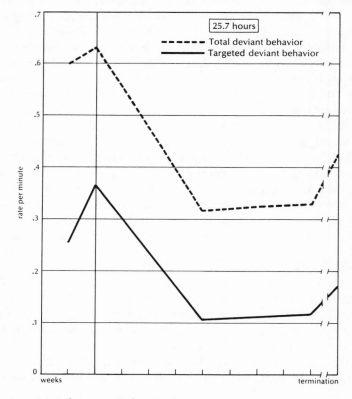

*Figure 1. Deviant Behavior Baseline and Intervention*

are rewarded by the parents' success. The greater the degree of control of the family by the child, the longer and more acerbic these initial interchanges. If the procedure is not effective within a week or two in reducing the rate of the target behavior to near zero, then the staff goes to the home to identify the errors being made in applying TO.

The parents are contacted each day by telephone to collect data, redefine behaviors if necessary, discuss the use of TO, to check on the use of social reinforcers, and to provide the parents with reinforcement for the work they are doing. The time spent on the telephone by the therapist averages about five to ten minutes per phone call. The calls are gradually faded out during the second and third programs carried out by the parents.

## CHANGES IN DEVIANT CHILD

For each identified child, the behaviors were listed which served as targets for supervised programs carried out during intervention. Rates were calculated for the total class of responses during baseline, the fourth-week probe, and for the probe at termination.

Figure 1 shows that there was a 46 per cent reduction in Targeted behaviors from baseline (total) to termination. A change equal to or greater than this magnitude occurred for 9 of the 13 families. The F value of 4.31 was highly significant, showing that the parents had been effective in reducing the rates of problem behaviors for which they had received specific training.

Both parents tended to perceive improvements along all the personality dimensions; they particularly emphasized changes in those factors related to out-of-control behaviors. The changes in the mothers' descriptions were analyzed by the Wilcoxin Test, which showed changes in their ratings to be significant at $p$ less than .05 on all of the factors. While the sample size for the fathers was too limited to permit statistical analysis, the results supported the findings obtained from mothers' ratings in suggesting that both parents had acquired a "general disposition" to view the deviant child in a more favorable light.

This experience suggests that the members of the social environment rather than the deviant child should be the appropriate targets for intervention programs.

## REFERENCES

Kopfstein, D. C.
1970    "The Effects of Natural Contingencies on the Social Behaviors of Trainable Retarded Children: A Learning Analysis." Unpublished doctoral dissertation, University of Minnesota.
Leitenberg, H.
1965    "Is Time-Out From Positive Reinforcement an Aversive Event?: A Review of the Experimental Evidence." *Psychological Bulletin* 64: 428–441.
Levine, G. R. and J. J. Simmons
1962    "Response to Praise by Emotionally Disturbed Boys." *Psychological Reports* 11: 10.
Patterson, G. R.
1965    "Responsiveness to Social Stimuli." Pp. 157–178 in L. Krasner and L. P.

Ullmann (eds.), *Research in Behavior Modification*. New York: Holt, Rinehart and Winston.

Patterson, G. R. and J. A. Cobb
1971    "A Dyadic Analysis of 'Aggressive' Behaviors: An Additional Step Toward a Theory of Aggression." *Proceedings of the Fifth Minnesota Symposia on Child Psychology*. Minneapolis: University of Minnesota. Pp. 72–109.

Patterson, G. R. and M. E. Gullion
1968    *Living With Children: New Methods for Parents and Teachers*. Champaign, Illinois: Research Press.

Patterson, G. R., R. A. Littman, and W. Bricker
1967    "Assertive Behavior in Children: A Step Toward a Theory of Aggression." Monographs of the Society for Research in Child Development 32, No. 5 (Serial no. 113).

Patterson, G. R., R. S. Ray, and D. A. Shaw
1968    "Direct Intervention in Families of Deviant Children." *Oregon Research Institute Bulletin* 8, No. 9.

Patterson, G. R. and G. D. White
1969    "It's a Small World: The Application of 'Time-Out from Positive Reinforcement." *Oregon Psychological Association Newsletter* 15, No. 2 Supplement.

Perkins, M. J.
1967    "Effects of Play Therapy and Behavior Modificaton Approaches With Conduct Problem Boys." Unpublished doctoral dissertation, University of Illinois.

Rausch, H. L.
1965    "Interaction Sequences." *Journal of Personality and Social Psychology* 2: 487–499.

Wahler, R. G.
1967    "Behavior Therapy With Oppositional Children: Attempts to Increase Their Parents' Reinforcement Value." Paper presented at the meeting of the Southeastern Psychological Association, Atlanta.
1968    "Behavior Therapy With Oppositional Children: Love Is Not Enough." Paper presented at the meeting of the Eastern Psychological Association, Washington, D.C.

Walker, H. M. and N. K. Buckley
1970    "Investigations of Some Classroom Control Parameters as a Function of Teacher Dispensed Social Reinforcers." University of Oregon, in preparation.

Walker, H. M., R. H. Mattson, and N. K. Buckley
1969    "Special Class Placement as a Treatment Alternative for Deviant Behavior in Children." In F. A. M. Benson (ed.), *Modifying Deviant Social Behaviors in Various Classroom Settings*. Eugene, Oregon: University of Oregon, No. 1.

# CHAPTER ELEVEN
# The Family and
# Violence in the Future

## 37. *Alternative Family Structures and Violence-Reduction*
**ROBERT N. WHITEHURST**

The political philosophy of a democratic society runs counter to the idea that social scientists should determine the future shape of society. Nevertheless, social scientists can importantly aid citizens and government in making choices about the future. One of the most important such contributions consists of spelling out the probable consequences of different alternative patterns of society. This can be done by making use of relationships already demonstrated through research and putting them together in a theoretically consistent fashion.

In the following article, Whitehurst suggests that "alternative family structures"—that is, families which contain more people than the traditional husband-wife-children combination (such as communes and group marriages)—might reduce the potential for family violence. His conception of alternative family structures also includes rejection of the hierarchical structure of the traditional family and greater interpersonal openness than in the traditional family.

Although Whitehurst is careful to indicate that his conclusions are tentative, even greater qualification is needed. We feel (and Whitehurst agrees) that a theoretical analysis of this type must be based on much more solid empirical evidence than is now available. For example, Whitehurst bases much of his discussion on the assumption that alternative family systems allow more autonomy to the individual than the nuclear family system does. Since this is a crucial assumption, it is essential that it be factually correct if the theoretical analysis using this assumption is to be valid. Unfortunately, evidence which would support this assumption is not available. If it were available, and if other similar starting assumptions were based on firm evidence, then we could have a much higher degree of confidence in Whitehurst's conclusions about the potential of alternative family structures for reducing violence.

Although evidence on the incidence and types of violence in conventional families is far from complete, it seems desirable to focus some of our energies on an attempt to understand the relation of counter-culture family styles to

SOURCE: This article was specially written for the present book.

violence. This is not merely in response to the increasing interest in alternate family forms expressed in a variety of professional and lay publications.[1] It is still uncertain if interest in communes and alternate marriage styles is more permanent than fad-like. However, whatever the future form of the family, there are likely to be long-lasting changes growing out of the present ferment. Among these changes may be an altered (and possibly reduced) potential for violence in family groupings. The essential goal of this article, therefore, is to provide a rationale for understanding the violence-reduction potential of alternate family patterns. Although the conclusions are highly tentative, they are based on widely accepted facts and theories of present social-science knowledge regarding the family; at the minimum, our conclusions may be viewed as hypotheses worth testing in the future.

There are some reasons to believe that the current counter-culture setting might lead to a set of values and patterns of interaction that will materially reduce the level of punitiveness and violence in family structures in the future. As a general hypothesis, the following can be suggested: insofar as families tend to make relatively public more segments of their interpersonal behavior, sanctioning reference groups are more readily available to reward the working-through of hostilities and tensions—therefore overt aggressiveness and violence will be decreased. The following comparisons are designed to show how typical situations may tend to work themselves out in both counter-culture and conventional families.

In conventional families—relatively isolated and under strain to produce both children and adults who can perform up to middle class standards—subtle forms of pressure to achieve can lead to fairly high levels of tension and hostility with a high violence-potential.[2] By contrast, one of the most salient features of nearly all alternate family forms involves a norm of autonomy, of evolving one's own life style in an idiosyncratic way. This norm of allowing the person to develop pretty much on his own without overt coercion (other than the singular mandate to "grow," which can also become a heavy burden depending on the situation) seems to make for a lessened possibility of one person intruding violently into the life of another or responding violently to subtle but intolerable pressure to achieve.

Another crucial factor involved in lessened violence potential in alternate families is the tendency to make more public and open one's highly personal interactions with significant others, such as spouses. This opening up of intimate networks is no doubt instrumental in making public certain problems which can be scrutinized by the group so that a wider variety of solutions are considered and encouraged than might be the case if problems remain in a privatized dyad. In the dyad, problems remain closed off, solutions often

---

[1]A working definition of "alternate family forms" would possibly include the following: any group of persons who consider themselves more or less permanently attached to each other in a living arrangement wherein all are enjoined in the struggle to create a social network in some respect extended beyond a nuclear group. This would include communes, triads, group marriages, and other extended non-kin networks in various intimacy groupings.

[2]Arelene S. Skolnick and Jerome H. Skolnick, *Family in Transition* (Boston: Little Brown, 1971), pp. 22–24.

seem circumscribed and in general are not as amenable to open disclosure and solution as is true of the open and intimate networks of alternate families. In part, this notion involves a simple expansion of the immediate social control network, the basic idea being that the more readily available are sanctioning reference groups, the more likely is the group to resolve potentially explosive issues and prevent violence. This also implies that there be in existence norms of working through problems instead of denial of problems.[3]

The need for husbands to control wives as well as children (and vice versa) is deeply implicated in familial violence. Insofar as alternate family norms make persons aware of their tendencies to control others and by interpersonal-encounter techniques lessen this need to control, violence may thereby be decreased.

## VIOLENCE AGAINST OUTSIDERS

Granted these violence-reducing potentials in alternative family systems, it is important to recognize that both alternative and conventional families can be the bearers of cultural norms which advocate violence—especially against outsiders. An extreme example of norms favoring violence against outsiders is to be found among the Nazi operators of concentration camps. They were unbelievably brutal to Jewish prisoners, but were reportedly able to relate as fully loving fathers and husbands to their own wives and children. This apparent style of schizoid-like behavior is likewise occasionally manifested on the commune scene. Roberts reports that in some instances, Weatherman communes and the Seattle Liberation Front members used violence or at least ideologically supported the use of violence.[4] It should be fully recognized that men can often fully compartmentalize their lives so as to achieve diametrically opposed ends, with disparate values governing the same person in even a very short time-span. An example of cruelty and violence in the external operation of a group is found in the case of the Manson "family." [5] These examples should alert us to avoid the notion that violence cannot somehow become part of the activities of alternative life styles. On the one hand are communes such as that described by Zablocki in *The Joyful Community,*[6] which have become so organized that violent actions are structured by religious means into such a place of irrelevance that hostility and violence are simply unimportant problems. On the other hand, some others—such as the Manson family as described by Sanders—have a very large component of their activities surrounded by quasi and real violence.

---

[3]It also assumes a norm of non-violence since the same group support and pressures can be applied with equal effectiveness to encouraging violence, as in the case of the cuckolded husband in some societies who, despite love for his wife, feels forced by family traditions and honour to kill her.

[4]Ron Roberts, *The New Communes: Coming Together in America* (Englewood Cliffs, New Jersey: Prentice-Hall, 1971), p. 84.

[5]Ed Sanders, *The Family* (New York: Avon Books, 1971).

[6]Zablocki, Benjamin, *The Joyful Community* (Baltimore, Maryland: Penguin Books, 1971).

It must be recognized that although groups can legitimize violence against others, there is always a limit to what the group can stand in terms of legitimized internal violence and survive. The main emphasis of this article is on internal violence; and we suggest that for structural reasons, there is a greater possibility of violence occurring within conventional as contrasted with alternative families. Roberts, in fact, points out that the collective can build on positive images within while girding itself for battle without: the following indicates one Seattle Liberation Front member's view of the role of the collective in political action:

It is only in collectives that we can develop ourselves as creative political organizers without the stifling atmosphere of mass-meeting based organizations . . . in transforming the movement into a tough and sensitive grouping prepared to withstand the repression and reach working-class constituencies in the seventies, the collective form will be crucial. It allows us to build trust, mutual love and struggle, and will liberate the creativity and imagination which must still be among our chief weapons.[7]

Thus, while action involving confrontation and potential violence is legitimized outside the collective, love reigns as the ideal within. Perhaps, if past sociological orientations have been correct in their appraisal of hostility and violence, internal violence can be kept at a minimum if external sources are available as scapegoats or objects on which to ventilate aggression, thereby preventing internal hostilities from arising.

The "peace through violence" rhetoric seems not always to be the special province of the conventional right-wing person. There is little doubt in this writer's opinion that by this point in the 1970's, violence as a legitimate means to achieve long-term revolutionary goals is falling into disfavor. More personal and subjective means of establishment-subversion seem to be in order. A greater variety of communal types appear to believe with Roberts that "the development of a revolutionary life-style is fundamental to the political revolution."[8] The range of definitions of the situation that fall into acceptable types of revolutionary activities include: drugs (more often in the 1970's, those defined as non-harmful or minimally harmful—such as wine and pot); hard-rock or other unconventional music; freaky dress; casual and informal life styles, sometimes on subsistence farms; and sex and family organization styles that are other than those touted by the establishment. The pleas for more militancy have followed a pattern of exhaustion in the light of radical events of the late 1960's. Disenchantment with violence has been fairly well internalized. This fact tends to support the basic argument of this paper—that alternative life-style family organization holds a greater potential for lessened violence than conventional family organization. By contrast, there is simply no evidence that any parallel change or increased awareness of the futility of violence has occurred to conventional families.

[7]Roberts, pp. 85–86.
[8]Roberts, p. 83.

To summarize the distinctions made above: although some alternate-style families (such as the Manson group, Weathermen, or Seattle Liberation Front) can increase violence—usually that vented upon outsiders—most are strongly committed to non-violence. If the norms of the group support non-violence, then members of such groups will tend to behave in accord with the norms. The more solid or cohesive the group, the more likely the response to its normative demands. Thus, the typical counter-culture family, which is opposed to violence, can be an extremely effective force for non-violence because it can bring the weight of the entire group to bear. In the case of the conventional family, the tensions engendered by its limited solidarity and other structural features—not its norms about violence—probably enhance the violence potential.

All of the above suggests, as at least a tenable hypothesis, that the structure of alternate family systems (including the norms and values supporting that structure) leads to lessened *potential* for violence in alternate families. A corollary hypothesis suggests that, whatever the potential, when this normative structure of alternate families is closely supported by visible reference groups and individuals, the *actual* level of violence will be lessened within the family. The chart on page 320 outlines more systematically the differences in the two forms which may be present and which need to be investigated. It is not suggested that violence never occurs in alternate families, but that due to the average variation in the conditions discussed and listed in this chart, that it is less lkely to occur in these alternative family forms.

Paradoxically, the emerging values of the 60's and 70's may, during the period of transition, increase the frustrations and violence potential in many families. As husbands and wives become more autonomous from each other in many respects, more tensions may be expected in the future. As children seek autonomous possibilities earlier—and freedom from parental control—violence potential increases. As women and children seek the freedoms long accorded men in this society, tension possibilities increase. Many family members seek in their apartness the relief from alienation and family control which they cannot cope with at home in the normal family settings. To achieve at once the feeling of belonging in a hassle-free setting becomes a major objective of many youth and some oldsters.

In the remaining portion of this decade, if we continue in conventional families to attempt to use outmoded legal and moral a priori answers to problems of life instead of rationally looking at the disparity of ends and means, we may well find more violence as a predicted outcome of family life.

This does not deny the probability that people who opt for life in alternate family structures will continue to have severe problems. At the same time, social scientists can do no less than explore and encourage any possibility for increasing human freedoms and relative peace in families of whatever structure; not to engage in theoretical analysis of the peaceful potential in alternate family forms or not to engage in comparative study of this issue would involve gross neglect of social scientists' responsibilities.

*Orientations of Conventional and Alternate Families Relating to Violence Potential*

| Conventional Families | Alternate Families |
|---|---|
| Live in relative privacy isolation—permits hidden, cloistered, non-solution to problems; denies existence of difficulties. | Live in relatively public life arena—less behavior hidden—denial of problems is more difficult. |
| Few tension-release mechanisms; those that do exist often become stilted, cyclical, and unlikely to produce break-throughs or change short of divorce. | Tension-release mechanisms often built into daily life structure; heavy norms of interpersonal honesty, peer pressures to resolve tensions and get on with living. |
| Major orientation to external sanctions and rewards—conformity related to rewards offered by outside world's goals. Heavy achievement ethic—behavior related to means to achieve. | Major orientation toward personal growth potential—sanctions (rewards) sought at hands of internal group; "achievement" is predicted on Gestalt assumption of filling out own life style. |
| Solutions to problems (intrafamilial) seen in terms of above rewards, establishment goals. A priori answers to problems sought in moral (Biblical) or legal codes. | Solutions to problems seen in Gestalt terms; group-defined, self-growth possibilities explored open-endedly. New answers sought in means-ends scheme. |
| Truncated (real) social control network (husband, wife, few outsiders, of real importance). External controls perceived as real, but are impersonal—in form of agencies, etc. These sanctioning reference groups not available for immediate help in crisis. | Expanded social control network includes significant others outside spouses. The sanctioning reference groups are real and intimate in the lives of family members; are immediately available for crisis help. |

# 38. Violence Research, Violence Control, and the Good Society
**MURRAY A. STRAUS AND SUZANNE K. STEINMETZ**

Alternative family forms are far from the only—or even the most important —events which could alter the level of violence between family members or the effects of family patterns on violence outside the family. Indeed, a social system perspective on the question of the future of violence in the family immediately tells us that if we are to have any real glimpse of what is likely to occur, we must consider a great many things beyond the internal structure of the family—important as that is.

The "System Model of Intra-Family Violence" on pp. 18–19 is a *partial* listing of some of the many factors which must be considered. The word "partial" is emphasized because there can be no question that many more factors must be considered if we are to even come close to predicting the future level of violence. But, for the moment, assume that the factors listed in this diagram are a sufficient set. We could still not get an accurate estimate of the future level of violence because information on even this limited set is so incomplete. In addition, even if we know the present relation of a given factor to the level of violence, we still do not know what the future level of that factor will be. For these reasons, it would be foolhardy to try to make any specific predictions about the future level of violence and intra-family violence in American society.

It may not be many years, however, until such predictions are possible. Social scientists are rapidly developing system models of various aspects of society which use the tremendous capacity of modern computers to simulate the processes set in motion by changes in one or more elements of the system. The work on models of the economic system for which Tinbergen won a Nobel prize is an example (J. Tinbergen, 1964). Another example is the simulation models of urban social structure being developed by Jay Forrester (1969).

The same type of analysis can, in principle, be carried out in relation to intra-family violence. Even the computer simulation techniques available at this moment would probably be sufficient *if* only we knew the values to enter into the equations. But we do not. We do not, for example, know with enough accuracy the level of even the type of intra-family violence on which there has been the most research: physical punishment of children. Even more crucial, we do not know with enough accuracy just how physical punishment is related to such things as the income level of the husband, number of brothers and sisters in the family, and the employment of the mother. We *do* know that as income level goes up beyond the poverty level, physical punishment tends to go down; and that as the number of children goes up, so does physical punishment. But such general propositions are not sufficient for social forecasting, just as it would not be sufficient to know that as investment in capital goods goes up, so does employment level. The economic system models work because it is possible to estimate *how many* jobs are created for every million dollars of capital investment. That figure becomes one of the many equations which enter into the model, and (since it is a *system* model) in turn is affected by the other equations in the model. In the introduction to his comprehensive propositional inventory of family research, William J. Goode puts the issue as follows: "Without at least crude measures of *how much* is exchanged between subsystems, we can do little more than Parsons or Smelser have done, that is, diagram speculatively a set of hypothetical "boxes" or subsystems and label the *kinds* of output and inputs each gives or receives from the others" (Goode, 1971: xxi).

It should be obvious that a vast amount of research will be necessary to provide the quantitative data on the level of each of the factors in the diagram on p. 18 and the specifics of how many units of change in one of these factors is produced by a given change in another of the factors. If funding agencies and social scientists were to take up the issue of violence to a greater extent than the limited current level of research, such knowledge could be accumulated in a relatively short time—perhaps a decade.

Unfortunately, there is little likelihood that the massive research effort needed for a breakthrough in a decade will take place. In addition, even if we could know that such a research effort were to take place and that it would reach a successful conclusion in only ten years, we need not and should not wait the ten years. A decade may be a short time in the history of science, but it is a long time in the life history of persons exposed to violence. In each of the four parts of this book, there are articles and discussions of specific steps which can be taken *now* to reduce violence. Some of these steps are based on little or no research evidence. Others are based on fairly solid evidence, even if not precise enough to provide values to enter into the equations of a simulation model. We can make a start with these, especially if they are steps which are socially desirable in their own right. Thus, as we pointed out in Part One, a reduction in economic insecurity is likely to reduce the level of violence in families headed by economically insecure household heads. We do not know just how much of a reduction this will bring about. The violence-reduction potential of reduced economic insecurity might even be counteracted by other changes set in motion by the steps taken to reduce economic insecurity. But since a basic minimum level of income is a social good in its own right, the society will have gained even if such a move turns out to have no effect on the level of intra-family violence.

## VIOLENCE AND THE GOOD SOCIETY

Our view of the good society is one with a minimal level of violence—in the family or elsewhere. The selections included in this last part of the book all tend to show that violence is learned in the family context. Moreover, the behaviors observed and acted out in the family have a pervasive and lasting influence. So it is essential to understand and reduce the level of violence between family members if we have any hopes of achieving a generally less violent society.

But non-violence is only one of the characteristics of a good society. Our view of the good society also specifies that it must be open to change and to correcting inequities. There are occasions and situations in which the value of non-violence and the value of equity and openness to change conflict. It is in these situations that violence can have important positive contributions to human welfare (Coser, 1966). The riots of the late 1960's by blacks locked into the urban slums were clearly a powerful factor which forced public attention to oppressive conditions and generated at least some needed social changes.

So one can go too far in condemning violence. We must not lose sight of the fact that violence, like other aspects of human relations, has both positive and negative consequences. Within the family, for example, violence can serve as a means of communication and as a catalyst bringing about needed changes when all else fails. Take the situation of a family in which there is a serious problem between a husband and wife, but the husband just doesn't listen, or get the message, or ignores the message and the problem. Finally, in desperation, the wife throws something at him or hits him. At least in middle class families, that is such a shocking event that the husband can no longer ignore the seriousness of the problem. It is like the hoisting of a danger signal which cannot be ignored (or is very difficult to ignore).

But perhaps even then the unignorable is ignored or merely superficially patched over. Months later, another and more violent episode occurs—one which is so violent that there is an injury or the neighbors call the police. As a result of this violent episode, the family is referred to a marriage counselor or other mediating agent, with the result that a viable solution is worked out. In this sequence of events, violence has served as a catalyst to bring into action forces which would not otherwise have been present.

In principle, there should never be a situation when all else fails. In practice, such situations do exist because alternative modes of resolving conflicts and inequalities are either unknown to the persons involved, unavailable to them, or unavailable until some violent act serves as a catalyst to bring non-violent methods of change into the picture. Therefore, unless we are prepared to live with inequity and injustice, it is almost inevitable that violence will remain a part of the human condition because there will probably always be situations in which only violent acts can trigger needed changes. Our view of the good society and of desirable family relations makes such situations few and far between. It calls for the development of social relations and institutions which will make violence unnecessary. Realism, however, compels us to conclude that a truly non-violent society will be a long time in the making. It may, in fact, be impossible except in a completely static society. At the same time, "realism" has its dangers. It can be a self-fulfilling prophecy or a sophisticated defense of the status quo. We believe that the contents of this book show not only the nature of the problem of violence between family members, but also gaps in our knowledge of violence, and steps which can be taken now to achieve immediate progress toward the creation of a non-violent society.

REFERENCES

Coser, Lewis A.
  1966    "Some Social Functions of Violence." Pp. 8–18 in Marvin E. Wolfgang (ed.),
          *Patterns of Violence: The Annals of the American Academy of Political and
          Social Science,* Vol. 364 (Philadelphia: American Academy of Political and
          Social Science, March, 1966).
Forrester, Jay W.
  1969    *Urban Dynamics.* Cambridge, Massachusetts: MIT Press.
Goode, William J., Elizabeth Hopkins and Helen M. McLure
  1971    *Social Systems and Family Patterns: A Propositional Inventory.* New York:
          Bobbs-Merrill.
Tinbergen, Jan
  1964    *Central Planning.* New Haven, Connecticut: Yale University Press.

# Author Index

# Subject Index

Printer and Binder: Braun-Brumfield, Inc.